Agnes Bowker's Cat

Travesties and Transgressions
in Tudor and Stuart England

David Cressy is Professor of History at Ohio State University, USA.
He has also written *Birth, Marriage, and Death: Ritual, Religion, and the
Life-Cycle in Tudor and Stuart England* (1997).

Agnes Bowker's Cat

Travesties and Transgressions in Tudor and Stuart England

David Cressy

OXFORD
UNIVERSITY PRESS

OXFORD
UNIVERSITY PRESS

Great Clarendon Street, Oxford OX2 6DP
Oxford University Press is a department of the University of Oxford.
It furthers the University's objective of excellence in research, scholarship,
and education by publishing worldwide in

Oxford New York

Athens Auckland Bangkok Bogotá Buenos Aires Calcutta
Cape Town Chennai Dar es Salaam Delhi Florence Hong Kong Istanbul
Karachi Kuala Lumpur Madrid Melbourne Mexico City Mumbai
Nairobi Paris São Paulo Singapore Taipei Tokyo Toronto Warsaw

and associated companies in Berlin Ibadan

Oxford is a registered trade mark of Oxford University Press
in the UK and in certain other countries

Published in the United States
by Oxford University Press Inc., New York

First published as *Travesties and Transgressions in Tudor and Stuart England* 2000

First issued as an Oxford University Press Paperback 2001

British Library Cataloguing in Publication Data

Data available

Library of Congress Cataloging in Publication Data

Data available

ISBN 0-19-282530-5

1 3 5 7 9 10 8 6 4 2

Typeset by Best-set Typesetter Ltd., Hong Kong
Printed in Great Britain
on acid-free paper by
Cox and Wyman Ltd., Reading

To see a World in a Grain of Sand
And a Heaven in a Wild Flower,
Hold Infinity in the palm of your hand
And Eternity in an hour.

William Blake, 'Auguries of Innocence'

Acknowledgements

Dozens of scholars have helped me to locate sources, clarify my ideas, and to turn seminar papers, lectures, and essays into the chapters in this book. I would like to thank everyone who helped me with criticisms and suggestions. I am especially grateful to the National Endowment for the Humanities for the grant of a full-year fellowship, and to the Huntington Library in California for providing me with funding and facilities for research.

'Agnes Bowker's Cat: Childbirth, Seduction, Bestiality, and Lies' was the subject of a workshop at the Huntington Library in May 1993 and a plenary address to the Mid-West Conference on British Studies at the University of Minnesota at Hallowe'en 1993. A version of this chapter appeared as 'De la fiction dans les archives? Ou le monstre de 1569', in *Annales. Économies, Sociétés, Civilisations*, 48 (1993). Elyse Blankley helped me see Agnes Bowker's case from a feminist point of view. Norman Jones helped me to frame it within the complex world of early Elizabethan politics. Deborah Harkness helped me understand its medical and scientific dimensions. Sybil Jack directed me to local materials relating to Elizabethan Leicestershire. Barbara Shapiro made useful suggestions about contemporary criteria for credible report.

Earlier versions of 'Monstrous Births and Credible Reports: Portents, Texts, and Testimonies' were delivered as the Phi Beta Kappa University Lecture at California State University, Long Beach, in March 1993 and as the Eighth Annual Renaissance Conference of Southern California Lecture at the Huntington Library in May 1993. I am grateful for all subsequent comments and suggestions, especially for those from colleagues in English literature.

The chapter on 'Mercy Gould and the Vicar of Cuckfield' benefited from the advice of Robert Bucholz, Patrick Collinson, Sybil Jack, Kevin Sharpe, and Christopher Whittick.

Earlier versions of 'Cross-Dressing in the Birth Room' were delivered at the Huntington Library British History Seminar in May 1994, at the North American Conference on British Studies at Vancouver, British Columbia, in October 1994, and at a conference on 'Virtual Gender: Past Projections, Future Histories' at Texas A & M University in April 1996. The chapter includes material published as 'Gender Trouble and Cross-Dressing in Early Modern England', in the *Journal of British Studies*, 35 (1996).

I posed some of the questions in 'Who Buried Mrs Horseman?' at a conference on 'The Final Hour: Death in Medieval and Early Modern Europe' at Arizona State University in February 1992.

The chapter on 'Mocking the Clergy' was the basis for my remarks at a conference on 'Religion, Culture and Society in Early Modern England' at St Mary's University College in April 1998. I am grateful to Christopher Haigh, Peter Marshall, and John Morrill for helping me make improvements. I also used some of this material for a paper on 'Clergy, Laity, Tradition and Discipline' at a conference on 'State Religion and Folk Belief in the Early Modern World' at the University of Minnesota in May 1998.

I am grateful to Lori Anne Ferrell and Sears McGee for their insights into 'The Atheist's Sermon: Belief, Unbelief, and Traditionalism in the Elizabethan North'. I explored this case in a seminar at the University of California, Santa Barbara, in November 1997, and in discussion and correspondence with Patrick Collinson, Eamon Duffy, Christopher Haigh, Peter Marshall, and William Shiels.

I presented an early version of 'Baptized Beasts and Other Travesties' at a conference on 'Reading Riots' at Manchester Metropolitan University in June 1997. I am particularly grateful to John Bolland, Peter Marshall, and Bernard Capp for their comments.

Christopher Haigh and Lori Anne Ferrell read earlier versions of 'The Battle of the Altars' and steered me away from error. Another version was prepared for the Huntington Library British History Seminar in October 1998.

I discussed earlier versions of 'The Portraiture of Prynne's Pictures' in seminars at All Souls College Oxford, in March 1991 and at Claremont Graduate University in March 1998. Neil Roberts taught me about metonymy. Michael MacDonald helped me think about the power of images.

I presented various versions of 'The Adamites Exposed' at the Huntington Library in January 1997, the University of Adelaide in February 1997, La Trobe University in March 1997, Princeton University in April 1997, and the North American Conference on British Studies at Asilomar, California, in October 1997. I am particularly grateful to Christopher Hill, Ann Hughes, Peter Lake, Frank McGregor, and Keith Thomas for steering me towards useful sources.

'Rose Arnold's Confession', 'Another Midwife's Tale', 'The Essex Abortionist', and 'The Downfall of Cheapside Cross' are presented here for the first time. I alone am responsible for any remaining errors. Spelling and punctuation have been modernized, and the year is taken to begin on 1 January.

Contents

List of Illustrations

Introduction

This book brings to life some of the strangest and most troubling incidents from the byways of Tudor and Stuart England. Through a series of linked stories and close readings of local texts and narratives, it examines the ways in which early modern society coped with cultural difficulties and dealt with bewildering phenomena. Among the topics under discussion are bestiality and monstrous births, seduction and abortion, ridicule and paranoia, mockery and invective, symbolic violence and iconoclasm, atheism, excommunication and irregular burial, nakedness and cross-dressing. These were issues that challenged the orderly, Protestant, hierarchical society of post-Reformation England. They disturbed the margins, cut across the grain, and set the authorities on edge.

When incidents of this sort caught the attention of diarists, came before the ecclesiastical courts, or entered the realm of printed discourse, they were often surrounded by questions. What was the truth of the matter, what exactly had happened, and what did it all portend? What were the limits of credibility, and whose account should be believed? What did it mean, for example, when Leicestershire villagers asserted that a woman in their community gave birth to a cat? Why was a Sussex parish so divided over midwifery, plague remedies, and religion, and why was the fate of their minister bound up with accounts of an illegitimate birth? Why was an Oxfordshire woman refused Christian burial, and why were her neighbours so uncooperative when their bishop tried to find out who had secretly invaded the church to bury her at night? What explains the mocking invective flung at a Yorkshire clergyman, the insults suffered by Kentish churchwardens, and the venomous language some pastors directed at their flocks? And what was at stake at Chester in 1637 when the authorities gave public execution to five empty picture frames?

Behind these questions lay stories and counter-stories that were rooted in local struggles and shaped by contests over gender, authority, deference, and belief. But each episode also touched issues of national significance, that engaged the attention of the magistrates, the bishops, the crown, and the court. Their telling embroiled the centre and the periphery, the mainstream and the marginal, engaging both public and private spheres.

There are stories here about sex and violence, faith and folly, birth and death. But this is not a conventional history of any of these topics. It is rather a project in creative listening. Rather than constructing a standard historical narrative of social and cultural development I have chosen to immerse myself in a sea of stories. Rather than approaching my subject through the usual historiographical protocols of problem and hypothesis, I have allowed the voices of the past to whisper and beckon, and sometimes to rant and rave. Sometimes the cacophony is excessive, but at other times the silence is intolerable. Part of my project is to capture and calibrate historical noise.

My stories have a host of authors. They include people in distress, neighbours in trouble, the anxious, the alarmed, the confused. They speak as preachers of sermons, writers of letters, hawkers of broadsheets, and authors of popular pamphlets. More often they are defendants or witnesses, litigants or deponents, telling their tales to the secular or ecclesiastical courts. Each case affected the teller's reputation, and sometimes their lives depended on what they had to say. Their voices are sometimes urgent and angry, more often faint and distant. Their utterances are often allusive and indirect, laconic and indistinct. Inevitably, they come to us filtered and redacted through the processes of archival or textual transcription. They never tell us everything we want to know. Some of my authors spin tales of deceit, all the time insisting on their veracity. Sometimes they embellish the truth, sometimes they treat it with great economy. What they say about their world can be arresting, illuminating, shocking, or strange. The following stories come from the reigns of Elizabeth I, James I, and Charles I, but they intersect only intermittently with the familiar political history of Tudor and Stuart England.

I, too, of course, am the author of these stories. At least, each chapter is mine. I have taken an incident, a tale, a dispute, or a dilemma as my starting point, and have then read everything else that the archives and libraries can offer to help me make sense of it. Sometimes it is like pulling on a tangle of thread to see what unravels, though there is also an element of knitting or stitching whole cloth. I am conscious of my own rhetorical strategies, as well as my academic professionalism, in shaping and ordering the record. The process of researching and writing is intended to clarify the past but it may also impose fresh distortions. My notes, I hope, are full enough for interested readers to reconstruct my path.

Sex and violence, faith and folly, birth and death: these are powerful themes. All human life is there. Yet these stories are more time-bound than timeless. However touched they may be by universal human concerns, they are also rooted in the immediacy of their particular historical context. Each story emerges from the contested culture of post-Reformation England, and each reflects the strains and stresses of its local time and circumstance. From the mid-sixteenth to the mid-seventeenth century, England was beset by moral, spiritual, and religious difficulties, economic and demographic problems, cultural and political crises. It was, for all that, a literary golden age. The reigns of Elizabeth I, James I, and Charles I saw tussles for power within the aristocracy and arguments galore about the behaviour and beliefs of the common people. Religion generated endless disputes. The shift from Catholicism to Protestantism was traumatic for England, with many issues of belief and worship, ceremony and discipline, left undigested. God and the Devil still fought for people's souls, in a world of providences, wizardry, and wonders. The hierarchies of gender, status, and authority were subject to test and question, while parishioners negotiated the demands of family, Church, and State. A good many people showed indifference to the religious and ideological struggles of their era, and focused instead on the accumulation of wealth and the pleasures of the flesh. They too are the actors and tellers of stories.

Whereas my last book, *Birth, Marriage, and Death: Ritual, Religion, and the Life-Cycle in Tudor and Stuart England* (1997), dealt largely with routine rituals and normal expectations, *Agnes Bowker's Cat* is concerned with abnormal circumstances and rituals that went wrong. By investigating peculiar occurrences, extraordinary phenomena, and what Shakespeare described as 'maimed rites',[1] I hope to learn more about the workings of early modern society. The stories gathered here shed fresh light on how early modern parishioners construed their local universe and how they coped with crisis. Each episode illuminates its actors' enmeshment with authority and their myriad entanglements with each other.

The keywords in my sub-title require some glossing. They are not chosen only for their phonic or alliterative grace. 'Travesties', by one definition, are literary compositions which aim at exciting laughter by grotesque or burlesque treatments of serious subjects. Another definition addresses the element of disguise, of trans-vestment or cross-dressing, of assuming an alternative costume. For stories that involve mockery and deceit, and the occasional misuse of clothing, it seems an appropriate and felicitous word. The women who arranged the birth of a cat, the boys who took beasts to be baptized, the manservant who dressed as a woman, and the writers who gave us the Adamites and the sufferings of Cheapside Cross, were all involved in travesties of one form or another.

Much of the behaviour they report was deeply transgressive, crossing the bounds of propriety and offending religious, social, legal, or customary norms. The villagers of Holton transgressed when they countenanced an illegal burial, though they might claim that the church was at fault for its lack of accommodating charity. Other parishioners transgressed when they bad-mouthed their ministers, and clergymen exceeded the bounds when they returned the verbal fire. Iconoclasts transgressed when they assaulted Cheapside Cross, though they might argue that the authorities were at fault for permitting an idol in their midst. The advocates and opponents of Caroline religious policy, from William Laud to William Prynne, were also guilty of transgressions, according to one's viewpoint, as much as the installers and breakers of altar rails. The records abound with transgressions, great and small, though one person's fault could be another's moral imperative.

Early modern society was governed by principles of order and consensus, but countervailing tendencies of discord and dissension also gnawed at its heart. The stories and incidents under examination here highlight these disruptive stresses. Many of my chapters feature communities in discord, where harmonious relationships had temporarily broken down. The musical meaning of discord is also suggestive, evoking the sounds of confusion and clashing, in a project attuned to the recovery of historical noise. Social and religious dissension, as well as sexual and domestic discord, concerned the governors of Tudor and Stuart England. The following chapters indicate how well they succeeded in bringing it under control.

Chapter 1, 'Agnes Bowker's Cat: Childbirth, Seduction, Bestiality, and Lies', examines the claims and confusions when a woman in Leicestershire in 1569 allegedly gave birth to a cat. We have testimony from midwives and market women, servants and shopkeepers, clerics and magistrates, and from Agnes Bowker herself. The story so troubled local officials that they referred it to higher authorities, the case eventually reaching the attention of Queen Elizabeth's Privy Council and the Bishop of London. One of the investigators of this incident declared that 'there is nothing so secret it shall not be made open', but the convolutions of the story raise challenging questions about credulity and credibility, and the processing of doubtful information.

Chapter 2, 'Monstrous Births and Credible Reports: Portents, Texts, and Testimonies', pursues the themes of natural and supernatural childbirth by examining popular broadsheets and pamphlets from the mid-sixteenth to the early seventeenth century. Often luridly illustrated and laden with sensationalist religious verse, these printed texts took great trouble to establish the authenticity of the phenomenon they were describing. Though readers and viewers might be fascinated by gynaecological catastrophes, they were repeatedly instructed that England's monsters were messages from an angry and judging God.

Chapter 3, 'Mercy Gould and the Vicar of Cuckfield: Domestic and Clerical Pleading', examines letters written from a deeply divided Sussex community to officials at court between 1578 and 1581. The crisis that began with an unmarried servant's stillbirth or abortion (or perhaps her illness and treatment) grew to involve the local clergy, rival gentry and their wives, rivals in the iron business, the Bishop of Chichester, and Queen Elizabeth's secretary Francis Walsingham. Depending on which story prevailed were the honour and reputation of both men and women, control of the parish church, and the fate of local evangelical Protestantism.

Chapter 4, 'Rose Arnold's Confession: Seduction, Deception, and Distress in the Heart of England', rehearses the story that another unmarried servant told to a Leicestershire magistrate in 1608. Its ingredients include power and dependency, sex and violence, attempted abortion, attempted murder, suspected infanticide, and the construction of an exculpatory narrative.

Chapter 5, 'The Essex Abortionist: Depravity, Sex, and Violence', probes deeper into these issues through stories told to the Colchester borough magistrates in 1638. Lydia Downes gave a damning account of her sexual adventures and partnership in crime with the cunning man, abortionist, and poisoner, Richard Skeete. Corroborative testimony from witnesses, and evidence from the archdeaconry court, reveals a five-year spree of sexual depravity, infanticide, and murder, for which both Lydia and Richard were hanged.

Chapter 6, 'Another Midwife's Tale: Alcohol, Patriarchy, and Childbirth in Early Modern London', is a story of sexual dalliance, jealousy, and female sociability that came before the London archdeaconry court in 1635. It is a tale of strong drink and strong women, made all the more remarkable because its central character was employed as a midwife, and made claims about her midwifery practice to bolster her reputation. Here again we have tales within tales, and contested claims to the truth, as women argued in public about affronts to their honour.

Chapter 7, 'Cross-Dressing in the Birth Room: Gender Trouble and Cultural Boundaries', begins with the extraordinary case from 1633 of a young male servant discovered in female disguise in that most gender-segregated environment, the birth room. The midwife, her daughter, and the servant himself testified before the Oxford archdeaconry court. Other discourses that shed some light on this case include godly reformist complaints against cross-dressing, scenes of male cross-dressing on the early modern stage, and kindred cases from the archives. An issue of some moment was whether cross-dressing was an abomination unto the Lord, whether it undermined gender boundaries, or whether it was harmless fun. These are matters more commonly treated by literary scholars than historians, so problems of interdisciplinary discourse also arise.

Chapter 8, 'Who Buried Mrs Horseman? Excommunication, Accommodation, and Silence', explores the problem that confronted an Oxfordshire village in 1631 when the corpse of an excommunicated recusant gentlewoman was illicitly and secretly buried inside the parish church. At issue was the sanctity of consecrated ground, the flexibility of ecclesiastical discipline, and the clash between neighbourliness and law. 'God's blessing on them that buried the dead, it is fit the dead should be buried', remarked a sympathetic observer; but it took the bishop of Oxford several months of frustrating inquiry before he could guess who had performed the deed.

Chapter 9, 'Mocking the Clergy: Wars of Words in Parish and Pulpit', presents an array of incidents in which laymen berated and insulted their ministers, and a smaller number of cases when clergymen poured verbal venom on members of their congregation. These altercations shed fresh light on community discourse, and expose the strains in lay–clerical relations. Laymen sometimes mocked their ministers in jest, in anger, or in hopes of reforming their conduct. Some clerics, on the other hand, accepted 'tongue-smiting' as part of the price of their calling. Honour was once again at issue, along with matters of pastoral style and social discipline.

Chapter 10, 'The Atheist's Sermon: Belief, Unbelief, and Traditionalism in the Elizabethan North', concerns a Nottinghamshire landowner who was accused in 1590 of a slate of offences including atheism, slander, brawling, and conjuring. Perhaps his gravest offence, which set him at odds with the parish minister, was his reading of a midsummer sermon or homily which perpetuated an unreformed Catholic theology and a discredited devotion to the saints. The incident raises questions about the progress of the Reformation and the practices of popular religion.

Chapter 11, 'Baptized Beasts and Other Travesties: Affronts to Rites of Passage', collects together a number of incidents in which cats and dogs, calves and horses, were profanely taken into church and mockingly administered the sacrament of baptism. Some of these cases reflect youthful high spirits, while others in the early 1640s were connected to assaults on the established Church by sectarian reformers and parliamentary soldiers. Reports of these incidents are sometimes inflammatory, sometimes apologetic, as they position themselves for legal or polemical effect.

Chapter 12, 'The Battle of the Altars: Turning the Tables and Breaking the Rails', comes closest to the mainstream concerns of modern historians of the politics of religion. It addresses the local parochial consequences of the Caroline altar policy, and examines objection and resistance to the relocation of communion tables as altars and to the erection of communion rails. While thousands of parishioners willingly collaborated with the Laudian–Caroline regime, thousands more objected to changes of liturgical custom. When the political world shifted in 1640 the ceremonial altar furnishings came under attack, with widespread destruction of altar rails. Court records, petitions, sermons, and memoirs document this zone of cultural and religious contention, and capture the voices and stories of many of those involved.

Chapter 13, 'The Portraiture of Prynne's Pictures: Performance on the Public Stage', continues to examine reactions to government policy in the reign of Charles I. It focuses on the sufferings and triumphs of the polemicist William Prynne, and pays particular attention to the political theatre enacted through his body and his image. This is a story of mutilation and martyrdom, victimhood and vindication, that mobilized large sectors of public opinion between 1634 and 1641. One of its high points was the public ritual burning of the frames from which Prynne's portraits had already been removed.

Chapter 14, 'The Downfall of Cheapside Cross: Vandalism, Ridicule, and Iconoclasm', studies a spate of physical assaults on one of London's most venerable civic monuments. It combines satiric and religious pamphlets from the early 1640s with earlier accounts of iconoclasm to explore a variety of sensitivities and passions. When the Cross was finally dismantled in 1643, with public ceremony, it was treated as heathen idol and as a sentient being that could also suffer pain and dishonour.

Chapter 15, 'The Adamites Exposed: Naked Radicals in the English Revolution', examines one of the most startling phenomena of the English revolution, the appearance, or alleged appearance, of a sect of revolutionary fundamentalist nudists. Stories about this group appeared in the popular press in 1641, with reports of their sexual and religious perversions. Other authors discussed their antecedents in ancient Christianity, medieval heresy, and the more recent radical reformation. Adamite elements appeared among the Ranters and Quakers of the early 1650s, though it is doubtful that any such sect as the Adamites actually existed. Like many of the stories in this book, the tale of the Adamites involves engagement with highly dubious information. Questions arise not only about the truth of the matter, but also about the moral, political, and religious climate in which the Adamite phenomenon was discussed.

Most of this material will be new to most readers, and some may wonder why an historian of Tudor and Stuart England should attend to such marginal phenomena. One answer would be the pleasure in encountering historical actors like Agnes Bowker and Lydia Downes, Thomas Salmon and John Whippe, and the delight that comes from remarkable stories. A more serious answer would advance the claim that the margins illuminate the centre, and that the cultural history of early modern England is incomplete without hearing from people on the edge. Each episode provides a point of entry, a moment of leverage, for exploring a world we have lost.[2] I have certainly acquired a richer appreciation of village discourse and domestic politics, popular religion, and popular culture, in the period between Reformation and Revolution, and I hope to share that with my readers. Fresh insights and new information can be found about a complex and fascinating society by detouring along roads less travelled.

I am not, of course, the first to venture into this kind of territory. One of my Cambridge teachers, H. C. Porter, used to say that the history that most interested him was the history of 'the quirky bits'. By paying attention to curious and unusual phenomena, to oddities, puzzles, and aberrations, one might find a path to the past that other historians may have missed. Another, the great G. R. Elton, pioneered the practice of micro-history, though he would have been horrified to have been saddled with that reputation. Elton's *Star Chamber Stories* (1958), threw light on 'the lives, the habits and the speech of men and women in the sixteenth century... who would never ordinarily make the headlines'. And their stories in turn illuminated the legal and administrative history of their day. *Star Chamber Stories* is the most neglected of Elton's books, but it may outlast the controversies of his others.[3]

A more recent generation of European historians has examined the margins of early modern history to expose all sorts of relationships, beliefs, and tensions. Natalie Zemon Davis, for example, revealed the religious, social, occupational, and sexual tensions behind carnival processions in sixteenth-century France.[4] David Sabean was able to show how the sacrificial burial of a bull in an eighteenth-century German village exacerbated strains between local and regional authorities, between official and popular religion, and competing views on public health and sympathetic magic. Sabean's stories in *Power in the Blood: Popular Culture and Village Discourse in Early Modern Germany* (1984) allowed him to probe 'the dynamics of power and hierarchical relations' among peasants and officials from the sixteenth to the eighteenth century.[5] Robert Darnton likewise deployed stories about eighteenth-century France as a means of entering a lost symbolic world. Darnton's quarry was the *mentalité* that underlay the so-called 'Age of Enlightenment', and his stories in *The Great Cat Massacre and Other Episodes in French Cultural History* (1984) enabled him to expose 'an alien system of meaning' and to explore its complex 'ways of thinking'.[6] Italian historians have adopted the label 'micro-history' to describe a technique of extracting large and demanding questions from small and unpromising beginnings, and English historians are adept at case studies and incisive accounts of particular episodes.[7] The archives are full of surprises, stores of stories, and almost any point of entry can be chosen for building a world from a grain of sand.

1

AGNES BOWKER'S CAT: CHILDBIRTH, SEDUCTION, BESTIALITY, AND LIES

This is a story about stories, about versions of evidence and fragments of information that circle around the telling of an historical tale. It begins in the village culture of Elizabethan England, detours through the realms of gynaecology, midwifery, and ecclesiastical justice, spills over into ephemeral pamphlet literature, and ends up in the files of Elizabethan Privy Councillors. Along the way it raises questions of truth-telling and evidence, credulity and credibility, authenticity and verification, and the elusiveness of historical narrative. It is a story that links the concerns of local worthies and central governors, lay and ecclesiastical magistrates, and the intersecting spheres of men and women. It is also one which challenges the historian to think creatively and humbly about the possibility of ever making sense of the past. Whatever else we may learn from this material, it forces us to think about the foundations of knowledge and the criteria of 'credible report'. One of the participants in this story concluded, 'there is nothing so secret it shall not be made open', but even he was uncertain what actually to believe.[1]

In telling this story, and the others in this volume, we face several problems of procedure and rhetoric. We could summarize the incident, gather what seems most interesting from the record, and attempt to relate it to the mainstream history of the period; in this case the story throws an unusual sidelight on one of the most troubled years of the Elizabethan regime. We could impose a specialized interpretative framework on it, and relate the evidence to local history, legal history, the history of childbirth, the history of sexuality, and so on. Or we could lay out the information, in as complete a form as possible, and follow it wherever it leads. We may then find ourselves dealing with a fractal narrative, with endlessly multiplying connections and connotations, thickening layers of significance, and no clear sense of closure. Madness may lie in that direction, but so too might a richer sense of the complex culture of early modern England.

The story starts simply enough in the late 1560s, with the unwanted pregnancy of an unmarried domestic servant. The circumstances, to begin with, were unexceptional. Most young women were employed in household service in the years before they were married, and some of them, at some stage, became sexually active. If a servant became pregnant and was unable to conceal her condition, two considerations usually followed; first, her dismissal or removal, to safeguard the honour of the house; and second, investigation of the identity of the father. She might then take to the road or return to her family; she might hope for a miscarriage or attempt an abortion; but eventually, in most cases, she would be in need of a midwife. Not enough is known yet about the social and cultural history of bastard-bearing, about pregnancy-management and the availability of abortifacients, but the church court records contain fragments of testimony which illuminate various parts of this process. It is well established (by historical demographers) that up to 3 per cent of all live births were illegitimate in mid-Elizabethan England, and a goodly proportion of these were born to servants. Literary and cultural historians may think this 3 per cent figure is surprisingly low, but the measured percentage was even lower in eastern England and fell further in the generations that followed.[2]

This, however, is not a story of statistics (themselves beset by varying degrees of uncertainty and confidence) but rather of a unique and unsettling incident. It concerns the Leicestershire servant Agnes Bowker who in 1569, at Market Harborough, gave birth to a cat. Whether this really happened, whether such a delivery was physically possible, what it portended, and what other wickedness was attached to it, became matters for local and national authorities. The great cat delivery became a short-lived cause célèbre, attracting popular, clerical, and political attention. The case originated before the court of the Archdeacon of Leicester within the Diocese of Lincoln, a court that was normally occupied by minor violations of ecclesiastical discipline and good order, but also had jurisdiction over local midwives.[3] The church courts dealt frequently with fornication, bastardy, and sexual incontinence, but rarely with humans who gave birth to cats. So strange was the testimony, and so troubling, that the archdeacon's commissary sent a full transcript to the Earl of Huntingdon, along with his own notations and commentary; Huntingdon sent it to the queen's principal secretary, William Cecil, for consideration by the Council, and he referred it to Edmund Grindal, then Bishop of London, for further advice. Eventually the packet was filed in Lord Burghley's papers, now British Library Lansdowne Manuscript 101. The account was further embellished with a life-size, blood-red depiction of the cat, rendered on parchment and attached to the sheaf of papers.[4]

Agnes Bowker became pregnant some time during 1568 and after some wandering adventures, some of which will be related, came to term at the beginning of 1569. After something of a false start the ceremony of childbirth apparently

1. Anthony Anderson's depiction of Agnes Bowker's cat, accompanying the transcripts he sent to the Earl of Huntingdon, 1569

proceeded normally, with midwife and other mothers in attendance, until the horror of the monstrous feline birth. I am quoting the testimony in the order that it was heard by the court, rather than reconstituting it into some kind of master chronology, in order to better understand how the story unfolded to its original hearers and readers. By laying this out with minimal processing, I hope to capture some lost voices and anxieties from early modern England. I will then suggest some analytical avenues which may help us to understand this amazing and convoluted tale.

This is what we are told. Agnes Bowker, aged 27, daughter of Henry Bowker of Harborough, appeared before the archdeacon's court on 22 January 1569 and reportedly said as follows: 'That she was delivered of this monster (for so she called it) the 16th day of January between the hours of six and seven at night; and further sayeth that one Randal Dowley, servant to Mr Edward Griffin, had to do with her at Braybrooke over the porter's ward at Michaelmas was twelvemonth.' Agnes reported further sexual encounters with Randal Dowley in the porter's ward, in the maltmill, and, most recently, 'upon the grange leas as she was gathering sticks one month before pease harvest last past'. This appears to be remarkably candid information about servant sexuality,[5] with telling details about the time and place of sexual congress and calendrical prompts to memory, and it would seem to pin down Randal Dowley as the father of the child. But, as we hear, there was no child born, but rather a monster or cat, and other putative fathers enter the picture as the story unfolds.

Agnes, it is clear, was no wandering stranger but belonged to the Harborough community. She had worked as a servant in several local house-holds. Her father was dead but her mother was close enough to consult at the time of her delivery, and her godmother came to see her soon after. Neighbours may have found the story especially disturbing for coming from one of their own.[6]

Agnes explained to the court 'that a cat had to do with her six or seven times betwixt Michaelmas was twelvemonth and a month before Harborough fair last past.[7] Further she saith that on a time she willed Randal Dowley to be good to her in her great necessity, being by his only procurement brought thereunto, who utterly forsook her and departed from her. She being greatly amazed with these his words, went into a certain wood called Boteland and there with her girdle would have hanged herself, but the girdle brake.' Wandering the lanes in midwinter, distraught and suicidal, she 'came to Little Bowden, and there went before her a beast in likeness to a bear . . . and a little after she came into the street and to her seeming the same bear went before her into pond, and she followed it and was almost drowned.' (Her rescuers later testified that they pulled her out from water that was barely waist deep, and that she showered them with falsehoods, including the claim that she was already married.)

Eventually Agnes returned to Harborough, in urgent need of a midwife, and met with Margaret Roos, a gentleman's wife who supplied informal gynaecological services.[8] Mrs Roos told the court that she 'handled' Agnes Bowker soon after New Year's Day, 1569, 'and found somewhat to be in her body besides the natural course thereof, but what it should be . . . she could not tell or well discern'. A few days later Agnes came to her again, this time 'in extreme labour'. Searching her body, Mrs Roos said, 'she did feel a thing but whether it were child or water she could not tell', but, rather ominously, whatever it was pricked her finger. Mrs Roos's opinion on this occasion was that Agnes already 'hath had a child of late, and this is the afterbirth'. Perhaps she had attempted to induce an abortion. Whatever it was, the labour apparently stopped, and commenced again eight days later under the guidance of a different midwife.

This introduces a key witness, Elizabeth Harrison, aged 60, midwife of Bowden Parva, and either colleague or competitor with Margaret Roos. Midwives were women of wisdom and authority, supposedly ecclesiastically licensed, who normally took charge of the business of childbirth. They commonly attended bastard-bearers as well as respectable married women, and they were answerable to the court and the community for improprieties in the birth room. In contemporary literature their reputations ranged from interfering crones to competent helpers, but only in the imaginations of misguided modern writers were midwives associated with witchcraft.[9] Ecclesiastical court records provide a remarkable window into midwives' routine activities, and in this case there was plenty to explain. We have already met with sexual conduct, attempted suicide, bestial visions, and gynaecological examination. Before this story is over we will encounter a broad range of topics that recent scholarship has rarely explored.

Elizabeth Harrison testified 'that on Tuesday the 11th of this January (she) was sent for by the wives of Harborough, Margery Slater being the messenger, to come to Agnes Bowker being in labour. She saith that she asked this Agnes who was the father of her child . . . who answered it is one Randal Dowley, for he had had many times the use of her body carnally; and further (she) saith that the said Agnes told her these tales following'. It was by custom the midwife's duty to discover the paternity of an illegitimate birth. But no other Elizabethan midwife heard, or participated in, anything so transgressive as the story that followed.

We now have tales within tales, or testimony within testimony, that shift with the teller and the telling. This is what the midwife told the court that Agnes had told her—filtered, like all such accounts, by memory and reshaped for strategic and rhetorical purposes, then further rendered into writing and conformed to legal conventions by the clerk to the archdeacon's court. This is the midwife's tale:

There came to (Agnes) divers and sundry times a thing in the likeness of a bear, sometimes like a dog, sometimes like a man, and had the knowledge carnal of her body in every such shape. Also she saith that Agnes Bowker told her that . . . as she walked abroad the country (she) met with an outlandish woman, a Dutch woman, and the stranger asked her the cause of her sadness. Agnes answered, I have good cause for I am with child; then the stranger said, Nay thou art not with child, but what wilt thou give me, I will tell thee what thou art withal. Then Agnes said I will give thee a penny, and so did, and the woman stranger said Thou art neither with man child nor woman child, but with a Mooncalf, and that thou shall know shortly, for thou hast gone forty weeks already, and thou shalt go eleven weeks longer, and then at the same hour the moon changeth or thereabout, get thee women about thee, for it shall then fall from thee.

And the midwife said that as soon as she heard this story she relayed it to the other women about her.

What are we to make of this? That Agnes had been engaged in bestial relations with shape-shifting animals, as well as relations with Randal Dowley, and that parturition would follow a fifty-one-week pregnancy? By the lights of sixteenth-century science, such things were not impossible, however uncommon.[10] Should we assume that Agnes had sought out a cunning woman (in other testimony a 'Welsh' woman rather than a Dutch woman) to guide her through her troubles? Or had she (or the midwife) made the whole thing up? The stranger's prophecy, as told by the midwife, was a vital element in Agnes's story. Listeners would know that a mooncalf, or mola, was a mass of malformed tissue, believed to be the fruit of forbidden couplings, faulty seed, or a vicious conception. Some might even have seen pictures of such things in sensationalist broadsheets, or in medical handbooks whose engravings of gynaecological horrors added to their prurient interest.[11] And they would be prepared for an abnormal outcome. It was a nice touch to say that delivery would coincide with the time of the turning of the moon, which occurred in the middle of January. Agnes began labour on 11 January, intermitted for almost a week, and then gave birth to the cat, if that is what happened, on 17 January 1569.[12]

Resuming her testimony, Elizabeth Harrison named the other women present during Agnes Bowker's delivery, and described their efforts to bring forth the monster, 'the hinder part coming first'. She said that 'when the women saw this strange sight they fled', but the midwife 'boldened them and willed them not to go from her, and then she said to the monster thus: In the name of the father and the son and of the holy ghost: Come safe and go safe and do no harm, now in the name of God what have we here?'

What indeed? It is often said that midwives possessed special skills including the uttering of certain charms, but this is unique in being quoted in the records. Echoing key words from the service of baptism—a service that Elizabethan midwives sometimes performed *in extremis*—this incantation took on the properties of an exorcism or spell.[13] Its effect must have been chilling to everyone present, signalling that something strange and unnatural was being born. Foretold as a mooncalf, drawing blood from the first midwife's finger, and presenting itself abnormally, 'the hinder part . . . first', this utterance from Agnes Bowker's womb might well prompt the question, 'what have we here'. The women might well run away if they feared that the sight of a monster would somehow contaminate their own wombs.[14]

To learn more about this incident and to augment the testimony of the midwife the court summoned several women who had been present at the birth. Six such women acknowledged helping with the delivery, but none could tell for certain what had happened. All recalled being afraid. The testimony in this case confirms our impression of childbirth as a female collective experience, with goodwives gathered together in a darkened room attending and watching the midwife.[15] Only the outcome was strange. Joan Clement, aged 50, was 'going away' when the midwife called her back with her prayer. Emma Buttrick, aged 40, was 'standing by in the house with her child in her arms' when the monster cat appeared, 'but she saith she dare not affirm or say it came out of [Agnes's] body'. Margaret Harrison, aged 30, said 'that she was at the birth of the monster with her child in her arms, and the wives willed her to fetch a candle for they had not light . . . and when she came in with the candle she saw the monster lie on the earth, and she thinketh it came out of Agnes Bowker's womb'. Isabel Perkins, aged 30, was also present with her child in her arms, 'and saw the monster . . . when the midwife drew it from under the clothes of Agnes Bowker'. None of these women actually saw the monster emerge, on this dark January evening, but the product was there for all to see, dead and shrivelled on the floor and resembling nothing so much as a skinned cat.

That it was a cat was obvious to everyone, though most preferred to refer to it as a monster. The question was, had Agnes Bowker given birth to it? If so, how, and if not, what? This is where the men came in. So far this has been entirely a female story, except for the runaway Randal Dowley and the officers of the archdeaconry court. Now the men of Market Harborough would offer their wisdom—clergymen, shopkeepers, and magistrates. Together they embarked on an empirical examination, a remarkable exercise in improvised investigative pathology, to answer the midwife's question, 'what have we here'. Their testimony too forms an important part of the record.

The curate, Christopher Pollard,[16] told the court that he 'was present when the entrail of the cat was opened, and there did he with others see and take forth very straw out of the gut, to the number of three or four'. George Walker, innholder, 'ripped the maw of the cat, pulling it out of the body thereof, and there he did see certain meat congealed, and also in the same maw a piece of . . . bacon'. William Jenkinson supported this testimony, observing 'the piece of meat that came out of the maw of the cat, or monster if it were one, and to his judgment he saith it were a piece of bacon sword, for he might very easily and perfectly discern of both sides of the bacon the bristles or hairs, and farther he saith that Edmund Goodyear of Harborough, baker, will depose the same'.[17] Such details may curdle delicate stomachs, but they indicate the pragmatic and materialist manner with which one group of Elizabethans approached the problem, as well as the confidence the church court placed in their testimony. Theirs was a hands-on investigation, untroubled by medical or religious theory. It may also indicate a gendered epistemology, in which the men considered the cat as an object to be investigated while the woman looked on the birth as a mysterious though not impossible event. Observing the bacon and straw convinced these men that they were dealing with a real cat that had earlier been foraging in the lanes of Leicestershire, not some misshapen monster gestated in a poor woman's womb. Furthermore, they introduced evidence that Agnes had recently tried to borrow a cat, and that a neighbour from whom she had begged now found his cat missing. The solid businessmen of Harborough had little doubt where it had gone.

On 27 January, five days after the first ecclesiastical court hearing, the secular authorities took up the case. Their primary concern was to investigate whether there had been a crime. Sir George Turpin, knight, and Edward Griffin, esquire, examined some of the same parties, and recorded pretty much the same statements as before.[18] A few more witnesses fleshed out the story, including Christopher Clarke, husbandman, who helped save Agnes from drowning (to whom she then lied about her marital status), and Agnes's friend Joan Dunmow (to whom she lied about having already had the baby, saying 'her child was at the nurse at Guilsborough' in Northamptonshire). These examinations add little to the account, except to expand our appreciation of Agnes's gift for storytelling. Edward Griffin, esquire, would seem to have been Randal Dowley's erstwhile master, and his property the place of Agnes's fall, but none of that was mentioned, or at least not entered into the record.

Examined yet again on 4 February by Sir George Turpin, Agnes Bowker elaborated her tale of bestial-supernatural conception. She now said 'that a thing came unto her as she was in bed and lay the first night very heavy upon her bed but touched her not. The next night she saw it and it was in the likeness of a black cat. By the moonlight it came into her bed and had knowledge of her body' on several occasions. As to the foetus, the fruit of this cross-species coupling, she told the Justice, 'it was dead in her from St Thomas's day in the Christmas until she travailed, and yet that it was sweet when it was born'. The story of what she had delivered, and when she delivered it, was covered with as much confusion and obfuscation as the tales of her impregnation.

Not until 12 February, once more before the archdeacon's commissary Anthony Anderson, did anything approaching the truth emerge. And once again the truth was elusive and slippery, as much a construction of language and rhetoric and a means of satisfying particular audiences as an objective account of 'what actually happened'.

During the weeks following the delivery of the cat, Agnes lay-in at various houses in Harborough, the subject of much curiosity and scrutiny. Rumours stretched from those who believed that the monstrous birth was a portent or supernatural message to the embattled Tudor state, to those who suspected that the whole business was a cover-up for infanticide. The gentry wives were especially anxious to untangle the mystery, and both Mrs Roos and Lady Turpin secured private interviews with Agnes Bowker. So too did Agnes's godmother,

Emma Walker, wife of George Walker, innholder, the man who discovered the bacon.

Emma Walker testified that on 10 February she visited Agnes 'to give her counsel to discharge her conscience'. Her words, in the form we have them, are as much a product of court procedures and selective memory as all the others, but they mark a turning point in the narrative. Lady Turpin, it transpired, had told Agnes 'it was not possible this cat could come from her' and Emma Walker agreed. 'Surely even so think I,' she told her god-daughter, 'but thou hast had a child and it is made away and this cat by some sleight or sorcery is conveyed to thee. Then the said Agnes said, Alas godmother, I was conjured . . . I dare not tell you nor disclose the matter, for I have promised to keep the thing secret, and have given myself both body and soul to the devil if ever I utter the matter any further than I have already.'

Two days later Agnes was ready to talk. She responded to twenty articles drawn up by the archdeacon's commissary, and told yet another version of her story that had not been heard before. Whether it was true, or partially true, or a complete fabrication, was still a puzzle to the authorities. 'Whether this tale . . . be true or false, yet it seemeth to me that in such a fardel [i.e. a pedlar's bundle] here is great store of wares such as they are, as whoredom, witchcraft and buggery; if besides there be none other, which hath tied up this fardel and given it her to bear?' So pondered Anthony Anderson, the diligent archdeaconry commissary; and the puzzle is ours as well. This is what Anderson recorded:

(Agnes) saith that in time past [*some time in the mid-1560s*] she dwelled with one Hugh Brady sometime dwelling in Harborough and was schoolmaster there . . . This Brady she saith was a very vicious man and did lie with his maids often, and committed adultery with them; and she knowing his facts, told her mistress on him, and her master therefore entreated her evil, and there the falling sickness [i.e. epilepsy] took her, and her mistress did send her to . . . London to dwell, because her master should no more so evil entreat her. After this she saith she came to Braybrooke and dwelt there, when the Queen's majesty came on her grace's progress thither,[19] and being at the court gates this Hugh Brady saw her and came to her and gave her two shillings, and bad her go to the grange yard close and he would meet her there.

She saith she went there and he came to her and cast her on the ground, and had his carnal pleasure upon her and bad her be merry, and he would get her a boy, and would send for her where she should live in better state all the days of her life. Further she saith he said to her, hath thy disease left thee yet? No, saith she. Well, saith Brady, if thou wilt be ruled by me and not betray me I will help thee of thy disease. There is no remedy, thou must needs have a child first and then thy disease will leave thee, and another thing thou must do.

(Agnes) asked Mr Brady what she must do further. Marry, saith he, thou must forsake God and all his works, and give thyself wholly to the devil, and within two or three years thou shalt be whole. Further, she saith that this Mr Brady promised to send to her a thing, which should come to her in the likeness of a man into that close, one day, where she should meet him, and to him she must give her promise that she would from thenceforth forsake God and his laws, and betake her to the devil body and soul, and also must give and offer to him some part of her blood and then she should have the same thing . . . when she would, and should not need to be afraid thereof.

She saith that about two years after this she went one day into that close, and came to her, toward the night, a trim man [i.e. someone neat and well-furnished] and said he was come to her for her promise made to Brady, and then she saith she did give him her faith, that she would forsake God and all his works, and give herself from that time forth to the devil fully and wholly. She saith that then at that time she tickled her nose and made it to bleed, and dropped her blood upon a rag, and gave it to the man, which man then lay with her, and after came, as Brady had said he should, like a greyhound and a cat, and had to do with her sundry times carnally.

Nor was this the end of the affair.

(Agnes) saith that about Candlemas last past, viz. 1567 [8] or the Lady's day in Lent, she had been at Harborough for grout [i.e. coarse meal] and in St Mary's lane this Brady and two other with him came riding, and when they saw her he reined back his horse and gave her sixpence and bad her come to St Mary's church, which standeth in the field, and so she did, and his servants went softly before, and he lighted there (and) in the porch of the church aforesaid he had, saith she, his carnal pleasure upon her.[20]

She saith that he then asked her if she yet had not a child, and she said, No not yet. Well, saith he, thou shalt have shortly, and at the time of thy travail thou shalt have much more mind to one woman than to all other to be thy grace woman, or midwife, and the same woman unto whom thou shalt have such mind shall deliver thee of the child, and then will I take thee away where thou shalt be kept in a little better case than thou art now, all the days of thy life. She saith that he told her he was going to Lincoln, and so went toward Dingley [*the next village to the east*], and since that time she saith she never saw him.

This, then, is a seduction tale, the story of a woman's downfall. Though structured in answer to legal interrogatories, and paced by the procedures of the court, it has elements in common with sensational folk-tales and ballads.[21] We are given, through Agnes's words, the sexual predator and manipulative teacher, thwarted only briefly by his long-suffering wife; we see the vulnerable young servant, bent on virtue yet drawn too easily into corruption; we even glimpse the monarch, the Virgin Queen on her royal progress, and the irony of the local celebrations that led to Agnes's ruin; we learn of Agnes's falling sickness—epilepsy—and Brady's remarkable prescription for its cure;[22] and we have the vivid account of the second seduction in St Mary's lane and a further demonstration of the versatile use of church porches. The tale concludes with Brady's promise to take good care of his victim, and his almost inevitable failure to make good on it (similar to the desertion by Randal Dowley). In its structure and content this story is reminiscent of popular morality tales, on which Agnes may have modelled it, though that does not necessarily undermine its credit.

When asked by Mrs Roos, the gentlewoman who had previously searched her body, 'I' faith, Agnes, did thy Mr Brady never bewitch thee or deal by sorcery with thee?' Agnes Bowker replied, 'No, never,' and 'I am right glad thereof', saith Mrs Roos. Considerations of witchcraft would permit another possible range of explanations, and they hover at the edge of this particular narrative. But despite the contemporary fascination with witchcraft, and reports of recent trials,[23] the investigators at Market Harborough preferred to believe that Agnes Bowker's case involved victimization, duplicity, and delusion rather than witchcraft, sorcery, and supernatural manipulation. They had no body to examine, apart from the cat, and no obvious victim of infanticide or *maleficium*. Though Agnes had already admitted to her godmother that she had been 'conjured', and the stories of diabolism and shape-shifting might have led to further interrogation, the authorities decided that secular forensic proceedings would suffice.[24]

Finally, Agnes turned to the outcome of her pregnancy, the only subject on which other witnesses could testify. Once again, she told contradictory stories. At the beginning of her account Agnes acknowledged that 'three weeks before Christmas . . . one Thomas Dawe's . . . wife seeing her before having a great belly, and now the same very small and gaunt, asked her whether she were delivered of a child, and she said, yea, and my child is dead and is buried at Little Bowden'. (She had told earlier questioners that her child was alive and at nurse at Guilsborough, while according to the mainstream account she was still pregnant at this time.) But at the end of her testimony Agnes returned to her dealings with the midwife and the story that she had given birth to a cat. Her account throws interesting light on the treatment and choices faced by expectant single mothers in early modern England, even if her particular circumstances were decidedly unusual. Rather than being denied proper attention, Agnes enjoyed the support of respectable married women and a remarkable choice of gynaecological assistance.

'(Agnes) saith that when she began to travail she had much need, and many midwives she had in sundry towns through which she travelled, but none could do her any good till she came to Harborough; and she saith that her mind was ever to Elizabeth Harrison of Bowden Parva, to have her to be her midwife, after she had heard of her, above all others, and liked none but her. She saith that Elizabeth Harrison, her midwife, tarried the longest with her of any other, and did indeed help her and deliver, as she thinketh, and saith that she could not be delivered till this midwife came.' It is not absolutely certain that Elizabeth Harrison was the midwife or grace woman Hugh Brady had urged Agnes to seek out, but it seems highly plausible that the midwife and the seducer were in cahoots. Agnes claimed not to know what was going on, in the midst of her labour, and 'saith that she is not certain and sure that this cat-monster came out of her body; but the midwife told her it did come from her, and she thinketh it did, but upon her oath she is not sure thereof'. And if Agnes herself was not sure whether she had actually given birth to a cat, what hope has anyone else to make a determination? Discovering whether Agnes Bowker was simple-minded, profoundly evil, or glibly duplicitous became a central aim of the inquiry.

Commissary Anthony Anderson, who conducted Agnes's examination, glossed it with the following remark. 'All and every the premises came of herself, without threats or favourings; but suddenly moved by such pieces of scripture as it pleased God to give me to tell her of, she fell down on her knees, with weeping tears abundantly, and so uttered this before written; at the end whereof she said, Now am I forever damned, for I have uttered this which I promised I would never disclose; but I comforted her so well as I could, and before her departure she seemed comforted, notwithstanding I perceive there is more yet that hereafter may be got from her.' Notwithstanding the abundance of testimony, the story remained incomplete: true or false, or a mixture of half-truths and fabrications, the authorities had no way to determine. The schoolmaster Hugh Brady was nowhere to be found, the servant Randal Dowley had left the district, and no more credible information was forthcoming. The women could not agree what had happened, and those present at the birth could not even testify with confidence to what they had seen. Lady Turpin and Emma Walker appear refreshingly level-headed with their doubt whether such a cross-species delivery was possible, and with their unexamined suspicion of infanticide. Anthony Anderson smelled a rat, but all he had left was the cat, and the spreading notoriety of the incident.

On 18 February, a month after the emergence of the monster and a week after Agne's last examination, Anderson referred the entire case to Henry Hastings, Earl of Huntingdon, the nobleman most closely involved in Leicestershire affairs.[25] Anderson told Hastings, 'there hath been of late and is yet abroad, right honourable, set forth in print a printed pamphlet, describing the shape of a monster born at Harborough ... the which neither in form pictured or lines printed expresseth the truth, but otherwise falsely reporteth the matter, as may appear by this picture which is the very true proportion of the thing (surely a cat).' Somebody had evidently gone quickly into print with a broadsheet or pamphlet, now lost, about Agnes Bowker's monstrous birth. But the writer, like sensationalist journalists everywhere, had got the details wrong. Anderson wanted to quench misleading rumours and set the record straight, and his finest asset was the material remains of the monster itself—'surely a cat'—a pitiful creature with its gut pulled out and all of its hair removed. The picture, life-size and drawn in the colour of red brick or dried blood, would anchor the affair in some kind of certainty, or at least verisimilitude. 'This picture . . . containeth the full length, thickness, and bigness of the same, measured by a pair of compasses; and for the more credit of the matter I have set forth the seal used in my office . . . so the cat (so I think it to be) yet kept will warrant this shape.'

If this was not enough, Anderson reported the results of his own laboratory experiment to prove that the monster was indeed nothing but a barnyard cat. He never charged explicitly that the mother and midwife were lying, but that suspicion clearly underlies his actions. The townsmen, in their zeal for the truth, had disembowelled the original cat to find out what was in its stomach. Now the commissary reported, 'I caused another cat to be killed and flayed, and betwixt the one and the other in the whole this was the difference and only the difference, the eyes of my cat were as cats' eyes that be alive, and the monster cat's eyes were darker than blue. I cast my flayn cat into boiling water, and pulling the same out again, both in eye and else they were altogether one.' What more could be asked of the scientific method, in this country version of Renaissance laboratory craft? And who could believe after this that the cat was a monster, or that it issued from Agnes Bowker's womb? Something strange and wondrous may have happened, but it was not to be classified among the other monsters for which early Elizabethan England was famous.

Anderson's package of transcripts, complete with the picture of the cat, made its way from Lord Hastings to Secretary of State William Cecil, who turned for advice to Edmund Grindal, the Bishop of London. What did it mean to them? Why should these powerful figures concern themselves with such bizarre reports from Leicestershire? The answer reveals the vulnerability of the Elizabethan regime as well as its vigilance and caution, and it underscores the link between local happenings and central government. It also suggests that these magistrates, like the shopkeepers of Harborough and the clerks of the archdeaconry court, were anxious to discover and interpret the truth. Bishop Grindal received the 'examinations about the supposed monster' at the beginning of August 1569 and reported a fortnight later, 'for the monster, it appeareth plainly to be a counterfeit matter; but yet we cannot extort confessions of the manner of doings'.[26] Despite their scepticism, the bishop and the Council were no more successful than commissary Anderson in fully establishing what had happened. Agnes Bowker soon returned to oblivion, her subsequent history unknown.

It mattered little to Cecil whether Agnes gave birth to a bastard or to a beast, or whether she had murdered her baby; but it became a matter of public concern when people saw threatening portents in this apparent violation of nature, and when credulous Catholics gained ground by exploiting a dubious story. Abnormal births and bestial intrusions were shocking reminders of the unpredictability of the universe and of the power of hidden forces to subvert everyday routines. At times of crisis they assumed political dimensions, as auguries of 'alteration of kingdoms' and portents of 'destruction of princes'.[27] It should come as no surprise, then, to find the government attempting to control or neutralize such reports in 1569.

What else was happening in the winter of 1568–9? English Protestantism was struggling to make headway, while traditional Catholicism still thrived in many parts of the country. The Elizabethan regime was but tenuously established, the queen unmarried and the succession perilously uncertain. Relations with Spain were fast deteriorating, Mary Queen of Scots had recently arrived in England, and the northern earls were festering rebellion. The real monster of 1569, from the government point of view, may have been the many-headed monster of insurrection, for which mooncalves and monstrous births might be portents.[28]

There is nothing in the record to link directly the Leicestershire cat with the nation's uncertainties, but it may be significant that commissary Anderson took the case to a courtier politician, Lord Hastings, rather than to his ecclesiastical superiors in the Diocese of Lincoln. Anthony Anderson was a rising evangelist minister,[29] and Hastings a patron of puritans. Grindal was known for his Protestant activism, which in 1570 would win him the archbishopric of York, and Cecil, by no means a puritan, was staunchly Protestant and alert to the dangers of popular Catholicism.[30] None of the principals in this case is specifically identified in confessional terms, nor is religion an explicit part of the testimony, but Agnes Bowker and her women clearly belonged to the traditional folk culture of wonders more than to the sceptical culture of the Protestant Reformation. Agnes's story, if not vigorously countered, could feed the flow of rumour and credulous apprehension that held back godly Protestantism and nourished hopes of a Catholic restoration.

The Leicestershire incident followed a spate of reported monstrous births earlier in the 1560s that are discussed in more detail in the following chapter.

Cheap publications described 'two monstrous children born at Herne in Kent' and the 'shape of a monstrous child which was born in Northamptonshire' in 1565; graphic broadsides depicted 'two monstrous children' born in Buckinghamshire and another in Surrey in 1566, and 'the shape and form of a monstrous child born at Maidstone' in 1568. None of these had animal shapes, but they were horridly incomplete or malformed, sometimes incompletely separated twins. Commentators attributed these accidents to divine anger against England's wickedness, as warnings of retribution and signs of a disordered world. 'Unnatural shapes', the broadsheet writers insisted, contained 'lessons and schoolings for us all, as the word monster showeth'.[31] Monstrous births demonstrated that the nation was in trouble, with deformities in newborn children matching deformities in the body politic.

The Leicestershire monster could be seen as belonging to this genre, though deviating significantly from it. In the same dangerous year of 1569 appeared a compendium of *Certaine Secrete Wonders of Nature* illustrating freaks and monsters from continental Europe and from classical antiquity, including some with animal features, parts of a dog, the face of a cat, tails, etc. Monsters appeared to be sprouting up all over, as part of a fecund but putrid cultural landscape, and the publicity they enjoyed may have helped Agnes Bowker to construct her story and her auditors to interpret it.[32]

The monster literature of the 1560s laid great stress on the reliability of its information. Reports, however grotesque, were invariably asserted to be 'true'. The deformities described in the broadsheets lay beyond the common realm of experience and hovered on the margins of credibility, but illustrations, physical descriptions, and the names of supporting witnesses worked hard to establish or reinforce their bona fides. Establishing the truth of the matter was a necessary preliminary to spelling out its lessons. By contrast, in the case of the Harborough monster, establishing that Agnes Bowker's story was *not* true might rein in the spread of rumours and undercut assertions about its moral and religious consequences.

It would help, to be sure, to find the pamphlet against which Anthony Anderson reacted, but searches have so far proved unsuccessful. Either it was suppressed and withdrawn, or it went the way of the 80 per cent or more of the early ephemeral literature that has subsequently disappeared.[33] The incident was widely cited, however, as a scandal of popish credulity and ignorance, and was mentioned in other mid-Elizabethan writings. Barnaby Googe, in *The Popish Kingdom* of 1570, castigated the Catholics, 'for mark what things they do believe, what monsters they do frame'. William Bullein, in his *Dialogue Against the Fever Pestilence* was much more specific. Bullein's characters Roger and Civis join in the following exchange:[34]

Roger: What a world is this? How is it changed! It is marvelous, it is monstrous! I hear
        say there is a young woman, born in the town of Harborough, one Bowker, a
        butcher's daughter, which of late, God wot, is brought to bed of a cat, or have deliv-
        ered a cat, or, if you will, is the mother of a cat. Oh God! How is nature repugnant to
        herself, that a woman should bring forth a very cat (or a very dog, etc., wanting
        nothing, neither having more than other dogs or cats have), taking nothing of the
        mother but only as I guess her cattish condition.

Civis: It is a lie, Roger, believe it not; it was but a cat. It had bacon found in its belly, and
        a straw. It was an old cat, and she a young quean [i.e. a strumpet]; it was a pleasant
        practice of papistry, to bring the people to new wonders. If it had been a monster,
        then it should have had somewhat more or else less; but another cat was flayed in the
        same sort, and in all points like, or as it were, the self same. Thus can drabs do some-
        times when they have murdered their own bastards, with help of an old witch bring-
        ing a cat in its place. A toy to mock an ape withal. Roger, it should have been a kitling
        first, and so grown to a cat; but it was a cat at the first.

Roger: Yet there are many one do believe it was a monster.

Roger and the citizen, or their author Bullein, evidently had details based on
Anthony Anderson's transcript (or from the now-vanished ballad), in which
the townsmen's discovery of the bacon and the commissary's experiment with
a duplicate cat became evidence against popular belief in monsters. In appro-
priating Agnes's story they explode its mysterious power, and in debunking it
they dispose simultaneously of female fantasy and Catholic caprice. If the
evidence for a monster falls apart, along with it goes any need to think of
warnings, portents, and judgements on England.

An annotation to Anderson's illustration of the cat reads, 'there is nothing so
secret that shall not be made open'. But perhaps this is wishful thinking. Neither
Grindal nor Anderson could get to the bottom of the matter, and without firm
evidence or a clear confession they were not about to voice their suspicions. No
wonder Burghley just filed it away in his collection of oddities. So where does
one go from here? How does the historian decide what questions to ask, what
lines of inquiry to pursue? A deeper political and religious contextualization
might throw more light on the strains of the late 1560s. A detailed local social
and cultural account might usefully locate Agnes's pregnancy within the
mental and domestic environments of southern Leicestershire. Comparative
reading of the history of bastardy, abortion, and infanticide might help us to
better understand Agnes Bowker's predicament. More work on sorcery and
diabolism might provide analogues for some of her amazing stories. Certainly,
we have ways of bringing the episode under some kind of control. But does it
unlock the story to ask 'what really happened', or does such a common-sense
question sidestep its potential significance?

Who impregnated Agnes Bowker—the servant, the schoolmaster, or the thing in the likeness of a beast? Perhaps all three 'had to do with her'. Bestial or demonic intercourse was not thought impossible in the sixteenth century, nor was a superfetation, the formation of a second foetus some months after another. Was Agnes really pregnant for fifty-one weeks, rather than the normal thirty-nine, and what explains the varying calendar of her labour? By some accounts she was delivered of child in December, went into labour again in January, and finally gave birth to the cat a full week later. This might be explained by reference to miscalculation, to superfetation, or to the delayed expulsion of a defective twin, although it seems more likely that Agnes concealed a dead baby and then developed a conspiracy with the midwife.

How do we answer Elizabeth Harrison's question, 'what have we here?' Contemporary childbirth manuals are filled with grotesque happenings, not all of them unknown to modern science. It was commonly held that a woman's imagination could have damaging effects on her offspring, so that thinking of a black cat during intercourse or pregnancy could result in a child with dark and feline features. Modern medical explanations might even be brought to bear on the problem, if we wanted to stay within the bounds of gynaecological probability.[35] None of this gets to the bottom of the Agnes Bowker story, or the midwife's insistence that she really did give birth to a cat. The 'truth' remains bafflingly elusive, even if one harbours one's suspicions.

It is not necessarily helpful to say that women do not give birth to cats and therefore the whole tale is an imposture, the monstrous delivery a fraud or a cover for a violent crime. Medical science and folklore alike believed in the possibility of hybridization and bestial conception. Religious authorities acknowledged cross-bred prodigies as signs of God's providence. Women in Renaissance Europe were believed to have given birth to dogs, pigs, and toads. Writing in 1635 Thomas Heywood reported the fourteenth-century case of a woman who was 'delivered of cats'. A Norfolk woman allegedly gave birth to a cat in 1668, and a Hampshire woman brought forth a toad and a serpent in 1675.[36] As late as the 1720s the celebrated Mary Toft and her managers convinced some of the most distinguished physicians in England that she really had given birth to a litter of rabbits.[37] That leads us back to the 'what really happened' kind of question, which may be less significant than what people at the time thought was going on, and how they reacted.

It is possible to venture a feminist analysis which sees Agnes Bowker as a strategist, and not just a victim, her sexual promiscuity and verbal inventiveness as means of empowerment or retaliation. Though weak and vulnerable, guileful and gullible, and prone to epileptic seizures, this unmarried servant held the stage against her neighbours, accusers, and judges. Against a world of

male sexual predators, male employers, and male investigators, Agnes deployed
the powerful weapon of words. Her stories gave her authority and protection,
deflecting charges of infanticide while distancing and manipulating men. It
was she who framed the narrative, she who shaped the action, she, if you like,
who midwifed her own text. Her female associates, friends, grace women, and
companions in birth gave her attention and solidarity, being willing to countenance the cat story even while wondering about its truth. But Agnes's words,
and all the other words of women in this episode, are only available to us in a
form set forth by men. Although this record seems to bring us within listening
distance of veiled female voices, we are constantly aware that the forum and the
format, the historical record, were both controlled by male professional clerical
and legal processes. Nor is this simply a feminist objection, since every judicial
process imposes order on events and recollections that were originally much
more chaotic.

There may be other avenues to follow, other theoretical and methodological
paths to explore. Should we engage in a literary analysis of rhetoric, genre, and
narrativity without worrying too much about the events that lay behind them?
Would it be a mark of desperation to invoke the symbolic significance of cats
as female domestic companions or as familiars and stand-ins for the devil,
observing that 'cat' is the opening syllable of the word 'Catholic'? Is it time to
reject the 'minimal processing' that I have advocated, and deploy instead the
conceptual tools of critical theory and post-modern analysis? Perhaps we
should jettison the notion of 'truth' as a cultural construct, and simply amuse
ourselves with stories. What then happens to history if we treat the whole
episode as mere discourse and text?[38]

Perhaps the most fruitful strategy, or one branch of it, is to posit a double set
of negotiations, a nested epistemology, involving present and past. At one level
we are concerned with Elizabethan villagers and governors and their problem
of making sense of what happened in 1569 and the processes they engaged in to
explain what they saw and heard. But at another level, closer to home, we are
faced with methodological problems of our own. Without giving up the ship by
saying that historians are ineffably estranged from the past, we may admit to
engagement with something alien and elusive. The discourse subverts interpretation, resists one's attempts to bring it to order. Agnes Bowker's testimony
takes us into the realms of uncertainty, indeterminacy, and ambiguity, the shifting grounds of bewilderment and wonder, in which the telling takes precedence to the tale.

The more one learns the more difficult it is to establish what happened, and a
point arrives where establishing 'the truth' recedes behind the equally challenging task of interrogating the story. It is satisfying, of course, to be drawn to this

position by the historical record, the documents themselves, rather than by post-modern literary theory. The records of this case yield abundant documentation—some twenty-five folios of handwriting—but one hesitates now to call it 'evidence'. While reconstructing the past may be beyond our reach, and traditional magisterial explanation may verge on hubris, a more modest description of our enterprise might be 'negotiated engagement', involving give and take and a willingness to probe and feint. Nor does this prevent pursuit of the more conventional branch of my strategy, to find out as much as possible about the parties involved, their backgrounds, interconnections, and cultural assumptions. The testimony in this case touches a range of issues: normal and abnormal childbirth, gender relations and sexuality, monsters and the imagination, the proceedings of ecclesiastical justice, community discourse and authority, storytelling and the standards for establishing truth. The story of Agnes Bowker's cat takes us on a tour of the margins of Elizabethan society and culture. It exposes a variety of transgressions, violations, suspicions, and doubts. However much we aspire to believe that the secrets of the past may be laid open, we are left with a pedlar's pack of mysteries, a fardel or farrago of fictions, some of which may never be fully untangled.

Dramatis Personae

THE WOMEN

Agnes Bowker, 27, servant, of Harborough, Leicestershire
Elizabeth Harrison, 60, midwife, of Bowden Parva, Northamptonshire
Margery Slater, messenger
a Dutch woman, also described as a Welsh woman, prophetess
Margaret Roos, gentleman's wife, unofficial midwife
Lady Turpin, magistrate's wife
Joan Clement, 50, attended the birth
Emma Buttrick, 40, attended the birth
Margaret Harrison, 30, attended the birth, fetched a candle
Isabel Perkins, 30, attended the birth with her own child in her arms
Joan Dunmow, Agnes's friend
Emma Walker, Agnes's godmother, wife of George Walker
one Thomas Dawe's wife

THE MEN

Randal Dowley, servant, Agnes's lover
Hugh Brady, schoolmaster, Agnes's seducer
Christopher Pollard, curate

George Walker, innholder
William Jenkinson, tradesman
Edmund Goodyear, baker
Christopher Clarke, husbandman, helped save Agnes from drowning

OFFICIALS

Anthony Anderson, clerk, Commissary to the Archdeacon of Leicester
Sir George Turpin, magistrate
Edward Griffin, esquire, magistrate
Henry Hastings, Earl of Huntingdon,
William Cecil, Privy Councillor and Principal Secretary
Edmund Grindal, Bishop of London

2

MONSTROUS BIRTHS AND CREDIBLE REPORTS: PORTENTS, TEXTS, AND TESTIMONIES

When Margaret Mere of Maidstone gave birth to a horribly deformed baby in 1568 her neighbours immediately attributed it to the filthiness and iniquity of her behaviour, 'who being unmarried played the naughty pack'. But the broadsheet writer who described the child also construed it as 'a warning to England'. Agnes Bowker's remarkable delivery of a cat in 1569 not only set off a round of inquiries into her sexual background but also much pondering of the monster's wider significance. A misshapen child born in the Isle of Wight in the following year prompted fears of the final millennium and the imminence of God's 'day of wrath'. The body of yet another monstrous child was brought up to London as a travelling exhibit, and the parents—in this case an 'honest' couple—were treated with curiosity and compassion.[1] Elizabethan audiences reacted in widely different ways to the strangeness of severe malformation, making multiple responses to the monstrosities in their midst. As local crises became matters of public moment it was crucial for readers and listeners to determine whether 'strange and true' stories were based on credible report.

This chapter sets out to uncover the cultural responses to malformed births and their representation in print in Elizabethan and early Stuart England. It attempts to explain how private gynaecological disasters gained widespread public attention, and how foetal abnormality in remote English villages became newsworthy topics in the metropolis. It traces the representation of these phenomena at the intersection of elite and popular culture and examines their accommodation into social and religious experience. It concludes by considering how learned authorities, churchmen, politicians, villagers, and popular authors evaluated information about phenomena they found strange and distressing.

Malformed babies, defective tissue, irregularly shaped children, and incompletely separated twins, which might nowadays be regarded as genetic mistakes, chromosomal aberrations, or perhaps the consequence of chemical or radioactive contamination, invariably prompted sixteenth-century Europeans to think of 'monsters'. Founded on classical scholarship and ancient tradition, nuanced by apocalyptic medieval bestiaries, and quickened by print and polemic in the Renaissance and Reformation, the European debate on monsters spanned popular and academic cultures. Elizabethan England developed a vernacular version of this fertile continental tradition and adapted it to home-grown problems.[2] Competing systems of explanation—some based in the alehouse, some the university, and others the evangelical pulpit—jostled for control of their meaning. Monsters, by definition, were expected to demonstrate something, and different cultural interests appropriated abnormal phenomena in various ways. In England, in the century following the Reformation, they were mostly harnessed to the needs of evangelical Protestantism.

Dysmorphogenesis continues to fascinate modern readers, in a tradition linking *The Problemes of Aristotle* to the *National Inquirer*. Our own culture's appetite for monsters, both scholarly and popular, has strong roots in the age of Elizabeth I. In recent years a growing interdisciplinary scholarship has engaged with historical teratology, relating monstrous births and other prodigies to medical history, the history of science, the history of ideas, and literary representation.[3] It is argued, for example, that the early modern era saw a shift of attention from material to metaphorical monstrosity, and a change from superstitious to scientific attitudes to monstrous births.[4] Later Stuart observers became increasingly willing to treat such matters as natural phenomena rather than as signs of divine chastisement, although the exact admixture of attitudes—lay and clerical, male and female, popular and elite, scholarly and folkloric, etc.—still calls for investigation.[5]

Early modern midwifery manuals, mostly continental in origin, gave graphic space to the most gruesome abominations of natural abortions, mooncalves, molas, and monsters. Their illustrations reached prurient as well as professional eyes, and helped people visualize the worst that nature could threaten. Alongside popular broadsheets announcing monstrous births, medical texts displayed a gallery of horrors that compounded the normal terrors of childbirth.[6] To ward off these horrors churchmen offered prayers that may have been common on expectant parents' lips. 'Give unto this woman thy handmaid neither a monstrous, a maimed, or a dead birth . . . let thy blessing be upon it,' prayed the Jacobean Robert Hill. Daniel Featley similarly prayed, 'that the notes of the parents' sin be not seen in the marks, maims, and defects of the child'.[7] Oberon's consecration of the lovers in *A Midsummer Night's Dream* invoked this tradition when he prayed that 'the blots of nature's hand | Shall not in their issue stand; | Never mole, hare-lip nor scar, | Nor mark prodigious, such as are | Despised in nativity, | Shall upon their children be.' The counterpoint to this was the womb-invading curse, mobilized by Lear against Goneril: 'If she must teem, create her child of spleen, that it may live and be a thwart disnatured torment to her.'[8]

More than two dozen publications describing monstrous births survive from the mid-sixteenth to the mid-seventeenth century, and several more are known to have existed. The principle titles, in chronological order, were the following:

The true reporte of the forme and shape of a monstrous childe, borne at Much Horkesleye, a village three myles from Colchester, in the county of Essex, the xxi daye of April in this yeare, 1562 (1562; STC 12207)

John Barker(?), *A discription of a monstrous Chylde, borne at Chychester in Sussex, the xxiiii day of May. This being the very length, and bygnes of the same* (1562; STC 6177)

The Description of a Monstrous Pig the which was farrowed at Hamsted besyde London, the xvi day of October (1562; STC 12737)

William Fulwood, *The Shape of ii Monsters* (1562; STC 11485)

John Barker, *The true description of a monsterous Chylde, borne in the Isle of Wight* (1564; STC 1422)

The true discription of two monsterous chyldren Borne at Herne in Kent (1565; STC 6774)

William Elderton, *The true fourme and shape of a monsterous chyld, whiche was borne in Stony Stratforde, in Northamptonshire* (1566; STC 7565)

John Mellys, *The true description of two monsterous children, laufully begotten betwene George Steuens and Margerie his wife, and borne in the parish of Swanburne in Buckynghamshyre* (1566; STC 17803)

The true discripcion of a Childe with Ruffes borne in the parish of Micheham in the Countie of Surrey (1566; STC 1033)

The discription of a rare or rather most monstrous fishe taken on the East coste of Holland, the xvii of November (1566; STC 6769)

The forme and shape of a Monstrous Child born at Maydstone in Kent, the xxiiii of October (1568; STC 17194)

Pierre Boaistuau, Englished by Edward Fenton, *Certaine Secrete Wonders of Nature, containing a description of sundry strange things* (1569; STC 3164.5)

John Phillip *A Meruaylous straunge deformed swyne* (1571; STC 19071)

John Brooke, trans. (attributed to Martin Luther and Philip Melanchthon), *Of two Woonderful Popish Monsters* (1579; STC 17797)

A right strange example of the handie worke of God, by the birth of three children, born in Paskewet in Monmouth (1585; STC 20127)

A Most certaine report of a monster borne at Oteringham in Holdernesse, the 9 of Aprill last past (1595; STC 18895.5)

I.R., *A Most straunge, and true discourse, of the wonderfull iudgement of God. Of a Monstrous, Deformed Infant . . . borne at Colwall, in the County and Diocesse of Hereford* (1600; STC 20575)

A True Relation of the birth of three Monsters in the City of Namen in Flanders (1608; STC 18347.5)

Strange Newes out of Kent, of a Monstrous and mishapen Child, borne in Olde Sandwich, upon the 10 of Iulie last (1609; STC 14934)

William Leigh, *Strange News of a prodigious Monster, borne in the Towneship of Adlington in the Parish of Standish in the Countie of Lancaster, the 17 day of Aprill last* (1613; STC 15428)

Gods Handy-worke in Wonders. Miraculously shewen upon two Women, lately deliuered of two Monsters . . . within a quarter of a mile of Feuersham in Kent, the 25 of Iuly last, being S. Iames his day (1615; STC 11926)

A Wonder Woorth the Reading, or, A True and faithfull Relation of a Woman, now dwelling in Kent Street, who, upon Thursday, being the 21 of August last, was deliuered of a prodigious and Monstrous Child (1617; STC 14935)

Thomas Bedford, *A Trve and Certaine Relation of a Strange Birth, which was borne at Stone-house in the Parish of Plimmouth, the 20 of October* (1635; STC 1791)

John Vicars, *Prodigies and Apparitions. Or Englands warning Pieces* (1643)

Edward Fleetwood, *A Declaration, Of a Strange and Wonderfull Monster: Born at Kirkham Parish in Lancashire* (1645).

Sensational reporting fed on itself, in bursts and clusters, so that reports of one incident led to another and another in a chain. Their settings and circumstances were local and specific, but their meaning and manner was global and generic. Reports from the continent mingled with news from home, and a few monstrous beasts joined the parade of malformed human infants. Most of these publications were broadsheets, single large sheets of paper printed on one side in black letter, often with a banner headline, a gruesome picture, and some sensational moralizing verse. By the seventeenth century they were more likely to be multi-page pamphlets, though stylistically and graphically linked to the earlier tradition. Collectively they have some of the flavour of supermarket magazines or junk TV, from a time when only the minority of the population was literate. Their purpose, however, was not just to amaze or to entertain but to teach.

Before proceeding further we need to consider some important questions about the relationship between texts and events, and about the milieu of reading and writing. What was the interface between oral report and printed

The true description of two monsterous children,

lawfully begotten betwene George Steuens and Margerie his wyfe, and borne in the parish of Swanburne in Buckyngham shyre, the.iiij. of Aprill. *Anno Domini,* 1 5 6 6. the two children hauing both their belies fast ioyned together, and imbracyng one an other with their armes : which children wer both a lyue by the space of half an hower, and wer baptized, and named the one John, and the other Ioan.

I Read how *Affrique* land was fraught
    for their most filthy life,
With mostrous shapes, confusedly
    that therin wer full rife.

But England now pursues their vyle
    and detestable path,
Embracyng eke all mischiefs great
    that moues Gods mightie wrath.

As these vnnaturall shapes & formes,
    thus brought forth in our dayes :
Are tokens true and manifest,
    how God by dyuers wayes :

Doth styrre vs to amendment of
    our vyle and cankred lyfe ;
Which is to to much abused is,
    in man, in chylde, and wyfe.

We wallow in filthie sin,
    and naught at all regarde :
No; wyll not feare the threats of God
    tyll we for iust rewarde :

Be ouerwhelmd with mischiefs great,
    which ready bent for vs
Full long a go decreed wer,
    as Scriptures doth discus.

Both tender babes & eke brute beastes,
    in shape disfourmed bee :
Full manie wayes he plagues the earth,
    (as dayly we may see)

Thus mightie *Ioue*, to pearce our harts
    these tokens straunge doth send,
To call vs from our filthie lyfe
    our wicked wayes t'amend.

And thus by these two children here,
    forewarnes both man and wyfe :
How both estates ought to bewaple,
    their vile and wretched lyfe.

For sure we all may be agast,
    to see these shapes vnkynd :
And tremblyng feare may pearce our harts
    our God to haue in mynd.

For yf we printed in our brest,
    these signes and tokens straunge :
Wold make vs from our sinnes to thinke
    our liues a new to chaunge.

But some proude boastyng Pharisie,
    the parents well detect :
And iudge with heapes of vglie vice
    their liues to be infect.

No no, but lessons for vs all,
    which barely offend :
Yea more perhaps, then hath the friends,
    whom God this birth did lend.

For yf you wyll with single eye,
    note well and view the text :
And marke our Sauiours aunswer eke,
    that thereto is annext :

Where his disciples ask'ed him,
    to know therein his mynd :
Yf greatter wer the parents sinnes,
    or his that was borne blynd.

To whom Christ aunswered in a brief,
    that neither hee, nor they :
Deserued had that crooked fate,
    although they sin each day.

But to the end Gods glorie great,
    and miracles diuine :
Myght on the earth apparaunt be,
    his workes for; to define.

Such lyke examples moued me,
    in these forgetfull dayes :
To rue our state that vs a mong,
    vice beares such swings and swayes.

Wherein the goodnesse great of God
    we way and set so light :
By such examples callyng vs,
    from sin both day and night.

Where we doe runne at randon wyde,
    our selues flatteryng styll :
And blazyng others faults and crimes,
    yet we our selues most yll.

But if we doe consider right,
    and in euen balaunce way :
The ruine great of hartie loue,
    among vs at this day :

And well behold with inward eyes,
    th'embracyng of these Twinnes :
That God by them vpbraides vs for;
    our false dissemblyng sinnes.

We would with Niniuie repent
    our former passed peares,
Bewaplyng eke our secret sinnes
    in sacke cloth and in teares.

Therfore in time amend your state,
    and call to God for grace :
Bewaple your former lyfe and sinnes,
    while you haue time and space.

FINIS. ᶴ *Iohn Mellys Nor.*

Imprinted at London by Alexander Lacy, for william Lewes : dwellyng in Cow lane aboue Holborne cundit, ouer against the signe of the plough.

2. The true description of two monstrous children, born in Buckinghamshire in 1566

text, and how did news of this sort circulate? Who were the authors of these sensational works, and who their intended audiences? What kind of tension existed between narrative and commentary, news-gathering and didacticism, sensationalism and profit, and what did the writers intend their readers to believe? Why was the story worth reporting, why was the broadsheet or pamphlet worth buying, and what was it supposed to signify? How much common cultural ground lay between the original local witnesses to these births and the metropolitan and clerical writers who memorialized them? How much time elapsed between the birth of a monstrous child and the appearance of a publication describing it? How accurate was the written account, how sympathetic its treatment, and how true to life were any accompanying illustrations? Were there reasons to doubt the information offered, and what criteria applied for evaluating its claims to truth? We may not be able to answer all these questions, but simply by asking them we challenge the notion that monstrous birth belonged to a simple genre and elicited a univocal response.

Broadsides and pamphlets should be understood as interventions in popular culture, or contributions to popular culture, as well as reflections of popular beliefs and attitudes. The very fact that they were printed products, mediated through the market place and infused with godly morality, should make us question their credentials. They may provide a surrogate account of popular concern, and they may have been snapped up at popular bookstalls and fairs; but the broadsides were also crafted works with evangelical and commercial ambitions, and with different audiences in mind. Several of them took pains to distinguish between the simple rustics, midwives, and women who were the initial witnesses to a monstrous birth, and the reputable townsfolk, gentry, and metropolitan readers who were better prepared to receive its moral and religious message. The authors, many of them clergymen or clerically trained commentators, may have adopted a popular voice and format, comparable to that used in ballads, but their work was primarily an inter-cultural mediation, an imposition of meaning and significance, flavoured with spiritual, social, and gender condescension. These were traits they shared with many of the murder pamphlets so effectively analysed by Peter Lake and Francis Dolan, and the witchcraft publications examined by Jim Sharpe, Clive Holmes, and others.[9]

Some of these publications show signs of hasty production, indicating that they were written while the news was hot. The monstrous child born in Essex on 21 April 1562 was said to be still living at the time when the broadsheet was printed. News of the Isle of Wight monster born in October was printed on 7 November 1564. The account of a monstrous child born with ruffs on 7 June 1566 went to press on 20 August. *The forme and shape of a Monstrous child born at Maydstone* on 24 October 1568 was printed in London within two months of its occurrence on 24 December. These dates are printed on the broadsides themselves, as advertisements of their authentic currency (or current authenticity). News of the Oteringham monster, born on 9 April 1595, was reported in a letter dated 6 May that soon found its way into print. The account of the Herefordshire monster born on 6 January 1600 was prepared for the press on 30 April. The pamphlet describing the Kent Street monster of 1617 dated its birth to 'Thursday last' suggesting that the pamphlet was penned within a week of the child's delivery. These publications apparently had short shelf lives, even if they dealt with perennially interesting issues.

The common theme of these publications—one might say their obsession—was severe foetal abnormality that issued alive from unfortunate women's wombs. The broadsheets set out the circumstances of each birth and attributed it to a particular place and date. They recounted the physical form of the newborn creature, and described in detail its monstrous features—missing or misshapen limbs, webs of skin or folds of flesh, dicephalic or horribly conjoined twins. Usually they identified by name the parties involved, the parents of the monster, the midwife and other women who helped bring it forth, the minister who baptized or buried it, and the neighbourhood worthies who served as witnesses. Were it not for the hideous deformities that made these monsters unviable, these accounts might serve as useful descriptions of the everyday circumstances of childbirth in early modern England.[10]

Having described the monster, often with graphic engraving, the broadsheet's next task was to explain it, to gloss it, to give it spin. And for this they drew upon several streams of interpretation. Contemporaries expected to find moral, religious, or political meaning in aberrations of nature, and would have been disappointed by accounts that failed to draw lessons. 'A true description of a monstrous child' was not simply news, but news you could use—use to understand the inscrutable workings of God, to predict the future in an unstable world, or to amend your sinful life. Comments on the message and elucidations of its lessons were important parts of this reporting. Finally, in case anyone doubted the truth of these strange stories (and thereby the truth of their moral message or religious warnings), the writers went to considerable trouble to establish the veracity of their reports.

We have no exact figures for the incidence of monstrous births, nor reliable estimates of the probability of their occurrence, but in most human populations they are mercifully rare—perhaps one in several million.[11] There is no evidence to suggest that gestational deformities occurred more commonly in one historical period than another, and it seems highly unlikely that their actual numbers went up in England in the second half of the sixteenth century.

It is remarkable, however, that in the 1560s alone at least eight spectacular monstrous births were recorded, each memorialized with its own breathless broadsheet, followed by a second concentration in the reign of James I and a third in the 1640s. How should we explain these surges? Although Renaissance England was distressed by disease and dearth, and was sometimes flush with alcohol, it experienced no medical or environmental catastrophe, no Thalidomide or Chernobyl, that would account for a clustering of birth defects. If there was something in the atmosphere that made early modern England particularly susceptible to monsters it was more likely to be found in the miasma of political conflict, religious anxiety, and cultural tension than in the water, the diet, or the air.

As we have already noted with reference to the investigation of Agnes Bowker, early Elizabethan England was wracked by anxiety, fear, and guilt over the pace and direction of its religious reformation. During the 1560s the situation was aggravated by uncertainty about the health of the queen, the succession, Mary Queen of Scots, religious faction, enemies at home and abroad, threats from Rome, Spain, and France, economic problems, and plague. It hardly seems surprising that this should prove a fertile time for monsters. Similarly, the Jacobean period experienced religious stress, moral strain, and political conflict, which may have stimulated the audience for portents and prodigies. The 1640s too was a time of religious and political crisis, when an unfettered press documented the descent into civil war. But what of other troubled decades, like the 1590s and 1630s, when social, religious, and economic problems compounded together? Why were they relatively free from concentrations of reports of monstrous births? Although England experienced profound cultural disruptions at various times in the sixteenth and seventeenth centuries, along with a rising population and periods of economic distress, no simple environmental, political, or chronological treatment can account for waves of attention to monstrous births.

Monstrous births might mean many things, but they could not be allowed to mean nothing. Contemporaries were accustomed to considering a range of possible meanings, a hierarchy of plots and sub-plots, in which natural law, divinity, and human corruption intertwined. Multiple explanations were not incompatible, each derived from a culturally acceptable logic. In Elizabethan and early Stuart England 'the monstrous and unnatural shapes of these children' suggested at least six lines of explanation that were not mutually exclusive but collectively and cumulatively reinforcing. They could be seen as freaks of nature or as manifestations of divine power; they could be interpreted as judgements and punishments against individual sinners, usually the parents, or as generalized warnings to the community at large; they could be seen as portents or prognostications, looking forward to some earthly catastrophe, or as precursors of the latter days, foresignals of the end of the world. And finally, for people who were moved by none of these explanations, the monster babes provided opportunities for freak-show entertainment, occasions for idle amusement.

Sixteenth-century Europeans knew that nature was bountiful, abundant, and teeming with vitality. Under God's guidance, the natural world operated according to accustomed regularities. The cycle of birth and death, like the cycle of the seasons, was mostly normal, conformable, and predictable, though subject to occasional surprises, freaks, and quirks. Regular patterns were a sign of good order, all right with the world. Irregular occurrences indicated disturbance, possibly to the good—like the appearance of a new star over Bethlehem—but more likely baneful, a disruption of the great chain of being. Violations of the natural order—like the appearance of animal features on a human, or the birth of a child with two heads—were likely to instil fear. As John Brooke wrote in his account of 'two wonderful Popish monsters', a borrowing from the continent published in London in 1579, 'among all the things that are to be seen under the heavens . . . there is nothing can stir up the mind of man, and which can engender more fear . . . than the horrible monsters, which are brought forth daily contrary unto the works of nature'.[12] Disorder in nature was one of the most fearful things one could imagine.

'Natural' interpretations of monstrous births enjoyed a respectable ancestry from the ancient world to the age of the Enlightenment, and found particular favour among the medical and scientific elite. The procession of deformed babies, unseparated twins, and human and bestial monsters could be seen as sports of nature, or products of 'nature's spite'.[13] This was the view espoused in Edward Fenton's *Certaine Secrete Wonders of Nature* (adapted from the French of Pierre Boaistuau in 1569), which promised to expose 'sundry strange things, seeming monstrous in our eyes and judgment, because we are not privy to the reasons of them'. Popularizing a natural teratology, it depicted such horrors as a two-headed woman from 'the ancients of old time'; a monster with human and animal features, allegedly taken out of the Tiber in 1496; a 'hideous monster . . . most horrible, deformed and fearful', born in Poland in 1543; a Swiss child born in 1556 with the head of a dog or a cat; and a child born in Flanders in 1567 with two heads and three arms.[14]

Authors in this tradition found their explanation in humoral theories of medicine and reproduction. Moral and religious explanations were still possible, indeed were almost inseparable, but natural philosophy shaped their fundamental assumptions. The most common theory linked monstrous births to sexual intercourse during a woman's period, when the man's wholesome seed became contaminated by the woman's menstrual blood. This was a gendered physiological explanation, linking menstruous and monstrous, which threw most of the responsibility for the misfortune onto the woman. An associated theory, linking mind and body, attributed monstrous births to 'an ardent and obstinate imagination which the woman hath while she conceives her child'. The results could still be blamed on the woman. Thinking bad thoughts or glimpsing loathsome creatures during intercourse or pregnancy could cause a mother to give birth to a bestial or deformed child. These ideas were strongly entrenched in medieval and Renaissance medicine. They were repeated in most of the textbooks and continued to influence gynaecological theory beyond the eighteenth century.[15] This may explain why the women attending Agnes Bowker fled in horror when she apparently brought forth a monster, as if their own wombs could become infected by witnessing something so transgressive.[16]

For the writers of popular broadsheets, natural philosophy was inadequate. Contemporary monsters were not simply things 'for us to gaze and wonder at, as things happening either by chance or else by natural reason, as both the old and our philosophers also hold nowadays, and without any further heed to be had thereto'.[17] To say so would be to miss their supernatural significance and the urgency of their moral and religious message. Instead the religious culture of post-Reformation England, at least that part of it which controlled the popular press, resisted mere secular and philosophic explanations of 'nature's spite'. Indeed, the author of *The true discripcion of a Childe with Ruffes* in 1566 set up such an explanation only to pull it down.

> By nature's spite, what do I say?
> Doth nature rule the roost?
> Nay God it is say well I may
> By whom nature is tost.[18]

The early Stuart preacher Thomas Bedford, reporting the *Strange Birth, which was borne at . . . Plimmouth*, likewise insisted that 'the special hand of God' disposes secondary natural causes, and that 'God over-ruleth the stars'. Indeed, he argued further, the secular philosophers and physicians were mistaken because they 'would attribute all these impeditions and alterations of nature to secondary causes: either internal, as the defectiveness or excess of seminal materials, or external, as the dullness of the formative faculty, or indisposedness of the vessels, or strength of conceit or imagination'. Natural philosophers, he observed, gave insufficient attention to the workings of providence and to the active intervention of an angry god. In this they were little better than astrologers, who turned to 'the constellations of the planets and configuration of their aspects' to explain occurrences in this sublunary world.[19] Bedford's contemporary Francis Bacon proposed to examine 'all monsters and prodigious births of nature' as part of the *Novum Organon*,[20] but this was far removed from common curiosity and the preoccupations of evangelical Protestantism.

Religious authors regarded marvels and monsters as evidence of divine dominion. According to the broadsheet of 1562 the Essex monstrosity was wrought by the 'mighty hand' of God. The 'monstrous child' brought forth in the Isle of Wight in 1564 was likewise a demonstration of God's wondrous works:

> Where nature's art doth not her part
> In working of her skill
> To shape aright each lively wight
> Behold it is God's will.

The Northamptonshire broadsheet of 1566 asserted, in equally bad verse, that

> God that can in secrets show the sign
> Can bring much more to pass by power divine.[21]

These were neither original nor profound formulations, but they sustained the opinion that monstrosity originated in the supernatural rather than the natural world.

Broadsheets taught popular audiences to see spiritual significance in these physical phenomena, and to appreciate God's power to do whatever he willed with his creation. 'These strange and monstrous things almighty God sendeth amongst us that we should not be forgetful of his almighty power,' explained *The Description of a Monstrous Pig* in 1562. 'These strange sights' were 'wonderful tokens' of divine omnipotence, explained the author of *The Shape of Two Monsters* the same year. 'It pleaseth God . . . to work wonders . . . as plague, pestilence, war, famine, scarcity, dearth, new sickness and diseases, comets, blazing stars, flashing lights, shooting and streaming in the air, monsters of man and beast,' claimed the report of 'a monstrous deformed infant' born in Herefordshire in 1600.[22]

There was nothing in nature to withstand God's omnipotence. 'He who bad the sun retire, and it obeyed . . . who reared up the divided waters like walls of brick, and made a pathway through the deep . . . who graspeth the thunder in his right hand, and the rainbow in his left . . . whose throne is heaven, whose footstool is earth . . . this terrible God, I say, who created all of nothing, can as easily divert the usual and orderly course of procreation, into dreadful and hideous deformity.' So wrote the author of *A Wonder Woorth the Reading, or, A*

True and faithfull Relation of a Woman, now dwelling in Kent Street in 1617. The author of *Gods Handy-worke in Wonders. Miraculously shewen upon two Women* in 1615 repeated the point that God can do what he pleases, like the potter shaping his clay. Devoutly interpreted, a monstrous birth was not to be seen as an error, as if God were 'a bungler in some common trade'. Rather, like all life, it came from 'the great master, in whose hand it lies to make a beggar or a king, a beautiful body or a monstrous'.[23] Monstrosities were clearly providential signs from God; the only difficulty lay in how to interpret them.

A refinement of this view saw monsters not only as demonstrations of God's power, but also as pointed demonstrations of his anger. That anger could be focused directly on an individual sinner, commonly a wicked woman, or directed more generally against the country or population at large. The Fenton–Boaistuau compilation went beyond secular philosophy to aver, 'it is most certain that these monstrous creatures, for the most part, do proceed of the judgment, justice, chastisement and curse of God, which suffereth that the fathers and mothers bring forth these abominations as a horror of their sin'.[24]

The 'common custom', according to one Elizabethan author, was 'to judge God only offended with the parents of the same, for some notorious vice or offence reigning only in them'. The Essex monster of 1562, for example, demonstrated God's anger against its parents for their 'want of honesty and excess of sin', rather than his general disappointment with early Protestant England. In order to make sense of deformity, to distil moral significance from an obscure rural misfortune (and also to warrant metropolitan publication), there had to be a readable lesson. In this case the parents were singled out for their fornication, and were made an example to the rest of 'this monstrous world'.[25] Even more specific was the case of Margaret Mere of Maidstone in 1568, 'who being unmarried played the naughty pack, and was gotten with child'. Unlike most other illegitimate children, hers turned out to be grossly deformed, 'which may be a terror as well to all such workers of filthiness and iniquity'.[26]

The *Monstrous, Deformed Infant . . . borne . . . in . . . Hereford* in 1600 was 'begotten by incestuous copulation, between the brother's son and the sister's daughter ... being both unmarried persons', and their grotesque and short-lived offspring proved 'a notable and most terrible example against incest and whoredom'.[27] In this case, however, God's anger was not confined to the fornicating couple, but also directed against the sinful society that nourished them. The parents' particular corruption, made manifest by the monstrous birth, also had broad social and political significance. Their individual 'sins of uncleanness' were warnings to the community at large. God's judgement on sinners put the whole kingdom on notice, proclaimed the Herefordshire pamphleteer, for 'by the gross iniquity of the people, (He) is provoked to send such monsters'.[28]

Sometimes it turned out that the parents were blameless. God was so powerful and so inscrutable that he could choose any decent Christian as the conduit
for his anger, selecting if he wished a woman 'of honest and quiet conversation'
as the vessel for a monstrous incarnation. Any mother might spawn a monster,
under influences beyond her control. Some people—'boasting Pharisees' one
broadsheet writer called them—would no doubt attempt to assign blame; but
'no, no' the writer insisted, the babes' deformities were 'lessons for us all'.
Neither the Buckinghamshire monsters of 1566 nor those from Sussex four
years earlier could be laid to the misbehaviour of their lawfully married
parents. The Oteringham monster of 1595 was fathered by 'a man of honest and
good disposition' and its mother was 'a woman of honest life and conversation'.
Correctly interpreted, these misshapen babes were signs of 'God's mighty
wrath', sent to rebuke the entire community for its 'vile and cankered life'. The
reader was led quickly from wonder at the grotesque anatomy to broader spiritual and political considerations. The basic message was that God, though
caring, was angry and that England had better reform. 'Thus mighty Jove, to
pierce our hearts | These tokens strange doth send, | To call us from our filthy
life | Our wicked ways t'amend.'[29]

This, indeed, was the most common and most forceful explanation. The
Kentish monster of 1568 was seen as 'a warning to England' as well as a judgement on its sinful mother. The creature was to be read as a coded message about
moral and political deformities, so that the 'gasping mouth' challenged 'ravine
and oppression', the 'gorging paunch' attacked greed, the fingerless stumps 'set
forth' idleness, and the foot climbing to the head chastised subjects 'most
vicious, that refuse to be lead'.[30] Given the common trope of the 'body politic'
and the normal hierarchy of head and members, it is not surprising that writers
of broadsheets and pamphlets presented these fleshly violations as signs of a
world turned upside down.

Most authors had no doubt that monstrous births were 'tokens' of God's wrath,
sent to rouse fear, to stimulate remorse, and to induce timely repentance. The
spate of Elizabethan and Jacobean monsters were taken to signify 'the ire and
wrath of God against us for our sins and wickedness'. They were 'threatenings
and foreshowings . . . the heralds and executors of God's justice'. Animal monstrosities, which could hardly be blamed on the sins of their progenitors, were
similarly interpreted as warnings of divine anger. 'We ought to be warned,'
advised one broadsheet, 'but if we will not be instructed by his word nor
warned by his wonderful works, then let us be assured that these strange monstrous sights do foreshow unto us that his heavy indignation will shortly come
upon us for our monstrous living.'[31]

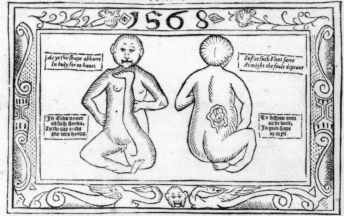

3. The form and shape of a monstrous child, born in Kent in 1568

Broadsheet after broadsheet announced that the monstrous child should be treated like a text, a message, a revelation. 'Let it to you be a preaching,' advised the broadsheet proclaiming the Isle of Wight monster of 1564. The message of the Northamptonshire monster of 1565 was that 'all is not well'. The Oteringham monster of 1595 was 'sent of God to forewarn us of our wickedness'. Though dead and mute, the Plymouth monster of 1635 was designed to 'speak and tell'.[32] The mainstream position was that these 'unnatural shapes . . . are lessons and schoolings for us all'. They operated as admonishments from God, 'to amendment of our lives, no less wicked, yea many times more than the parents of such misformed be'. Sin abounded everywhere and the land cried out for 'repentance and correction of manners'. A monstrous birth on the Welsh borderlands in 1585 was a sign 'to move us sinners to amendment of our wicked ways'. Another in London in 1609 showed that God 'is highly offended with us, in that he thus changeth the secret workings of nature'. A pamphlet of 1613 asked if any should wonder if 'nature . . . perverted her order . . . in the procreation of children, when men unnaturally go out of kind in the acts of sinning'.[33]

It was all very well to say that was God was angry, but what was he angry about? Most of the authors drew attention to defects and lapses, but they were usually more vague than specific. It was often left to the reader to pick up hints and make connections. When a 'monstrous fish' was taken in Lincolnshire in 1566, for example, it was naturally interpreted as a portent, but its exact meaning was left unspecified. There is a curious coyness about this particular publication which suggests that the writer was pulling his punches. He evidently disapproved of the Elizabethan religious climate but did not dare to say so forthright. Instead he directed attention to God's anger at recent developments in which Englishmen were now turned monsters, 'their manners mad and monstrous', as they broke with 'ancient custom'. If someone miraculously returned from the dead, he suggested, from 'forty years before'—that is, from before the Henrician Reformation—they would be amazed at England's decline. The monster fish was allegedly taken on 17 November, the anniversary of the triumph of Elizabeth's accession, but the significance of this date was not directly addressed. By contrast, *A Meruaylous straunge deformed swyne* displayed in 1571 became 'an exhortation or warning to all men, for amendment of life', particularly in light of the monstrous behaviour of recent Catholic conspirators and northern rebels.[34]

The vice that most troubled the writer of the 'true description of two monstrous children' born in Kent in 1565 was 'the great decay of hearty love and charity' in early Elizabethan England. The position of the innocent babes, 'the one as it were embracing the other and leaning mouth to mouth, kissing', was taken to upbraid us for our 'false dissembling', and to 'exhort us to sincere amity and true friendship'. The Buckinghamshire babies of 1566 also drew attention to 'the ruin great of hearty love', and their embracing posture 'upbraids us for our false dissembling sins'. The child born with folds of flesh like ruffs likewise exhibited God's special anger at 'this ruffling world' of pride and noxious fashions.[35] These were long-standing complaints, related to the 'puritan' reformation of manners, but also shaped by nostalgia for a more charitable England that was believed to have existed in the pre-Reformation past.

'Never was the world so wicked as it is now,' pronounced the bearer of *Strange Newes* from Lancashire in 1613. Like earlier unfortunates, these latest conjoined twins were attributed to their parents' sins of adultery and fornication. But the monster also reflected God's anger at the English nation at large. 'Forbidden sins are most of all practiced, and sins committed that are not to be named,' wrote the preacher William Leigh.[36] Another early Stuart pamphlet, *A Wonder Woorth the Reading* of 1617, similarly presented 'a monstrous message . . . from the king of glory . . . sent from the almighty for our further admonition and instruction'. In addition to heralding God's general anger at England's abuses and abominations, the hideously deformed child born in Kent Street was taken to target London for its profane neglect of the sabbath.[37]

Monsters served to predict the future as well as to punish 'sins and offences past'. Readers were taught that each monstrous birth offered 'true foresignification of some notable event to follow'. Prodigies were portents, inviting divination. This the ancient world knew well, as Cicero wrote, 'Quia enim ostendunt, portendunt, monstrant, praedicunt, ostenta, portenta, monstra, prodigia dicuntur.'[38] Something terrible was about to happen, and a few Elizabethan writers thought they knew what it would be. The *Discription of a monstrous Chylde, borne at Chychester* in 1562 claimed that things 'so strange' and 'out of kind' were indications of the final days, the end of the world, for which all Christians had to be prepared.

> The Scripture saith before the end
> Of all things shall appear
> God will wondrous strange things send
> As some is seen this year.

The Isle of Wight monster two years later likewise signalled the onset of 'these latter days' and the coming of 'the day of wrath'. It was tempting to see horrific malformed babies as harbingers of Christ's second coming. Though this was a muted theme in most reports, the Hereford author of 1600 knew that 'towards the latter days, iniquity shall increase', and that monsters were a sign of the end.[39] By contrast, the account of *Gods Handy-worke in Wonders*, published in 1615, took an explicitly counter-millennial position, denying that these monsters had any eschatological significance, and reassuring readers that 'the end is not yet'.[40]

It is remarkable that none of these publications attributed monstrous births to Satanic power or treated them as manifestations of witchcraft. Despite the ever-lurking abundance of *maleficium*, their origin lay with God, not the Devil. This may explain why the babies themselves, the actual monsters, were more often viewed with compassion than with loathing. Rather than seeing them as malignant pollutants, deserving extinction, the local communities generally treated the products of monstrous births as innocent and pathetic fellow creatures, however hideously they were deformed. One of the monsters born in 1562 was described as 'a guiltless babe . . . of good and cheerful face'. The Kentish twins of 1565 were baptized at home and were buried the next day by the minister. The Northamptonshire monster of 1566 'was christened by the midwife' and lived two hours. The Buckinghamshire babies of 1566 'were baptized, and named the one John, and the other Joan', and 'were both alive by the space of half an hour'. No less than three midwives attended the birth of the deformed child born in Herefordshire in 1600, and instead of fleeing when they saw that the creature was not likely to live, they sent for the minister who hastily christened the child 'What God Will'.[41] Once christened the creature belonged to the Christian community; and even those that died unbaptized may have been buried, for charity's sake, in consecrated ground.

Not everyone took the appearance of monsters so seriously as prodigies or chose to read them as messages from God. The very earnestness with which most of these publications proclaimed themselves as miniature sermons suggests that some streams of opinion remained to be convinced. The broadsheets and pamphlets engaged with popular culture and emulated its forms, but, as we have seen, their programme was didactic and reformist. The author of the 1562 Sussex broadsheet knew enough about popular irreverence to anticipate that this monstrous child might be taken as a source of idle entertainment rather than a warning of divine anger.

> But if we lightly weigh the same
> And make but nine days wonder
> The Lord our stoutness soon will tame
> And sharply bring us under.

Mockery and levity would earn the sternest reproach. 'His wondrous works we ought not judge as toys and trifles vain,' warned a pamphlet of 1571, implying that many ignorant people did indeed just gawp and scoff. The monstrous child born in Kent in 1609 was properly to be construed as an awful warning, 'yet carelessly we still run astray, regarding nothing at all these 'larum bells sent from our gentle redeemer'.[42]

The most vulgar reaction, most offensive to the broadsheet commentators, was to treat monstrous deformity as popular entertainment. 'The common sort make no further use of these prodigies and strange births than as a matter of wonder and table talk,' complained the Reverend Thomas Bedford in 1635. He appealed beyond 'the common sort', mired in illiteracy and irreligion, to the sophisticated audience that was accustomed to reading sermons. Significantly, Bedford's pamphlet, the only one describing a monstrous birth in the reign of Charles I, is among the few to be printed in Roman type rather than the more rudimentary black letter.[43]

Monstrous children, like grotesque beasts and prodigious fish, were sometimes exhibited for amusement and profit, their bodies displayed where they would attract most traffic. Instead of being interred as God's creatures they became the ware of hucksters. The Northamptonshire monster of 1566 was 'brought up to London, where it was seen of' many. The remains of the malformed triplets born in Monmouthshire in 1585 were reported to be 'seen at

London'. Gentlemen and commoners alike abandoned their sports at the cockpit to gawp at the Lancashire monster of 1613, and 'at the least five hundred' came to see the spectacle when its body was exhumed. 'Thousands of people came from all places' to see the monstrous children born in Kent in 1615, 'the misery of the sad mother being relieved by much money, which out of Christian compassion many bestowed upon her'.[44] Indeed, no cloud lacked its silver lining.

Local records occasionally illuminate or corroborate these stories. In Shrewsbury, for example, a child with cloven feet was displayed at the abbey fair in 1579, and in 1583 a travelling merchant brought 'strange and wonderful sights' to the town including 'a dead child in a coffin which had two heads and . . . two backbones'. The Norwich authorities licensed the display of 'a strange child with two heads' in 1616, but attempted to regulate the attendant publicity of drums and trumpets. Every few years there was a 'monster to be shown' that followed the circuit of travelling freaks and deformities.[45]

The author of *A Wonder Woorth the Reading*, who had serious news to impart, anticipated a derisive and incredulous reaction to the monster born in Kent in 1617. 'Should any meet my discourse with a scoff, and revilingly say, "This is an usual trick put upon the world for profit, and that this monstrous child birth . . . was begotten in some monster-hatching brain, produced for a Bartholemew Fair baby . . . to be nursed at the common charge of the news-affecting multitude," let them know (it) to be a merciful message sent from the almighty for our further admonishment and instruction.'[46] Here, locked in conflict, were the culture of Godly reformation and the culture of vulgar tradition. The reformers wrote the pamphlets and so gained control of the printed record, but the common folk continued to flock to spectacles and fairs.

It became 'a case of conscience', debated early in the seventeenth century, 'whether monsters and misshapen births may lawfully be carried up and down the country for sights to make a gain by them' and 'whether the parents of such births may sell them to another . . . to be prostituted to the covetousness of any'.[47] Shakespeare may have been playing with these ideas when Trinculo and Stephano in *The Tempest* imagine capturing Caliban, their misshapen 'moon-calf', and putting him on display for money. Ben Jonson invoked the same tradition when he satirized the attractions and fabrications at London's *Bartholomew Fair*.[48]

Establishing the credibility of reports about monsters was doubly important for the authors of broadsheets and popular pamphlets. At one level they had to counter the scoffers who doubted that such an event had ever happened. At another, they sought to lay claim to an uncontested truth in order to promote their evangelical message. Their claims about God's anger or his impending judgement only worked if they rested on reliable reports, yet the very form in which they operated, akin to the broadside ballads, was notorious for interlacing lies and truth.[49] The remainder of this chapter deals with the burden of authentication, and the strategies contemporaries employed to establish the trustworthiness of their texts.[50]

When the scholarly evangelist Stephen Batman published an historical catalogue of prodigies in 1581 he attempted to establish their veracity by grounding them in Christian faith. To any reader who might find these prodigies 'absurd' or 'altogether repugnant to natural reasons', Batman advised, 'that thou use not man's reason in searching out God's works, for the marvellous works of the Lord are great and incomprehensible'. Their very strangeness ought to command pious belief. However, 'lest in these my gatherings thou mayest find lack of credit and authority of the thing,' he added, 'I thought good to [supply] all authors, from whose watchful works set forth long agone I have gathered mine.' In other words, like modern scholars, he appended an apparatus of notes and references. Finally, with regard to contemporary prodigies, Batman relied on things that 'I myself have seen in my time, or have received of my special friends men of good credit'. In the last resort, scholarly discussion rested on no firmer epistemological grounds than the popular press, and left the reader to engage or suspend his belief. As an early reader noted on the Huntington Library copy of Batman's book, 'multa vera, multa falsa, sed omnia vere utilia'.[51]

A common authorial strategy was simply to assert that the story was true, and then to supply details of text and illustration that were capable of being verified. The very fact that the matter appeared in print might be taken as validation for, as the shepherdess Mopsa told Autolycus in *The Winter's Tale*, 'I love a ballad in print, a-life, for then we are sure they are true'.[52] The eye-catching titles—*The true form and shape . . . , The true description . . . , A most certain report . . . , A true and certain relation*, etc.—announced their veracity and bullied readers into credulity. One of the earliest examples of this genre, the report of the monstrous child born in Essex in 1562, set the pattern by announcing itself as a 'true report'. Its woodcut of the deformed child, along with a detailed limb-by-limb description of deformities, helped buttress the author's claim to authenticity. It grounded the occurrence in the particular, providing a specific report of time, place, and circumstance which curious or sceptical readers could check. The broadsheet tells us the date of delivery, 21 April 1562;

the location of the village, Much Horkesley, three miles from Colchester: and the names and circumstances of his parents, Anthony Smith, husbandman, and his wife. Notwithstanding the child's massive handicaps, this 'monster' was born alive, was said to be able to feed, and was reportedly still living at the time of printing.[53]

The broadsheet about the 'monstrous child' born on the Isle of Wight in 1564 likewise promised a 'true description', as did the account of the 'two monstrous children born in Kent' in the following year. The account of the 'monstrous child' born in Northamptonshire in 1566 was said to depict its 'true form and shape', and the descriptions of the children born in Buckinghamshire and Surrey that year were similarly asserted to be 'true'. Along with the obligatory pictures, each publication located its subject in place and time, identified a particular date and parish, and added substantiating details about the names and occupations of the parents, whether the child was born alive, how long it lived, who saw it, and whether it was christened. The report of the Herefordshire monster in 1600 likewise promised to satisfy the reader 'how, when, and where this strange thing was done, with every other circumstance thereto belonging'.[54] Remarkable confirmation of *The true discription of two monsterous chyldren* of 1565 comes from the parish register of Herne, Kent, which records that 'John Jarvys had two woemen children twynnes baptised at home, ioyned together in the belly and having each the one of their armes lyinge over one of theyr owne shoulders, and in all other parts well proportioned chilldren, buryed August 29.'[55]

Credible witnesses were essential to a credible report. Autolycus knew this when he assured his ballad customers that his preposterous printed tales were true. One had 'the midwife's name on it, one mistress Tale-porter, and five or six honest wives that were present'. Another had 'five justices' hands at it, and witnesses more than my pack will hold'.[56] Broadsheets and pamphlets supplied similar corroborative testimony. The Northamptonshire monster of 1566 was 'brought up to London, where it was seen of divers worshipful men and women of the city, and also of the country, to witness that it is a truth and no fable'. The Surrey baby born with ruffs 'was to be seen in Glene Alley in Southwark being alive and ten weeks old'. Witnesses to the Kentish child of 1568, which lived twenty-four hours, were 'William Plomer, John Squier, glazier, John Sadler, goldsmith, besides divers other credible persons both men and women'. The Oteringham monster of 1595 was 'averred by the credible testimony of divers gentlemen of worship' and others now present in London, and could also be certified by application to the local ministers.[57] A hierarchy of validation emerges from these publications, endorsing the stratified ranking of gender, status, reputation and credit and confirming the social foundations of truth.

The testimony of a gentleman, a minister, or a worthy citizen, counted more than that of an ignorant rustic; men's testimony counted more than women's; fisherfolk and foreigners might be doubted, but witness by an Englishman of credit was sufficient to make the implausible seem true.

The 1609 pamphlet, *Strange Newes out of Kent*, was especially concerned to establish its credentials, perhaps because its illustration was so crude and the monstrous child so dramatically misshapen. This creature, 'most strange and dreadful to behold . . . resembled no proportion of nature, but seemed as it were a chaos of confusion'. But the account could be warranted, the writer insisted, not only by 'the inhabitants of that country there dwelling which beheld it', who might be dismissed as credulous rustics and foolish women, but also by 'the reports, now most truly certified, by men of credit and substantial reputation', whose very credit and substance could be taken as a guarantee. Readers themselves could be drawn into this process of authentication. 'Let me entreat you,' the author continued, 'that both your eyes and ears may be gentle witnesses to the truth of this strange wonder in nature, and that your hearts and minds may be bent to a repentant understanding, for the discourse here following is both strange, true, fearful, and full of much wonder; and because there shall be no doubt made of the verity thereof, I have placed down the names of such personages of credit, now dwelling in London, that were eye-witnesses thereof.' There then followed a list of six 'such witnesses that saw this monstrous child', including Michael Dickson, a cooper in Thames Street, near to St Dunstan's church, Richard Rawson, waterman dwelling in East Smithfield, and Alice Smith, dwelling in Bishopsgate Street. Any diligent reader, jaded by Bartholomew Fair babies or patent fabrications, could search out these individuals to have their doubts relieved. The pamphlet describing the monster of 1617 similarly promised 'a true and faithfull relation . . . and if any curious censurer call in question the truth hereof, let him enquire at (John Ladyman's house in Kent Street) for his better satisfaction'.[58]

Crucial information about the Lancashire monster of 1613 included the claim that the creature had been seen by many, including 'certain gentlemen and many of the common people'. William Leigh, an Oxford divine and court preacher, tutor to Prince Henry and author of numerous sermons, was also 'an eye witness of the same', and his endorsement added dignity to the front cover. The author (perhaps Leigh himself) added that in order to give 'full satisfaction to some people that were incredulous of it, unless they might be made also eye witnesses of such an unheard of accident, the grave was opened again wherein it had been buried, and the body laid to the view of a great number of beholders; which were at the least five hundred, that not only bear a bare report, but can also give true testimony of this occurrence'. The circle of 'true testimony' widened from the women at the childbirth to the country-folk who 'came flocking', from the minister who performed the burial to the masses who witnessed the exhumation, until finally the pamphlet entered it into printed culture as trustworthy 'news'.[59] Whether this was news for people to use, and whether it reflected the anxieties of a troubled and divided culture, is a subject for continuing research.

3

MERCY GOULD AND THE VICAR OF CUCKFIELD:
DOMESTIC AND CLERICAL PLEADING

Some time around midsummer 1577, perhaps on St John's Day following the traditional Midsummer merriment, Mercy Gould, a domestic servant of Cuckfield in Sussex, became pregnant. By the following spring her condition was difficult to hide. About Easter, at the end of March 1578, Mercy Gould was dismissed from service. She found shelter with a neighbour, and there gave birth to a child. Whether this child was born dead or died soon after birth, or whether it was helped to that end by wicked practices, became one of many subjects of contention. The baby was quickly and secretly buried. But secrets were also short-lived in this rumour-rich ironweald village. The story of Mercy Gould's pregnancy, its management and outcome, and the efforts of her former employers and neighbours on her behalf, sent ripples of disturbance through the Cuckfield community. Embittered clusters and factions coalesced around conflicting and expanding versions of the narrative. Within a year the ripples of rumour had risen to a cataract of accusation and counter-accusation, sweeping the vicar of Cuckfield and even his brother the Bishop of Chichester into the flood. Mercy Gould's predicament became submerged amidst a welter of claims and counter-claims concerning personality, politics, preferment, and religion. The breaking waters of her pregnancy released a surge of local discontents, with effects that reached the Privy Council, the High Commission, the Assize Sessions, and the royal court.[1]

According to one account, advanced by a bevy of leading gentlewomen, Mercy Gould's ordeal was unfortunate but not exceptional; nature had taken its course and nobody was to blame. A rival group of women, including the village midwife who had not been summoned to the birth, suspected evil deeds. Mercy Gould's sin in bearing a bastard, a fairly commonplace occurrence,[2] was compounded by suspicion of serious crime relating to the child's unwitnessed arrival, death, and burial. And Mercy's former mistress, Elizabeth Bowyer, wife of one of the richest men in Cuckfield, was vehemently suspected of administering to her a potion that induced premature labour and sickness, and that may have been intended to secure an abortion. Each of these accounts was framed in the form of a deposition that ranged one sector of the Cuckfield community against another. Local magistrates attempted to get to the bottom of the matter, while advancing their own alliances and interests, but soon found themselves engaged in a political game with potentially higher stakes.

Mercy Gould's story, and the stories told by her neighbours and betters, gained the attention of leading Elizabethan Privy Councillors. Domestic and parochial dealings in Cuckfield intersected, for a time, with the higher affairs of the kingdom. The crisis in Cuckfield illuminates several areas of current historical interest, not least the relationships of clergy and laity, men and women, and the politics of patronage and the law in the mid-Elizabethan phase of the English Reformation. The leading families—Bowyers and Curteyses—were deeply enmeshed in a struggle which involved gender, religion, and reputation. The following account, which gives full voice to contemporary complainants and correspondents, draws mainly on the central repository of State Papers. The church court records, which might have told a different version, are unfortunately missing for the period concerned.

This is the confession of Mercy Gould taken the 19th day of April 1578 before Mrs. Mitchell of Tyes, widow, and Mrs. Bowyer, Mrs. Chaloner the younger and Mrs. Mitchell of the town and goodwife Gateland and Mrs. Mitchell of Anstey, the which we have taken by your commandment: by the which as far forth as we can perceive, that there is no fault in her of her child's death, but that it came only by the visitation of God. For the night before she was delivered she was very sore sick and in such case that she was not able to turn herself in her bed without help, as the goodwife of the house and her servants will be sworn unto, and that the child was never seen alive in this world, but by all likelihood she was upon the quickening, which was the only cause of her sudden deliverance.

Ten days later this statement had reached the office of Secretary of State Francis Walsingham, where it was endorsed, 'The confession of Mercy Gould, a lewd woman about Cuckfield in Sussex.'[3]

It took almost a year for the competing statement to reach London, by which time community cohesion in Cuckfield was sorely stretched. Other village women were suspicious from the outset, and far from sharing Mrs Bowyer's bland account of Mercy Gould's confinement suspected the gentlewoman herself of vicious complicity. The focus of attention shifted from the hapless Mercy Gould to her former mistress, and the hostile counter-account was endorsed, 'Witnesses deposing against Mr Bowyer's wife.'

The women's testimony was as follows:

May it please you to understand to whom these presents shall come, that about Easter was twelvemonth being in anno 1578, one Mercy Gould, servant unto Henry Bowyer the elder of Cuckfield in the county of Sussex, ironmaster, was with child in her foresaid master's house and being suspected thereof, the wife of the said Bowyer gave her a purgation and afterwards sent her away, and the said Mercy Gould came to one Boniface's house in the said parish, whose wife sometime was servant to the said Bowyer; and within a few days after the coming of the said Mercy to the said Boniface, there to abide, she was delivered of a man child in the night without knowledge given thereof to women. And the child so born, the said Boniface buried it in the fields, and concealed the same.

After bruit and rumour was spread that the said Mercy was delivered, certain women went to search her, as namely Denis Clarke, midwife, Isabel Chaloner, gentlewoman, Marjorie Chaloner, gentlewoman, Joan Curteys, Alice Rowland, Joan Bassett, Joan Mercer, and Eleanor Parson; all these came to Boniface's house and finding Mercy Gould winding of yarn by the fireside, the said Denis Clark the midwife said unto her, in the presence of all the women, truly hanging is too good for thee. Then the said Mercy Gould being also presently asked of the said midwife where her child was, she stubbornly denied and said she had none. Then being further burdened and straightly charged by the aforesaid women, she fell down upon her knees, and confessing indeed that she had a child, besought them to be good unto her, or else she should be cast away; to whom the said midwife answered, arise up for we are no gods, and cry to God for mercy, and repent.

Then the said midwife asked her who was the father of her child, the said Mercy answered, John Orgle, Mr. Bowyer's man. She was asked further what manner of drink was it which your mistress gave (you), then the said Mercy Gould said it was a cruel hot drink, a cruel hot drink, twice, with great sighing, which provoked me oftentimes to be delivered of my child. Also Isabel Chaloner, one of the foresaid women, said unto her was not the drink which thy mistress gave thee for the plague, unto whom she answered no, no. There were none that had of this drink but I and another maid called Agnes. These words with others unmeet to be set down, the said Mercy Gould spake, as the said women have witnessed, and also will testify their oaths whensoever they shall be called thereunto.[4]

Eight women appended their names to this statement but in one version Joan Curteys, though mentioned in the text as one of those interrogating Mercy Gould, was not among them. By the time this statement was made in the spring of 1579, her husband, the Reverend Edmund Curteys, was fighting to retain his position as incumbent, and Henry Bowyer was struggling to maintain his ascendancy in the community.

We should pause at this point to consider the issues that underlie this testimony. Was there more to this story than rival narratives of an unfortunate bastard birth? What were the circumstances of Mercy Gould's employment and how did she come to be dismissed from the Bowyer household? Was her fellow-servant John Orgle indisputably the father of her child, or was there someone else unnamed who had had sexual relations with her? (Their self-defensive

language in subsequent letters, and their strident labelling of Mercy Gould as a
strumpet, makes one wonder whether Henry Bowyer or even Edmund Curteys
was entirely innocent in this regard.) What was the nature of Mercy Gould's
sickness in the final weeks of her pregnancy, and what was the content and
purpose of the medicine administered to her by Mrs Bowyer? Was it, as the
Bowyers claimed, a remedy against plague, or was it rather, as the Curteys
faction suggested, an evil abortifacient? Other Elizabethan gentlewomen are
known to have dispensed physic to their neighbours and servants, but none
with so violent an effect.[5] What other resources could a forsaken child-laden
woman summon, upon what other options could someone in Mercy Gould's
condition call? How did she secure shelter and a place to give birth, and why did
the Bonifaces open their house to her? Was their action a common courtesy,
a charitable provision of hospitality that met with community approval, or
might they be liable at law for harbouring a bastard-bearer and for hiding the
details of her delivery? What prior relationship existed between the Bonifaces,
the Bowyers, and Mercy Gould and others in the Cuckfield community, and
what were the respective roles of men and women, masters and servants, as
they were drawn into this drama?

What were the social circumstances of Mercy Gould's childbearing? Why
were no other women summoned, why no midwife to supervise the delivery?
Other sources from this period indicate that pregnant single women, even
wandering women, were normally afforded the company of midwives and
women when they came to term. This neighbourly attention helped to ease the
pains of labour and provided witnesses to the birth, but it also allowed the
midwife to demand the name of the child's father and helped the parish to allo-
cate responsibility for its upkeep.[6] Was Mercy Gould's covert confinement a
violation of community standards, an affront to the professional position
of the midwife as well as a botched attempt at secrecy? Did she compound
her offence by rejecting womanly solidarity and by attempting to veil the
child's paternity? Whose behaviour warranted criticism when a storm of angry
women invaded Boniface's house and interrupted Mercy Gould's post-partum
recovery, and why should her placid but useful winding of yarn prompt
thoughts of death by hanging? An important question, lively in village conjec-
ture and vital before the law, was whether Mercy Gould was delivered of a stillbirth or a live child that soon died, and if the latter, how did the child come by
its death? Was this a case of infanticide as well as fornication, bastardy, and
attempted abortion? Does this explain the vehemence of the midwife's remark
that hanging was too good for her? Later law assumed the worst, suspecting
infanticide of women whose dead babies were born without witnesses. Even
without a charge of infanticide (and the suspicion was never fully voiced in the

documents and no legal accusation made), what was the proper way to dispose of a stillborn or perinatally deceased infant? The churchyard was reserved for baptized members of the Christian community (although exceptions were sometimes made), so Boniface's decision to bury the child 'in the fields' may have been less sinister than at first appears.[7]

Cuckfield, like other bustling Elizabethan villages, was awash with 'bruit and rumour'. A servant's pregnancy, her dismissal from service, her arrival in someone else's house, and the painful drama of birth and death, were almost impossible to hide. Even if secrecy was intended there were too many eyes and ears, too many talking tongues, for news not to find its way. Mercy's fellow-servant, 'another maid called Agnes', was said to have shared the medical potion and no doubt knew of Mercy's departure, and she could easily have provided a conduit of information to listeners outside the household. In this case, too, the flames of rumour were fanned by faction. The Bowyers had enemies, perhaps chief among them the Curteys family, who would leap at all ill news from that source. The vicar's wife, we will learn, was the instigator of the interrogation of Mercy Gould and may have been foremost in fomenting suspicion against the Bowyers. What were the causes of the quarrel between Bowyer and Curteys, and to what lengths would they take it? Was the dispute about Mercy Gould a surrogate contest conducted by their wives?

The conflict between Joan Curteys and Elizabeth Bowyer, expressed here through alternative strategies for coping with a servant's pregnancy and competing accounts of its outcome, rapidly expanded into challenges to their own and their husbands' reputations. Two competing narratives jostled for dominance. The Curteys group intimated that Mrs Bowyer was a liar, an abortionist, and keeper of a disorderly household, while the Bowyer faction charged Edmund Curteys with disabling deficiencies as a priest. Both sides marshalled support within the community, and both reached outside to influential friends and relations to gain political advantage and to promote their version of the story. In order to understand the vectors of this quarrel we ought first to learn more about the principal protagonists and their social and political resources.[8]

Cuckfield was a prosperous farming and iron-working village in the Sussex weald. The parish of Cuckfield covered a much wider area than Cuckfield village. At the time of this incident it reported eight hundred communicants (a suspiciously round number), which, if it can be trusted, converts to approximately 1,325 inhabitants. The leading gentry families, besides the Bowyers, were the Chaloners and the Mitchells, who were intermarried. All three families competed in the strategically significant iron business as well as in the accumulation of land. A critically divisive issue between them was the control of raw materials, especially water and wood for charcoal, and this may have shaped some of their alliances. Roger Manning's account of the Cuckfield controversy paints Henry Bowyer as a rough traditionalist who made a surprisingly late conversion to the puritan cause; but there are repeated indications from the 1570s that he more than the vicar was an advocate of parochial reformation. Elizabethan Sussex was notorious for its Catholic traditionalism, but recusancy was more concentrated in the western part of the county than in well-connected iron-working centres like Cuckfield.[9]

The Bowyers were an armigerous family, aggressively expanding their estates and influence like so many others in mid-sixteenth-century Sussex. It helped that they were early supporters of the Protestant cause. Assisted by Archbishop Cranmer, John Bowyer, Henry's father, secured the profitable lease of the rectory of Petworth. A further fortune built on rich ore workings and forges led the Bowyers to be known as 'ironmasters' as well as 'gentlemen'. Henry Bowyer married Elizabeth Vaux, daughter and heir to Thomas Vaux, comptroller of the household to Henry VIII, and together they had three sons and two daughters. Through his own and his wife's family Henry Bowyer maintained broadly useful connections. Henry's brother Simon Bowyer was a gentleman usher at the court, who could provide access to powerful patronage, and who would prove vital in maintaining his local reputation.

By 1564 Bowyer was able to purchase Bentley Park and other lands in Cuckfield from Lord Bergavenny, and in 1573 he acquired a fourth of the manor of Cuckfield from the Earl of Derby. Additional properties were added in the following years, bringing his holdings to almost 1,000 acres besides iron mills, messuages, gardens, and tithes. It appears that the Bowyers were only recently established in Cuckfield at the time of their difficulty with the vicar. They had moved quickly to a position of social and economic dominance, perhaps stirring resentment among longer-settled families. Their great house, Cuckfield Park, was under construction between 1574 and 1581, at the very time of the clash with the Reverend Curteys. The house was an ostentatious announcement of their position. The initials H and E.B. for Henry and Elizabeth Bowyer carved on the dining-room chimney piece served as another public representation of their marriage. A later deposition, unrelated to the present case, recalls that Henry Bowyer may have taken some of his building stone from a derelict wall in Cuckfield churchyard without waiting for the incumbent's permission. Later, after the defeat and dismissal of Edmund Curteys, Bowyer made amends by giving the church a chapel.

Henry Bowyer died in September 1588, rich in honour and estate. His will reveals him as a puritan or at least a godly layman, and supports the suggestion that his dispute with the vicar was rooted in a clash of religious style and opinion as well as an argument about the behaviour of women. He writes, 'I commend my soul into the hands and tuition of my heavenly father . . . to be placed with his saints in his kingdom . . . I commit the burial to the discretion of my executors over which I will have no manner of pomps and glory which I leave till I rise again at the last day. Above all things I charge my son he faithfully serve God and reverently embrace the gospel of Christ.' This was not the style of a lukewarm conformist or a crypto-Catholic. Bowyer's legacies included ten pounds toward local highway repair (perhaps an infrastructure investment for the ironworks), and ten pounds for the poor of Cuckfield to be distributed by Mr Waterhouse, Curteys's eventual successor as vicar. Brass memorials in Cuckfield church display Henry Bowyer's coats of arms and devotional images of his wife and children, with the words 'O praise the lord'. The ensemble proclaims gentility, domesticity, and piety. Had Curteys continued as incumbent it is questionable whether Bowyer's reputation would have been so secure. An accompanying marble inscription reminds churchgoers that Mrs Bowyer was daughter and heir to the distinguished Thomas Vaux. Any residual hint of scandal from the episode a decade earlier is silenced by these powerful monuments. Elizabeth Bowyer outlived her husband, to continue in comfort at Cuckfield Park until her own death in 1601.

Edmund Curteys (also spelled Coortesse or Curtis) was admitted to the vicarage of Cuckfield in February 1571 and also made prebendary of Thorney, appointed by his brother Richard Curteys the newly installed Bishop of Chichester. The appointment was controversial from the beginning, 'against the mind of the dean and certain of the chapter'. The elder Curteys was instrumental in advancing his younger brother's career in spite of some physical disabilities. Ordained while still a student in 1563, and in his midthirties at the time of the collision with Bowyer, Edmund Curteys had served parishes in Cambridgeshire and Huntingdonshire before moving to Sussex, and could call on clerical connections in several dioceses. Whether he was fit for the ministry, or suited to the parish, were questions that soon would be raised.[10]

Even before the business with Mercy Gould, Curteys's competence had been challenged and he had been called before the High Commission.[11] Why else would his supporters draw up an apologetic testimonial on his behalf? The following statement was dated May 1576 but it was reintroduced in 1579 when Curteys was struggling to keep his place.

We whose names are subscribed are able to witness and testify unto your grace that Mr. Edmund Curteys vicar of Cuckfield in Sussex hath been lame and sickly even since his first coming hither until this time. Who notwithstanding hath by himself as far forth as

his infirmity would suffer him, and also by others procured this parish so well to be
served that we have good cause to think well of the zeal and behaviour of the said Mr.
Edmund Curteys in discharging his duty in his calling, and also of his diligence in
procuring service to be truly and duly said according to the queen's majesty's laws.
Moreover, because of his infirmity and sickness he is not able to take such pains in
preaching and teaching as we hope, if it please God to restore him to his health, he
would do: yet not withstanding, these are to certify your grace that of late he the said
Mr. Edmund Curteys himself hath preached both godly and zealous sermons at divers
times amongst us. Thus testifying a truth (as charity bindeth us) we most humbly direct
the tenor hereof to your grace's wisdom. The four and twentieth day of May anno
domini 1576.[12]

We do not know the circumstances that prompted this testimonial but it
was signed or marked by thirty-three principal parishioners. The document
was a useful statement of support, though only carrying the names of a small
minority of householders. Mistress Joan Mitchell, widow, was the only woman
among the subscribers and her name stood at the top of the list. Five of the men
identified themselves as gentlemen, including her kinsmen Ninian and John
Chaloner,[13] who signed their names, and Edmund Chaloner, who made a
mark. Twenty-two of the subscribers were yeomen, and all but one of them
made marks. One of those testifying on behalf of the vicar, by mark rather than
signature, was John Boniface, who may be the householder who later took care
of Mercy Gould. No Bowyers spoke up for the vicar.

If the Bowyers were lay puritans it is easy to understand their dissatisfaction
with the Reverend Edmund Curteys. Here was the incumbent of an important
rural parish, jobbed in by the bishop with clear signs of nepotism if not simony.
His ailments are not specified, but even his friends conceded he was 'sickly
and lame'. For parishioners who expected strong pastoring, Curteys may
have been physically inadequate for the task. At best he was a disappointment.
More important were his spiritual qualifications and his inability to command
the pulpit. Those testifying on his behalf were evidently satisfied if their
priest read the services or provided a curate for that duty, and were content to
hear an occasional sermon. More progressive Protestants wished for an active
preaching ministry, less rigorously tied to the Prayer Book, and may have
assigned Edmund Curteys to the company of 'dumb dogs'. This was ironic, for
Richard Curteys, Bishop of Chichester, was reputedly a promoter of preaching
and clerical improvement, though only of the most conformist sort. Parishes
throughout England were negotiating the tension between reading and
preaching in the wake of the Admonition controversy and the Prophesying
movement, and it should not be surprising to find associated stresses in rural
Sussex.[14]

Bishop Richard Curteys was a conformist scholar who had earlier come to attention by complaining against ecclesiastical irregularities at St John's College Cambridge. He served as a royal chaplain and as chaplain to Archbishop Parker before being advanced to Chichester in 1570. As bishop of Chichester Curteys was constantly at odds with the Sussex gentry, engaging in lawsuits and disputations over coastal wrecks, church attendance, and forbidden Jesuitical books. He attempted to use episcopal authority to cleanse his diocese of 'Machiavels, papists, libertines, atheists, and other such erroneous persons' and, not surprisingly, made dozens of enemies in the process. Godly reformers were no more pleased with him than Catholic recusants or 'irreligious and backward persons', and he sent waves of hostility through the magisterial bench.[15] Bishop Curteys's enemies were no doubt delighted in June 1577 when he was forced to secure a testimonial that he was not drunk at John Sherwyn's house, as witnesses alleged.[16] The imbroglio with his brother, that reached its climax in 1579, gave his opponents further cause to scorn. Bishop Curteys's relations with Secretary Walsingham were already brittle, and were soon to become further strained.

On 3 October 1578 Henry Bowyer lodged written complaints against the vicar of Cuckfield at the Quarter Sessions at Lewes. Bowyer's information, repeated in notes that reached councillors, judges, and episcopal lawyers in London and Chichester, characterized Cuckfield as follows:

The number of communicants there 800.

The people well affected in religion.

The living sufficient for a learned preacher.

The pastor now *Idolum*, void of all learning and discretion, for reading insufficient, a profaner of the sacraments, a depraver of preachers, a scoffer at singing of psalms, a common alehouse haunter, accused of incontinency, a maintainer of strumpets' causes, a seeker to witches, a drunkard, a quareller and fighter, convicted for a common barrator, infected with a loathsome and contagious disease, his talk is of ribaldry, *consignatus a natura*, and a contemner of her majesty's laws and justices.[17]

(Barratry involves quarrelsome brawling and malicious raising of discord among neighbours. The complaint against the vicar was referred to the Sussex Assizes, where Curteys was indicted as 'a common barrator and a sower of contention', the indictment being certified into Queen's Bench in Trinity term, 1579.)[18]

This was a raft of charges, designed to discredit Edmund Curteys and to bring about his dismissal. It represents not so much anticlericalism as exasperation with this particular priest. The references to preaching and psalm-singing, demeaned by alehouse-haunting and ribaldry, differentiated godliness from malignancy and clearly put Curteys on the wrong side of the puritan reformation of manners. The reference to seeking to witches, whatever its truth, associated Curteys with the practices of unreformed credulity and *maleficium*. The vicar's alliance with the midwife may also reflect his integration into the traditional world of popular culture.[19] Endorsed by some of the leading magistrates and gentlemen of Sussex, these allegations convinced the government in London to pressure the Bishop of Chichester to remove this unsatisfactory incumbent, his brother, and to prefer someone else to his place. Not surprisingly, the vicar retaliated. The surviving correspondence is incomplete but enough remains of this remarkable record to show both sides in the dispute enlisting the support of kin and contacts, exploiting the procedures of the law, and seeking to gain control of the narrative for their advantage. Some of it reads like an epistolary novel.

On 20 January 1579 Edmund Curteys, 'clerk vicar of Cuckfield within the county of Sussex', wrote 'to the right honourable the Lord Chief Justice of England and to the rest of the honourable of the Bench' as follows:

That whereas your said orator ever since the time whilst he hath continued vicar there, hath continually employed his study and endeavour to the profitting of Christ's flock committed unto his charge, in preaching and teaching so far forth as God hath given him utterance and knowledge and also hath led his life in such honest sort as doth best become his vocation; by which his diligence and good conversation, he hath won the hearts of most part of his parishioners, for verifying whereof your said orator doth and will refer himself to the testimony made by his said parishioners under their hands to the most reverend father in God the Lord Archbishop of Canterbury grace hereunto annexed, being urged thereto through the complaint of one Henry Bowyer of Cuckfield aforesaid, his friends and adherents who together with his said complices have been a continual professed enemy and persecutor of your said orator by the space of these six or seven years (who vowed about three years ago, that as long as he had a heart to think, or a tongue to speak, or a groat to spend, he would never have your said orator goodwill, nor give him over. And that he would spend five hundred pounds but he would deprive your said orator of the ministry) working by all means possible as well secret as open to take away and impair the good name and credit of your said orator and to get him deprived of his living hath bestowed great costs and charges not only in procuring a Commission against your said orator, but also in furthering since from time to time complaints.

Also the said Henry Bowyer through want of sufficiency of good matter to bring to effect his intended purpose hath continually laboured by all manner of practices to withdraw the heart and goodwill of such as were well affectioned towards your said orator, and hath linked himself in league with such persons as have found themselves aggrieved with your said orator for charitably admonishing them of their licentious and dissolute life to the intent that either by one means or other at the length he might touch your said orator, and bring his good name into question. For the accomplishment whereof the said Henry Bowyer and his accomplices have surmised and put in writing certain articles both forged and false, and have exhibited the same to the Queen's majesty's Justices of Peace at the Quarter Sessions holden at Lewes in the county aforesaid the third day of October last past. And thereof have accused your said orator being a lame man to be faulty, and him indicted as a common barrator, upon the oaths or not oaths of the procurers of this matter, and their said partakers. Certainly persuading themselves of the countenance of certain of the Justices of the bench then sitting namely Sir John Pelham, George Goring esquire, Henry Barkley esquire, and Doctor Overton who are known to be open enemies to the right reverend father in God Richard Bishop of Chichester, your said orator's natural brother.

For the penalty of which indictment, although your said orator might have easily enough come to his fine by protestation, etc., yet considering your Lordship's accustomed clemency and this honourable Court in administering of true justice he hath rather chosen with great labour and costs to the utter undoing of your said orator, his wife and children, to crave determination of his just complaint, before so honourable a court than by fine to be adjudged guilty, betraying and condemning his ministry without desert. May it therefore please your good Lords and this honourable Court, favorably to admit this his complaint, and answers made to their pretended articles, granting to your said orator such space and time of proof for which redress of his griefs, as by law and favorable Justice may be permitted. And your said orator shall be bound both he, his wife, and poor children to pray unto God for the daily increase of your Lord's honour with prosperous success in all your honour's affairs as long as they shall live. Dated the 20th day of January 1578[9]. Lastly your said orator most humbly beseecheth your honours to grant unto him a Commission, both to examine the Articles whereof he was indicted and also the rest of his life. For he reserveth himself to be tried by his parishioners, and other parishes adjoining.

By your most humble and poor orator, Edmund Curteys.[20]

This, then, was the first line of Curteys's counter-attack, leaving in reserve the story of Mrs Bowyer's treatment of Mercy Gould. The story of the suspicious childbirth is temporarily set aside, as a sub-plot rather than the central action, which will return to centre stage from time to time. For the most part the vicar presents himself as a diligent minister at odds with an unruly faction, a man unjustly maligned, the victim of Bowyer's vendetta and a partisan magisterial bench. The parish was severely divided, with the vicar claiming the support of the 'most part' against the implacable enmity of Henry Bowyer and 'his friends and adherents'. But the grounds for the quarrel are not explicitly explained. Curteys presents Bowyer as a man determined to ruin the vicar, prepared to spare no expense to that end. Bowyer's allies include people the vicar has admonished for their 'licentious and dissolute life', a reference that hints toward Mercy Gould. Bowyer is further presented as being in league with a faction of magistrates (including William Overton, the treasurer of Chichester Cathedral), who were using the Cuckfield case to attack the Bishop.[21] The case, as Curteys casts it, is political in the local if not the national sense of that term.

Mr Secretary Walsingham now had two accounts of the problem at Cuckfield to consider, conflicting versions of the developing tension. As a puritan supporter himself, and no friend to inadequate clergymen, he was disposed towards Bowyer's position, and as a gentleman lawyer he was inclined to favour testimony from people of his kind. Both sides continued to polish the narrative, either directly or through intermediaries. Some of the Cuckfield gentlemen applied to Lord Treasurer Burghley for Curteys's removal, while others expressed their support. Councillors, judges, episcopal lawyers, and members of the High Commission engaged in the process that would lead to Curteys's dismissal, a matter that was made unusually sensitive because the vicar was the brother to the bishop. And before this was over the bishop himself would face suspension.

By 6 March 1579 Walsingham had determined that Edmund Curteys should be replaced. On that day he wrote to Richard Curteys, Bishop of Chichester, 'for the removing of the ill vicar of Cuckfield and placing one Robinson in his room', as follows:

After my hearty commendations to your lordship, having ['been' *crossed out*] of late by some gentlemen ['of your diocese' *crossed out*] of ['very' *crossed out*] good credit received a very hard information against the vicar and minister of Cuckfield in your diocese not only for his insufficiency in knowledge ['and unworthiness in every respect' *crossed out*] for the charge of that great flock, but also for his unworthiness to have any such pastoral charge at all in the church, his ignorance being so great and his life so vile as for modesty sake I spare to name some particulars delivered to me for the proof of the same; I was so much the more grieved with the said information as I understood this ill minister to be near to your lordship in blood and kindred; and yet as well for that I am assured that be he never so near tied [?] to you in nature you will notwithstanding prefer the care of the church before all natural respects, as also for the love I bear your lordship: I thought good to let you understand what I have heard, and doubting but you will have that care with it requisite for the removing of so great an offence not only from the good gentlemen and people of that parish, which as I hear be in number 800 communicants, but also clean ['out of your diocese' *crossed out*] from all ecclesiastical function within your diocese. But because it is not enough to remove the ill, except there be a care likewise to plant some good and fit man in his place, I have been moved to recommend unto you one Robinson, a bachelor in divinity of very rare gifts as well in knowledge and utterance as in conversation of life ['for the ministry' *crossed out*] to be preferred to the said vicarage. Whom it shall please your lordship to admit to that room after the removing the incumbent that now is, being so unworthy a man. You shall not only do a very acceptable thing to that whole parish and commendable to yourself but prevent also such ill rumours as peradventure may by the common enemies of our profession, the papists and men of malice than for any good respect be spared of your lordship for suffering so unmeet a minister to have any pastoral charge in your diocese. And that hoping you will accept this my writing in such part as I have meant the same, that is to say, as a token of ['plain' *crossed out*] my unfeigned goodwill, enforcing me to let you know both what I have heard and what I wish to be by you done in this case. I commend your lordship most heartily to God, from the court, the (6th) of March 1578[9]. Your lordship's loving and assured friend.

In support of this letter Walsingham enclosed a copy of the complaint about the vicar's insufficiencies.[22]

Walsingham's letter was a masterly piece of exhortation, flattery, cajoling, and manipulation. But it failed to accomplish its primary purpose. Bishop Curteys wriggled away from the dishonour of depriving his brother, and on 30 March wrote back to the Secretary with procedural smoke and alternative suggestions:

Your honour doth lovingly for that you have heard, and tenderly for the furtherance of God his church, advise me to remove the vicar and minister of Cuckfield, and to place a more sufficient and worthy man in his room. Truly right honourable, these causes have been heard before Archbishop Parker, Bishop Sandys, then Bishop [Grindal? *paper torn*] this Archbishop at his first coming, Dr. Watts and Dr. Yale and now (as I am informed) depend before the High Commissioners in Paul's from whence an inferior judge cannot well call the same.[23] But if the matter were never commenced anywhere, yet seeing by order of the Council I was contented to my great charge to refer over all the dealing in Jurisdiction to Mr. Dr. Becon, a man as very well liked of me, so specially commended and named by your honour, I most humbly beseech your goodness, that following my preaching I may neither herein, nor in any like matter be troubled hereafter; the rather for that I hear now, upon the end of controversies, between the Bishop of Norwich and him, Dr. Becon purposeth very shortly to come into this country, who I take indifferent to execute justice uprightly without partiality to any person. As the man hath deserved in law to be displaced, I will prefer the care of God his church, before natural respect. I mind not to be a mediator for him. And yet it is not in me to give the living, if he were removed tomorrow. And they which understand the truth know that I have not that interest for the mans [?] direction which the world would judge my place requireth. And therefore I fear (right honourable) some men rather to alienate that honourable loving affection, which they know or hear your honour hath borne me of late to my great comfort, than for any likelihood of ability in me to perform their request, have preferred this suit to your honour, if through ignorance they deal not in an unknown matter. I live to my book, prayers and preaching, my jurisdiction and disposition of other livings in my gift granted over to others, my only desire is to live in quiet, wherein I will not forget in my daily prayers to commend your honourable services to God his most merciful protection and direction. At Cherisworth the 30th of this March 1579.[24]

If the bishop's choice had been to remove his brother Edmund or accept suspension himself, Richard Curteys had chosen the honourable path.

About this time Edmund Curteys played his other card. He attempted to discredit his opponent by revealing the evil behaviour of Henry Bowyer's wife. The Cuckfield women's testimony, with the midwife's remarks and the compromising account of Mrs Bowyer's deadly medicine, was sent up to London in the spring of 1579. This may have been the first that Walsingham and the other officials knew of the business with Mercy Gould, and it certainly muddied the issue. Two connected stories, one about the suspicious outcome of an illegitimate pregnancy, the other of conflict between clerk and laity, now became entwined at both the local and the national level. Henry Bowyer was now on the defensive, and he wrote to *his* brother with a somewhat frantic summary of developments. With unconscious symmetry, both Henry Bowyer and Edmund Curteys called on their brothers to help preserve their reputations, and the brothers were obliged to assist because *their* reputations too were inevitably embroiled. Simon Bowyer held no administrative office but his position at court opened doors that would be useful in a close kinsman's cause. By contrast, the Bishop of Chichester's power was already constrained by rival ecclesiastical officials and was further reduced by his informal suspension; though still a royal almoner he had no parliamentary business at this time and diminishing opportunities to press his own or his brother's case in London. During the crisis when Edmund Curteys most needed him, his brother the bishop was politically hobbled.

In response to Curteys's move, Henry Bowyer wrote on 15 June 1579 to his brother Mr Simon Bowyer, 'gentleman usher and daily waiter to the queen's majesty at the court'[25] enclosing 'the confession of Mercy Gould', taken fourteen months earlier, 'whereby may appear how unjustly he is charged by Curteys the vicar of Cuckfield'. This long and rambling letter, hastily written and short on punctuation, reveals the apparent change of fortune and the urgency of Henry Bowyer's position. Written in an exceptionally difficult hand (perhaps Walsingham's quick copy), the letter supplies a lot more detail, shaded by special pleading, about the events that precipitated the crisis. It takes us back to Mercy Gould's pregnancy, her dealings with her former mistress, ministrations of local pharmacology, and the manoeuvres of the Cuckfield magistracy and gentry. Community cohesion in Cuckfield had become so unravelled that neighbouring gentlemen no longer thought each other fit to share the sacrament of holy communion. The letter reads as follows:

After my very hearty commendations, I received your letter whereby I understand that our vicar to purge himself, which he can never do, hath shamefully belied and slandered others, which he can never prove, whereof I thank God I am nothing offended, knowing it is the old practice of his master the devil to bring himself clean down. The matter that toucheth my wife is so untrue and odious that I must needs bring him to his answer therein to his utter overthrow. The strumpet he writeth of was sometime my wife's servant but of such untowardness as she was sent home ['delivered' *crossed out*] to her mother, and she being there her mother and father-in-law [i.e. her stepfather] died both within the space of six days or thereabouts, which being in the time of the plague at Cuckfield it was much doubted that it was the plague. Upon the death of her mother and father in law, she being alone came to an honest woman within Cuckfield who was her acquaintance and desired of her to help her to a service and she promised to do what she could for her, not hearing how suddenly her father and mother was dead before, and she went to Mr. Boordes and there got grant to receive her to service and that she should come the Monday following. This was the Friday or Saturday.

The Sunday night or Monday morning this strumpet fell very sick and the good wife of the house now hearing of the sudden death of her father and mother feared it was the plague, and as it was a common thing for such as were visited, to send to my wife when she was at home or else to my house for metredation [mithridate] of dragon water and other things which I had always ready for the sick, she sent her boy to my wife to desire her to have some metredation of dragon water for such a one was fallen sick in her house and she feared it was the plague, and sent for a bottle of beer also. My wife sent metredation of dragon water and a bottle of beer according to her request. This wench lay very sick certain days and within certain days was ill of a child dead born which was thought to be never quick; the woman of the house came to my house and told my wife how the strumpet had abused her and her house, and what was come to pass of her sickness, and that the magistrates might be advertised of the case. My wife imparting the matter to me, the constable was then with me. I sent him presently to the Justice Mr. Covert that the matter might be examined to effect, and I took my nag and met him there. The Justice sent the constable presently to the chief of the ['parish' *crossed out*] gentlewomen and others of the parish to examine the strumpet and others in the house she lay of her sickness and the ['manner' *crossed out*] state of the child which there died and certified the matter in writing, a copy whereof I have sent unto you herein. Afterwards Mr. Covert and Mr. Bartlye sent for all the gentlemen of the parish and sent for the party as soon as she was recovered and examined the matter very straightly both touching the child and the father and proceeded to punishment according to the statute, the Justices are to answer in this matter who I think did their duties as thoughtfully as they could do.

But now I will show you the vicar's lewd practice. Whilst the woman of the house came to my house to show my wife what was happened and that I should show the matter to the Justices, the vicar's wife hearing of the matter, for it was made openly known presently, she took three or four like herself and went to the house and into the chamber to the wench and examined her whether she had taken no sorcery nor drinks to destroy the child, and she said no but such as her old mistress sent her, which was the metredation of dragon water that was sent for; and upon this the vicar and that wicked rout amongst themselves have slanderously spoken, whereof I hearing desired the Justices at their last examining her to examine her thoroughly of it where it did appear she could take no hurt thereby, so that I am so shamefully misused herein that now he justifieth it I must and will follow it as far as I can by law, and surely all that he hath is never able to make my wife undone whose credit I must defend, for I know that she would not have consented to such a matter for all the goods [?] in the world.

Touching Mr. Ninian Chaloner, whereas I hear that in Curteys's letter to Mr. Secretary he writeth that I bear with Mr. Chaloner you know that is most untrue, for he took part with the lewd vicar against all the gentlemen of the parish for which he is worthily plagued, and when I first explained the matter to the Justices, for that the matter was very suspicious, the vicar only upheld him and the strumpet he is charged withal, which now being before the High Commissioners he is to be tried of, and I have thought ill of him and his doings always, and as you know, whereas he sayeth that Mr. Chaloner received the communion with others this Easter I and Mr. Hussey and others were grieved [?] when we heard it, but I saw it not and he is not yet convicted of the crime is laid to his charge, but surely I would advise him not to have come to the table before he had either purged or submitted himself both to the order of law and the congregation; but this I will so assure you, that he hath written nothing touching me nor my wife nor Mr. Hussey nor such as seek in the fear of God his reformation, and removing that he is able to prove but shall answer to his shame, and all that we allege shall be sufficiently proved; wherefore pray you presently to show to Mr. Mills the whole content that Mr. Secretary (to whom we think ourselves so much bound) might be presently advertised, I pray assist my brother Mitchell in his business who can show you all things and what Mr. Chancellor hath or can do; and so I commit you heartily to God, with hearty commendations from my wife and all the rest of your friends here, this 15th of June 1579, your assured loving brother Henry Bowyer.[26]

Charge, counter-charge, and rumour focused on the medicine that Elizabeth Bowyer gave to Mercy Gould. Was it noxious or benign, normal or unconventional? Did it operate as a precaution against plague, as Mrs Bowyer contended, or was this concoction designed to induce an abortion or worse, as the midwife and vicar's wife said they feared? Elizabethan countrywomen were familiar with a large pharmacopoeia of herbal remedies, and could be expected to know what prevented diseases and what would cause 'abortement'. A variety of medicines was used 'to bring down or provoke a woman's flowers', to stimulate menstruation, or 'to hasten the bringing forth' of a child from the womb, and this knowledge was widely distributed through printed herbals and through women's lore. Plague remedies and domestic first-aid were equally well known.[27]

According to Joan Curteys and company, Mercy Gould and her wombchild were sickened by the ill effects of a 'purgation' that Mrs Bowyer administered to her before expelling her from the house. Being asked 'what manner of drink' it was which her mistress gave her, 'then the said Mercy Gould said it was a cruel hot drink, a cruel hot drink, twice, with great sighing which provoked [her] oftentimes to be delivered of [her] child. Also Isabel Chaloner, one of the foresaid women, said unto her was not the drink which thy mistress gave thee for the plague, unto whom she answered no, no.' The implication was that something sinister was at work. But Elizabeth Bowyer's account, repeated by her husband, was that she merely provided a common household medicine, which Bowyer kept in store, in response to Goody Boniface's request and in line with Mercy Gould's need. In this version, the woman of the house where Mercy Gould was lying sent her boy to Mrs Bowyer 'to desire her to have some metredation of dragon water for such a one was fallen sick in her house and she feared it was the plague, and sent for a bottle of beer also,' and Mrs Bowyer obliged out of charity. This 'dragon water', which sounds so fearsome, was most likely derived from *dracunculus*, dragonwort or 'dragon', a garden or pond plant with valued properties. According to a standard herbal, distilled dragon water 'hath virtue against the pestilence or any pestilential fever or poison, being drunk blood warm with the best treacle or mithridate'. (Mithridate was a honey-based electuary composition regarded as a universal preservative or antidote against infectious disease.) A popular Elizabethan directory of medicines prescribed a concoction of dragon water with treacle, washed down with ale, as 'a sovereign drink against the plague'. This is exactly the usage that Elizabeth Bowyer prescribed. But the herbal also warns that dragon root 'scoureth and cleaneth mightily', that it 'causeth the humours which stick fast in the chest to be easily voided', and that 'the smell of the flowers is hurtful to women newly conceived with child'. It was not so efficient an abortifacient as spurgewort, sowbread, fern, or some others, but was thought to have had the effect of making a pregnant woman ill and thereby loosening her child.[28] It is possible, then, that both accounts approximate the truth, that the dragon water was administered with goodwill as a precaution against the plague, but that its unfortunate side effects caused premature labour and irreversible damage to the baby. The midwife was entitled to be furious, for most communities deferred to her expertise in these matters, and live births were essential to her good reputation.[29]

Simon Bowyer would accept his brother's explanation and would present his version of the struggle with the vicar to any who would usefully listen.

Evidently he had Walsingham's ear. Against this lobbying campaign, Edmund Curteys made a last attempt to rescue his reputation, to establish his bona fides, and to cling to his position as vicar. He wrote from Cuckfield on 31 May 1579, appealing 'to the honourable and my very friend Secretary Walsingham at the Court or elsewhere', as follows:

My most humble duty remembered unto your honour, thinking myself most bounden, that it pleased your honour to have such care over me, my wife, and poor children, as to write unto me being a poor minister as it seemeth unto me upon mere goodwill. Notwithstanding whereas your honour chargeth me (as you have been misinformed) both with insufficiency of learning and also with ill demeanour. These are to certify your honour that I was made minister by the right reverend father in God the Bishop of Ely sixteen years ago being then student in St. John's College in Cambridge. And I was then thought meet to be in the ministry by the said right reverend father and also by Mr. Doctor Whitgift, at that time being his proctor, both for my learning and religion; and also for conversation and good behaviour. And I continued therein seven years after the minister of St. Giles, being parish church to Magdalene College. And after that I was preferred to a benefice in Huntingdonshire by my Lord Keeper late deceased, a parish of great worship called Yaxley. And from thence I was preferred by my Lord Bishop of Ely to a benefice called Swavesey a little from Cambridge. All this time (I thank God for it) my good name was never called into question, though mine enemies of late in all these places have searched my life. And my conversation is no other now than it was then, which I doubt not but to prove by the testimony of mine honest neighbours, if I might obtain a Commission for the trial of my good behaviour and not by the false information of mine enemies upon forged articles be condemned. Indeed, the cause of all this my trouble is for that I have sought the punishment of certain wicked men, which have two wives apiece now alive, whereof the one is a gentleman linked in kindred with the rest of mine enemies with whom they have received the communion together, and with whom also they are daily conversant. And for these and other abominable vices am I by mine enemies thus persecuted. Wherefore I most humbly beseech your honour to suspend your judgement until I have tried myself by law. And then I trust their malicious dealing and dissimulation will be known. Thus most humbly desiring your honour to tender my case, my poor wife and children, I commit your honour to the tuition of almighty (god) wishing you health in the Lord with increase of honour. From Cuckfield the last day of May. By your honour's most humble orator Edmund Curteys.

A postscript moved from personal history to the matter in hand.

As touching the talk which my Lord of Buckhurst had with me concerning resignation of my vicarage, these are to advertise your honour that I can not resign it in such sort as my Lord of Buckhurst would have me without committing simony, as both Mr. Doctor Ford and other learned men hath certified me. Which thing also I told my lord when I talked with him. And thereupon he willed me to take a fortnight's deliberation to ask my counsel. Wherefore seeing that I can not do so I beseech your honour of your lawful favour that I may set a learned preacher under me to serve the cure and preach.[30]

It was not to be. The Bowyer faction won, perhaps because their political ammunition outmatched the resources of their opponents, and perhaps, too, because they told a more persuasive story. At its meeting on 16 January 1581, attended by Secretary Walsingham and eight others, the Privy Council directed a letter to the Dean of St Paul's, the Dean of Arches, and other ecclesiastical officials, requiring them to examine Edmund Curteys in person and to consider the complaints against him. By 5 February the Council had reached a decision and instructed the Bishop of London and other High Commissioners that, 'considering the enormity of the faults, which are, as it is informed unto their lordships, sufficiently proved against him, and whereof there is no hope of amendment, for avoiding of further offence and slander his lordship and the rest are required by virtue of their Commission Ecclesiastical to proceed to the deprivation of the said vicar of Cuckfield both from his benefice and vicarage of Cuckfield, and also from exercising any function ecclesiastical in the ministry elsewhere'.[31]

Curteys and his supporters faced humiliation, but they did not give up without a rearguard action. Nor was the parish of Cuckfield calmed by this judgement. Edmund Curteys stayed on in the area, licking his wounds and attempting to restore his fortunes. His supporters bore grudges and continued to use whatever legal and political resources they could find to restore their advantage or to harm their enemies. Parish communions, which were supposed to be occasions of charity and harmony, were fraught with ill will. Bishop Richard Curteys reluctantly instituted a successor to the vicarage, one Alexander Southwick who pleased nobody, while another minister, George Closse, claimed that the vicarage was still vacant and attempted to secure it for himself.[32] Meanwhile, in respect of his poverty and lack of maintenance, the authorities allowed the deprived Curteys to continue in the vicarage house for a year and to enjoy the benefit of the glebe land, even after his successor was appointed.[33] For several months the parish continued in turmoil, with uncertainty about rights of institution and payment of tithes. This struggle for control of the parish erupted into violence on 25 June 1581, the Sunday after St John's Day, when rival factions fought for possession of the pulpit. The surviving documents tell only one side of the story, and that only in outline, so we have to recreate the scene in our imaginations.

Henry Bowyer, esquire, John Hussey, gent., Henry Mitchell, gent., Thomas Turner, tailor, Thomas Jenner, yeoman, Edward Roberts, yeoman, John Johnson, husbandman, and Alexander Green, yeoman, all parishioners of

Cuckfield, were indicted before the Sussex Assizes held at East Grinstead on 7 July 1581. These men were the activists in the Bowyer camp and they represent a wide social spectrum. Hussey was the owner of the impropriated rectory of Cuckfield and therefore had an interest in the vicarage and a right to the tithes. All were indicted for riotous assembly and for 'interrupting a celebrant during divine service, contrary to statute, when on 25 June 1581 they riotously assembled in Cuckfield parish church during morning prayer, assaulted George Closse, clerk, prevented him from giving a sermon, and forcibly ejected him from church'.[34]

Notwithstanding the possibility that something of this sort really happened, Bowyer was able to convince his friends in London that the indictment was false and the prosecution malicious. The Privy Council had summoned three of Bowyer's enemies, Messrs Ninian Chaloner, Thomas Mitchell, and John Henslow, under warrant from Secretary Walsingham on 2 July, and put them on notice not to proceed against Bowyer. On 10 July, three days' after the Sussex indictment, Chaloner and Mitchell were ordered back to London to answer for their contempt, and on 16 July they were committed to the Marshalsea prison. Ten days' detention was enough for flexing the ligaments of power, and on 26 July, 'upon their submission and promise not to intermeddle hereafter in the matter of the vicarage of Cuckfield [they] were with some good lessons to behave themselves more dutifully hereafter, dismissed and set at liberty'.[35]

It was during this period that Edmund Curteys, now late vicar of Cuckfield, resurrected the business of Mrs Bowyer's treatment of Mercy Gould, in hope of demeaning his enemy. The Privy Council heard that 'the wife of Henry Bowyer . . . is very desirous to clear herself' and that the relevant written testimonies had been collected, but by this time the Curteys faction was so discredited that no such examination was necessary. Once again Henry Bowyer turned a potentially troublesome situation to his advantage, and with the help of the Privy Council made his mastery of the Cuckfield community more secure. All that was needed to complete his triumph was a progressive preacher to occupy the vicarage, and this was supplied by the institution of John Waterhouse on 25 September 1581. Waterhouse, who served Cuckfield from 1581 to 1607, was everything Curteys was not. According to his obituary, Waterhouse was 'a most rare and excellent preacher, greatly admired for his zealous and godly speech'. The godly found him sympathetic and protected him from episcopal interference, and it was not until 1605 that he was presented before the archdeacon for 'not wearing the surplice nor using the cross in baptism'. It was to Waterhouse that Henry Bowyer entrusted his charitable legacies, and it was during his incumbency that Bowyer contributed to the further edification of the church. If, at the heart of the matter, this dispute that began with Mercy Gould's pregnancy was about advancing the Reformation, then moderate puritans, among whom both Bowyer and Waterhouse might be numbered, can be seen to have been the victors.

Bishop Richard Curteys attempted to reinstate his brother to his prebend, but the canons of Chichester refused to have him in residence. Further pressure from London may have hardened them in their decision.[36] The bishop died on 30 August 1582, discredited and effectively suspended. His younger brother Edmund, for whom he took so much trouble, lived out his days in the vicinity of Cuckfield, a recipient of charity, and was buried in the parish he had formerly served as vicar on 17 May 1605.

Of Mercy Gould's subsequent history we know nothing. The record is silent whether she lived and thrived as a resident of Cuckfield, whether she moved on, whether she married, or when she died. No Cuckfield parish registers can be found before 1598 so the marriages, baptisms, and burials of our protagonists cannot be traced. Mercy Gould's ordeal was soon over, but its consequences set households, neighbours, parishioners, and magistrates in a struggle for righteousness and legitimation that exposed their alliances, stresses, and contradictions. The story of Mercy Gould and the vicar of Cuckfield is a story that illuminates power relations, great and small, in the underside of Elizabethan England. It reminds us how tightly related were personal and public morality, local and national politics, and the religion and culture of the humble and the elite. It reminds us, too, of the danger of distortion which arises when historians try to write about these topics in isolation from each other.

Dramatis Personae

BOWYER FACTION

Mercy Gould, servant to Henry Bowyer (formerly servant to Edmund Curteys)
Henry Bowyer, Cuckfield ironmaster and landowner
Elizabeth Bowyer, Henry's wife
Simon Bowyer, Henry's brother, gentleman usher at court
John Boniface of Cuckfield, gave shelter to Mercy and buried her dead child
Boniface's wife, former servant with Mercy
John Orgle, servant, putative father of Mercy's child
Mrs Mitchell of Tyes, widow
Mrs Mitchell of the town
Mrs Mitchell of Anstey
goodwife Gateland
John Hussey, gent.
Thomas Turner, tailor

Alexander Green, yeoman
Thomas Jenner, yeoman
Edward Roberts, yeoman
John Johnson, husbandman

CURTEYS FACTION
Edmund Curteys, vicar of Cuckfield, 1571–81
Joan Curteys, Edmund's wife
Richard Curteys, Edmund's brother, Bishop of Chichester
Denis Clarke, midwife
Isabel Chaloner, gentlewoman
Marjorie Chaloner, gentlewoman
Alice Rowland
Joan Bassett
Joan Mercer
Eleanor Parson
Edmund Chaloner, gent.
John Chaloner, gent.
Ninian Chaloner, gent.
Thomas Mitchell
John Henslow

MAGISTRATES AND CLERICS
Sir Francis Walsingham, Secretary of State; William Cecil, Lord Burghley; Lord
    Buckhurst; Sir John Pelham; Sir Walter Covert; George Goring, esq.; Henry
    Barkley, esq.; Mr Gooch; Archbishop Matthew Parker; Bishop Edwin
    Sandys; Dr William Overton; Dr Ford; Dr Watts; Dr Yale; Dr Becon; Mr
    Robinson; John Waterhouse; Alexander Southwick; George Closse

4

Rose Arnold's Confession:
Seduction, Deception, and
Distress in the Heart of England

This story cuts to the heart of economic, social, and sexual relationships in early modern England. It could serve as a morality drama about exploitation, a scenario for a play about survival and endurance, but it comes, like so many tales of distress, from the ecclesiastical archives. Its themes are gender and power, love and deception, sex and seduction. The story exposes the relationships of gentility and dependency, coercive male mastery and the vulnerabilities of female domestic service. Its ingredients include unwitnessed spousals, concealed pregnancy, attempted abortion, attempted murder, thoughts of suicide, a bastard birth, and suspicions of infanticide. Other topics exposed in the course of its unfolding include subterfuge and resistance, bribery and forgery, the misuse of literacy, and the threatened misuse of the law. The story even has religious dimensions involving the swearing of oaths, invocation of the Devil, recourse to the Bible, and a popular misrepresentation of the doctrine of predestination. The central character, Rose Arnold of Scraptoft, Leicestershire, told her story to her mother, to her minister, and to a magistrate, before retelling it, after much rehearsal, to the clerks of the diocesan court. Here, with minimal processing, is Rose Arnold's confession, recorded late in 1608.[1]

Whilst I was a servant to Mr. Lane of Tilton I was importuned by Mr. Francis, son of the said Mr. Lane, and upon his promise made unto me, to make me his wife, I granted unto him the loss of my chastity. Proving with child, I told him thereof; whereto he answered, 'I know so much by my calendar; notwithstanding, I have read in a book that if a woman in such a case will but immediately drink a draught of well water it would cure her of such a disease.' Which I willing to prove, went forth out of my master's house into the kitchen adjoining to a well therein, there to have drunk water. Whitherto he following me, the well being by him already uncovered, it being dark, and I stooping to take water, violently offered to have cast me therein. But I catching hold of the furniture of the well, and striking a blow withal, he desisted from his purpose. And asking him if he meant to murder or drown me, he answered, praying me to forgive him, that the devil was great with him for that purpose, but he was already sorry for the same.

This being about Martlemas time [*St Martin's Day, 11 November, a traditional time for servants' contracts to expire*], he then prayed me, and every day after more and more urged me to depart from his father's house. Howbeit, I continued there still his father's servant until the first week in Lent [*mid-February in 1608*], when my fault beginning to be apparently seen, he persuaded me earnestly to leave the town of Tilton, which request I granted. And he, still promising to marry with me, gave me twenty shillings of money and a passport which testified that I was late wife to one Jannill, and that I had sustained great losses by fire, and that my husband, affrighted therewith, died leaving me comfortless. So that I was constrained, as appeared by my passport, to travel towards Lynn to certain of my dead husband's friends. He willed me also to go to a place called Coton in Cambridgeshire where he would presently meet me and provide for me all things necessary. [*Here the manuscript is torn, a stage in the narrative missing. The rendezvous apparently went amiss.*]

Rose Arnold admitted that she would, so far from home,

by some vile means have taken away my life, but [I] wandered up and down in Northamptonshire until I was delivered of childbirth, and that child died, which was about midsummer last. Then I returned into Leicestershire to Scraptoft to my mother, who in my absence, being suspicious thereof, and finding by tokens that I had lately been delivered of a child, reported the same, so that it came to the ear of the minister of the town whose name is Mr. Fisher.[2] [He] privately examined me who was the father of the child, to whom I answered truly, Francis Lane of Tilton.

The news of my coming to Scraptoft being spread abroad, Francis Lane sent secretly unto me one Francis Bullivant, who willed me to meet the said Francis Lane in a place near Newton. Where we being met, he after some speeches refused to marry with me. Only, he would give me twenty pounds if I would lay the child to one James Dallywater, late servant to his brother in law John Blount of Tilton. Which I refusing to do, saying, 'I have related the truth to Mr. Fisher,' he answered me, he could deal well enough with him. And he would still give me twenty pounds if I would but deny my speech before the said Mr. Fisher, and withal lay the child to Dallywater. And that I might the better do it, he did assure me that the said Dallywater was already hanged.

I relying on his promise of marriage withstood these his offers and temptations. Then he flatly told me that he must either forsake his country or forswear the act. And rather than he would forsake his country he would absolutely forswear it. For, saith he, 'I find it in one place of scripture, if I be born elected, whether I swear or not swear, I shall be saved.' Moreover, he threatened me if I would dissent from these motions made he would call me before a Justice and there lay to my charge that I had stolen certain things out of his father's house at my departure.

Before making this confession to ecclesiastical officials, Rose told her story to the magistrate, Mr Cave, who enjoined her 'to go to Luddington where I was delivered of child, from thence to bring him under the minister's hand a true certificate of the same, and what was become of the child. But before I came thither Mr. Francis Lane had procured one from thence to Mr. Cave, whereof I have true copy.' It is not clear what happened next, or whether anyone was charged or punished. Since there was no live bastard and no dead body, and no other account of this misery besides Rose Arnold's, it was hard to see how secular or ecclesiastical justice could proceed. At the end, Rose no longer had a baby to support, but may still, despite everything, have wanted Francis to marry her. Marriage to the son of a gentleman, the father of her lost child, would raise her status and esteem, even if it entailed a life of domestic misery. Perhaps she would rather be miserable in comfort. For the vile Francis, marriage to a former servant, one he had so grievously abused, would undermine his self-esteem and bar him from making a more advantageous alliance among families of his own landed class. Unlike a staged drama, this story ends inconclusively, as do so many other accounts of vulnerable women's ordeals.[3] Like an earlier Leicestershire servant, Agnes Bowker, Rose Arnold's strength lay in her ability to command narrative, as well as to endure a heap of distress.

Dramatis Personae

Rose Arnold, servant, of Scraptoft
goody Arnold, Rose's mother
Mr Lane of Tilton, Rose's master
Francis Lane, Rose's seducer
Francis Bullivant, friend of Francis Lane
James Dallywater, servant
Mr Cave, magistrate
Nicholas Fisher, clerk

5

The Essex Abortionist:
Depravity, Sex, and Violence

Richard Skeete and Lydia Downes were hanged for murder early in 1639. There was no gory pamphlet to describe their deeds, no lurid report of their performance on the scaffold. But a story survives, entered in the Colchester borough records, which offers Lydia Downes's account of the entanglements that took her to her death. Like Agnes Bowker's confession of her dealings with the schoolmaster Hugh Brady and Rose Arnold's account of her relationship with her master's son Francis Lane, this is a tale of exploitation and distress, told by a woman in trouble. In the course of its unfolding Lydia Downes's story exposes dark areas of the medical, sexual, and criminal underworld of early modern England. The familiar ingredients of dependency, seduction, pregnancy, and illegitimacy are joined by mysterious illnesses, desperate cures, attempted abortion, attempted suicide, serial infanticide, and murder. Like other confessions and depositions that illuminate the past, Lydia Downes's statement also reveals the rhetorical skill of the teller and her negotiation with the authority of the law. Historians have occasionally cited this case with reference to murder and abortion, but Lydia's words, redacted for the magistrates, have not previously been published in full. They make a chilling tale.[1]

Examinations taken the 12th day of November anno domini 1638, before John Furley, gentleman, mayor, etc., and Henry Barrington, gentleman, Justice of the Peace of our sovereign lord the king, etc., for the town Colchester etc.

Lydia Downes aged 24 years or thereabouts, being examined confesseth and sayeth that about five or six years since her brother in law, one William Hardy (who is now dead), did come to Richard Skeete in the parish of St. Mary's, and told him in what condition she this examinant was then in, and her said brother in law told Skeete that she was to go to Chelmsford to a woman there for cure. And Skeete told her brother that it was in vain to go to that woman of Chelmsford for she could not cure her . . . but if her brother would bring her to him he would cure her for twenty shillings. And her brother telling Skeete that [she] was not able to come, Skeete sent her by her brother a paper with crosses to hang about her neck that night, and the next day that paper to be burnt, and she . . . to be held over it (which was done), and then she might come to him without any danger.

And after that was done, then she and her brother did come to Skeete's house (about two of the clock in afternoon) and that night (after the said Skeete had caused her to take an oath upon the testament that she should not reveal his secrets, otherwise he could not cure her) the said Skeete did let her blood, but she bled but a little (in regard she was so frightened with that which she then saw and heard, for that night the said Skeete did cross papers and burnt them, and cut off some of the hair of [her] head and burnt it, and Skeete said then some words which she understood not), and after a great noise and a mighty tempest of wind the candle and fire went out, and then there appeared some thing in the likeness of a man (which she thought was the devil or some evil spirit). And [she] rising up to awake her brother (lying then sleeping upon Skeete's bed), Skeete beat her down, and bade her sit still, and said to her, cannot you sit still and be quiet, he going about to cure her, and then pulled her out of the chair wherein she then sat and carried her into the yard. When she was in the yard she fell down with fear, and Skeete left her and (as she thought) went into the house.

And after Skeete had awaked her brother and those that were in the house and sent them away, the said Skeete did throw her upon his bed, and there had the carnal knowledge of her body, and after that gave her physic and sent her home. And the Saturday following [she] with her said brother came to Skeete's house, where he gave her a second oath of secrecy, and let her blood, which blood [she] would have spilt, but Skeete would not let her, and told her that she came to him for help, but would not let him alone, and then he took her blood and burnt it with pins and needles, and after that had the carnal knowledge of her body and kept her at his house till the Monday following, and in which time Skeete had the use of her body several times.

And after which time [she] proved with child, and had a child by one Tunbridge, and after she was up again and was to come to the spiritual courts (having been warned thither), Skeete sent to speak with [her], and when her mother and she came to the court, Skeete came to them, and they went together to the house of one Coker, and there supped, and Skeete paid for their suppers, and that night [she] lay at the said Coker's house with her mother. And the Saturday following she . . . did lie with Skeete at his house all night, and that then he had again the use of her body, and soon after she proved with child. And upon the quickening she told Skeete she was with child, and he bade her take savin (which she did) but that did her no good. And about six weeks after she was quick with child, and then Skeete told [her] that she must take some physic, and he gave her physic which she took, but it prevailed not.

And then she told Skeete she would never come to shame again, and thereupon she took ratsbane (which she had at her brother's, he being a farrier) at Skeete's house, unbeknown to Skeete, and after she had taken the poison (being then fearful of death) she told Skeete of it, and he gave her salad oil and the kernel of hazel nuts which expelled the poison, that it wrought not. But yet the child was not killed within her, but afterwards (at the house of the said Coker) she was delivered of a child (which was born alive), and none was with her at the time she was in travail but Skeete and Coker's maid (whose name she knoweth not). But whether Skeete was with her at the instant time of her delivery she remembreth not (for she was much troubled with her convulsion fits), but presently after her delivery Skeete and the said maid asked [her] what they should do with the child, and she told them what they would, and she said to them that she . . . was not so hard hearted as to make it away, but Coker's maid said tush, it was not the first that she had made away. And then after they had wrapped up the child in [Lydia Downes's] apron, they carried it away, and as she thinketh put it into the ground in Coker's yard.

And also [she] sayeth that afterwards she was with child by Skeete, and was delivered thereof at Skeete's house, and that when she was delivered of that child there was then present only Skeete and one Keeler's wife, and that presently after that child was born Skeete gave it something in a spoon which he told [her] was water and sugar, but presently after the child swelled and died, but what became of it afterwards she knoweth not, but Skeete and Keeler's wife conveyed it away. And [she] further sayeth that Skeete before she was delivered of the said child, by physic often assayed to destroy the said child within her, and that before the time she was delivered of the child Skeete had purposely sent his wife away to Mersea that [Lydia Downes] might lie in at his house where she stayed about fourteen days. And also [she] sayeth, that after the said Keeler's wife had looked to her about a week she (being [her] keeper), fell sick and died. But before her death she would have revealed the murthering of the child, but that Skeete and [Lydia Downes] would not be from her for fear thereof, until she was dead.

And further [she] sayeth, that Skeete did give to her poison to give to his wife, and told her that if his wife were dead he would marry [Lydia Downes]. But she threw down the poison and would not give it to his wife. And then Skeete entreated [her] to go away with him, and he would leave his wife and that he had with her, and they did go away together, and were gone together about six days. And then she being terrified in her mind, would stay no longer with him, and gave him good words to bring her home again, being afraid that he would make her away. And also [she] sayeth that after Skeete's wife was dead, Skeete told [her] that he had given his wife such a draught, that was the last she drank. And that the said Skeete before his said wife was buried, sent for [Lydia Downes] to come to his wife's burial, and sent her word that if she would come he would marry her. Lydia Downes, her mark.

Lydia Downes's story is remarkably rich yet tantalizingly incomplete, but even this brief narrative suggests several directions for study. She lived at Dedham, just a few miles north of Colchester, but had no part in the puritan culture for which that community is famous. Indeed, religion is absent from this story. We may wonder at the nature of the malady that required Lydia Downes to seek medical attention. It was evidently serious enough for members of her family to want to help her to a cure. Her brother-in-law (married to her sister Alice) was going to take her to the 'woman of Chelmsford' before Skeete intervened with his therapy. One possibility is that Lydia Downes, like Agnes Bowker, suffered from epilepsy or falling sickness. She was, she said, 'much troubled with her convulsion fits' during labour, though this could equally refer to her birthpangs. Another possibility, to which she herself alluded, is that she suffered from smallpox. The most likely suggestion, however, is that Lydia was already pregnant, carrying the child fathered by Tunbridge, and that the 'cure' she was seeking was an abortion.

The Colchester archdeaconry act books record Lydia's earlier encounter with the ecclesiastical authorities when she was cited in April 1634 'upon a common fame of committing fornication or adultery with Matthew Tunbridge of Abberton'. Lydia confessed to the court 'that while she lived with her sister Alice Hardy of Abberton [*a few miles south of Colchester*] about St. James tide last past, the said Matthew Tunbridge came thither and had the carnal use of her body three several times, once in the barn and twice in the lower room, and begot her with child; of which child she sayeth she miscarried by reason she had the smallpox.' None gainsaying this account, which may have been Lydia's first experience of telling her tales in court, she was ordered to perform public penance in Abberton church, which she duly performed.[2] Her later history suggests that the miscarriage may not have been so innocent as it appears. Lydia's testimony to the Colchester magistrates suggests that she first met Richard Skeet while carrying Tunbridge's child, and that Skeete enjoyed Lydia's body while she was already pregnant.

Richard Skeete, a weaver, was evidently renowned as a cunning man or practitioner of occult and herbal remedies. He was also a specialist in finding lost treasure. At twenty shillings his services did not come cheap. His repertoire of cures involving amulets, fire, and blood belonged to an established tradition of popular medical magic that Reformers associated with Roman Catholicism. The Elizabethan author Henry Chettle had long since ridiculed the use of paper charms, blessed and burned, that promised 'to expel the spirits, purify the blood, and ease the pain'. The preacher Robert Humston had similarly warned against the 'popish superstitions' and 'Romish sorceries' of country magic, 'as though the wearing or bearing about us these names of God, written in virgin parchment, with crosses and characters were of force to cure maladies, to chase away bugs and cast out devils, which in truth is blasphemously to abuse and take in vain the holy name of God to our own destruction'.[3]

Half a century later, as Lydia Downes attested, such cures were still employed in the heart of puritan East Anglia. Skeete's use of crosses written on paper, his instruction that Lydia sleep with the amulet about her neck, his burning of the paper the next day, and his follow-up treatment with hair-clippings, blood, and pins and needles, all belonged to a ritual of exorcism, designed to rid the patient of evil spirits. Skeete's repeated oaths of secrecy and his utterance of incomprehensible words invested the treatment with awe and mystery. Who is to say that the 'great noise' and 'mighty tempest' that doused the candle and fire and which ushered in a 'thing in the likeness of a man' belonged to a charlatan's theatre of mystification rather than a sick woman's imagination? Readers who recall Hugh Brady's ministrations to Agnes Bowker in Elizabethan Leicestershire, and his similar demand of blood and secrecy, should not be surprised that the treatment concluded with 'carnal knowledge'.[4]

As soon as she was cured—or as soon as she recovered from her pregnancy with Tunbridge's child—Lydia renewed her relationship with Skeete. She appears to have spent the next four years as his mistress and companion. Historians have posited, and some have questioned, the existence of a 'bastardy-prone sub-society' in early modern England; Lydia Downes would seem to fit the bill.[5] At least five times in this period she quickened with child, and at least four times Skeete destroyed her baby by medicinal or physical violence. It is testimony to the woman's robustness, and also to the inexactitude of popular pharmacology, that Skeete, though skilled in spells and poisons, was not always successful in inducing an abortion and was driven to resort to infanticide.

Lydia Downes's confession to the magistrates was a damning testimony, enough to hang Skeete and his associates several times over. Not surprisingly, when the magistrates confronted Skeete with Lydia's testimony, he protested that her story was 'false and untrue'. Though admitting to sexual relations with Lydia Downes, 'at her own house several times, and once at the house of William Coker', he insisted that everything else was a fabrication.

Lydia Downes, however, had not finished telling her story or digging her lover's grave. Three weeks after her first examination, she was back before the magistrates with further information. Lydia's second testimony is as extraordinary as her first, not least for its graphic account of childbirth in distress, infanticide, and murder. Readers who wish to be spared gruesome details may be advised to skip this part of Lydia's confession.

[T]hree years since or thereabouts she was with child, but whether it was by Skeete or one Richard Bryant, a feltmaker, she knoweth not for both of them had the use of her body. And as Skeete and Bryant and she were going along by the house of one Crankes of Abberton at the end of the mean wood (since which time the said Crankes was hanged for felony) she fell in travail, and so they went into the said Crankes's house, and there she was delivered of one female child which was born alive; and at the birth thereof there was with her Skeete and Bryant, but whether Crankes's wife was with her when the child was born she knoweth not. But Skeete told her that he would make away the child, and she told him that she would not consent to have it murdered. And Skeete told her that if she would not consent to have the child made away, she should never go home again to tell tales. And then Skeete took the arm of the child and put the hand of it into the mouth, and strangled it. And Bryant consented to the death of the child, and promised never to reveal it. And the next day when they went from Crankes's house, Skeete and Bryant showed her the place in mean wood where they had buried the child.

She also confesseth that before she was delivered of the child which she had at the house of the said Crankes, she was with child by Skeete, and before she was delivered she was carried away by Skeete and Bryant. As they were going towards London, beyond Chelmsford at an alehouse, she was delivered of a man child, and there was with her three or four women, and that child lived four days and then died and was buried in the churchyard there; and she stayed in that alehouse about a fortnight. And Bryant told the folks of the house and the women that were at her labour that she was his wife. And Skeete and Bryant left her at that alehouse and went away, and about three or four days after Bryant came thither to her, and stayed there with her until they came from thence to Colchester to Skeete's house, where Bryant left her and went his way.

Under further examination Lydia elaborated her story, incriminating Skeete and company in yet another act of infanticide. 'Concerning the child she was delivered of beyond Chelmsford [she said] that after she was delivered of it, that Bryant and Skeete both of them came to her and threatened her that if she would not give her consent to the murdering of the said child that they would make her sure for ever going home herself; and that thereupon she bade them do with it what they would; and presently after the said Skeete and Bryant strangled the child, and after they had done it they brought it up to her and she saw that it was dead.' In saying this, Lydia had as good as condemned herself to death.

Turning to another part of her narrative, Lydia said

that when Keeler's wife lay sick she was desirous to drink some wine with sugar, and thereupon one Joan Collins did fetch half a pint of white wine and she [Lydia] went for sugar, and they delivered the wine and sugar to Skeete. And Skeete put some of the wine into a glass, and put into it something that was white like sugar . . . and gave it to her [Lydia] to give it to Keeler's wife. And she [Lydia] offering to taste of the wine in the glass, Skeete would not let her, and said she, Keeler's wife, shall not drink of your dregs, and she did not drink it but gave it to the goody Keeler; and [Keeler's wife] perceived something swimming in the glass, supposing it to be sugar, said to [Lydia], what can you not stir the sugar but let it swim, and thereupon [Lydia] with Skeete's knife stirred it in the glass, and then Keeler's wife drank it up, and died within an hour . . . After the goody Keeler had drunk up the wine in the glass she [Lydia] would have put some more wine into the glass intending to drink it herself, but Skeete would not suffer her, but took the glass of her hand and washed it and threw some of the water down upon the ground, and a cat that was there lapped some of that water and swelled and some of her hair went off from her. And when Skeete and [Lydia] was gone from Keeler's house, Skeete said to her, we have been a long time afraid of her [Keeler's wife], but I have given her in the wine some mercury, that she will tell no more tales.

Tales, however, kept surfacing as other witnesses addressed the borough court. Joan Collins, who served as 'keeper' or attendant to Keeler's wife during her last illness, testified that Richard Skeete and Lydia Downes were 'daily conversant with [Keeler's wife] all the time of her sickness'. The patient died, she said, 'within three hours after the drinking of the said wine . . . but whether by reason of the drinking of the said wine her death was hastened she knoweth not'. Elizabeth Coker, who had often hosted Richard Skeete and Lydia Downes at her house, reported that one time Skeete said to Lydia, 'when they were drinking together, that when his old wife was dead she [Lydia] should be his next wife'. Another witness, Robert Brittaine of Colchester, gave further testimony about Skeete's practice as a cunning man and finder of lost money. But it was Lydia's testimony, detailed and compelling, that took her and Skeete to the gallows.

Richard Bryant, who had been Skeete's friend and accomplice and who may have fathered Lydia's last child, made one last appearance, though he seems to have escaped the judgement of the court. Lydia first told her story to the magistrates on 12 November 1638. Word no doubt got out, and Bryant tried to spirit her away. Testifying again on 7 December, Lydia Downes said that Bryant came to her at Dedham on 28 November,

and was very desirous to have her go away with him, and told her that if she would go with him he would come the Friday after and bring a horse and carry her away; and she promised him to go away with him, but she did not intend to go away with him, but told him so because she was desirous that he might be taken. . . . Bryant, according to his promise, did come with a horse that Friday he appointed, about ten o'clock of the night, to carry her away. But she having revealed it to Mr. Waterhouse, Mr. Waterhouse did lock her up so that Bryant could not come to her; and so Bryant went away and did not see her nor speak to her, but she knew it was he that came for her for that he told her . . . he would gumble against the wainscot in the entry, and so he did . . . three time before he went away.

Bryant, presumably, rode his horse to safety and oblivion, and might have taken Lydia with him. Instead, by the end of January 1639, both Lydia Downes and Richard Skeete were sentenced to hang. Lydia, by her testimony, had almost suicidally purged herself, taking the poisoner-murderer-abortionist lover with her to oblivion of a different sort.

I have presented this tale with minimal processing, to allow Lydia Downes and her associates to speak for themselves. Readers may make of it what they will. The story may be read as an episode in the history of crime or as a chapter in human morality. It offers a vignette into early-modern gender relations and sexual violence on the eve of the English Revolution, with both Lydia and her lover responsible for multiple transgressions. The tale may also be treated as a remarkable personal narrative, an exculpatory confession with a dramatic structure and rhetorical flair of its own.

The magistrates who tried this case, Barrington and Furley, may have listened with fascinated horror at this tale of depravity in their midst. Both were members of the godly elite who later became active in the parliamentary cause, Barrington becoming a Congregationalist and Furley a Quaker. The case came before them in 1638 at a time when the Laudian ascendancy seemed unshakeable and when godly preachers at Colchester were being silenced.[6] Was this a warning of England's peril if reformed religion were not upheld?

Dramatis Personae

Lydia Downes, singlewoman, of Dedham, aged 24 in 1638, hanged
(pregnant by Tunbridge, allegedly miscarried; pregnant by Skeete, delivered in Coker's house, child killed; pregnant by Skeete, delivered in Skeete's house, child killed; pregnant by Skeete, delivered in alehouse, child killed; pregnant by Skeete or Bryant, delivered in Cranke's house, child killed)
Richard Skeete of Colchester, weaver, poisoner, aged about 50 in 1638, hanged
Goody Downes, Lydia's mother, accompanied her to Colchester
William Hardy, farrier, of Abberton, married to Lydia's sister Alice, dead by Nov. 1638
Mary Skeete, Skeete's wife, died from poison
Matthew Tunbridge of Abberton, fathered a child on Lydia Downes, 1634
Richard Bryant, feltmaker, Skeete's friend and Lydia's lover
Crankes of Abberton, harboured Lydia, hung for felony
William Coker of Colchester, provided hospitality for Lydia and her mother
Elizabeth Coker, wife of William, aged 62
Mary, Coker's maid, assisted at birth and disposal of child's body
Anne Keeler, wife of Thomas Keeler of Colchester, labourer, assisted at next birth and disposal of child's body, poisoned by Skeete
Joan Collins, wife of Edmond Collins of Colchester, 'keeper' to Anne Keeler in her last illness
John Furley, mayor of Colchester, magistrate
Henry Barrington, Justice of the Peace

ANOTHER MIDWIFE'S TALE: ALCOHOL, PATRIARCHY, AND CHILDBIRTH IN EARLY MODERN LONDON

In July 1635 the London archdeaconry court heard that Elizabeth Wyatt of Newgate, a married woman, was 'keeping company at unlawful hours and in suspicious places' with Abraham Brand, a married man, and that they often drank and took tobacco together in taverns and victualling houses until late in the night. Elizabeth Brand, Abraham's wife, became so fed up with this squandering of family resources, this diversion of her husband's affection, and her own public humiliation, that she obtained a warrant to keep the offenders apart. The charges and counter-charges in this dispute cast an extraordinary light on the world of the street and the alehouse, on matronly solidarity and female jealousy, and on gender relations and neighbourly interaction in early modern London.[1] It provides strong support for those historians who see cross-currents and contradictions in patriarchal relations, and who find women sometimes to have been each other's own worst enemies.[2] Even more remarkable, this testimony sheds fresh light on the cultural performance of childbirth and the veiled female world of the birth room, for Elizabeth Wyatt was a midwife, and part of the case turned on estimates of her skill and suitability for that task.[3]

As so often turns out with church court records, the trail of citations, charges, answers, and judgements is incomplete. Elizabeth Wyatt became subject to judicial investigation and half a dozen women gave evidence about her; but it is not immediately clear whether her social, moral, or professional shortcomings were the central subject of concern.

The midwife's principal accuser was Elizabeth Brand, aged 44, the wife of Abraham Brand of the parish of Christ Church, London. She acknowledged that Elizabeth Wyatt had 'used the office of a midwife about a year or thereabouts . . . but whether she were licensed or not she cannot say'. The purpose of this vague and dismissive testimony seems to have been to undercut the midwife's professional standing, and to prepare the ground for the following assault on her character.

Goodwife Brand told the court that Elizabeth Wyatt 'much frequenteth taverns' and that she was often 'overtaken by drink'. Furthermore, she alleged, she 'has been found and seen at unlawful hours and unfitting hours in the night in taverns and victualling houses in company of Abraham Brand', the accuser's husband. She herself had 'found them so divers times', implying that she had gone looking for them when her husband failed to come home. Elizabeth Wyatt, she charged, had 'caused her said husband to spend his estate, so as he hath been fain to leave the City and his diet and his children'. The Brand household was ruined, so it seemed, because instead of providing for his family another man's wife 'was beneficed by his diet'.

Other housewives from the Holborn area amplified these allegations. Sarah Lee, aged 35, of the parish of St Sepulchre, deposed that Elizabeth Wyatt was 'a great frequenter of taverns and alehouses' and that she had 'divers and sundry times observed [her] to be very much overcome with drink'. Specifically, she said, 'about Christmas last past, 1634, [Elizabeth Wyatt] was so far overcome with drink at the Red Cross [alehouse] in the parish of Christ Church, that she was unable to go steadfastly, but reeled and staggered up and down the streets as she went home to her own house'.

Alice Harrison, aged 34, the wife of John Harrison of St Sepulchre's, confirmed that Elizabeth Wyatt was 'a great company keeper and common frequenter of taverns and alehouses, and a great taker of tobacco. And in her drink she hath in a bravado given out and said that she had, or that she could take tobacco with a lord for a companion, and he or she that could not was a companion for a dog.' Elizabeth Selby, aged 19, the wife of a scissor-maker of Christ Church and, as it turned out, one of the midwife's clients, also reported that Elizabeth Wyatt was so drunk on occasion that 'as she hath gone along the street the market women have called out to have someone or other to hold her for fear she should fall in the street'.

Judith Simnell, aged 50, of the parish of St Giles, Cripplegate, told the court that the midwife was often overcome by drink, and that her company-keeping with Abraham Brand 'at unlawful hours' had continued over the past three years. For example, she alleged, they had been seen together 'at the Queen's Arms in Newgate market until the hours of twelve in the night or one, revelling and laughing in so much that the room wherein they did sit had been washed with wine, to the great expense of the said Abraham Brand and the undoing of his wife and children'. Furthermore, claimed Judith Simnell, 'by the instigation' of Elizabeth Wyatt, Abraham Brand 'hath demeaned himself very harshly, scurvily, abusively and inhumanly unto his wife, by kicking her, being great with child, beating of her black and blue, that she hath lain in great extremity for the space of a seven night'.

Abraham Brand, then, was a wife-beater as well as a drunkard, a philanderer who brought ruin on his family by years of carousing with Elizabeth Wyatt.

Midwife Wyatt appears no better, in this barrage of hostile testimony, and is charged with leading Abraham astray. There is no overt suggestion of sexual impropriety between them, but evidence abounded of their general unruly behaviour. As a married woman and *femme couverte*, Elizabeth Brand could do nothing in law to rein in her errant husband. If there was a shouting match between them it is lost to history, nor is any charivari known to have brought the husband to shame. The goodwife was not, however, entirely without judicial resources, and used the processes of both secular and ecclesiastical justice to bring pressure on her husband's drinking companion.

Judith Simnell recalled that Elizabeth Brand 'complained to Sir Martin Lamb, one of the Justices of Peace for the city, of the said great abuses, and hereupon a warrant was granted by the said Justice'. The warrant, however, was not against the husband, who was expected to govern and discipline his wife, but against Elizabeth Wyatt, the disturber of domestic harmony. As Elizabeth Brand recounted before the archdeacon, the midwife 'was brought by a warrant by a constable before Sir Martin Lamb, knight, one of the Aldermen of the City of London and Justice of Peace'.[4] There Sir Martin allegedly said, 'that she was fitter to be sent to Bridewell than any whore was, and had not the husband of the said Elizabeth come in and entreated for her, the said Sir Martin had sent her to Bridewell. And upon her promise and the promise of her said husband that Elizabeth Wyatt would not keep company with the said Brand any more, the said Sir Martin released her. But the next day and divers times since she hath frequented [Elizabeth Brand's] husband's company.'

The women's testimony paints Elizabeth Wyatt as a boozer and a home-wrecker who was lucky not to be imprisoned; they cast her as a woman lacking self-discipline who showed no respect for the vows of matrimony or for the majesty of the law. There was, they said, a 'common fame' in the parish of Christ Church and environs of Newgate and Holborn, that she was too often in her cups. On top of this, they also cast doubts on her probity and effectiveness as a midwife, alleging several cases of negligence and incompetence.

Several witnesses made the point that Elizabeth Wyatt was not actually a licensed midwife, but served merely as assistant or deputy to the local official midwife, Anna Brown. Sarah Lee deposed that though Elizabeth Wyatt practised midwifery 'for three years or thereabout' she was 'never sworn or lawfully authorized for the same, but only practiceth under her pretence of a deputation from one Mrs. Brown living upon Snow Hill'. Elizabeth Brand, the instigator of the case, purported not to know 'whether she were licensed or sworn', but Anna Brown herself, in a brief appearance before the court, confirmed that Elizabeth Wyatt had been her deputy for three years, and 'practiceth now for herself, she being not licensed'.[5] Furthermore, the midwife deposed, she 'never saw the said

Elizabeth Wyatt in drink'. Many women, it seems, practised midwifery to the general satisfaction of their clients, and only sought out a licence when required to do so by the Church.

As testimony to Elizabeth Wyatt's unfitness for the office of midwife, Sarah Lee gave the following report. 'That a year since or thereabout one Mrs. [*blank*] of the parish of [*blank*] being in labour sent to Mrs. Brown, midwife, to help her in her great extremity of pain and travail, and [Mrs. Brown] sent [Elizabeth Wyatt], being [herself] not well or else otherwise employed, to the said Mrs. [*blank*]. And at her coming, by reason of her weak judgement, said that [Mrs. *blank*] was not in travail, and would not stay at all but went from her and left her in great danger of her life, and then half an hour later the said Mrs. [*blank*] was delivered by another midwife, she [Sarah Lee] being at the same time present.'

This was not especially damning or compelling testimony, since the witness could remember neither the name of the mother nor the location of the parish. In any case, a misjudgement about the progress of labour was no ground for judicial action. The main burden of the story was to add further damage to Elizabeth Wyatt's reputation, and it was corroborated by Annis Cox, aged 70, a widow of the parish of St Andrew by the Wardrobe, who also served as a midwife.[6] Annis Cox told the court that she 'being sent for to one Mr. Bennett's dwelling on the back side of the shambles to deliver his daughter, being in labour, the said Elizabeth Wyatt came into the room where the said Mr. Bennett's daughter lay in labour, and there said that [she] was not in labour and that her labour would not be of three days, and presently left the room and went her way. But as soon as she was gone, or within an hour after, (Annis Cox) delivered the said Mr. Bennett's daughter of a man child.'

Mr Bennett's daughter turned out to be Elizabeth Selby, age 19, whose voice we have already heard. Her deposition before the archdeaconry court added detail to the story of Elizabeth Wyatt's incompetence, and spread further incriminating rumours about the midwife's failings.[7] 'Mrs. Wyatt came to [Elizabeth Selby's] father's house in Newgate market the night before [she] was in labour', she said, 'so drunk that she made mouths and played very unseemly tricks'. She returned the next day, apparently sober, 'and affirmed before one Mrs. Cox, a midwife that was then sent for, that [Elizabeth Selby] was not in labour, and that she would not be brought to bed not this night nor the next night nor the next night after that, and so went away leaving [Elizabeth Selby] in peril of her life, had not other women been present.'

Elizabeth Selby was naturally prejudiced against a midwife who had served her so ill. She was not content, however, to speak only from her own experience, but related other matters of which 'there hath been a common voice and fame'.

Dredging up every charge that would cast ill light on the midwife, Elizabeth Selby told the court that she 'hath heard that the said Elizabeth Wyatt did bring a woman to bed privately in her house without any company, the which child was never baptized so far as [she] believeth, but was privately conveyed away out of the parish, for which she was questioned at the sessions'. Unwitnessed childbirth, the possible harbouring of an unmarried mother, and avoidance of the sacrament of baptism, were serious violations of law and custom. Here, at last, was something with which the archdeaconry court might be legally concerned. Midwives were subject to ecclesiastical jurisdiction, and it was an offence for them, or any one else, to assist in the concealment of a birth or the avoidance of baptism.[8]

Given the chance to answer these charges, Elizabeth Wyatt testified, 'that she hath practiced as a midwife for the space of these five years and that she is not yet licensed, for she is but a deputy to one Mrs. Brown with whom she conditioned to serve seven years, and at the expiration of the said years she intendeth to obtain licence'. There must have been dozens of such women in early modern London, midwives in training who developed private practices of their own. The seven-year term bespeaks a kind of apprenticeship, appropriate for a skilled and reputable profession but unregulated by any guild or sorority.

Far from having anything to be ashamed of, Elizabeth Wyatt related with pride the story of her role in the mysterious childbirth to which Elizabeth Selby alluded. The story, in her telling, points to her skill and resourcefulness in fulfilment of her duty, rather than transgressive behaviour that required examination. It happened, she said, that

she delivered one Christian Hoare, widow (living in Purpoole Lane at the sign of the Harrow), suddenly taken in the street with the pangs of childbirth; and being against this widow's door [she] received the said Christian Hoare into her shop, where she delivered her of a man child. And at the doing of the premises there was present Catherine Wyatt [her] daughter and Catherine Morris [her] maid. Other women also were called, but she was so speedily delivered that all the business was dispatched before they came, for [it] was done in less than a quarter of an hour. Also she saith that the said Christian Hoare was delivered at the least eight weeks before her time, and that the child was so weak it was not like to live an hour; whereupon she sent her maid to get a minister to christen it, who meeting in Newgate market with Mr. Barnes, an ancient minister who she believeth is curate of St Giles in the Fields, brought him . . . to [Elizabeth Wyatt's] house, and then (she) desired the said Mr. Barnes to christen the said child, which he did, and the child was named Edward.

It was especially important, in this testimony before the archdeacon's court, for the midwife to point out her orthodoxy and diligence in attending to the spiritual needs of the child. She did not neglect its baptism, nor did she attempt to perform the ritual herself, but secured a minister of the church. These were sensitive matters in the religious politics of the 1630s, when senior churchmen insisted on the sacramental importance of baptism, and insisted too that it could no longer be performed by women.[9]

Continuing her account, Elizabeth Wyatt explained what happened to baby Edward. 'Which child the said Christian Hoare delivered to Katherine Cole-bank, the wife of John Colebank, bricklayer, living in Purpoole Lane in Hol-borne, and desired the said Katherine Colebank to nurse the said child, which [she] did undertake, and carried it away with her to her house . . . where the said child died the next morning, and was buried in the parish church of St. Andrew in Holborn.'[10] All above board, the child was delivered to a wet-nurse, and joined those tens of thousands who succumbed to London's high infant mortality.

Somewhat later, the midwife continued, 'there was a fame raised by the churchwardens about this business, within this fortnight, who questioned [her] at the sessions to know what became of the said child, and before that time she answereth and believeth there was no fame concerning this business'. By her own account she was diligent and competent, and had behaved accord-ing to the rules of her culture, her religion, her gender, and her profession. Indeed, she recalled, 'when the Lord Mayor and Mr. Recorder of this City had well examined the business they commended [her] for harbouring the said Christian Hoare in her great extremity'.

Finally, to the charge of her philandering and carousing with Abraham Brand, she retorted 'that she never kept [him] company at unlawful hours nor in suspicious places, but confesseth that about three years since she used to go to his house to visit his wife, who was then distracted, and then with other neighbours she did keep [Abraham Brand] company.' This seems to have been disingenuous, in light of abundant testimony about her drinking habits. Her tippling, however, was no concern of the court, provided it did not take place in time of divine service, and did not disgrace her calling.

The depositions take us some small way into the veiled world of childbirth in early modern England. They reveal both community and competition among urban midwives, and the previously unknown practice of midwife training. They point to the guesswork and skill midwives used in the management of pregnancy and labour, and the problems and customs of attendance, witness-ing, and fulfilment of legal and religious obligations. Far removed from the clinical advice of contemporary childbirth manuals, testimonies like these bring us closer to the social and cultural practices of early modern England. In this case they illustrate, with remarkable specificity, how women in travail could find succour, how other women would gather for a birth, and how the midwife (at least by her own telling) was scrupulous in securing a minister to baptize a failing child. Elizabeth Wyatt was dogged by rumours about her professional incompetence, and about her possible collusion in covering the birth of a suspected bastard child, but it seems that the gossip had more to do with her carousing with Abraham Brand than her ministration in various London birth rooms.

There is strong evidence here of the independent social life of metropolitan women. City comedies and misogynist tracts often point to the unruly behaviour of citizens' wives and their gossips, and some claim that they were notorious for their unbridled licence and lust.[11] The church court records help put these more sensationalist allegations in context by showing us women and men in all manner of situations, at work, at worship, and at leisure. Laura Gowing has made brilliant use of defamation depositions to reconstruct the sexually charged language of insult, and the same records can be used to show the social settings and mix of company where offensive words were uttered.[12] They take us into such social spaces of early Stuart London as the Red Cross and Queen's Arms alehouses, Newgate market, and the shambles in the parish of St Andrew by the Wardrobe.

The allegations and answers in these cases also remind us of the importance of reading around and across the record. We may gain knowledge from this episode even if, like the civil magistrates and church court judges, we are not quite sure whose testimony to believe. Elizabeth Wyatt described herself as upright and efficient; but her enemies, in this tangle of jealousy and neighbourly intrigue, depicted her as feckless and incompetent. The competing stories, at one level, are about female honour, displayed not through women's sexuality but through their status, activities, abilities, and callings. They reinforce Garthine Walker's expansion of the boundaries of female honour in early modern England,[13] for Elizabeth Wyatt defended her honour as a midwife while Elizabeth Brand sought restitution of her honour as a wife.

The case also reveals some of the weaknesses and pitfalls of patriarchy. Elizabeth Wyatt was a married woman (not a widow) but her husband is so entirely effaced that we do not know his name. Despite his nominal domestic superiority, he was unable to prevent his wife from spending evenings with Abraham Brand, and he only intervened when the magistrate threatened to send his wife to Bridewell. He seems to have played the role of cuckold, with an accommodating set of horns. The carousing and philandering took place in public, over several years, to the shame and dishonour of all concerned. Elizabeth Brand was humiliated and abused, and at least once physically attacked, but she did not remain silent and obedient. The records show vividly how an aggrieved and angry woman could employ the resources of the state to help to recoup her respect. Elizabeth Brand was not entirely powerless in the face of her husband's ill-mannered behaviour, and she engaged the magistrates, the archdeaconry authorities, and the testimony of female neighbours to air her complaints and to secure some redress. The City magistrate, Sir Martin Lamb [or Lumley], was willing to intervene on behalf of good neighbourly and domestic relations, but he directed his injunction not against the errant husband but against the formidable Elizabeth Wyatt, whom he seemed to think the stronger vessel.

Dramatis Personae

Elizabeth Wyatt of Newgate, unlicensed midwife (a married woman)

Abraham Brand of the parish of Christ Church (Elizabeth Wyatt's drinking companion)

Elizabeth Brand, 44, wife of Abraham Brand (Elizabeth Wyatt says she had been 'distracted')

Sarah Lee, 25, of St Sepulchre's

Alice Harrison, 34, wife of John Harrison of St Sepulchre's

Judith Simnell, 50, of St Giles, Cripplegate

Elizabeth Selby, 19, wife of a scissor-maker of Christ Church, daughter of Mr Bennett of Newgate

Anna Brown, 58, of Snow Hill, licensed midwife, wife of William Brown

Annis Cox, 70, of St Andrew by the Wardrobe, midwife, widow

Christian Hoare, widow, mother of Edward Hoare

Catherine Wyatt, daughter of Elizabeth Wyatt

Catherine Morris, maid to Elizabeth Wyatt

Mr Barnes, minister of St Giles in the Fields

Katherine Colebank, wife of John Colebank of Holborn, nurse

Sir Martin Lamb [or Lumley], Justice of the Peace and Alderman

The Lord Mayor and Recorder of London

The Archdeacon of London

CROSS-DRESSING IN THE BIRTH ROOM: GENDER TROUBLE AND CULTURAL BOUNDARIES

The story that opens this chapter involves gender and generational relations, limits and breaches of customary activity, normal and abnormal ceremonies of childbirth, and one of the most extraordinary cases of male to female cross-dressing recorded in early modern England. It illuminates social and legal responses to deviant behaviour and, if pushed hard enough, may be made to expose cultural tensions and social accommodations in the reign of Charles I. To understand it we need to consider the customs and culture of childbirth, puritan polemic about transvestism, comedy on the early Stuart stage, and the practice of the ecclesiastical courts. Following the threads of this story—unravelling the tangle of transgressions—involves confrontation with a variety of problems and engagement with the interests of several academic disciplines.

Pursuit of these issues entails further exploration of the archives, an historical excursus into drama, and sharp disagreement with the findings of some literary cultural historians. It introduces that rarest of rare birds, an actual (or non-fictional) cross-dresser, caught in the act, in early Stuart England. Since it comes from the archives it belongs to a genre traditionally labelled as 'evidence', but given our awareness of the fictionality of court reporting, it may be better to call it a 'story'. Like many such stories, it serves for more than entertainment or delight, since it opens a window on complex cultures of the past. What makes a story significant, rather than merely interesting, is the landscape it illuminates, the contours it reveals, and the opportunity it presents to examine opaque attitudes, conduct, and speech.

Our window opens at Tew Magna, Oxfordshire, on 7 December 1633 where Francis Fletcher, midwife, the wife of Edward Fletcher of Tew, appeared before the archdeacon's court to answer some serious charges. As a midwife her behaviour fell within ecclesiastical cognizance, and she may have had a licence awarded by the Church. Francis Fletcher admitted that

she doth practice midwifery . . . at such times as her neighbours do require. Being further demanded whether she did help Hugh Rymel's wife of Tew to be delivered, she sayeth she did; and being further interrogated whether Thomas Salmon her servant did come to the labour of the said Rymel's wife, or presently after she the said Rymel's wife was delivered, disguised in woman's apparel, she confesseth he did come into her chamber some six hours after she had been delivered so disguised, but by virtue of her oath she sayeth at his first coming she knew him not, but afterwards, she discovering by her daughter-in-law her clothes which the said Thomas Salmon had on, she made him to depart the room, and was no way privy to his coming or to his disguise.[1]

The incident was outrageous on several counts. It was inherently disorderly, even if it did not lead to a ruckus. It was an affront to the traditions of child-birth, discourtesy to the mother and her friends, demeaning to her husband and family, and discredit to the profession of midwifery. Whether it was also a threat to the stability and sanctity of gender identity, an abomination unto the Lord, and a symptom of sexual disorder, will be among the concerns of this discussion.

The village of Tew Magna—Great Tew—is best known in the reign of Charles I as the literary retreat of Lucius Cary, Lord Falkland, who was lord of the manor in the 1630s. In an important essay on this community Hugh Trevor-Roper (Lord Dacre) remarks that 'we have all heard of the Great Tew Circle', an observation that sadly now has diminishing force. Falkland's 'Great Tew Circle', which included philosophers, churchmen, and poets, was renowned for its high-minded reflection and learned conversation, '*convivium philosophicum*, or *convivium theologicum*'.[2] Humbler inhabitants of Great Tew make no appearance in Lord Dacre's version of cultural history; so it is both startling and rewarding to encounter Great Tew villagers in a tale of transgression which cuts to the heart of gendered identity and social practice in early modern England.

Recent work on the cultural history of midwifery and gynaecology has emphasized the degree to which childbirth was a gender-segregated event. Women normally gave birth in the company of other women and celebrated their safe delivery in a conclave of sisterly visiting. The childbed room was a place of 'mysteries', a privileged female domain from which even the father of the child was excluded. Men had no place there, and remained ignorant of how women conducted themselves behind the veil. The birth room belonged entirely to women, except in dire medical necessity. Any male presence was transgression.[3]

How could midwife Fletcher have allowed Thomas Salmon's unprecedented invasion? To what degree was she responsible for this rupture of the traditional ceremony of childbirth? As keeper of the ceremonies, was she answerable for losing control of the customary process? Was she in any way liable at law? Had she failed to uphold the standards of her profession and the provisions of the midwife's oath which, among other provisions, required her to 'be secret, and not open any matter appertaining to your office in the presence of any man, unless necessity or great urgent cause do constrain you'?[4] Worse, was she complicit in this compound violation of gendered costume and female space, in which her own servant and daughter-in-law were principals? By permitting her cross-dressed manservant to sit with the newly delivered mother and her gossips midwife Fletcher was accessory to grave misbehaviour, for Thomas Salmon's offence lay in his presence as well as his gender-bending disguise.

With understandable delicacy, the court sought to resolve several problems. How did a man come to intrude into the female domain of the birth room, and what was the meaning or significance of his cross-dressing? How did the intruder conduct himself, and why was he not immediately recognized? Why did his face, voice, or manner not discover him, and his subterfuge only collapse when his mistress belatedly attributed ownership to his clothing? What were his feelings and intentions, who were his accomplices, and what did it all betoken? What can such an unusual incident tell us about the culture of the 1630s?

The next witness before the court was Elizabeth Fletcher, the wife of John Fletcher of Tew Magna and daughter-in-law to the midwife. In the course of describing the conventional social courtesy whereby neighbouring women crowded the chamber of a newly delivered mother—in itself rare documentation of a delicate and opaque topic—she explained how that practice was violated. Being asked,

whether she did help Thomas Salmon, her father-in-law's servant, to put on woman's apparel and go to goodwife Rymel's house, she being then in labour or newly delivered, she sayeth that she herself being at her labour about two of the clock in the afternoon, seeing her well laid in her bed, came home to her own house and stayed there till nine of the clock the same night, and at nine of the clock she this examinate saying that she must go to Rymel's house to be merry with the other women there, Thomas Salmon her father's servant then replied that there would be good cheer, desired that he* might go along with her.

(*At this point the court scribe, anticipating the climax of the story, and evidently confused by shifting gender, wrote 'she' instead of 'he' and then crossed out the letter 's'.)

Elizabeth's testimony continued: 'and afterward, at the request of the said Thomas, she helped to dress him in woman's apparel and consented to let him go to the said Rymel's house, intending only merriment thereby'. Whether she meant merriment for herself, or amusement for Thomas Salmon, or laughs all round, is not immediately clear. But it is evident that Elizabeth Fletcher was of a younger generation, perhaps no older than the servant. She had scant respect for her mother-in-law's position or the dignity of midwifery, and she certainly did not behave with the gravity expected of a respectable married woman. At best, by her own account, the younger woman helped to perpetrate an outrageous practical joke; at worst, by the standards of contemporary reformers, she had colluded in a most sinful abomination unto the Lord. The Bible warned that cross-dressing of any sort was abominable, and contemporaries who were familiar with the text of Deuteronomy might have thought to apply that chastisement to the case at hand.[5]

The final statement came from Thomas Salmon himself. The court described him as '*nuper de* Tew, *nunc de* South Newton', so apparently he moved to another village after the scandal (or perhaps after his servant's contract expired; we have the date of the court hearing, but not the date of the birth room incident. Nor, unfortunately, do we know his age, which may be a critical factor in the story.). When asked, 'who was privy to the dressing of him in woman's apparel', he answered, 'that at the said time he hearing that there would be good cheer at the house of Eleanor Rymel who was then lately brought a-bed, wished that he might be there; whereupon his dame Elizabeth Fletcher said he should, and then fetched her apparel, and he put off his doublet and he came to the said house where the women met, and bid them say that he was Mrs Garrett's maid, and that his mistress sent him to see how she did, which he did; and he stayed there in the room but a little, but he continued in that apparel about two hours.'

If Thomas Salmon can be believed, no offence was intended. But people under investigation by the ecclesiastical courts commonly sought to minimize the gravity of their offence and to mitigate its circumstances. (For example, people presented for refusing to kneel at the altar sometimes claimed arthritis, and those presented for keeping their hats on in church said they had cold heads.) Salmon admitted that he had insinuated himself into the most private and secret of female gatherings, but claimed innocence of evil or deviant intentions. No man had been present at the vital moment of parturition, or had sight of the mother's privities, so the gynaecological mysteries of the birth room were preserved. The young servant understood that there would be good cheer at the post-delivery lying-in, and that, as usual, the drinking, eating, and gossiping would be enjoyed exclusively by women. He simply wanted some of that good cheer. His cross-dressing, from this perspective, was a response to scarcity, a means to temporary betterment, comparable to that of certain disadvantaged women from time to time who are known to have passed themselves as men.[6]

Egged on by Elizabeth Fletcher, Thomas Salmon impersonated a neighbouring maidservant, and was permitted by the assembled women to take his seat among the gossips. His ruse was helped by the customarily low light level in the dimly lit birth room, after nine o'clock at night. If the gossips had been drinking, as by custom they would, the intruder's disguise might be still more secure, especially if Elizabeth Fletcher was prepared to support his pretence. Only the midwife's recognition of her daughter-in-law's clothes on a visitor purporting to be someone else's maidservant aroused suspicion, and led to the intruder's dismissal. This may sound disingenuous (both his account and mine), but there is not enough evidence to judge whether Salmon was devious or deviant, a simple-minded innocent or a pervert seething with complex desires.

Having heard from the midwife, the court let her go without punishment. She, as much as the other women of Tew, was a victim in this affair. Her daughter-in-law, Elizabeth Fletcher, was ordered 'to make acknowledgement of this her fault in such manner as shall be delivered her'. And the court accepted Thomas Salmon's confession and assigned him a formal penance. The incident was closed with punishments that were remarkably mild. The court had done its duty in disciplining youthful folly, but found nothing gravely amiss by the laws of Church or State.

Is this a case, like the Sherlock Holmes mystery, of a dog that did not bark? Should we expect to find a greater sense of outrage in the ecclesiastical records? Why was the gravity of the offence downplayed? Should we assume, following recent critical suggestions, that Thomas Salmon was effeminized by his wearing of women's clothing, that his male identity was compromised and an alternative self revealed? Should we be sensitized to the unleashing of erotic energies, attuned to the notion of pollution, and alert to cries for retribution in the outraged community of Great Tew? Was Salmon himself, or anyone else, sexually aroused by this activity? What did the other Great Tew circles think— the women, the men, the clergy, the gentry—when Thomas Salmon's transvestite behaviour was exposed? Even if we cannot find the answer it is well worth asking how the young man felt while his mistress's daughter-in-law dressed him in women's clothes? And why did he continue to wear the borrowed garments for two hours after his sex had been discovered? Did he delight in his unaccustomed costume, was he parading or carousing at the alehouse, or was he simply unable to undo the points without assistance and so could not get the borrowed clothing off? There is nothing in the record that explicitly relates Thomas Salmon's offence to the virulent prohibition on apparel-switching set forth in Deuteronomy, and nothing that makes overt connection to the complaints about cross-dressing that had reverberated for more than fifty years. Yet, if recent literary scholarship is to be believed, cross-dressing was high on the cultural agenda of early modern England, gender identity was subject to intense and troubled scrutiny, and Reformers were quick to denounce violations of gendered apparel. The case of the Great Tew cross-dresser provides a point of leverage for examining several of these suggestions.

Thomas Salmon's violation of clothing conventions and customary behaviour—his transgression of gendered dress, gendered space, and gendered social activity—followed a period that some scholars have labelled 'the transvestite controversy'.[7] From the 1570s to the 1620s, during the reigns of a manly queen and a queenish king, England is said to have been challenged by disorderly people presenting themselves in public in a gender-confusing manner. Late Elizabethan and Jacobean England emerges, especially in some gay and feminist literary history, as a golden age of cross-dressing. Whether the available evidence bears some of the interpretations that have been strung on it remains a matter for critical discussion. A review of recent critical assessments may expose the social and sexual confusions of transvestism, throwing fresh light on the cultural contests of early modern England and perhaps on those of our own day too.

A celebrated article in *Shakespeare Quarterly* opens with the question, 'How many people crossdressed in Renaissance England?' Jean Howard, who posed this intriguing question, suggests that disruption of the semiotics of dress, gender, and identity during the late Elizabethan and Jacobean periods points to 'a sex-gender system under pressure' and a patriarchal culture disturbed by profound anxieties and contradictions. Even if the answer to her question turns out to be 'very few', the discourse surrounding the practice reveals an area of critical and problematic unease. Female transvestism on the streets of London, male transvestism on the stage, and vituperative attacks on cross-dressing by Protestant reformers, are among the symptoms that indicate that 'the subversive or transgressive potential of this practice could be and was recuperated in a number of ways'. Dressing boy actors for female roles, for example, was not simply 'an unremarkable convention within Renaissance dramatic practice', as some scholars have suggested, but rather a scandalous 'source of homoerotic attraction' arousing 'deep-seated fears' of an 'unstable and monstrous' and feminized self.[8] Whether in real life or in literature, by this account, cross-dressing involved struggle, resistance, and subversion, as well as modification, recuperation, and containment of the system of gendered patriarchal domination. Renaissance cross-dressing involved ideological work of a complex kind which ultimately, in Howard's materialist feminist analysis, 'participated in the historical process eventuating in the English Revolution'.[9] This is a claim that may make English historians gasp, but it is one that they cannot ignore.

Literary Renaissance scholars are fascinated by cross-dressing, by men wearing women's costumes or women dressed like men. Whether they focus on boy actors taking female roles, female characters donning male attire, male characters wearing drag, or London prostitutes sporting mannish attire, literary scholars often argue that cross-gender clothing signalled subversion, resistance, and transgression, and that the sex-gender system of early modern England was in a state of flux. Cross-dressing, we are told, upset patriarchal values, assaulted cultural boundaries, and unravelled the sexual separators of ambivalence, androgyny, and eroticism. Historians, by contrast, have shown little interest in these matters.[10]

Two types of cross-dressing have recently caught the attention of literary scholars. First, the women of Renaissance England who 'began adopting masculine attire'; and second, the boys and young men who took female parts, and dressed in female costume, in the course of dramatic performances on stage. The first is represented as a challenge to patriarchal values, a bold assault on oppressive cultural boundaries; the second as marking the sexual ambivalence, androgyny, and muted eroticism linking actors, dramatists, and playgoers in a sexually charged subculture of transgression. Both phenomena were disturbing to moralists and Reformers, and both offer interpretative opportunities to modern cultural critics. Not surprisingly, they open avenues to politicized discourse about sexuality, self-representation, and gender which have become increasingly fashionable in our own contested culture within the last dozen years.[11]

Linda Woodbridge has identified not simply isolated and ambiguous cases of women 'masking in men's weeds' but a full-blown 'female transvestite movement' in early modern England. Its indications were everywhere, she finds, not just in literary polemic and satire but in 'real life' too, becoming 'a fairly permanent feature of the Jacobean landscape'.[12] Women dressed as men, Woodbridge suggests, for a variety of admirable reasons: to plead at law, regain a fortune, or practise a profession barred to women; to advance a stratagem, win back lovers, or fight a duel; to travel alone, avoid rape or molestation, and to have adventures. The cross-dressed women, in this rendition, were bold and ingenious, their actions commendably shrewd. The evidence that supports this depiction comes mainly from literary sources, especially plays like *The Roaring Girl* by Dekker and Middleton, read against anti-theatrical misogynist writings like Stubbes's *Anatomie of Abuses*. The degree to which this creative or polemical literature was grounded in social practice is never convincingly shown, although it is somehow held to reflect 'real-life fashion' and 'contemporary reality too'.[13]

Several related studies of Elizabethan and Jacobean literature suggest that early modern England was preoccupied with problems of gender and costume,

The Roaring Girle.

OR
Moll Cut-Purse.

As it hath lately beene Acted on the Fortune-stage by
the Prince his Players.

Written by *T. Middleton* and *T. Dekkar.*

My cafe is alter'd, I muft worke for my liuing.

Printed at *London* for *Thomas Archer*, and are to be fold at his
fhop in Popes head-pallace, neere the Royall
Exchange. 1611.

4. Mary Frith, the original roaring girl, in masculine attire, 1611

and that the theatre provided special sites for the exploration of sexual problems. Shakespeare, one scholar tells us, invited his audience 'to view themselves as gendered subjects acting out a drama of sexual difference'. Shakespeare's world, another tells us, was tormented by 'the problematics of the flesh'. The theatre, says a third, was 'a medium for the release of transgressive erotic impulses'.[14] The cross-dressed male was a familiar figure in literature, and was used, so it has been suggested, to explore themes of 'erotic androgyny' and homosexuality that could not be treated more directly. Early modern culture appears to have been obsessed with 'images of androgynous breakdown' in which 'the hermaphroditic actor becomes the embodiment of all that is frightening about the self'. 'Cross-dressing', Jonathan Dollimore suggests, 'epitomizes the strategy of transgressive reinscription' addressing 'intense anxieties' about the 'unsettling of gender and class hierarchies'. 'Cross-dressing', Susan Zimmerman adds, 'had a disturbing, anarchic potential'.[15]

Many of these threads come together in a recent study by Laura Levine, *Men in Women's Clothing*, which endorses the claim that the theatre dissolved and effeminized masculinity through changes of dress. Male characters who went as woman became reduced, powerless, or degenerate because their masculine identity itself was fluid, pliable, and unstable. 'It is as if femaleness were the default position,' Levine suggests, 'the thing one were always in danger of slipping into.' Puritan polemicists, she argues, betrayed their fear that clothing could actually alter gender, since cross-dressing supposedly had the 'power to alter and unman the male body itself'. Early modern culture, including the drama, was animated by anxiety about 'castration, porousness, effeminization, otherness', and above all by 'the terror that there is no masculine self'.[16]

Observations of this sort abound in Renaissance literary studies but are rarely made by historians. Partly, I suspect, this has to do with disciplinary rhetorical conventions. But it also reflects different ways of reading texts, different ways of discussing evidence, and different ways of thinking about gender.

Contemporary moralists knew exactly what was wrong, and fumed at unnatural and outlandish violations of costume. If it was unsettling, in an age of ambitious self-fashioning, that people used clothing to misrepresent their social status,[17] it was downright disturbing if they misrepresented their gender by dress. It was unconscionable that the sign should mis-signify, the costume deceive. Worst of all was the unnatural impiety involved, in violation of the law of God, since outward apparel intimated inward characteristics and the wearer of cross-sexed clothing trod the slope to monstrous degeneration. Was it not written in Deuteronomy that transvestism was an abomination unto the Lord? Most of this diatribe was directed against representation and misrepresentation in the theatre, but it was generalized in polemical discourse to indict all disorderly costuming, off-stage as well as on. One did not have to be a puritan to ask, with George Gascoigne in 1576, 'What be they? Women? masking in men's weeds? . . . They be sure even *Wo* to *Men* indeed.'[18]

Writing in the middle of the Elizabethan era, Stephen Gosson argued that it was an 'abomination unto the lord' to counterfeit the opposite sex. 'The law of God', he protested, 'very straightly forbids men to put on women's garments.' Garments, Gosson explained, 'are set down for signs distinctive between sex and sex; to take unto us those garments that are a manifest sign of another sex is to falsify, forge and adulterate, contrary to the express rule of the word of God.'[19] William Harrison reported meeting 'some of these trulls in London so disguised that it hath passed my skill to discern whether they were men or women. Thus it is now come to pass that women are become men and men transformed into monsters.'[20]

Men who attired themselves in 'the habits and ornaments of women', wrote Thomas Beard in his thrice-printed *Theatre of God's Judgements*, became 'lascivious and effeminate . . . monstrous . . . dishonest and ignominious'.[21] Continuing the attack at the end of Elizabeth's reign, John Rainolds found women's clothing 'a great provocation' to wantonness and lust. 'A woman's garment being put on a man doth vehemently touch and move him with the remembrance and imagination of a woman', stirring up uncontrollable feelings of lechery, a sensation Rainolds may have recalled from acting in woman's clothes as a youth.[22] 'What do they teach or stir up in us but lusts,' asked the preacher Adam Hill of stage players, 'whose bodies being made weak and wanton in imitating the going and apparel of women, do counterfeit unchaste women with unhonest gestures?'[23] Cross-dressing clearly touched a raw nerve, and produced, in these Reformers, a recirculating rhetoric of anxiety and fear.

Philip Stubbes, furious at multiple abuses, likewise fulminated against women who dressed like men and men who dressed like women. Transvestism, Stubbes reiterated, was offensive to God. 'It is written in the 22nd. of Deuteronomy,' he reminded his readers, 'that what man soever weareth woman's apparel is accursed, and what woman weareth man's apparel is accursed also.' Male and female costumes were divinely ordained as God-given markers, so their misapplication subverted the fundamental structure of God's universal plan. For a man to wear effeminate costume made him 'weak, tender and infirm', indeed, womanish. For a woman to dress like a man undercut the established order. 'Though this be a kind of attire appropriate only to man, yet they blush not to wear it, and if they could as well change their sex and put on the kind of man, as they can wear apparel assigned only to man, I think they would as verily become men indeed, as now they degenerate from godly sober woman, in wearing this wanton, lewd kind of attire, proper only to men.'[24] Female apparel-switching, in Stubbes's view, violated fundamental boundaries and distinctions; male transvestism diminished masculine character and imprinted inferior values; and both brought down clouds of divine retribution.

Stubbes, of course, overreacted, and it is easy to follow his lead. But a generation later it appeared that certain types of cross-dressing had got out of control. King James himself was so disturbed by female accessorizing with masculine attire that in 1620 he ordered the clergy 'to inveigh vehemently and bitterly in their sermons against the insolency of our women, and their wearing of broad-brimmed hats, pointed doublets, their hair cut short or shorn, and some of them stilettos or poniards, and such other trinkets of like moment'. And shortly after, John Chamberlain reported from London, 'our pulpits ring continually of the insolency and impudence of women . . . the king threatens to fall upon their husbands, parents or friends that have or should have power over them, and make them pay for it'.[25] Whether this was in response to a resurgent female transvestite movement or a short-lived fashion craze inspired by revivals of *The Roaring Girl* is not yet clear; but whatever its origins, the kingly intervention precipitated a flurry of misogynist pamphlets, *Hic Mulier*, *Haec Vir*, and *Muld Sacke*.[26]

The author of *Hic Mulier* suggested that female transvestism was rampant, 'for since the days of Adam women were never so masculine'. Vain and foolish women, the author charged, 'have cast off the ornaments of your sexes, to put on the garments of shame'. They cropped their hair, sported broad-brimmed hats, donned doublets, pulled on boots, and equipped themselves with swords. Habitués of theatres and brothels were particularly guilty of this mannish self-fashioning but, *Hic Mulier* alleged, 'It is an infection that emulates the plague, and throws itself amongst women of all degrees, all deserts, and all ages, from the Capitol to the cottage.' Like Stubbes's *Anatomie of Abuses*, *Hic Mulier* saw experimental fashion as a violation of divine as well as social order. Gender-specific costume—'a coat for the man and a coat for the woman'—was mod-elled by the 'great work-master of heaven'. Dressing in the wrong coat called in question the entire design of the cosmos.[27]

By the time of Charles I the transvestite controversy appears to have died down, but it was revived in 1633 by a new spate of puritan attacks on the stage. William Prynne's contentious *Histrio-Mastix*, published in the same year as Thomas Salmon's invasion of the birth room, refocused attention on costume and gender, authenticity and representation, and sinfulness and deceit. Prynne poured scorn on men who would 'adulterate, emasculate, metamorphose, and debase their noble sex' by acting womanish parts or putting on female costume. Like Gosson and Stubbes before him, Prynne cited Deuteronomy 22: 5 to prove that 'God himself doth expressly inhibit men to put on woman's apparel, because it is an abomination to him.' Even someone 'who puts on a woman's raiment but to act a part, though it be but once, is doubtless a putter on of woman's apparel . . . and so a grand delinquent against God.' The effect of such abominable behaviour—inevitably in Prynne's view—was to shame nature by making men monstrous and effeminate, and to unleash the sins of lustfulness, sodomy, and self-pollution. He would rather die, said Prynne at his trial, than put on woman's costume.[28]

This fundamentalist critique, which forms a buttress of the literary scholarship on transvestism, would appear to cement the case that cross-dressing was a sign of moral and cultural distress. The Caroline preacher Daniel Rogers concurred that 'effeminate disguisings and arrayings of one sex in the other's attire' were among the 'extravagances of senses and sensuality' to be abhorred at all times.[29] Fastidious godly students like Samuel Fairclough in James I's reign and Simonds D'Ewes under Charles I 'purposely avoided' dramatic performances at Cambridge that required actors to be clothed as women lest they 'hazard the loss of the light of God's countenance'.[30] But the Jeremiad is not necessarily the most accurate reflection of social reality. In order to contest this case I would like to introduce my own reading of some early modern plays and some more examples of transvestite behaviour from the archives.

In reconsidering this topic we need to differentiate kinds of behaviour that the moralists deliberately blurred. We need to distinguish occasional deployment of items of cross-gender costume from full gender-bending transvestism, while recognizing, with the moralists, that divine wrath knew no such discrimination. We need to understand when apparel was designed, like a provocative accessory, to heighten the wearer's sexual identity (as with *The Roaring Girl*) and when, by way of disguise, to hide it (like Thomas Salmon). We need to know what messages were sent by dress, what signals received, and how costume could be used to entice, to shock, to entertain, to convince, or to confuse. What, for example, was the cultural charge of a codpiece or doublet, a petticoat or bodice, points and ruffs, and how did their resonance change when items were appropriated by the opposite sex? Robert Herrick, Prynne's contemporary (and Thomas Salmon's), wrote that 'a sweet disorder in the dress kindles in clothes a wantonness', and went on to fetishize his lady's petticoat, stomacher, and shoe strings. In another poem Herrick is almost overcome by the 'liquefaction' and 'brave vibration' of 'Julia's clothes', as if the texture and swish of the garments was directly erotic, not just because Julia was wearing them.[31]

It is still something of a novelty for social historians to engage with creative literature, particularly in light of Peter Laslett's strictures on looking 'the wrong way through the telescope'.[32] Many of us have been warned away by our own disciplinary training, by our hesitation in the face of fiction, and by our sense that colleagues elsewhere in the academy have signed it 'off limits'. But the printed output of English Renaissance drama provides a huge trove of text, almost entirely neglected by historians, that calls for cautious investigation. Representations of male cross-dressing on the early Stuart stage may supply a distant analogue for Thomas Salmon's behaviour at Great Tew, as well as a model for responses to his offence.

Whereas female dramatic characters who dress as men are usually presented as admirable, resourceful, and effective—one thinks of Shakespeare's Rosalind or Viola—it is commonly argued that men who dress as women are more often rendered as comic or ridiculous, their circumstances degraded and their manhood diminished by a feminizing costume.[33] Similarly in Renaissance romance, it is suggested, cross-dressed heroes fall victim to ridicule and degradation. Rosicleer in *The Mirrour of Knighthood* (1580) dresses as a noble wife in order to deceive a tyrant. Don Belianis in *The Honour of Chivalrie* (1598) disguises himself as a woman in order to effect his escape. Sir Arlanges and Prince Agesilan in *Amadis de Gaule* (1577) impersonate young ladies in order to pursue a loved one at court. Pyrocles in Sidney's *Arcadia* disguises himself as an Amazon for similar reasons. But their female costume unmans them, and in their cross-dressed state they begin to adopt womanish traits and both men and women fall in love with them.[34] On stage too, the temporary transvestism marks humiliation, as in the case of Falstaff, who is dressed as the old woman of Brentford in *The Merry Wives of Windsor*.

But this is not always the case. Rather than being effeminized, the cross-dressed man is more often rendered as proactive, virile, and effective. His dissimulation is a means to advancement, not downfall. In Jacobean comedy (though not in dramatic criticism) the transvestite male appears more energized than emasculated by his temporary change of clothes. (So, *mutatis mutandi*, is Mary Frith's remarkable womanhood both problematized and intensified by her cross-dressing as *The Roaring Girl*.) More than two dozen plays from the Elizabethan and Jacobean stage feature a man disguised as a woman who becomes the perpetrator rather than victim of practical jokes, outwits an opponent through ludicrous mistaken wooing, or achieves sexual success through the comic infiltration of female society. Most commonly the cross-dressing is played for laughs, without suggestion of a gender system in trouble.

Thomas in Fletcher's *Monsieur Thomas* impersonates his sister. Welford in Beaumont and Fletcher's *Scornful Lady* impersonates his friend's fiancée. Iustiniano in Dekker and Webster's *Westward Hoe* adopts his wife's attire. Wily dresses as a seamstress's maid in *The Comedy of George a Green*. Walgrave becomes Susan in Haughton's *Englishmen for My Money*. Bold is disguised as a waiting woman in Nathan Field's *Amends for Ladies*. Follywit takes the guise of a courtesan in Middleton's *A Mad World, My Masters*. And in Ben Jonson's *Epicoene, or the Silent Woman*, the subject of considerable recent attention, the central character is a male disguised as a woman who mingles freely with the ladies.[35] Even if male to female cross-dressing was rare in the streets and villages, it was a common device on the London stage.

In one of the earliest plays, *George a Green*, also known as *The Pinner of Wakefield*, George's servant Wily enters Grime's house 'disguised like a woman', a seamstress's maid, to help Grime's daughter Bettris run away to her lover. The ruse works so well (despite Wily's face being covered as if 'troubled with the tooth-ache sore') that Grime calls him/her 'a pretty wench of smiling counte-nance', and works up a proposal of marriage. The cross-dressing achieves its comic end, deceiving Bettris's father, and is approvingly described as 'this subtle shift' when Wily reveals himself to be a boy. Follywit's impersonation of a courtesan in *A Mad World, My Masters*, is applauded as one of his admirable 'mad tricks'. ''Tis an Amazonian time', he remarks, combining his own mascu-line doublet with part of a gentlewoman's costume (Act III, Scene iii). Cross-dressed to gull his grandfather, he also allows himself to be courted and kissed by his grandfather's steward (IV. iii). The satire is cruel and amusing, skewering both gullible men and predatory women; but Follywit himself is unaffected by his temporary change of attire.

In Ben Jonson's *Epicoene* neither audience nor most of the characters know until the very end that the *Silent Woman* is, like Wily, a boy in disguise. Mistaken wooing is the central joke of the play. Unlike the other male cross-dressers in Jacobean drama, Epicoene has no prior independent role as a male until he is revealed as an instrument of Dauphine's plotting. As a woman he/she appears 'exceeding fair, and of . . . sweet composition . . . loving and obedient' and, at first, silent, satisfying all of Morose's requirements in a wife (II. v). In his feminine role Epicoene is adopted by the ladies' collegiate to learn their 'secrets', including 'those excellent receipts, madame, to keep yourselves from bearing of children' (IV. ii), and is apparently initiated, more than Thomas Salmon ever was, into the subculture of female fertility. Ultimately, of course, Dauphine reveals Epicoene's true gender—'a boy, a gentleman's son, that I have brought up this half year, at my great charges' (V. iv)—a relationship that may hint at bisexuality and homoeroticism. But gendered cultural bound-aries are preserved by Epiceone's promise not to reveal 'any mysteries' he has learned of the women. Like George a Green's 'subtle shift', Dauphine's ruses in *Epicoene* are applauded for their 'bravery and a wit' (II. iv) and for 'sport' that is 'full and twanging' (V. iii). True-Wit, who takes the role of a choral commentator, leads the audience in applause for 'concealing this part of the plot', a forerunner of the 'surprise' in the film *The Crying Game* (1993).[36]

Cross-dressing is also a matter of 'sport' in John Fletcher's *Monsieur Thomas* (first performed about 1610). This play features an on-stage robing scene in which Thomas, like Thomas Salmon, is dressed by his female accomplice. Dorothy and her maid paint Thomas's face and help him dress in woman's clothing, in a knockabout scene with jokes about breeches, points, and buttocks. Coached in female graces and taught to curtsey like a woman, Thomas asserts his manhood by filling the room with a monstrous (and masculine?) fart (V. i). But attired as a woman, Thomas is confident in his female disguise: 'Everyone takes me for my sister, excellent' (V. ii). But the disguise is far from perfect. The audience knows about it from the beginning, Thomas's femininity is grotesque, and other characters quickly see through his imposture. 'I saw his legs, h'as boots on like a player, under his wenches clothes; 'tis he, 'tis Thomas in his own sister's clothes,' cries the servant Launcelot, betraying Thomas to his father (V. i).

The disguise, however, is good enough to trick Valentine, the father of Thomas's beloved Mary, and Hylas, a lecherous old gentleman, who is persuaded that the 'lady' is in love with him. (Hylas describes his bride-to-be as 'fair gentlewoman' and 'the sweetest woman, the rarest woman, and the lustiest but wondrous honest', and before being cruelly humiliated excuses Thomas's rough cheeks and lips when he kisses him/her (V. vi, ix).) Thomas's woman's clothes admit him to Mary's bedroom, and indeed to her bed, but the women of the house, who know perfectly well who he is, play a trick upon him (V. v). More successfully, his cross-dressed disguise also allows Thomas to enter a nunnery where he 'plays revel rout', as one nun tells the abbess, like 'the fiend . . . among us'. He certainly makes no attempt to hide his sex, once he has gained entry to this female sanctum, although, like Thomas Salmon at Great Tew, he remains in female costume. Cellide, a novice, asks him, 'what are ye . . . and . . . what would ye with me?' Thomas: 'Any thing you'll let me.' Cellide: 'You are no woman, certain.' Thomas: 'Nor you no nun, nor shall be' (V. x).

What is evident from all this is that Thomas, despite his woman's apparel, is not the least unmanned. Indeed, his lustiness is enhanced, his libido uplifted, by the tricks he describes as 'sport'. He ridicules others, and is himself made ridiculous, in the interest of the trickeries of the plot. If there is a sexual charge to *Monsieur Thomas's* cross-dressing it is in the access it gives him to female bodies, not in any erotic frisson from the women's clothes themselves. The play may help answer Peter Stallybrass's question, derived from Rainolds, whether woman's clothes on a man awaken desire *for* a woman or *to be* a woman.[37]

By the same token Walgrave in *Englishmen for My Money*, subtitled *A Woman Will have her Will*, is not the slightest bit effeminized by dressing in woman's apparel. Rather, his dressing as Susan wins him Mathea, his heart's desire, and his masculine potency is vigorously aroused and satisfied by the effectiveness of his disguise. Still wearing woman's clothing, after a night in bed with Mathea, Walgrave seeks blessing from her father, Pisaro, 'for I have blessed you with a goodly son; 'tis breeding here, i' faith, a jolly boy'. Walgrave's disguise as the neighbour's daughter Susan had so convinced Pisaro that the old man courted her and called her/him 'sweeting', a joke that everyone but Pisaro could share (Scenes xi and xii). Walgrave's cross-dressing, like Monsieur Thomas's and Wily's, is a sport, a jest, a trick, a stratagem, which earns him his reward, congratulation from most of the other characters, and the humiliation not of himself but of others thought deserving to be humbled.

Nor is Welford unmanned when he dresses in woman's clothes and pretends to be espoused to Loveless in Beaumont and Fletcher's *The Scornful Lady*. Welford's cross-dressing, like most in this comedic genre, is another stratagem, 'a slippery trick', designed to 'overreach' and 'be even' with the Scornful Lady herself (V. i). Dressed in woman's clothes, Welford makes a virtue of his unwomanlike 'ugliness' by claiming to 'use no paint, nor any drugs of art', and appears as 'a good plain wench' in need of comfort after being jilted by a lover. Martha, the Scornful Lady's sister, takes pity on this seemingly distressed gentlewoman, and charitably invites her indoors: ' 'Tis very late, and you shall stay all night. Your bed shall be no worse than mine; I wish I could but do you right' (V. ii). And you can imagine the rest. Next morning Welford reports, 'what a pretty fury she was in, when she perceived I was a man; but I thank God I satisfied her scruple, without the parson of the town', and Martha and Welford are forthwith married. The Scornful Lady, herself now won by Loveless, admits to being completely taken in by Welford's disguise: 'What a dull ass was I, I could not see a wencher from a wench; twenty to one, if I had been but tender like my sister, he had served me such a slippery trick too.' And addressing Welford she continues, 'my large gentlewoman, my Mary Ambree, had I but seen into you, you should have had another bedfellow, fitter a great deal for your itch'(V. iv). Mary Ambree, frequently mentioned in these plays, was an Elizabethan woman who passed as a soldier and was thus an archetype of gender disguise. The 'itch' too was replete with sexual meanings.

Nathan Field's comedy *Amends for Ladies* is even more a riot of cross-dressing and complex gender reference. In the course of this drama Frank, 'attired like a woman', pretends to be married to his brother Ingen, who is trying to win the love of Lady Honour, and even allows Ingen to kiss him/her (II. iii, III. ii). Lady Honour herself later takes the disguise of a footboy and is wounded by her unknowing brother, Lord Proudly (IV. iii). Lord Feesimple dresses 'like a lady, masked', and is farcically courted and kissed by his own father, the count who responds, "'Sfoot! She has a beard! My son?' (V. ii). The play even features a topical appearance by Moll Cutpurse, the roaring girl, a woman dressed up as a man and addressed as 'Mary Ambree' and 'Mistress *hic* and *haec*', referring to the *Hic Mulier* controversy (II. i). But the central action of the play concerns Bold, a gentleman suitor who spends most of the drama in woman's costume.

Bold first appears 'disguised as a waiting gentlewoman', and it is not clear how the audience would know that he was a man cross-dressed as a woman, rather than a conventional male actor playing a female part. Perhaps there was some stage business to tip the wink, like Monsieur Thomas with his farcical curtsies. Lady Bright, however, the object of his attentions, takes Bold at her/his word as a waiting gentlewoman named Mary Princox (another name with sexual connotations) and accepts her/him into her service. Princox claims to be escaping Bold's attempt at seduction, allowing the suitor, though dressed as a woman, to assert his lusty manhood while reportedly attempting to seduce himself. Bold's disguise is so good that Lord Feesimple, convinced of her 'truth and honesty', himself pays court to her: 'an't please God, that thou wert not past children' (I. i).

Ensconced in Lady Bright's service, Bold as Mary performs the duties of a waiting gentlewoman, pinning and unpinning her mistress, all the while chatting of feminine topics. The scene is heavy with satire, irony, risqué jokes, and double entendre, with considerable discussion of clothes. Eventually Lady Bright concludes, 'well, well, come to bed, and we'll talk further of all these matters,' to which Bold says, aside, 'Fortune, thank thee . . . now she is mine indeed' (III. iii). Given Thomas's attempt on Mary, Welford's bed-trick with Martha, and Walgrave's overnight success with Mathea, one might expect to find Bold having his way. But Lady Bright is not so easily taken on finding her female bedfellow to be a man. The Lady defends her honour, threatens to cry rape, wields a sword (itself a masculine accoutrement), and bids the intruder begone. Bold's stratagem is comically undone and his sexual ambition 'foiled and disgraced' (IV. i, ii) before, in their final reconciliation, Bold and Lady Bright agree to be married.

Once again, the device of cross-dressing wins the audience's applause. The male character's 'putting on of woman's apparel' is a matter of mirth, his artificial femininity a source of 'good cheer'. Welford, Walgrave, and Bold are not made womanish by putting on woman's costume. Nor do they appear to be eroticized by the clothing itself. But wearing it gains them admission to intimate feminine circles, and the sexual opportunity it gives them makes them decidedly aroused. These, after all, are plays about courtship, about winning wives and property, and the overall dramatic framework within which they work is resolutely heterosexual, even if that cannot be said of all members of the acting company.

Theatrical cross-dressing is not portrayed as threatening, effeminizing, and certainly not an abomination unto the Lord. But how should it be otherwise, since plays were not the voices but the targets of Reformist propaganda? Theatre treated costume playfully without the moral and religious weight of *Histrio-Mastix, The Anatomy of Abuses* or Deuteronomy. Transvestite plotting toys with the conventions of gender distinction, but does not profoundly interrogate them. Yet even in comedy the cross-dressed male may be a source of unease, and his behaviour leads to dramatic complications. Though not himself humiliated or ridiculed, the butt of his deception is cruelly abused. And that may be the core of Thomas Salmon's offence too, not the risk of emasculation he took on himself but the potential harm he did to others.

The prevalence of the disguise motif in early modern literature, with its jokes about sex and costume, suggests that the inner and outer signs of gender identity formed a topic of continuing concern, at least among playwrights and playgoers. It may even reflect anxiety. When the comedy invites us to laugh, is it the laughter of idle amusement, the laughter of venom, of disquiet, or uncomfortable self-recognition? One does not have to endorse the extreme view, that the crisis in the sex-gender system of early modern England was part of 'the historical process eventuating in the English Revolution' to agree that the putting on of female apparel could be both mildly amusing and profoundly problematic.

Moving from the stage to the street, from literature to social behaviour, what were the circumstances in which men and women could be clothed in the costume of the opposite sex? Is any kind of answer possible to Jean Howard's question, 'How many people crossdressed in Renaissance England?' And did they compromise their gender or risk the sanctions of Deuteronomy by such actions? Was there a context in which Thomas Salmon's outrage at Great Tew might be explained or excused?

Men sometimes burlesqued in female clothing during carnivals and pageants. 'Both men and women change their weeds, the men in maids array, and wanton wenches dressed like men do travel by the way,' reported Barnaby Googe in 1570 with reference to the Shrovetide revels.[38] Men cross-dressed as 'May Marions' in the course of Maytide games, thereby earning the wrath of the Elizabethan critic Christopher Fetherstone.[39] The charivari or skimmington used cross-dressing to ridicule and to discipline disorderly neighbours.[40] Men dressed as women sometimes during enclosure riots or other public disorders, linking social protest to traditions of festive inversion, to taunt the authorities or to evade identification.[41] They might occasionally don an item of female dress, or have one put on them, while carousing or drunk, like Falstaff in *The Merry Wives of Windsor*. Prisoners sometimes dressed as women in order to escape.[42] Some men may have disguised themselves as women in order to infiltrate a forbidden place, or to make a rendezvous with a lover.[43] Some men may have worn women's clothes for the sake of erotic stimulation. Male actors, mostly boys, played women's parts on stage. Evidence can be found to document many of these situations, and imagination can supply the rest.

Women, in certain limited social settings, adopted items of masculine attire to shock, to allure, and to stretch the limits of permissible fashion. Prostitutes sometimes wore mannish gear to attract and arouse their customers. Women, too, may have dressed as men, or put on mannish costume, for pleasure, fun, or idle amusement. With more serious purpose they occasionally disguised themselves as men in order to travel, to serve in the army or navy, to meet or accompany a lover, or to avoid sexual attentions. Dutch sources from the seventeenth and eighteenth centuries record over one hundred cases of cross-dressed women in military service, at least a few of whom had taken female lovers or wives, and there are a few similar stories from early modern England.[44] Women passed as men in order to better their circumstances, to obtain the privileges or work of the opposite sex. There may have been an erotic charge for some transvestite women, just as there was for some men; but more commonly their transvestism was limited, temporary, and practical, addressing the needs of a particular situation. Though often associated with anxiety and disorder, not all cross-dressing was erotic or pathological or reflected a cultural system in distress.

Actual instances of women wearing male costume or men cross-dressed as women rarely appear in the English historical records. (Like flag-burning or communist infiltration, it may have been more feared than practised.) The London Bridewell and Aldermen's courts in the Elizabethan period made occasional references to prostitutes who 'went in men's apparel', who apparently used their costume to advertise their trade. Dorothy Clayton, for example, was a prostitute in 1575 who 'contrary to all honesty and womanhood commonly goes about the City appareled in men's attire'. She was ordered to stand in the pillory for two hours 'in men's attire', for public shame, and then committed to Bridewell. Another Elizabethan woman, Joanna Goodman, was punished in 1569 for dressing as a male servant to accompany her husband to war. These two incidents, grouped in Jean Howard's discussion as examples of 'actual' lower-class cross-dressing, in fact represent very different engagements with masculine clothing; the prostitute cross-dressed to entice her clientele, indeed to accentuate her available femininity; the soldier's wife wore male costume in an unsuccessful attempt at disguise; the first was a sexual provocation, the second a practical device or ruse.[45]

A cluster of incidents from the ecclesiastical courts of Elizabethan Essex involved women who dressed like men. Susan Bastwick of Stondon in 1578, 'whilst she was in service with her father about Allhallowtide last in a merriment came on horseback in a cloak disguised and demanded of him if he had any good ale'. The court ordered her to seek her father's forgiveness before she next received communion. At Littlebury in 1585 a female servant 'did wear man's apparel disorderly in her master's house'. The churchwardens of Great Chesterford reported in the same year 'that Hunt's wife, contrary to God's law, did put on man's apparel and went forth from one house to another so ungodly and shamefully, with other naughtiness of words'. In 1592 the court heard that James Cornwall's wife of Terling, cited for sexual incontinence with John Burles, 'useth to wear young men's garters and said she would so to do until they came for them'. In 1596 the three daughters of Thomas Day of Great Wendon were cited 'for going disguised a mumming', presumably in cross-dressed attire, and their father was cited 'for suffering them to go'. Also in 1596, in the season of Maytide merriments, Joanna Towler of Downham, was 'detected, for that she came into our church in man's apparel upon the sabbath day in the service time'.[46]

In 1612 another Essex woman, Catherine Bank, servant to John Whitebread of Grays Thurrock, was similarly presented, 'for coming in man's apparel into the church . . . to the contempt of religion, thereby dishonoring God and disturbing the minister and congregation'. I would guess that like Joanna Towler she was wearing a festival costume rather than participating in any Jacobean 'female transvestite movement'. The court ordered her to perform penance 'in her usual apparel with a paper on her breast' proclaiming her fault.[47]

These were mostly minor offences, more jests and pranks than challenges to the gendered social order; and their punishment was appropriately mild. Cross-dressing here involved mockery and high spirits and provocative disrespect for patriarchy and propriety, but it is hard to see it as subversive or seriously transgressive. In most cases it was associated with seasonal merriments of Hallowe'en and Maytide and mumming from house to house, and only attracted notice if it crossed the line from sanctioned to irresponsible behaviour, like Joanna Towler wearing her May games outfit to church. If fathers, masters, neighbours, churchwardens, or ministers were offended when young women flaunted mannish costume, and normal patriarchal discipline proved insufficient, they had some redress in the ecclesiastical courts. But the courts, more interested in restoring charity and harmony than in meting out punishment, were content to secure acknowledgement of error and to pass out a mild rebuke. The stiffest punishment, like that enjoined on Thomas Salmon, was performance of public penance.

This, too was the official response to Mary Frith, the original Moll Cutpurse and model for *The Roaring Girl*, who was cited by the London Consistory Court in 1612 for disorderly revelling in masculine attire. An almost legendary historical character, Moll Cutpurse enjoyed celebrity status on the fringes of the London stage and became a character in several plays. It is significant that her cross-dressing was closely associated with the festive traditions of the theatre, and that her costume was designed to flaunt, not to efface her gender. Mary Frith had attended the Fortune theatre 'in man's apparel, and in her boots, and with a sword by her side'. But any who doubted that she was indeed a woman she invited to her lodging to put the matter to the test. She was also found in St Paul's church on Christmas night 'with her petticoat tucked up about her, in the fashion of a man, with a man's cloak on her . . . to the disgrace of all womanhood'. Before the court Mary admitted her roistering but denied more serious charges of lewdness and bawdry. Predictably she attracted considerable attention when she performed her penance at Paul's Cross, and, in keeping with her character, despite promising to behave 'honestly, soberly and womanly', she made a travesty of the punishment by turning up drunk.[48]

A smaller range of cases involved men who were cited for wearing women's garb. In practice the Church was less concerned that they had violated the sanctions of Deuteronomy than that their behaviour provoked disorder. Young men, like young women, took part in seasonal revels, May and summer games, mummings, burlesques, charivari, skimmingtons, and the village morality drama of skits and libels. Often these activities involved cross-dressing, and were lubricated with good cheer, and sometimes they got out of control. If there was any sexual frisson in this festive cross-dressing it remained well hidden. The evidence points not to homoerotic ambivalence and subversive androgyny but to problems of social discipline.

At Cawthorne, Yorkshire, in the summer of 1596, in contemptuous disregard of an order 'that no rushbearings, summer games, morris dances, plays, interludes, disguisings, shows or abuses should be used . . . in any church or churchyard or upon the Sabbath day', an unruly company assembled none the less in the church 'and there did arm and disguise themselves, some of them putting on women's apparel, and othersome of them putting on long hair and visards', and then paraded through the town drawing the people after them.[49] At Oxford in 1598, 'the inhabitants assembled on the two Sundays before Ascension Day, and on that day, with drum and shot and other weapons, and men attired in women's apparel, brought into the town a woman bedecked with garlands and flowers, named by them the queen of May. They also had morris dances and other disordered and unseemly sports.'[50] The following year John Wilkins of Whitstable, Kent, was cited 'for going about the street in woman's apparel, being the parish clerk at that time'. In his defence he explained that 'at a marriage in merriment he did disguise himself in his wife's apparel to make some mirth to the company', and this excuse appeared to satisfy the archdeaconry court.[51]

Matthew Lancaster, husbandman, offered a similar justification for his part in a Maytide procession at Wells, Somerset, in 1607 when he wore 'woman's apparel like a spinster'. Lancaster's outfit included 'a red petticoat, kerchief and muffler' and he carried a distaff to accentuate his borrowed gender. On this occasion the carousing became too raucous and ran to libellous mockery of some leading citizens, which is why it came to the attention of the court of Star Chamber. Using words that could have been spoken in dozens of similar incidents, Lancaster acknowledged his cross-dressing but insisted he did it 'in a merriment and not otherwise'.[52] The issue at law was behaviour, not costume. Less leniently treated was John Taylor of Chester, but the circumstances of his offence are not clear. Taylor was indicted before the civil authorities in 1608, 'for wearing women's apparel' and was sentenced to have his clothes cut and made into breeches, and to be publicly whipped through the town.[53]

Finally in 1633, the same year as Thomas Salmon's outrage in Oxfordshire, Christopher Willan of Burton in Kendall, Cumberland, was cited 'for bearing rushes to the church or chapel disguised in women's apparel'. This took place in the course of a traditional rush-bearing (the ceremonial garlanding of the church), and it is likely that the Reformers were more offended by Willan's perpetuation of a superstitious ceremony and its affront to ecclesiastical good manners than by his costume.[54]

The Church was concerned with order and discipline, the sanctity of the holy space, and the dignity of the sabbath.[55] Ecclesiastical regulators were preoccupied with propriety and decorum, and one of their recurrent concerns was to maintain limits. It may have been permissible to cross-dress on the green, but offensive if the celebrants came unchanged to church. Wedding guests might play with gender and clothing by way of 'merriment', but questions of propriety were raised when one of the merry-makers was the parish clerk. Mary Frith could get away with cross-dressing at the Fortune theatre, but masquerading in St Paul's church brought down the wrath of the Bishop of London. The primary offence that needed remedy lay not in the gender confusion or abomination of cross-dressing, but in the intrusion of inappropriate behaviour into privileged space. This is why the East Anglian women and the north country men were cited for coming cross-dressed to church, and it helps us to understand the issues surrounding Thomas Salmon's invasion of the birth room at Great Tew. What the village community found truly offensive was not that the manservant dressed as a woman, but that he used this disguise to enter a place where he did not belong. If dirt, as Mary Douglas has observed,[56] is a substance out of place, then Thomas Salmon may have been doing something dirty and his presence in the birth room a pollution. At issue was where he was, not what he wore. The critical matter in this case, then, may have been genre rather than gender, and the latter a subset of the former.

What is striking about the Great Tew case is that neither the church court nor the Oxfordshire community appeared to share the anxiety or outrage about cross-dressing exhibited by the London anti-theatrical critics. Prynne's vituperative strictures, though exactly contemporary with Thomas Salmon's dressing-up, seem to have occupied a different world. Nor does the report of the offence or the testimony of the witnesses suggest that gender disorder was anywhere near as serious as some recent scholars have assumed. Neither Thomas Salmon's behaviour, nor Elizabeth Fletcher's, fits the model of subversion, oppression, or opposition advanced by radical critics. Nor does it have much to offer champions of sexual liberation, resistance, and 'transgressive reinscription'. Instead we see a reasonableness and sense of accommodation that accorded with the style and philosophy of the better-known intellectual circle at Great Tew.

Of course, there were strains in early modern society, and questions about gender roles and identity, but it is hard to argue that they were more acute than at other times. Nor can it be claimed with confidence that gender mattered more than other social, economic, religious, and political problems. The evidence suggests that cross-dressing in practice was neither the subversive abomination nor the eroticized transgression that some scholars have claimed. Neither the records of ecclesiastical justice nor the London comedies reveal, in my reading, a sex-gender system in crisis. Indeed, one could argue that the system was robust enough to play with, with a measure of festive tolerance and allowance for good clean fun.

Other scholars may read the sources differently, and make more of the case of Thomas Salmon, but it would be misleading to claim him as grist for any particular mill. The danger, in these matters, lies in projecting present preoccupations onto the past, and in bringing our opinions to the evidence rather than deriving them from it. There may well be politicized transgressive energies at work here, but not all are confined to the sixteenth and seventeenth centuries.

Dramatis Personae

Eleanor Rymel, wife of Hugh Rymel, of Great Tew
Francis Fletcher, midwife
Elizabeth Fletcher, daughter-in-law to Francis
Thomas Salmon, servant, impersonated Mrs Garrett's maid

OTHER CROSS-DRESSERS
Dorothy Clayton, London prostitute
Joanna Goodman, soldier's wife
Susan Bastwick, servant, of Stondon, Essex
Joanna Towler of Downham, Essex
Catherine Bank, servant, of Grays Thurrock, Essex
Mary Frith (Moll Cutpurse), celebrity of the *demi-monde*
John Wilkins, parish clerk, of Whitstable, Kent
Matthew Lancaster, husbandman, of Wells, Somerset
John Taylor of Chester
Christopher Willan of Burton in Kendal, Cumberland

8

WHO BURIED MRS HORSEMAN? EXCOMMUNICATION, ACCOMMODATION, AND SILENCE

On the twelfth day after Christmas, in January 1631, Charles Wise, the parish clerk of Holton, Oxfordshire, went to church early to ring the bells for the Epiphany service. To his surprise, 'he found the belfry door had been unbarred, and the chancel door unbarred, and a grave digged and made up again, and the table [i.e. the communion table] set upon it'. Furthermore, he told investigators, 'he hath heard that Mrs. Horseman was buried there, but who carried her to the church or buried her there he cannot depose'.[1]

Who buried Mrs Horseman? Who broke into the church and made an illegal grave in the holiest of all possible locations, yet buried the body without canonical Christian ceremony? Who would undertake such illegal and sacrilegious action, and why? What laws were broken, what conventions violated, by this clandestine burial as the parishioners and officials of Holton struggled to understand the secret events of Twelfth Night? The ensuing investigation by the Oxford diocesan court produced a remarkable record of testimony and prevarication, dissembling and partial co-operation, as witnesses disgorged fragments of the story. We can almost hear the hesitation in their voices. Most of those questioned were illiterate, and none of their words would be known to posterity were it not for the bureaucratic practices of the ecclesiastical court. And the court would not have taken such pains to get to the bottom of this case had not Mrs Horseman been 'an excommunicated person' and therefore not entitled to Christian burial, let alone burial in the *sanctum sanctorum*.

This case permits a rare insight into the actions and processes of a seventeenth-century community, exposing both the protocols of neighbourly custom and the requirements of ecclesiastical justice when dealing with the excommunicated dead. The story of the burial of Mrs Horseman—a story that took several months to conclude and which had many modes of telling— reveals conflicting standards of decency and discipline and variable notions of community and exclusion, decency and pollution, as well as differing levels of truth-telling and alternative modes of action, as laity and clergy, women and men, negotiated the cultural distance between the bishop's chancery and the village street. Diocesan officials wanted the truth, or at least a satisfactory narrative, but, like modern historians, were forced to accept a tale full of gaps, redolent with unvoiced possibilities and suspicions.

According to ecclesiastical law the minister was obliged to bury any parishioner, but was excused from burying an excommunicated person. The canons of 1604 did not expressly forbid such burials, but if 'the party deceased were denounced excommunicated *majori excommunicatione*, for some grievous and notorious crime, and no man able to testify of his repentence', the parson was not obligated to accommodate him (or her) (Canon 68). Even lesser excommunication could stand in the way, for Canon 85 required the churchwardens to ensure 'that all persons excommunicated and so denounced be kept out of the church', presumably dead as well as living. The rubric in the Book of Common Prayer was silent on this matter, until modified in 1662 to exclude 'any that die unbaptised, or excommunicate, or have laid violent hands upon themselves'.[2] Even so, there was room for manœuvre and negotiation, as there was on so many other contentious issues.

The problem in Oxfordshire stemmed from a lack of consensus about how to deal with the legal and social consequences of excommunication. In early modern England a person could be excommunicated for a wide variety of offences. These ranged from failure to come to church to failure to pay tithes, from participation in irregular marriages to disregarding the directions of the ecclesiastical courts. One did not have to be a heretic or a major religious dissident to earn this penalty. Excommunication was a crude device that caught both serious and trivial offenders in its meshes. Offenders who ignored citations to appear before the church courts, or who refused to perform court-ordered penance, were routinely punished by excommunication. So too were godly parishioners who refused to conform to particular aspects of Church of England worship. Elizabeth Shipden of Norwich, for example, the wife of a puritan alderman, was excommunicated in 1622 for refusing to wear a white veil at her churching.[3] Christian Harper of Harborough, Leicestershire, was excommunicated in 1637 for refusing to receive communion at the altar rails rather than 'the accustomed place', and was still seeking absolution four years later.[4] Parishioners of Walsall, in the diocese of Lichfield, were excommunicated in 1635 for wearing a hat during service time, for laughing and talking in church, for not coming to church, for digging ditches upon St Mark's Day, and for carrying lime upon May Day, as well as for failure to answer when summoned.[5] In the early part of Charles I's reign, it has been estimated, some 1,500 people a year were excommunicated in the diocese of York, 1,600 a year in the diocese of Norwich, and more than 2,000 a year in the diocese of Chester, as the church courts became increasingly willing to impose this penalty. In some areas as much as 5 per cent of the population was excommunicated.[6] Reformers criticized the indiscriminate use of excommunication, but the frequency of its pronunciation and the ease with which its sanctions could be lifted encouraged many parishioners to regard excommunication with indifference.[7]

There were two grades of excommunication. 'Lesser' excommunication deprived the offender of 'the use of the sacraments and divine worship'; 'greater' excommunication was supposed to exclude the offender from 'the society and conversation of the faithful'. Excommunicates were not supposed to enter the church during worship, and, emphatically, they could not approach the altar. In principle they were excluded from the services of baptism, matrimony, and Christian burial. But they were rarely shunned by their neighbours or treated as outcasts, since ties of kinship and community offered more generous standards of judgement than the ecclesiastical courts. In most cases the Church worked hard to bring excommunicates back into the fold, and the sanction could readily be lifted through such processes of reconciliation as purgation, composition, penance, or simple acknowledgement of fault. In post-Reformation England excommunication operated more as a disciplinary stricture than a spiritual terror, an interim social inconvenience rather than a lasting threat to salvation.[8]

The Church could apply increasing disciplinary pressure on offenders if pastoral counselling or neighbourly pressure failed to bring about correction or submission. As Worcester diocesan officials explained in a memorandum of 1608, 'if they persist in their obstinance, then may you proceed to excommunication; but you must be circumspect to have the articles set down by a public notary'. For denunciation to carry weight the paperwork had to be in order and the procedures properly followed. Forty days later, in extreme cases, the Church might seek a Chancery writ *de excommunicato capiendo*, which could lead to action by the civil authorities, imprisonment, and attachment of the excommunicated person's property. But in order to proceed 'there must be a *significavit* from the bishop after contempt of the party by willful standing under the censure of excommunication'.[9] The writ *de excommunicato capiendo* was a heavy weapon, not usually worth the cost and complexity of the business, and in practice it was rarely used except against the most obstinate offenders.[10] No bishop was keen to transfer his cases to the secular courts.

Among the many ironies of post-Reformation England, Roman Catholics could be excommunicated by a Church they did not recognize, and so be barred from participating in services that they did not attend. Most English Catholics coexisted with their Protestant neighbours, paid their recusancy fines, and worshipped privately on the margins of the Christian community. Some even made occasional use of their ancient parish church and secured burial in its consecrated grounds. Roger Martyn, for example, a prominent recusant in Suffolk, was buried and memorialized in Long Melford church in 1616.[11] Roman Catholics suffered myriad penalties and indignities, but recusancy by itself did not necessarily lead to excommunication. Nor were Catholics automatically excluded from the community of the Christian dead. Indeed, anti-Catholic legislation of 1606 imposed a fine of £20 on 'any popish recusant man or woman not being excommunicate' who 'shall be buried in any place *other* than the church or churchyard'.[12] Only those Catholics who persisted in contempt of the established Protestant religion, or who appeared to be 'heads and leaders of the rest', faced the additional handicap of excommunication and its consequent sanctions and exclusions.[13]

What happened when an excommunicated person died? A determination would have to be made quickly before decomposition rendered the body 'loathsome'. In theory, being barred from the Christian community, an excommunicant was supposed to be buried outside of hallowed ground, in any garden, roadside, or convenient place; having forfeited the comforts of the rites of passage the body would be interred without the Prayer Book ceremony or the services of a priest. This was the fate of some Lancashire recusants in 1611 when, in the words of a later seventeenth-century co-religionist, 'a bitter storm of persecution extended its fury to the bodies of deceased catholics. The churches in all parts denied them burial. Some were laid in the fields, some in gardens, and others in highways as it chanced. One of these, as I have heard it credibly reported, being interred in a common lane, was pulled out by the hogs and used accordingly.'[14]

More often, in practice, to avoid such indignities, the matter was left to local discretion. In most cases an accommodation could be reached. The impulses of Christian charity and neighbourly solidarity commonly conspired to see that all dead bodies were decently buried, with proper placement, ritual, and respect. Whatever their former sins or status, these bodies were formed in God's image, served as vessels of the soul, and might be revived at the Resurrection. Common opinion, bordering on superstition, held that to bury anyone without ceremony and to inter them anywhere but in consecrated ground was to treat them like animals. Christians, observed a sixteenth-century theologian, did not dispose of human corpses 'as we be wont to carry forth dead horses or dead swine', nor bury their dead like carrion. 'I cannot endure that Christian people should be buried like a dog', protested a seventeenth-century Yorkshire minister.[15] This deep-rooted horror of bestial interment offset the worst sanctions of excommunication. So did the barely articulated belief that the souls or 'shades' of the dead might linger in torment if their burial was improper or incomplete. There were strong cultural pressures to find mitigating circumstances and to give deceased excommunicates the benefit of the doubt, as if they had intended repentance and would have secured absolution before dying. The saving clause of the canon—'and no man able to testify of his repentance'—allowed the possibility of posthumous reconciliation, and a speedy resolution to the crisis. (Similar generosity was often extended to unbaptized babies, though rarely to the burial of suicides.)[16]

In many cases, with the tacit agreement of parish elders and the silent acquiescence of the ecclesiastical authorities, an unreconciled excommunicate might be interred in the parish churchyard at night. The body would then lie forever in consecrated ground, in the 'dormitory of Christians', awaiting resurrection.[17] Doubts might be settled, the matter expedited, and uncertainties resolved by seeking a special faculty, permission, or dispensation. Payment of fees worked wonders; the separatist Katherine Chidley charged in 1641 that when anyone died while excommunicated, 'his friends must give money to absolve him after he is dead, or else he shall not be buried in the consecrated earth'.[18] But occasionally, as in the case of Mrs Horseman, the process of inclusion and integration was thwarted, as different layers of parochial and diocesan authority stood their ground.

Furthermore, no person, even the most unblemished Christian, was allowed to be buried inside the body of the church without the express permission of the incumbent. The chancel in particular was the minister's preserve. The church building and the soil beneath it was regarded as part of the parson's freehold, and a fee was required—normally 6s. 8d.—for interment therein. As freeholder as well as pastor, then, the minister of Holton could feel cheated and offended by the irregular planting of Mrs Horseman in his chancel. Since Mrs Horseman's residence at Wheatley, adjacent to Holton, lay technically outside the parish, her illicit burial in Holton church would add to the outrage of officials who guarded the incumbent's privileges in this regard.[19]

Against this background we can return to the problem at Holton and the secret burial of Mrs Horseman. The story sheds light on both routine and irregular practices of burial, exposes social relations and rhetorical strategies within this rural community, and illuminates the relationship of the parish to external authorities. The diocesan court was determined to get to the bottom of the matter, in the interest of religious decorum and discipline. The villagers responded with due deference but the minimum of co-operation. Formal interrogatories led to personal answers, and the clerks blended verbatim transcripts with legal phrasing to create the documentary record. The drama hinged on questions of authority and order as well as ritual practices and Christian beliefs.

On 15 January 1631, having heard from the parish clerk, the Oxford diocesan court examined others who might shed more light on the incident. Thomas Day, labourer, Edward Day, John Robins, and John Stacy testified that they had asked Bartholomew Price, the minister of Holton, to bury the deceased Mrs Horseman, and that Mr Powell of nearby Forest Hill 'would bear him out if it cost an hundred pounds'. They understood that there might be a problem, but as soon as it was resolved they were ready to do their parts as mourners, bearers, and bell-ringers. The gentleman neighbour Mr Powell, apparently, was determined that Mrs Horseman should have a proper burial, and was willing both to underwrite the expense and to answer for any irregularity. The witnesses knew that Powell had sent to the diocesan office at Oxford, six miles to the west, 'for a dispensation for her burial', but claimed to know nothing of the actual interment. Thomas Day in particular insisted that he had no more to tell.

Edward Powell himself, the highest-ranking witness called before the court, testified that he was not privy to the burial of Mrs Horseman, nor did he know 'who or what parties did carry the said Mrs. Horseman to church to be buried or were privy thereto'. He did say, however, that after the woman's death, and after the minister of Holton refused to bury her, he sent to Dr Hugh Barker, the Bishop of Oxford's Chancellor, 'to desire a faculty for the burial of the said Mrs. Horseman, which when the messenger brought word it would not be granted [he, Powell,] did advise one Edward Day and another of his servants dwelling in Wheatley to bury her, the said Mrs. Horseman, in the garden, intending, after leave obtained lawfully, to remove her body'. Private interment in domestic ground would have been the legally correct disposition for an unreconciled excommunicate, though many would say she was buried like a dog. On further questioning, Mr Powell denied offering a fee to the minister of Holton, 'to will him to suffer the said body to be buried in his parish church, promising that he would save him harmless'. Powell evidently understood the business of dispensations, faculties, and permissions, and expected to be able to negotiate a satisfactory outcome through his dealings with the ecclesiastical hierarchy; it was the failure of those negotiations that precipitated the crisis in this Oxfordshire woodland village.

Richard Winstow of Wheatley, labourer, told the court that when Mrs Horseman died 'in the Christmas time last, and before New Year's day' her maid, Mary Slyman, brought him 'a stick or rod which . . . was the measure of Mrs. Horseman's coffin wherein her body was put'. The rod was to indicate the length of the required grave, and it was Winstow's task to take this information to the parish clerk of Holton to arrange for the digging. Besides this he was non-committal, 'knew not' who buried Mrs Horseman, and on this typically inconclusive note the court adjourned.

Two months later the court resumed its investigation of the provocative clandestine burial. Charles Wise, the parish clerk of Holton, acknowledged that Richard Winstow brought him the measure and went with him, on Mr Powell's instructions, to ask permission of the minister that Mrs Horseman be buried in Holton church. But the minister, 'Mr. Price, refused to give his consent thereto unless he had order from Dr. Barker for her burial there.' And as we know, Dr Barker refused to grant the dispensation.

Meanwhile, as was customary after the death of a prominent parishioner, the church bells rang. The ringers—the same four men who had already testified in January to Edward Powell's intercession—now said that 'they rang for Mrs. Horseman, and that Richard Winstow brought the ringers beer to church', which was part of their usual reward. Then, to their amazement, three or four days later, 'they found that the chancel door of Holton had been wrested open and the belfry door unbarred and opened and the ground in the chancel had been opened under the communion table and a body buried there as [they] thinketh, and the communion table set over that place again'. This was on twelfth day, a remarkable Epiphany for the community of Holton. Besides this the ringers said they knew nothing, and to this they set their marks. In most parishes the bell-ringers formed a close-knit fraternity on the border of the sacred and profane, and these Oxfordshire labourers clearly knew more than they were telling.

The court needed other witnesses to bring it closer to the truth. 'Widow Ives of Wheatley watched with Mrs. Horseman in her sickness. Richard Hoskins of Wheatley dwelleth by Mrs. Horseman's garden wall and might know somewhat, if she were brought out that way', suggested a court memorandum dated 5 March. Mrs Horseman's servant Mary surely possessed more information, but so far she was either reluctant to speak or unavailable. Another neighbour, John Bolton, testified that the maid had requested the ringing of the death peal at Holton, and that the four men who rang had the minister's begrudging consent for their action. Bolton said that Mary had told him that 'Mr. Price [the minister] had promised Mrs. Horseman in her lifetime that he would bury her when she was dead', but, like everyone else, he insisted he knew no more.

Eventually on 19 March, almost eleven weeks after the secret night-time burial, the maid told her part of the story. Mary Slyman testified that her mistress had died on Friday morning, New Year's Eve, 'and was kept in the parlour of her house in Wheatley from that time until Monday both day and night; albeit she was put into a coffin on New Year day, yet by Monday she began to smell so strong that they could not endure her in the house; whereupon on Monday night they drew her corpse in her coffin out into the garden and the next morning drew her into the parlour again, and continued this course until Wednesday, and left her in the garden on Wednesday at night next after New Year's day last, from whence she was carried in the night and buried in Holton church as she hath heard; but by whom she was buried or who carried her away or who made her grave or were any instrument or furtherer thereof she cannot tell'. The maid had heard, however, 'that Mrs. Brown had sent her man to Master Doctor Barker to have authority or warrant from him for her burial, and [she] persuading herself that this warrant should be obtained did thereupon send one Richard Winstow with a measure of the length of her coffin to the parish clerk of Holton to make a grave, and he went about that message, but what success he had therein she cannot tell'.

John Stacy, who had already testified in January, now added that he accompanied Richard Winstow to obtain permission for the burial, but the minister refused to bury Mrs Horseman 'until he had leave and warrant from my Lord Bishop of Oxford'. The minister's wife, however, gave them the key to the church 'for them to ring', Mr Price 'being not then risen out of his bed'. On this dark winter morning we may imagine the minister taking refuge from conflicting duties by snuggling down deeper beneath the covers. Bartholomew Price, the minister of Holton, was no new appointee but had been rector since 1584. He was now an old man, most likely in his seventies, and did not want difficulties at the end of his career.[20]

The other bell-ringers confirmed Stacy's account, and said that they rang two or three peals for Mrs Horseman. One of the ringers, John Robins, added that 'there was a bottle of drink and a little loaf of bread brought them to the church which they did eat and drink, and he thinketh it came from Mrs. Horseman's maid'. But they still had no idea how Mrs Horseman came to be buried. Listeners who did not yet know that a prominent neighbour had died might easily confuse the early morning ringing with the traditional ringing-in of the New Year, itself a contentious practice. The normal procedure when someone died was to toll a passing bell, not to ring two or three peals.[21]

The case resumed again on 16 April with testimony from Anne Price, the minister's wife. She deposed 'that the Sunday morning next after Mrs. Horseman's death Edward Day, Thomas Day the younger, and John Robins and John Stacy came to [her] house before her husband was up and desired to have the keys to the church to ring a peal, and she asked them wherefore they would ring, and Edward Day made answer and said they would ring for Mrs. Horseman who would be buried there, and then [she] said you should first know whether she should be buried there or not before you ring for her, and then the said Edward Day, being Mr. Powell's man, said you will take my master's word will you not, meaning Mr. Powell of Forest Hill, and she said no she should not be buried in Holton church unless he brought a note from Dr. Barker to give leave for her to be buried there. And after this the same morning came Richard Winstow, Mr. Powell's man . . . and brought Charles Wise the clerk of Holton with him'. They asked if the curate could 'serve the turn' if Mr Price refused, to which Mrs Price answered that none should bury Mrs Horseman without a note from Dr Barker 'to signify his consent'. Anne Price appears here as a forceful character, gatekeeper to the minister's chamber, and adamant that no irregular service should be performed without permission in writing. She understood the protective power of written consent, but her own limited literacy was revealed when, like most of the villagers in this story, she wrote a mark instead of a signature when subscribing her deposition.

Richard Winstow had asked the important question, 'where shall we make her grave?' To which the minister replied, according to Mrs Price, 'there should no grave be made till they brought a note under Dr. Barker's hand for it. Then Winstow said I will go to my master and we will send away George Ball to Dr. Barker and then I will be here again presently; and he then charged clerk Wise, who had then the measure of her coffin in his hand, to take heed that he lost not the measure, and so they departed.' Evidently they expected the Chancellor to reassure or overrule the parish minister, so that they could get on with the important business of burying the corpse. But the actual burial site was not yet determined. The sexton's measuring stick represented the deceased Mrs Horseman and this symbolic instrument was carried from place to place throughout the village as the parties negotiated the problem.

Several witnesses mentioned Dr Hugh Barker, the Bishop of Oxford's Chancellor, to whom the villagers appealed to allow Mrs Horseman normal Christian burial. He had rejected the petition, and now, some months later, as both an interested party and the official in charge of the court, he was determined to get to the bottom of the matter. Not only had an excommunicant been buried, a church broken into, a communion table rudely handled, and the most sacred ground within the chancel violated, but his own express denial of burial for Mrs Horseman had been most shamefully ignored. Barker may also have been the official who sentenced Mrs Horseman to excommunication, although no record of this can be found.[22] Issues of professional honour and episcopal authority became bound up with matters of ecclesiastical law and custom, as the villagers mocked the court by maintaining their wall of silence.

Mrs Price, the minister's wife, in common with everyone else brought before the Chancellor, deposed that 'she cannot tell' who buried Mrs Horseman. But she concluded her testimony with the observation 'that on twelfth day last past in the morning by break of day or soon after [she] saw John Stacy of Holton . . . in the street with his boots on and his boots were all dirty'. Ann Price's glimpse of John Stacy's dirty boots might prove to be the turning point in this case.

Another witness, Eleanor Turner, the wife of John Turner, labourer of Holton, contributed some useful circumstantial evidence which also sheds light on gender relations, neighbourliness, moral sentiment, work, and gossip in this Oxfordshire village. Early in the morning on twelfth day she had gone to John Stacy's house 'to help to milk his cattle, and the sun being then up' she found Stacy only then getting dressed from bed. To her taunting question, 'you are now a good husband, do you rise but now?' Stacy said he had been out late drinking. No more than anyone else did Eleanor Turner admit knowing who buried Mrs Horseman, but 'in Shotover wood she heard Thomas George's wife of Holton say "God's blessing on them that buried the dead, it is fit the dead should be buried", but whom she meant she cannot tell for they had no particular speech of Mrs. Horseman'.

It was time to call back John Stacy, who had previously appeared before the court in January and March. John Stacy now 'sayeth that on twelfth day morning or night last past he being not well but loose-bodied rose in the night and went out his street door with his high shoes on without any stockings on, and the door is so hard to open that it makes a great noise when it is opened so as the neighbours that dwell near him may hear the opening thereof. And when he had done that which he went about, he came in again and went to bed. And he many times weareth his boots, the ground being dirty, but whether he had his boots on that morning or his high shoes he cannot remember.' It was a plausible story, at least giving pause to the suspicion that the dirt on Stacy's boots had come from digging in the church, and that his tardy rising resulted from clandestine night-time exertions.

Stacy's statement continued. 'And he further sayeth that about the Sunday at night before twelfth day last past there was preparation made at Mrs. Horseman's house for Mrs. Horseman's burial, and a great deal of meat made ready for the company that met there expecting her then to be buried. And [he, Stacy,] at her maid Mary Slyman's request helped with others to remove the corpse out of the parlour into a porch by the garden because the corpse savoured much. And for ought he knoweth it remained there that night. And [he] and the company there met supped there that night, but there coming no authority or warrant for Mrs. Horseman's burial she was not then buried.' But beyond this, he told the court, he knew no more.

Everyone involved had a chance to testify. None claimed knowledge, and nobody confessed. Village opinion was with Mrs Horseman and her helpers—

'God's blessing on them that buried the dead'—not with the minister or the episcopal court. But by this time the Chancellor had a fair idea of what had happened. Eventually on 23 July 1631 the ecclesiastical court pronounced judgement. John Stacy, Edward Day, and John Robins (three of the bell-ringers), Charles Wise (the parish clerk), Richard Winstow (the labourer with the measuring stick), and their neighbour John Bolton, were all cited '*quod fuerint assistents et consentients ad sepulturam clandestinam Maria* [a mistake for Elizabeth] *Horseman in cancella ecclesia Holtonis noctis tempore*'. Presumably, they all did it. All were ordered to acknowledge their offence and to perform public penance in Holton church, and to certify the court of their compliance. And so they did. None of the offenders was excommunicated, and Mrs Horseman was presumably left undisturbed in her place of honour. At least, there is no record of her disinterment, no surviving order to that effect. A body, once buried, belonged to God or belonged to no one, and could not be exhumed without official permission.[23] The investigative process had been aimed at disciplining the community, not at ridding the church of pollution. Given the gravity of their offence and their lack of candour before the court, the judgement against the gravediggers was remarkably mild.

We do not know what manner of offence earned Mrs Horseman her excommunication, nor when that sentence was passed. But it seems unlikely to have been serious enough to lose her the sympathy and respect of her neighbours. Evidently she died expecting a normal burial despite her alienation from the Church of England. Her nuncupative will of December 1630 included conventional payments to have 'her funeral expenses discharged',[24] and as soon as she passed away the standard funeral preparations were begun. According to her maid, the minister had promised Mrs Horseman a Christian burial, but such a promise would not have been necessary unless the matter was in some doubt. Elizabeth Horseman appears to have been a Catholic recusant, one of three identified in 1624 in the parish of Cuddesdon (which included Wheatley) and she may have stood excommunicate for half a dozen years before her death. She was certainly a neighbour, and perhaps an associate, of the Catholic activist Ann Curson (d. 1631) in the adjacent parish of Waterperry, 'one of the centres of Roman Catholicism in Oxfordshire'.[25] Roman Catholic activism was a continuing concern for the Oxford diocesan authorities in the reign of Charles I, and a nuisance for the rector of Holton.

The primary problem at Holton, however, was social and practical, not theological or spiritual. Mrs Horseman's prominence in the community, as a widowed gentlewoman, is confirmed by the generous bell-ringing at her death, and by the solicitous negotiations conducted on her behalf. The neighbours partaking of funeral refreshments on the night before twelfth day evidently expected the Chancellor to overrule their minister, so that they could proceed with the burial as planned. They may also have assumed that the body of Mrs Horseman, like those of other gentlefolk, warranted burial not just in consecrated ground but inside the church, at the centre of the community's worship.

Both the site and the circumstances of Mrs Horseman's burial were charged with significance that we cannot now fully decode. Their symbolic meaning is susceptible to multiple interpretations. Though the men who broke open Holton church may have been somewhat drunk after an evening of Christmastide festivity, on top of funeral refreshments, their action achieved what many of the villagers wanted. In effect they dissolved the distinction between communicant and excommunicate, Protestant and Catholic, inside and out, and reasserted the claims of common humanity. They took the problem into their own hands because the body was beginning to fester, because they agreed that Mrs Horseman should not be buried like a dog, and because they were impatient with the ecclesiastical impasse. It seems likely that the grave diggers saw themselves as unofficial servants of the community, engaged in an act of charitable and neighbourly obligation, and their subsequent silence a matter of decency and solidarity. Though the night-time burial was hugger-mugger its consequences were patent for all to see.

At the same time their action can be judged as sinister and transgressive. As well as acting charitably to the deceased, the men who conducted the clandestine burial effectively dramatized divisions within the community. In solving one problem they provocatively precipitated another. They did not just bury a problematic corpse but, rather, they *used* Mrs Horseman's body to proclaim a message of resistance and defiance. Their flagrant disregard of ministerial instructions and their trespass on the incumbent's freehold served as a dramatic reproach to a tired and uncooperative parish priest. Their violent intrusion into the church and their ostentatious desecration of the chancel sabotaged notions of reverence and decorum. Their action fired a salvo against ecclesiastical protocol and put religious rigidity to shame. By digging a grave at the very spot where the minister conducted holy communion, and then covering the grave with the communion table (no doubt manhandled with dirty hands), they sullied the sanctity that religious ceremonialists most cherished. They disparaged the beauty of holiness and exposed the most sacred part of the church to pollution. Laudian ceremonialists, whose influence was rising in Oxfordshire, would react with horror to this travesty of good liturgical order.[26] If the action at Holton undermined religious reverence, subverted priestly authority, challenged episcopal discipline, and allowed an unruly laity to thwart ecclesiastical sanctions, it threatened the established order in ways more profound than the protagonists may have imagined. From this perspective, the burial of Mrs Horseman was an act of revolt.

In order to provide a broader perspective for the case at Holton it may be useful to consider how other communities conducted themselves when dealing with similar problems. Ministers elsewhere did not always behave with the cautious rigidity of the reverend Bartholomew Price, nor were episcopal officials invariably as unyielding as the Chancellor to the Bishop of Oxford.[27] Neighbours were not always so insistent on burying excommunicates in consecrated ground, nor so secret in their actions if official permission was denied. No other case of this sort is so well documented as the one involving Mrs Horseman, but disputes over clandestine burials, hugger-mugger funerals, interment in the church or churchyard, and even, occasionally, exhumation of illicitly buried bodies, are sprinkled through the church court records. A surprising number come from the reign of Charles I, from a time when the Church was especially concerned about decorum, discipline, and ceremony. Reviewing these cases throws further light on lay and clerical relations, law and custom, and the negotiations and accommodations that were invariably involved in creating and resolving local difficulties. Further exploration of the church court records not only helps to contextualize the crisis at Holton, but also illuminates other strands of discourse and disagreement in early modern England.

Every problem had several possible solutions. Given goodwill and ingenuity, there was no difficulty that could not be resolved. Successful administrators knew that negotiation was preferable to confrontation, that concord was better than division, and that community was founded on accommodation. Not all churchmen, unfortunately, were blessed with this irenic spirit, nor were all laymen so readily given to compromise. Personal rigidity, religious scrupulosity, and stubborn bureaucratic legalism all had the potential to turn a problem into a crisis.[28] The records relating to the excommunicated dead expose these variable processes of problem-solving, crisis-management, and the restoration of community consensus.

The most effective resolution of the crisis was to lift the sentence of excommunication. Even for superficial Christians who made light of ecclesiastical penalties, it was profoundly unsettling to approach death not knowing where one would be interred, how one's body would be handled, or whether it would be treated with decency. Fears about salvation, anxiety about reputation, and concern about exclusion from the customary funeral processes led some people who had lived in a state of excommunication to seek timely absolution as they approached their final hour. Kinsmen and friends, who would otherwise be responsible for disposing of the body, and whose own honour was implicated in its burial, often interceded on their behalf. Ideally the sentence would be lifted before the person died, but it was also possible for the authorities to act a few days later. Several cases show associates arranging last-minute reconciliation or seeking posthumous assistance from the courts.

A case from the diocese of London reveals the anxiety an excommunicated woman felt about her impending death, and about the likely disposition of her body. Alice Chapman, a widow of Stepney, Middlesex, had been excommunicated for her contumacy in keeping a bawdy house on the outskirts of Jacobean London. By all accounts she lived a disorderly and immoral life. But on her deathbed in 1620, according to witnesses, 'she was very penitent and sorrowful for her sins, and heartily desired such as were present with her to see that she might be buried in Christian burial'. Whether or not her repentence was authentic, the effective aim of this statement was to enfold Alice Chapman back into the community of Christians. Evidently it succeeded. Similarly in 1624, we learn, when John Collins of Stepney was 'grievously sick and in danger of death', his wife and a neighbour appealed to the court that he might be 'absolved from the sentence of excommunication that is published against him'. Once again the appeal to the bishop's commissary was successful, so Collins, who had been excommunicated for failing to answer a citation, could now look forward to a normal Christian burial.[29]

The Oxford diocesan court, so intransigent when dealing with Mrs Horseman, acted favourably later in 1631 in the case of Richard Halloway of Long Combe. Halloway 'died excommunicate, and before his death was desirous to be absolved but was not able to come to Oxford for absolution and was desired to be buried in Christian burial'. This time the Chancellor granted the posthumous request, but whether in light of the modesty of Halloway's offence, or to avoid repeating the struggle at Holton, cannot be learned.[30] These were normative cases, embodying the twin spirits of Christian charity and bureaucratic flexibility; but not all such appeals were successful.

A chain of difficult choices followed when somebody died excommunicate, 'and no man able to testify of his repentence'.[31] Pressed by parishioners, the minister could respond favourably and agree to a normal burial. This would put an end to the matter unless somebody else complained. If the minister denied the burial, as Bartholomew Price denied Mrs Horseman, higher authorities might be called to intervene. The diocesan court had the power to grant a dispensation, but if it refused and all appeals were exhausted there was little to prevent the body from being disposed of like an animal. At any stage in these proceedings, however, the friends of the deceased might short-cut the process and take matters into their own hands by conducting a clandestine interment in the churchyard.[32] The secret night-time burial of excommunicates was patently illegal, but it could, in some circumstances, provide an acceptable solution to the problem. Faced with a *fait accompli* the authorities could choose to accept the matter as closed, or they could seek to discipline the offenders. In cases of bitter controversy and community division there might even be a contested exhumation. Removing a corpse, unless officially authorized, was also a matter for examination and discipline.

Some of the records reveal more hesitation than negotiation. Oxfordshire officials were not sure what to do with the body of Julia Piggot of Eiston, who was thought to be excommunicated and who was also suspected of having drowned herself in 1583. In this case the problem of excommunication paled before the serious suspicion of suicide. Some officials advised keeping Piggot unburied 'until such time as the coroner had enquired how she came by her death', but others of a more pragmatic spirit instructed the vicar to proceed with her burial forthwith, for 'if there were any cause found afterwards she should be unburied again'.[33] It was simpler (and more salubrious) to bury her promptly and disinter her later, if so ordered, than to allow the unburied body to fester.

Another Oxfordshire case from 1630, a year before the death of Mrs Horseman, shows how a corpse was disposed of when negotiations proved unsuccessful. Certain parishioners of Eynsham took it upon themselves to inter their neighbour, George Prescot, after their minister refused to give him Christian burial; but they did not take the body to the churchyard. One witness, Thomas Evans, told the court 'that he heard that the said George Prescot was excommunicate, and Mr. Lang refusing to bury him in the churchyard, he having been so long kept after he was dead that it was noisome to the house where he lay, hereupon he with others carried him out of the house and set him in a close called the park at the back-side of Eynsham Abbey, and there left the corpse'. Another witness, William Wiggington, added 'that he knew that George Prescot in his life time would not go to church, and that Mr. Lang refused to bury him, and he helped to carry him out into the park, and there left him'. Thomas Barncote helped the others to carry the body 'and made a grave and helped to bury him', while a fourth parishioner, Humphrey Cap, 'looked on'.

Prescot's offence is not specified here, but his long-time refusal to attend church points to Catholic recusancy. Lacking the social advantages and community support enjoyed by Mrs Horseman of Holton, Prescot's corpse was disposed of on wasteland when the stench of decomposition proved too much to bear. This was burial like a beast, the final indignity that most English Christians abhorred. Nobody was punished as a result of this episode, for Prescot was buried exactly as the law intended. But the incident was unusual enough to command the diocesan court's attention. The fact that Prescot was 'so long kept [unburied] after he was dead' suggests that his neighbours were not sure what to do, that some sort of argument was taking place, and that the men who disposed of the body thought that they were doing everyone a favour when negotiations failed.[34]

Burying the dead was a pastoral duty, and in problematic cases the priest could exercise his judgement and argue later with his ecclesiastical superiors. In a case from Elizabethan Yorkshire the minister of Almondbury was cited in 1598 'for burying Nicholas Littlewood, an excommunicate person, in the churchyard'. Here the minister had exercised his pastoral discretion, but his superiors called his action into question.[35] Another minister, Anthony Gorredge, the vicar of Tutbury, Staffordshire, was cited in 1636 'for burying an excommunicate person in the night'. But it is not clear in this case whether he was cited for being present, for conducting the service, or just for allowing it to happen.[36] In a Durham case in 1637 the archdeacon proceeded against the minister of Lanchester 'for suffering Eleanor Forcer, a grand recusant, to be buried in the choir'. The curate, Roger Willis, admitted that this had taken place, but said 'it was in his absence, and that Edward Willis, parish clerk, made the grave'. It rather sounds as if the parish leaders had colluded in Eleanor Forcer's privileged burial, and that confronted with official displeasure they had begun to run for cover.[37]

Daniel Letsham, the rector of St Peter's, Wallingford, Berkshire, protested that he did not know that the woman he buried in March 1634 was 'a person excommunicate and a recusant convicted'. He thought he was doing his duty. Mrs Austin, a Catholic widow, died in 'the college', the converted remains of the old collegiate church of St Nicholas within the castle precincts at Wallingford, where she was visiting Mr Michael Paine, a gentleman recusant. When Mrs Austin died Mr Paine asked the rector to bury her, and assured him that she was 'neither excommunicate nor convicted'. Paine made all the arrangements for the funeral, and met all the expenses of transportation, grave-making, and bell-ringing. Letsham told the court that he buried Mrs Austin on a Sunday between six and seven in the evening, 'according to the form prescribed in the book of common prayer, there being present a great company, viz. forty persons and upwards who did accompany the corpse to the burial'. Mrs Austin received a respectable funeral, a religious ceremony, and interment in consecrated ground. Only afterwards did the minister learn that she had been formally excommunicated, but by then it was too late. Had she been a regular parishioner he might have known her status, but in the circumstances he could only acknowledge his fault.[38]

Faced with intransigent ministers or unaccommodating authorities, lay neighbours, kinsmen, and friends were often prepared to act illicitly to bury their loved ones in consecrated ground. Catholic recusants in particular seem to have looked forward to burial in the ancient sacred enclosures. Churchyards were easily accessible and rarely monitored, allowing a determined burial party to dig a grave and to bury a corpse while nobody else was watching. Churches too could easily be entered, as parishioners discovered at Holton. Clandestine intrusions of this sort were hard to prevent, but the physical evidence was difficult to hide. Episcopal authorities usually made some effort to punish the perpetrators, but left the corpse where it lay. It was much easier to bury than to unbury someone, due to complex legal procedures governing exhumation.

A brief selection of cases will indicate the range of complaint and response in these circumstances. Robert Harwood of Banbury, Oxfordshire, was ordered to perform penance in 1610 after acknowledging 'that he is sorry for offending the law in interring his wife contrary to the law being excommunicate'. William Radhouse of Weedon Beck, Northamptonshire, dying excommunicated in January 1616, 'was buried by stealth in the night time in the churchyard . . . whereupon the church was interdicted a fortnight'. Here the court decided to punish the entire parish since they were unable to identify those responsible. Catholic recusants around Dorchester, Oxfordshire, buried several members of their families in the ancient churchyard during the 1620s. Parish officials reported these intrusions, but there was little they could do to prevent them. The Dorchester recusants were not necessarily excommunicated, and there is no evidence that the perpetrators were punished.[39]

Christopher Messenger of Great Marlow, Buckinghamshire, was cited before the archdeaconry court in 1633 'for bringing his wife into the churchyard, and burying her in the night time, she standing excommunicated'. The court ordered the churchwardens to find out who else was present when this violation occurred. Most belonged to a cluster of local recusants. Another Marlow resident, Silvester Messenger, who may have been involved in the night-time burial, himself died excommunicate and was also secretly buried. Similar charges were laid against Francis Gamon of Warborough.[40] Eleanor Bateman, a widow, 'excommunicate and convicted of recusancy', secured a private night-time burial at St Oswald's, Durham, in 1635. And friends and family members buried William Ward, another excommunicated person, in the church at Marchington, Staffordshire, in 1636.[41]

Covering the grave with earth was not necessarily the end of the matter. The body of an Essex woman was one of several to suffer interment, exhumation, and reburial as neighbours and officials argued about its proper disposition.

Elizabeth Chambers was buried in the churchyard of Pitsea, Essex, in 1632, 'in the dead time of night, she being an excommunicated person'. Upon discovering her grave the churchwardens dug it up, but then, when money changed hands, consented to her reburial. John Lane, one of the churchwardens, was cited 'for consenting to the taking up of the body of Elizabeth Chambers . . . and afterwards compounding with one Robert Cornish for 20s. for the burial of the said Elizabeth again' in the churchyard. There was no question of her having a Prayer Book ceremony, but considerable ambivalence about where her remains should lie.[42]

An horrific incident occurred in 1634 after the night-time burial of another excommunicated recusant at Thornton, in the archdeaconry of Cleveland, Yorkshire. A crowd of villagers accompanied the body of Ann Hodgson to her clandestine burial in the churchyard. (Among those cited were five labourers, a husbandman, a fuller, and a wright.) One of those present, Thomas Story, denied taking part in the burial, but claimed rather to have been sent by the rector, John Robinson, 'to take note of the business'. The minister apparently kept his distance, and certainly withheld his permission, but his representative was not content to remain passive. After the burial party had departed, Thomas Story and five other men 'took up the body of the said Ann Hodgson after it was buried and brought her back to the house, and broke her coffin wherein she was' and tipped her out on the ground. The report continues, 'that the swine tore the sheet off her and had eaten her if some neighbours had not come and laid her in the coffin again and after buried her'.[43]

It may not be coincidental that so many of these cases occurred in the reign of Charles I. In pressing its demands for discipline the Caroline Church identified many offenders while weakening its capacity for compromise, informal negotiation, and the exercise of charitable discretion. At a time when the church courts were increasingly profligate with excommunications they seemed less willing to give excommunicates or their friends the benefit of the doubt. Common to Mrs Horseman's case at Holton, George Prescot's case at Eynsham, and Ann Hodgson's case at Thornton, was the refusal by the ecclesiastical authorities to yield to popular sentiment or to exercise their wonted discretion. The high ceremonial style of churchmanship that became fashionable in the 1630s involved a fastidiousness that some members of the laity found offensive. Just as they railed off altars to prevent desecration by dogs, installed font covers to prevent contamination of the water of baptism, and required women at their churching to present themselves in veils, Laudian ceremonialists may have been especially insistent that excommunicates be separated from communicant Christians. They certainly insisted on the sanctity of God's precincts and the dignity of God's priests. In promoting the beauty of holiness the Caroline Church drew fresh attention to notions of sanctity and pollution, and may have followed stricter standards in dealing with the excommunicated dead.

Although many of these cases involve recusants, Catholics were not the only ones affected. Laudian officials were concerned to police the burial of excommunicates, no matter what the religious inclination or prior offence of the deceased. When a puritan activist died at Aldham, Essex, in the 1630s the Laudian rector, Daniel Falconer, 'refused to bury him, and sent his son to forewarn the sexton not to make his grave'. At Burrow, Lincolnshire, in 1634 the archbishop's commissioner noted 'many puritans', and when one of them died excommunicate he ordered an investigation of 'where she was buried and by whom'.[44]

Nor may it be entirely coincidental that so many of these cases involved women. Scholars may argue whether this reflects women's poverty in patronage and community support, the gendered dimensions of pastoral ministry, or another aspect of patriarchal domination. Women were no more likely than men to suffer excommunication, but the disposition of the bodies of excommunicated women appears to have been particularly controversial. Some Caroline churchmen found women's bodies embarassing whether they were alive or dead, and were unwilling to stretch the rules on their behalf.[45]

Similar problems occurred in the later seventeenth century when the restored Church of England faced challenges from dissenters and recusants. The Church still used excommunication as a sanction against offenders of all sorts, but its disciplinary effectiveness in the post-Restoration era was substantially reduced. The revised 1662 Prayer Book explicitly denied the funeral service to excommunicates but offered no guidance about where such people should be buried. As in previous generations, the matter was left to local discretion. Continuing the practice of revolutionary-era radicals, Quakers established their own burial grounds and shunned the Anglican church. But Roman Catholics still laid claim to the old churchyards and were prepared to seek burial by day or by night. In cases of difficulty parishioners sought guidance from their ministers, ministers referred problems to their bishops, and occasionally mediation was left to the archbishop. Many senior churchmen understood the virtues of compromise and the force of extenuating factors, and recognized that punctiliousness could be counter-productive. Others insisted that the bodies of excommunicates should not lie alongside their brethren, and ordered their removal to the common highway. Fewer cases of this sort came to court, and later Stuart church court records are generally more laconic; but ecclesiastical correspondence shows churchmen groping for a satisfactory combination of principle and pragmatism.

An episcopal letter of 1676 commended John Bennet, a Dorset minister, for his 'zeal, courage and prudence' in the face of troublesome papists. After two of these recusants died Bennet 'refused to bury them in the churchyard because they were . . . excommunicate persons, but their own gang came and buried them by a strong hand'. Faced with such disorder the minister sought advice from his bishop. Bishop Guy Carleton of Bristol referred the problem to Archbishop Gilbert Sheldon, explaining, 'he desires to be advised if they bury their excommunicated persons any more in the churchyard whether he may . . . cause them to be taken up and buried in the highway'.[46] We do not have the answer to this request, but the letter further testifies to the gravity of the problem and to continuing uncertainty how to deal with it.

Acting in strict accordance with the law Peter Mews, the Bishop of Bath and Wells, ordered 'the removal of the body of a papist who died excommunicate' in 1679, after the dead man's friends had secured his burial inside the church. Influential Catholics complained to the king, prompting this retort from the bishop: 'I am sure I did nothing but my duty, though the manner of doing it be represented under very ill but (which is my satisfaction) false circumstances.'[47]

Faced with a similar problem in 1675, Richard Exton, a minister in the diocese of Hereford, sought episcopal permission before proceeding with the funeral. 'Worthy Sir', he wrote to the bishop, 'there is a poor man dead in my parish that was excommunicated, and Mr. Reynolds said he cannot be buried without special licence, which if you please to grant I shall perform my office . . . The bearer will acquaint you with the deceased's condition.' A diocesan official endorsed the letter before sending it on to the registrar. 'I well know what direction we have in the Book of Common Prayer for the burial of the dead. Is a licence in this case usual? I find no canon to countenance such licence; but the bearer is in haste, instances in this case are rare; there is somewhat to be said for this man if the bearer speaks truth. I consent to what is irregular, then if you grant a licence I affix my *fiat*.'[48]

The negotiations, accommodations, permissions, and objections involved in burying the excommunicated dead are further illuminated by yet another incident from Oxfordshire in 1681. Roger Cooper (the parish clerk?) of All Saints, Oxford, was cited, 'that he did toll the bell and set open the church door and suffer [Ann King] the wife of Lawrence King of the parish of St. Martin to be brought through the church and put into the ground without any divine service.' Cooper responded that this was true, 'but doth allege that he first went to Dr. Marshall, Rector of Lincoln College and rector of the parish of All Saints, and advised with him what to do about her burial, being an excommunicated person, who gave leave, with the consent of the churchwardens, that she should be buried in the churchyard without divine service as an excommunicate person'. And Cooper displayed certificates from Dr Marshall and the church-wardens to satisfy the court. Ann King's body was transported through sacred space and buried in hallowed ground, but without the burial service from the Book of Common Prayer. Despite her excommunication, her burial was duly recorded in the parish register on 11 June 1681.[49]

Finally, mixing toleration, evangelism, and discipline, Bishop Edward Jones of St Asaph wrote to Archbishop William Sancroft in February 1683 about occa-sional practical modifications to the 'severity that we use toward all persons that die under excommunication. It was ordered at the last convocation in this diocese that whosoever dies excommunicate shall want burial in the church or churchyard, unless the bishop order the contrary in any particular case. This indeed is a punishment to the relations, and therefore where the relations are good conformable people I have suffered them to bring their dead in the churchyard (but by no means in the church) and that by night, without prayer or other solemnity. Yesterday some papists came to me for leave to bury one of their dead that died under excommunication. I endeavoured by that handle to bring them to church but after long discourse with them found them obstinate, and therefore refused them the use of holy ground for their dead.'[50] The bishop could exercise a discretionary power, even for excommunicated papists, so long as there was co-operation and goodwill. By seeking guidance, affixing fiats, giving leave, and consenting to what was irregular, these late Stuart prelates sought practical modifications to the law, of the kind that her neighbours sought for Mrs Horseman. By this time, however, the churchyard was no longer the only desired resting place, and dissenting groups who were subject to excommunication increasingly operated burial grounds of their own. Burying the excommunicated dead still posed problems for the Church and for the community, and their effective resolution still depended more on goodwill than on law.

These cases demonstrate, once again, that the 'final hour' of death was by no means the end of the story. A person's social presence continued *post mortem* through such processes as watching, carrying, burying, and memorializing. Whether privileged to be buried inside the church, or interred as was most common in the churchyard, villagers continued together as neighbours in the enduring community of the living and the dead. The collective burying ground of the churchyard was, as contemporaries sometimes described it, the 'dormi-tory of Christians' whence they would awake in joyful company on the day of resurrection. Local sentiment held that no neighbour should be denied this prospect because of the inconvenience or ill-fortune of excommunication. Our records make no mention of hovering shades, anxiety about pollution, or the baneful influence of the unburied, though ideas of this sort formed part of the ferment of popular culture. Instead, we see a determination to do what was best, by means official or unofficial, to resolve controversial problems, and to achieve community cohesion. The sentiments voiced in Shotover wood in 1631 may serve as a general epitaph, 'God's blessing on them that buried the dead, it is fit the dead should be buried.'

Dramatis Personae

Mrs Elizabeth Horseman of Wheatley, widow, deceased
Mary Slyman, servant to Mrs Horseman
widow Ives of Wheatley, watched at Mrs Horseman's deathbed
Edward Powell of Forest Hill, gent.
Dr Hugh Barker, Chancellor to Bishop of Oxford
Bartholemew Price, rector of Holton
Anne Price, rector's wife
Charles Wise, parish clerk of Holton
Thomas Day, labourer, bell-ringer
Edward Day, servant to Edward Powell, bell-ringer
John Robins, bell-ringer
John Stacy, bell-ringer
Richard Winstow, labourer
Richard Hoskins
John Bolton
Mrs Brown
George Ball
John Turner, labourer
Eleanor Turner, John's wife
Thomas George's wife

MOCKING THE CLERGY: WARS OF WORDS IN PARISH AND PULPIT

'Parson thou art an ass . . . I never saw such an ass as thou art,' proclaimed a Yorkshire yeoman to his parish priest in the late 1590s. Lincolnshire ecclesiastical authorities were scandalized a few years later when a layman reviled his vicar as a 'scurvy rascal knave'. A Buckinghamshire man in the 1630s dismissed his minister as 'tinkerly parson', while another in Northamptonshire addressed his minister as 'jackanapes'. A Norfolk parishioner railed at his rector in 1636 as 'a wide-mouthed rascal', while a Yorkshireman was cited in the same year 'for comparing his minister to a pedlar and his ministerial function to pedlars' wares'. Elaborating on this vocabulary a Dorset tailor in 1640 addressed his rector as 'a base knave, a dangerous knave, a base rogue, a dangerous rogue', while a Suffolk innkeeper called a clergyman 'knave, fool, jacksauce', before swinging at his head with a cudgel.[1]

In these and hundreds of similar confrontations, lay parishioners used the language of insult against ordained ministers, and were called to answer for their offence before the ecclesiastical authorities. Their remarks disparaged and demeaned the ministry, violated the norms of neighbourliness, and undercut the hierarchical, deferential, and reverential conventions on which English religious culture was based. Their words transgressed against decency, charity, and linguistic restraint, and bruised the honour of a sensitive professional caste. Whether they were also expressions of anticlericalism, rather than soured personal dealings or strained community relationships, is a question of some importance. Historians are currently inclined to see anticlericalism as a significant and robust phenomenon, and to treat it more as a consequence than a cause of the Reformation in England; but the altercations documented here point to frustration with particular clerics rather than generalized hostility to the clerical estate.[2] The collisions and exchanges were *ad hominem* rather than *ad clerum*, though especially fraught for being directed at men of the cloth.

This chapter probes more deeply into episodes of verbal confrontation. It sets ministerial precepts about priestly dignity against legal testimony, mostly in the ecclesiastical courts, in order to calibrate some of the tension between ministers and parishioners. It studies the vocabulary of derision, the choice of

insulting words and the circumstances in they were hurled, in order to understand the nature of abuse the courts described as railing, reviling, irreverent,
slanderous, or blasphemous. It also examines the obverse of this relationship,
ministerial contempt for the laity, and in particular the intemperate language
some preachers used against parishioners they considered to be obstructive,
rude, or reprobate.

The larger historical framework here, and throughout this book, is the
impact and progress of the Reformation and the struggle for social discipline in
the decades preceding the English civil wars. By paying attention to insult and
mockery we may throw fresh light on the relationship between the elite and the
popular, the godly and the multitude, and the occupants of the pulpit and the
pew. Though any neighbour could berate another, and secular officials like
constables and churchwardens could also be targets for abuse, the exchange of
insults amongst the laity lacked the religious edge—the frisson of blasphemy
and sacrilege—involved when a parishioner called his parson an ass.[3] These
verbal collisions were especially damaging in times of religious contest, when
ministers were seeking to achieve moral, liturgical, or disciplinary reforms.
Mockery of the clergy was especially disturbing because it undercut the spiritual authority of God's ministers on earth.

The relationship of clergy and laity in post-Reformation England was complicated by social, cultural, religious, and financial transactions, as well as by
problems of personality and style. For lay men and women there was no escaping the rhythms of the Prayer Book or the barrage of catechism and sermons.
Church attendance was mandatory, and adults could be sanctioned for irregularly coming to worship. The church was indispensable in managing and
sacralizing rites of passage—from the baptism of babies and the churching of
newly delivered mothers to the solemnization of matrimony and the burial of
the dead. Weekly and seasonal routines and the rituals of the life-cycle all came
within ecclesiastical cognizance, as did questions relating to sexual morality,
community relations, and probate. Furthermore, everyone had clerical neighbours. All but a few of England's nine-and-a half thousand parishes had resident ministers—in the rectory, parsonage, or vicarage—whose lives intersected
with those of their parishioners. Tithe-fat parsons could be sources of envy
while impoverished curates generated contempt, but the entire clerical order
laid claim to a dignity that set them apart. Gentle householders may have
looked down on their minister as a social subordinate, while humbler parishioners looked up to him as a member of the elite, but all could measure their
Christian duty in the outlay of rates and assessments, fees and tithes. Deeply
rooted structural tensions associated with education, income, and class were

compounded by passing differences over religious solemnity, devotion, and belief.

Not surprisingly, lay–clerical relations were often brittle and uncomfortable. Both sides were quick to find fault. For university-trained scholars,[4] preferment to a rural parish could seem like isolation in one of the dark corners of the land. For parishioners at home in their local community, their minister could appear as an overweening or incomprehensible outsider. In a world of tradesmen, artisans, and agriculturists, academic clerics (no matter what their taste in theology) were inevitably alien. They knew themselves, as did George Herbert in Caroline Wiltshire, 'to be both suspected and envied'.[5] Intellectually, socially, culturally, and often geographically, they did not belong.

Herbert was but one of many ministers to remark on the problem of pastoral communication, 'especially with country people, which are thick and heavy, and hard to raise to a point of zeal and fervency'. His parish of Fugglestone with Bemerton was a far cry from the intellectual refinements of Cambridge or the spiritual intensity of Little Gidding.[6] Even superhuman saints like Richard Greenham at Dry Drayton or Richard Baxter at Kidderminster spoke of the 'untractableness and unteachableness' of many of the people, and experienced their dealings with parishioners as battles of slings and arrows.[7] 'It is an heap of miseries and a very representation of hell to be continually vexed and exceedingly grieved with their wicked conversation', complained the Jacobean minister William Attersoll of his 'lewd' and abusive parishioners at Isfield, Sussex. John Thaxter's parishioners at Bridgham, Norfolk, were not deliberately offensive, but 'being wholly bent to the toil of manual affairs and the tilth of the ground', he complained, they were unreceptive to all catechism.[8] William Harrison's hearers at Huyton, Lancashire, were deaf to his sermons, preferring jests and fables to the solemn word of God.[9] 'I am seated in a barren place,' complained Ralph Cudworth from deepest Somerset.[10] What were the prospects for a minister in another 'dark corner' of the land like Cumberland or Westmorland, where, as one put it in the reign of Charles I, 'he sees his hopes shall be terminated and himself nailed fast'?[11]

Cultural, personal, and professional antagonisms often estranged ministers from their flock. Financial demands and exigencies kept them at odds. Clerical diaries, treatises, and correspondence of this period repeatedly reflect on the struggle against ignorance and irreligion, boorishness and intransigence, while church court records reveal some of the hostility and derision with which incumbents had to cope. Godly reformers and strict ceremonialists were equally likely to collide with parish intransigence, for neither puritans nor Laudians were exempt from being called an ass or a knave.

The clergy enjoyed a privileged place in the post-Reformation community, and expected due deference to their office and function. Despite early Protestant notions of 'the priesthood of all believers', the established Church of England maintained a strict distinction between clergy and laity. Ordination to the priesthood conferred the right to administer the sacraments and other services, while induction to a vicarage or rectory carried social as well as financial privileges. But attempts by social historians to locate the clergy in the socioeconomic spectrum from gentlemen to peasants often miss the point that the crucial differential was their calling and their relationship to God. The clergy were spiritual leaders, distinguished from ordinary mankind. This was a view that could unite radical presbyterians and Anglican sacerdotalists against the multitude to whom they ministered. A review of clerical perceptions of their role, and of their pastoral-sacramental relationship to the laity, may help to explain why ministers found mockery so unsettling and so offensive.

Late Elizabethan ministers took an elevated view of clerical dignity, which was taken to new heights of sacerdotal conceit by some of their seventeenth-century successors. Their high sense of spiritual and professional superiority may explain the frustration most clergymen felt when laymen subjected them to scorn. To Edward Dering, for example, 'The true minister is the eye of the body, the workman of the harvest, the messenger that calleth unto the marriage, the prophet that telleth the will of the Lord, the wiseman to discern between good and evil, the scribe that doth expound the law, the servant that occupieth his master's talents unto gain, the witness that beareth testimony of Christ to all people, the dispensers of the mysteries of God.'[12]

It became a commonplace of early Stuart preaching that the clergy were God's ambassadors, his husbandmen and builders, the Lord's soldiers and captains. 'The ministers are builders of the Lord's house, soldiers in the Lord's camp, husbandmen in the Lord's fields, watchmen in the Lord's city, and shepherds over the Lord's flock,' claimed the Sussex minister William Attersoll in 1612. The clergy were 'the salt of the earth, ordained of God to season men', asserted the Jacobean preacher George Downame, so that 'not to reverence the ministry is to dishonour God'.[13] Caroline priests made similar claims, like William Hardwick of Reigate, Surrey, who preached in 1638 that 'our God will have us reputed as his ambassadors, and as shining stars, yea, as angels'.[14] Small wonder that bold laymen thought to bring them down a peg or two!

Clerical authors devoted a considerable amount of time to discussing 'the smitings of the tongue', particularly when they themselves were its victims. In a work that was often reprinted between 1593 and 1634, the Cambridge theologian William Perkins lamented 'the abuse of the tongue among all sorts and degrees of men everywhere', in particular the 'swearing, blaspheming, chiding, quarreling, contending, jesting, mocking, flattering, lying, dissembling, vain and idle talking' that poisoned relations between Christians. Evil speech was explicable, he thought, because 'the heart of man by nature is a bottomless gulf of iniquity'. It had to be answered by loving correction and godly reproof.[15] 'Scoffing speeches, railing voices, and slanderous words' were especially serious, according to the Leicestershire minister Anthony Anderson, because they undermined 'the true church of God now in England', and eased the path for popery and superstition. Christ and his father were despised and the work of antichrist facilitated, he said, when 'the holy ministry is holden in contempt'.[16]

Calvinist theology helped many ministers to understand that reprobates were all around them. But one did not have to endorse the harsher nuances of predestination to believe that bawdiness, irreverence, and incivility divided the world between saints and sinners. Alehouse culture and common village life were worlds apart from the parson's study, notwithstanding the mitigating effect of popular religious ballads and the temptation some ministers felt to display good fellowship by sitting at the ale bench.[17]

Revilement and abuse were part of the parson's lot, a standard occupational hazard. 'Scoffers, scorners, mockers, and suchlike monsters' were to be found in every parish, wrote Charles Gibbon, with an eye on the inhabitants of Bury St Edmunds. 'We shall find our function to be full of labour and sweating . . . evil entreating and hard entertainments,' wrote the minister of Isfield, Sussex, who had to put up with 'reviling taunts' and 'railing and rotten speeches' while attempting to exercise his calling.[18]

'Dunghill scurrilities, quaffing compliments, ridiculous jeerings, obscene ribaldries [and] irreligious tongue-smitings' (the complaint is Joseph Bentham's) were only to be expected, especially in the polarized religious culture of early modern England. George Herbert remarked on 'the general ignominy which is cast on the [clerical] profession', but made it a badge of pride to share 'the portion of God his master and of God's saints his brethren' in suffering.[19] 'The vile railings and contradictions of Satan's revellers and popish insolency' had to be met with patience, 'generous magnanimity, and brave contempt', advised the Northamptonshire minister Robert Bolton. Against 'the language of hell, which consisteth in oaths, lying, slandering, in obscenities, railings, contemptuous insolencies against the ministry and ways of God', was to be set the judicious exercise of 'Christian reproof'.[20] But too often, as many a minister knew to his cost, reprimand of a parishioner produced another tongue lashing in return.

Assailed by a sea of profanity, harrassed and offended clergy consoled themselves by claiming to be on the side of the angels. Their enemies, by contrast, could be consigned to the darkness of reprobation or be bestialized as 'swinish wretches' and 'currish dogs'.[21] The experience of mockery confirmed anxious ministers in their own sense of righteousness and encouraged them to identify with the torments of the prophets, and even with the suffering Christ.[22] Revilement helped bond the puritan godly as a moral elite, gave Laudians a sense of common suffering in God's cause, and stiffened the ministerial sense of membership in a dedicated professional caste. Though weekly worship was supposed to unite the parish as a Christian community, hostile interactions left many a minister and layman glowering at each other across a personal and cultural divide.

Embattled clergymen could turn to their books and identify with Old Testament prophets. They could stand with Nehemiah against 'spiting Sanballat and menacing Tobiah', and take comfort in the fall awaiting mockers and scorners.[23] William Perkins cited various judgements of God against men's evil tongues. Dod and Cleaver's popular *Godly Forme of Houshold Government* repeated the warning that 'the two and forty children that mocked Elisha the prophet, saying come up thou bald head, were rent in pieces with bears', as if the same might happen to their own irreverent neighbours. Joseph Bentham's *Societie of the Saints* recalled the fate of the 'mocking Ishmaels, railing Rabshakehs, reviling Shimeis, scoffing children, backbiting dogs [and] slandering Tertullus', who 'escaped not the sharp and smiting punishments of the Lord'.[24] Providential anecdotes showed that God's anger was not only spent in the biblical past. He was still 'a visiting God' who vented his anger on his enemies. Thomas Beard's *Theatre of God's Judgements*, for example, included the story of John Apowel, 'sometimes a serving man', who was driven to the devil after 'mocking and jesting at the word of God'. Beard also reported the case of the gardener John Vintner of Godmanchester, 'one that would profanely . . . scoff at religion and abuse good men', who in July 1628 'fell from the top of a pear tree to the ground and brake his neck, and so died'.[25] These were things to think about while turning the other cheek.

Though ecclesiastical law as well as priestly rhetoric demanded reverence to the clergy,[26] leading churchmen recognized that their estate was perennially vulnerable to mockery and abuse. Jacobean bishops inquired at their visitations whether any parishioners had 'spoken slanderous and reproachful words' against their ministers, or used them 'unreverently' with 'violent hands' or 'contemptuous speech', as if such outrages were not uncommon. Archbishop Abbot's articles for the diocese of Gloucester in 1612 were typical in inquiring of the churchwardens, 'have any in your parish quarrelled or stricken or used any violence to your minister . . . or demeaned him disorderly in the church, by filthy or profane talk, or any other lewd or immodest behaviour? Or have disturbed the minister in time of divine service or sermon, or have libelled or

spoken slanderous words against your minister, to the scandal of his vocation?'[27] All such indignities were supposed to be punished if they could not be
endured.

In the early part of Elizabeth's reign, when the Church of England was barely
established, attacks on the clergy could be triggered by their commitment to
reform or their adherence to tradition, as well as perennial problems of payments and personality. New priests and new practices rubbed many traditionalists the wrong way, while married ministers were especially easy targets for
derision. By the end of the sixteenth century, when English Protestantism was
more firmly entrenched, laymen were more likely to berate ministers for their
slackness than for their zeal, though zeal too was often socially disruptive. Strict
Calvinist reformers clashed with parishioners they considered unregenerate,
ceremonialist innovators sparked nervous reactions amongst the laity, while
adherents of good fellowship picked quarrels with their more godly neighbours. Improving standards of clerical education and the beginnings of recovery in the economic fortunes of the clerical estate did little to ease social
difficulties.[28] The problem was exacerbated when high churchmen insisted that
their priesthood set them above and apart from the laity, on opposite sides of
the rail.

Writings by clergymen suggest that they often endured mockery and contempt,
but their printed works give few indications of what was actually said. The following discussion examines fragments from manuscript court records that
reproduce some of the words actually spoken in lay–clerical altercations. Allegations, answers, and depositions reveal something of the circumstances of
the altercation in which the offending words were uttered. The examples will
necessarily be selective, but they lead to an instructive lexicon of insult and a
profile of acrimonious interactions. Though the processes of ecclesiastical law
and the mediation of scribal recording somewhat rob them of immediacy and
inflection, the words and phrases may none the less be taken as an echo of
heated speech and a crude reflection of popular attitudes and beliefs.

The church court evidence makes clear that the laity commanded an escalat-
ing vocabulary of abuse—from the mildly offensive to the unrepeatable—that
could be unloaded on clergymen as well as anyone else. It exposes a variety of
situations and a hierarchy of places in which utterance of these words was especially sensitive or fraught, from the church itself to the churchyard to the public
highway. And it shows how insults directed at ministers could extend by trans-
ference to parish officers and to clergymen's wives. These were not 'instance'
cases, pursued by one aggrieved party against another over verbal defamation
or sexual slander, of the kind well known to social historians. Nor were they

gender-charged complaints, except to the extent that anyone thought the clergy 'womanish'.[29] Rather they were serious proceedings by the 'office' of the ordinary (usually the bishop), or even the High Commission, designed to deal with offences against the Church. They came to court not just because the words were personally defamatory or slanderous, but because they impugned ecclesiastical authority. The purpose of the proceedings was didactic as much as punitive, designed to police the limits of lay–clerical discourse, to restrain loose tongues, and to re-establish harmonious parochial relations. Behind these exchanges often lay a history of dispute and confrontation over money or religious practices, fees and tithes or liturgical conformity, as well as personality, temper, and drink. Occasionally, the boot was on the other foot, as a minister gave as good as he got, or even took the initiative in pouring abuse on his parishioners.[30]

Some early Elizabethan cases from the diocese of Canterbury provide a convenient place to begin. In the parish of Wareham, Kent, in 1561 William Black called his minister a 'knave'. This was a potent term of abuse imputing dishonesty, lack of principle, baseness, trickery, and deceit. After evening prayer one Sunday before Michaelmas, it was alleged, Black 'fell out with the parson for speaking against great ruffs and breeches, [and] said the parson ought to speak only of parish matters and not of the Jews or the Pope; and though advised by the parson and Thomas Harlackenden [*one of the churchwardens?*] to revoke his words, refused to do so.' Then on Michaelmas Day Black 'went out of church during reading of the Epistle, saying he could not abide the doctrine. He thought his heart would have burst.' This was evidently a clash between tradition and reform as well as between layman and cleric, triggered by a sermon on apparel. The parishioner seems to have taken the preacher's call for reform as an attack against him personally. William Black's social standing is not certain, nor do we know his taste in clothing, but his willingness to dispute with the minister and his sensitivity to criticism of fashion bespeaks a member of the gentry. His choice of the word 'knave', however, points to a loose tongue and a choleric temper as well as an offensive view of lay–clerical relations. The court ordered Black to apologize, and to re-establish himself in charity with his neighbours, but he died before he could complete his purgation.[31]

In the same year another Kentish parishioner, George Brysto of Stocksbury, misbehaved in church and reviled his minister with words that were irreverent, insulting, and threatening. He too called his minister 'knave'. The court heard that 'the Sunday before the feast of St Michael last past . . . being in the middle part of church, [Brysto] did play with a dog when the curate was in the pulpit reading of the paraphrases of the gospel, and the curate rebuked him of it. And upon Michaelmas Day after the said George did follow the curate out of the church gate and reviled him and called him knave above ten or twelve times . . . and afterwards did say afore his master that he would thrust his dagger through both the curate's cheeks.' This was a confrontation of a different sort, but it produced the same electric language. George Brysto, apparently, was a hot-tempered servant who carried a weapon. Like many an early-modern church-goer he thought nothing amiss with taking his dog to service, found the dog more interesting than the Gospels, and was upset to be singled out for correction in the face of the congregation. The curate, who remains anonymous, performed his duty in reading the word and in guiding his flock, in correcting a lax parishioner and in protecting the church from canine pollution. Though the conclusion of the case is unknown, the altercation can best be understood in terms of the unending friction between reformist ministry and secular youth.[32]

A report from the West Country in the mid-1580s cited extreme instances of what ministers had to endure from their parishioners. 'In all the western circuit of Cornwall,' it alleged, 'the ministers are so contemned, threatened, reviled, abused, that in many places they cannot go out of their doors.'[33] Several had been manhandled or assaulted, suffering bodily harm as well as verbal abuse. Robert Edbrooke, the curate of St Mawgan, 'was not only sundry times reviled' by parishioners who called him 'knave priest, rascal priest, polled priest', but also, 'as he was riding in the common highway' was 'struck . . . with a cudgel, down from his horse' and then beaten 'with many blows'. The rector of St Pinnock was likewise 'miserably beaten about the face', while the vicar of Phillack was struck on his 'head, face, body, arms and legs' and had to retire to his bed. William Drake, 'a learned preacher and vicar of [St] Just, walking in his own ground, had a naked dagger cast at him'. Nor was he the only Cornish priest to face 'the point of [a parishioner's] dagger'. Several preachers were interrupted in their sermons or dragged out of church, it was said, 'in great despite and contempt of the ministry'.

Most of the victims were described as 'learned preachers' or 'ministers of the word of God'. The code words suggest that they belonged to a minority of forward Protestants in a backward region, and the document was drafted on their behalf. With its Celtic heritage and proliferation of local saints, Cornwall possessed a unique religious culture, and western Cornwall, in particular, was long resistant to the godly reformation. Robert Edbrooke and his colleagues may have faced an especially unruly traditionalism, but it is by no means clear that they were hated more for their attempts at reform than for their collection of tithes. Several 'learned preachers' in Cornwall were set upon when 'they demanded their just and lawful tithe'. One of them, Ralph Kett, 'a godly preacher', had his sermons interrupted and 'his tithe corn taken from him by force'. Ministers suffered revilement for a variety of reasons—their personalities,

their churchmanship, their financial exactions, or their use of English—and
hostile parishioners might not tell which they hated most.[34]

Anthony Anderson, rector of Medbourne, Leicestershire, whose sensitivity
to revilement we have already noted, complained to the Bishop of Lincoln
in 1582 that John Pain, one of his parishioners, had abused him and attacked
him over the collection of tithes. The rector and the Pain family were already
engaged in protracted litigation over unpaid tithes of fleeces and sheep.[35]
Matters came to a head one September Thursday morning around harvest
time, when the reverend Anderson on horseback met John Pain 'riding in his
cart to fields'. Pain protested that his tithe was wrongly assessed and last year
'ignorantly' taken, which Anderson denied. Then the farmer lost his temper
and began to lash out with words. 'Was I a preacher?' Pain asked of Anderson,
'no I was a palterer, and my living was but in paltry, and I had no mind to mend
yet.'

To gauge the weight of this insult, we need to remember that a palterer
was a trifler, a huckster, a haggler, an untrustworthy person who played fast
and loose; paltry was worthless rubbish; so 'paltry' and 'palterer' were sharply
degrading words to apply to an ecclesiastical freeholder, the minister before
whom on other occasions the parishioner knelt to take the sacrament. Anderson tried to calm Pain down, saying, 'John, thou dost use thyself to me like a
boy, and not like a man,' but this patronizing tone, with its challenge to Pain's
manhood and its condescending use of his Christian name, had just the opposite effect. Overcome with rage, Pain moved from verbal to physical violence
and threatened to pull the minister from his horse. Anderson testified that he
appealed to Pain's own sense of honour and reputation. 'Thou wilt not strike
me having no weapon about me, said I, surely lest thou should be thought to
play the boy.' But Pain was not stayed, and the altercation moved from bad
blood to bloodletting, from animosity to violent assault.

It might be claimed that the rector was overbearing and insensitive, but there
is no excusing Pain's offensive words and actions. In Anderson's account, the
only version available, the minister presents himself as the restrained upholder
of clerical dignity and law, and his parishioner as the epitome of unguarded
temper. According to Anderson, 'he laid at me, railing upon me, and I having
nothing about me but a little willow stick to beat my horse was fain to bear off
his blows with my right arm, striving to get from him; but he did grievously
break my head, and worse bruise it, so as it is as soft as a sponge, and the blood
ran plentifully about my ears; and indeed, if rescue had not come, I think verily
he had purposed to have slain me.'

A few years later Anderson moved to become rector of Stepney, Middlesex,
and London diocesan records show him on no better terms with some of his

new parishioners. Anderson had, by this time, published several sermons and had been invited to preach in the Chapel Royal. Though evidently a divine of some distinction, he was no more able to command due pastoral respect. Early in 1590 the Bishop of London's Commissary heard that John Pye, a moneyer, 'did abuse Mr. Anderson, the pastor of Stepney, with opprobrious terms, and gave him the lie, and bade turd in his teeth, contrary to his duty to a man of his place so well deserving'.[36] 'Giving the lie', or calling the rector a liar, was deeply offensive to a minister of God's truth. Bidding 'a turd in his teeth' was a stinging scatological insult, the equivalent today of saying 'eat shit'.[37] In the course of the inquiry the churchwardens alleged that Pye had abused Anderson, in the minister's own house, 'in evil words', while Pye, on his part, denied the charge, except to acknowledge a slip of the tongue. According to Pye, it was the clergyman who used the words, 'thou lyest, thou varlet', to which Pye responded 'to the said Mr. Anderson, being sore provoked by him, why then thou lyest, and that was the worst that was said unto the said Mr. Anderson'.

'Varlet', like 'liar' and 'palterer', was a serious term of abuse whether used by layman or minister. It was a demeaning word, implying servile or menial status, and also carried connotations of rascally or knavish behaviour. Significantly, the defendant denied saying it, and his accuser did not press it. In this case, though the court was concerned to uphold clerical dignity, it seemed more interested in reconciliation than in punishment, and left Pye to the judgement of his employer, the Warden of the Mint.

Anthony Anderson was involved in another case of 'railing speeches' a short while later when he supervised the public penance of Thomas Nettleton of Ratcliffe, a hamlet within Stepney. Nettleton's original offence was keeping his shop open on the sabbath, but his mouth and his temper brought him into deeper trouble when he cursed the churchwardens who brought the charge against him. In his statement to the court Nettleton denied calling one of the parish officers a knave, but 'being moved by one Morris Ward, the churchwarden, with bad and threatening words, did answer him again with froward and unseemly words which he doth not now remember'. In this case Nettleton's lapse of memory did him more good than his earlier loss of decorum, and his acknowledgement of negligence and fault restored him to public harmony with the parish.[38]

A few more cases from the late Elizabethan courts add to this pattern of tongue-smiting. Zachary Some, we learn, 'uncharitably abused' the parson of Sandon, Essex, in 1592, calling him 'a prattling fool, for preaching against drunkenness'. 'Prattling' was the unshaped speech of babies, not of ministers, while 'prating', a cognate term, meant idle and boastful chatter. A 'fool', in early modern discourse meant someone clownish, simple, or light-minded. The words came together in the biblical proverb, 'a prating fool shall fall'.[39] Zachary Some went on to avow that 'he could if he had authority within a fortnight space make as good a sermon' as the minister, and he further distinguished himself 'by throwing pessocks [i.e. hassocks, kneeling cushions] at the head of the sexton and thereby brake his head'. Though not mentioned explicitly in the record, the use of these cushions to attack a parish officer implies strong contempt for the controversial practice of kneeling in church.[40] Behind Some's antics lay a view of churchmanship and clerical dignity very different from that of the incumbent priest.

John Whippe of Slaidburne, Yorkshire, likewise unnerved the reverend Thomas Banks in the mid-1590s by making 'great outcries, hallooings and shoutings' every time he met the minister in public. His laughter and mockery seemed designed 'to disgrace and bring into contempt the said Thomas Banks'. On one occasion Whippe addressed him, 'Thou art an ass, parson . . . I never saw such an ass as thou art,' which he repeated 'at least six or seven times over'. An 'ass' was notoriously clumsy, ignorant, stupid, and absurd, as well as a phoneme for 'arse', which is evidently what Whippe thought of his parish priest. He concluded, in a remarkable topsy-turvy version of the reformation of manners, 'I am ordained to plague thee, parson. Thou art learned, indeed, I confess. But thou wanteth worldly wit and discretion.' Using mockery, effrontery, and insult, the parishioner set out to humiliate, discredit, and discipline the priest.

Whippe, it seems, was a minor landowner and sheep-farmer, probably a superior yeoman, who rode a horse and enjoyed the leisure of hunting with hawks and greyhounds. The animosity between Whippe and Banks was fuelled by disputes about the tithe of sheep, cutting of wood, and about the ownership and treatment of hunting dogs. But it exploded over matters of religious decorum. The reverend Banks considered Whippe 'long time a slanderer and depraver of the minister of God's holy word', who in ten years residence in Slaidburne 'never received communion but once, and then most unreverently, departing out of the chancel with his hat upon his head'. Whippe, for his part, complained that the parson was neglectful of his cure, was often absent and rarely preached.[41] When Banks preached a pastoral sermon against 'opprobrious speeches and . . . all disdainful gesture and action', particularly directed at a parishioner, it only stimulated Whippe's campaign of ridicule and derision, and he persuaded other parishioners to join in the 'sport'. The discord climaxed in an incident of jostling on horseback on the road from York to Tadcaster, when Banks addressed Whippe as 'base fellow' and Whippe, with more 'evil and scornful words', repeated that the parson was an ass and threatened to pull him from his horse. The testimony of witnesses and participants is remarkably full at this juncture, allowing a partial reconstruction of their dramatic public interaction.

Banks and his servant and Whippe and his companions, all on horseback, met on the road from York to Tadcaster in October 1596. Predictably, there was hallooing and jeering on the one side, dignified discomfort on the other. According to Banks, the layman 'began to quarrel and brawl with him, and to rail and revile him', repeating his assertion that the parson was 'an ass . . . a bad man . . . an ass in man's shape'. Whippe, for his part, claimed that he merely offered a neighbourly greeting, 'well overtaken, parson', to which the minister responded, 'what dost thou here, thou base fellow? Get thee out of my sight.' Harsh words led to unwise actions, and it appears that Banks's servant interfered with Whippe's passage and deprived him of his cloak, while Whippe attempted to push past the minister 'and offered to lay violent hands upon him and to pull him off from his horse'.

The exchange was essentially trivial, but highly revealing of local social dynamics. A secular lawyer might see defamation, assault, and affray, but the Court of High Commission, a prerogative court for ecclesiastical affairs, was primarily concerned with Whippe's demeanour towards a man of the cloth. Like the preachers who spoke of clerical honour, the judges in High Commission would argue that contempt for a minister was contempt for the ministry, and tantamount to contempt for the crown, for Christ, and his Church.[42]

Whippe's behaviour was boldly insulting, but it did not necessarily indicate anticlericalism. Like other verbal assaults against ministers, it was personal and specific, more reproof of the man than rejection of his calling. Indeed, there are hints that Whippe expected more from his minister in terms of good preaching and good fellowship, and that his campaign of ridicule was directed at the shortcomings of the incumbent. Whippe might argue that he was as good a man as his minister, despite their difference in status, because he was a leader among farmers, sportsmen, and drinkers while the minister 'lacked worldly wit and discretion'. A different minister with a different manner might have been able to command his respect. There is nothing in the evidence to suggest that Whippe was a recusant, although he may well have been a traditionalist or church-papist. He may even have been a progressive Protestant, who was absent from his parish communion because he went gadding to more godly ministers. More likely he was observant but indifferent, a farmer who went to church and grumbled about his tithe, but whose true religion was greyhounds and sheep.

A few years later John Barker of Helpringham, Lincolnshire, another ill-disposed parishioner, heaped verbal assault on John Foster, the vicar of Wigtoft, in a confrontation on St James's Day, 1602 in the churchyard at Helpringham. Barker, it was charged, addressed the reverend Foster 'in angry, brawling, quarreling and chiding manner', calling him 'a knave, a rascal knave, a scurvy rascal knave', in ever-compounding dishonour. 'And being forewarned by some that stood by, did notwithstanding in despiteful manner reiterate the same . . . with many other railing speeches to the discredit of the said John Foster.' Whether Barker was drunk, on this high summer saint's day, whether there were underlying causes for his anger, or whether Foster had said something in church to upset his religious sensibilities, cannot, at this stage, be determined. Appearing before the bishop's court, Barker admitted that 'being in choler and anger by reason of some speeches that were then and there spoken to him, he did utter divers unreverent speeches to Mr. Foster, calling him knave'. Barker sought to represent his anger as an external mitigating force that made him beside himself, or outside himself, and therefore not fully responsible, but he would not go so far as to acknowledge his use of the contemptuous adjectives scurvy and rascal.[43] 'Scurvy' meant shabby, scabby, worthless, and contemptible, a sorry word to apply to a minister. A 'rascal' was a member of the mob or rabble, the meanest and least trustworthy member of society. No man of God could allow these words to attach to him, or to endure being called a knave.

Under Archbishop Laud's regime in the 1630s, with its heightened concern for sacerdotal and ceremonial reverence, mockery against the clergy acquired extra religious and political connotations. There were few new words of abuse, but ministers became quicker to take offence and bishops more determined to seek discipline. Caroline ministers seem to have been especially sensitive to laughter that detracted from the beauty of holiness and undermined the dignity of the clergy. Church court records of the 1630s contain dozens of charges against parishioners for laughing in church as well as for badmouthing their ministers.[44] But laughter, though disconcerting, could be the product of a merry brain or wandering attention and did not necessarily have to be construed as mocking, derisory, or hostile.

Thomas Massingberd of Simpson, Buckinghamshire, for example, was cited in 1635 'for laughing in the church upon a sabbath day in sermon time'. This was unnerving to the priest, and a patent assault on the dignity of God's worship. Massingberd sought to minimize the gravity of his offence, and confessed to the court 'that he did laugh in the church in sermon time, but not at the minister, nor by reason of any thing that he preached, and is sorry that he gave offence thereby'.[45] We do not know what the court decided. Mr Dooley, the minister of Elford, Staffordshire, had similar problems with Edward Denston, and cited him in 1639 'for laughing and scoffing in the church in prayer time'. Hauled before the episcopal court, Denston acknowledged 'that he did smile at time of catechising, but not at anything Mr. Dooley said'.[46] Without further evidence it is impossible to tell whether we are dealing with an exceptionally sensitive minister or a frivolous and irresponsible parishioner. But clearly, as Keith Thomas has shown, laughter, like ridicule, struck a raw cultural nerve.[47]

The churchwardens of Anstie, Leicestershire, presented John Middleton before Archbishop Laud's visitation in 1634 'for his great and gross abusing our painful, orderly and peaceable minister, in uncivil, unbeseeming and scandalous speeches, to the disparagement of the ministry'. Appearing in court, Middleton acknowledged that 'some angry words passed between him and Mr. Pole, but what words he knoweth not'. Prompted by the churchwardens that it was 'publicly reported that John Middleton called Mr. Pole rascal', Middleton admitted 'that he did give some ill terms' but would not repeat them. That the minister was not so 'peaceable' as is here depicted is suggested by another presentation sixteen months later in which Mr Richard Pole, clerk, was cited 'for striking one of the churchwardens in the churchyard with a naked sword many blows'.[48] In the same year the archdeacon of Norfolk cited several parishioners who called their churchwarden 'a rogue and a rascal' or 'busy fellow', and others who bid their minister 'a turd in his teeth' or who cursed the minister 'and that day he came to serve'. Christopher Blythe of Belthorpe, Norfolk, was excommunicated 'for abusing Mr. Dunn, clerk, in his ministerial function, saying he did not hold or account such a minister worth a fig or a rush'.[49]

Richard Dawson of Chenies appeared before the Buckinghamshire archdeaconry court in 1636 'for giving our minister Mr. Jay many base and ignominious terms, viz. tinkerly parson, and other such like scandalous words as the report goeth, these words he gave publicly in the street'. Dawson's defence reconstructed the scene and the conversation, in such a way as to deflate or deflect the charge. He explained 'that upon some pretended discourtesy taken . . . Mr. Jay called him in Chenies street twice or thrice, saying, "sirra, you are a saucy fellow," and again, "sirra, do you come hither blustering to get anything?" Whereto [Dawson] replied, "Sir, I am as good a man as yourself, and none but a tinkerly fellow will call me sirra," but as for other scandalous words or speeches [he] denieth that he spake any'.[50] To call God's minister 'tinkerly' was to describe him as bungling and unskilful, to associate him with disreputable itinerant metalworkers, and to disparage both his person and his calling. 'Your ministers be tinkers' was one of the charges Roman Catholic polemicists used to discredit the Church of England.[51] For the minister to address Dawson as 'sirra' and to call him a 'saucy fellow' was equally offensive, to anyone who stood on his dignity, for the words implied a contemptible and servile condition with an insolent and presumptuous demeanour.[52] Richard Driver of Gargrave, Yorkshire, similarly offended in 1636 'for comparing his minister to a pedler and his ministerial function to pedlers' wares sold for money', but in this case the minister accepted his apology and had the citation withdrawn.[53]

Another disrespectful layman, George Catesby, esquire, of Ecton, Northamptonshire, called his minister, William Churchman, a 'fool, ass and knave' and threatened to kick him in 1637 because of his support for Laudian ceremonialism.[54] In the same year Nicholas Darton, the vicar of Kilsby, Northamptonshire, complained to Archbishop Laud about parishioners who made his life a misery. When Darton attempted to teach his people 'the doctrine of Christian subjection to authority' and reminded them of their obligation to pay tithes, they called him a 'cheater' and said that he was one of 'a den of thieves'. When he 'exhorted the parish to pay his majesty's ship-money and not to be disobedient and rebellious to his majesty's prerogative', they responded with jeering and slander. Henry Jenkins spread rumours that the vicar was drunk, while Lawrence Hall 'called me to my face rebel and jackanapes' (meaning a ridiculous monkey). When he tried to get them to bow at the name of Jesus they railed against him, one of them invoking the biblical curse against Meroz for not coming to the help of the Lord. Darton endured what he called 'schismatical and seditious molestation' from a host of hostile parishioners, but aided by the Archbishop of Canterbury he was able to obtain their apologies. Lawrence Hall confessed that he had 'dealt very knavishly' with the vicar, thereby turning the language of opprobrium back on himself.[55]

In one last example of hostile interaction, visitation proceedings at Sudbury, Suffolk, were violently disrupted in October 1640 when an armed 'rout of prentices, say-weavers, and other poor rascals' broke down the altar rails and snatched at the visitors' books. In the ensuing mêlée one Hodgkins, keeper of the inn where the churchmen had earlier lodged, charged one of them 'with the name of knave, rogue, fool, jacksauce' and then broke a cudgel over his head. The word 'jacksauce', a derogatory term for a saucy or impudent fellow, was the sting in the tail of a line of compounded insults. The complaint was serious enough to come to the attention of the authorities in London, but by the autumn of 1640 the ecclesiastical courts were crumbling and the government of Charles I was no longer capable of punishing men who mocked or assaulted the clergy.[56] Speech offences paled besides other assaults on a Church that was trembling, root and branch.

These examples represent a large number of cases involving verbal exchanges that the Elizabethan and early Stuart authorities deemed offensive. Though places, names, words, and contexts all varied, the reports seemed to follow a similar formula. A dramatic confrontation took place in which a layman made heated remarks to a minister. The court, or the complainant, then described these words as 'unseemly, offensive, despiteful, opprobrious', or the like. These modifiers did powerful work in establishing the pejorative tone of the alter-cation and marking the offender as an enemy of good order. Other adjec-tives characterized the language as 'abusive, angry, bad, base, blasphemous, brabling, braving, brawling, cavilling, chiding, contemptible, contemptuous, contending, contumely, depraving, disdainful, disgraceful, evil, frowardly, ignominious, ill, incontinent, irreligious, irreverent, jeering, misbecoming, misbeseeming, outrageous, profane, quarreling, railing, reproachful, reviling, scandalous, scoffing, scolding, scornful, slanderous, taunting, threatening, unbeseeming, uncharitable, uncivil, unreverent, unruly, vile and wrangling'. These were words that set people's ears on edge. Often they were accompanied by gestures and actions that made them even worse. These were words that could wound, that undercut standards of community discipline, and chal-lenged the reverential dignity of the Church.

The actual alleged words were then introduced into the record, with conventional procedural framing, so that all could see and hear how de-meaning they were. They drew on a fairly limited vocabulary of abuse, most of which we have already heard. The standard repertoire included 'rascal, knave, arrant knave, lousy knave, scurvy knave, rascal knave, wide mouthed rascal, varlet, rogue, base rogue, ass and fool', with such refinements as 'palterer, cheater, liar, lying priest, beggarly priest, scurvy vicar, tinkerly parson, pedler's wares, pratling fool, shitten churchmaster, jacksauce, jackanapes, rebel, traitor and thief'. Related imprecations include the classic 'a turd in your teeth', 'I care not a fart for you', 'a fig or a rush', 'a pox on your church and you', and the timeless 'kiss my arse'. Many of these words had far more gravity, and were much more damaging, than they now appear in their weakened modern form. They were scandalous in any discourse, but especially disruptive when applied by a subordinate to a superior or by a layman to a minister of God. They associated the clergy with the filthiest and least reputable levels of the social order, and called into question the priest's honour, reputation, dignity, and calling.[57]

Unlike the sexual vocabulary common in defamation cases among women—'brazen-faced quean, hacking jade, filthy bawd, and hot tailed whore'—these words struck at the parson's professional standing, his aura of reverence, and his association with gentility. Whereas a woman's sexual behav-iour was 'the absolute centre of her integrity',[58] a man's honour or credit depended on his honesty, rectitude, and ability to command his household. In addition, a clergyman's honour was tied to his priestly dignity, the divinity of his pastoral calling, and the maintenance of authority over his flock. Insults called all these properties into question, undermining the minister's relationship both to his parishioners and to God. Ultimately they touched the honour of the monarch, supreme governor of the Church, which is why the prerogative court of High Commission became involved. In a rare case of sexual language used to demean a minister, George Bryan of Stepney, Middlesex, in 1608 'did call Mrs Bowers, the vicar's wife, quean and drab in contempt of the ministry' (the words implied harlotry and sluttishness). Bryan alleged that Mrs Bowers had 'called him a knave' and spat in his face, so that he was sorely provoked. Harmony was restored by the offender making a public confession of his fault in church, with the vicar officiating and his wife looking on.[59]

Usually the lay defendant denied the worst of the charges, or offered a milder version of the exchange, and claimed to have intended no offence. Sometimes the outburst was excused as being attributable to anger or drink. Occasionally we learn that it followed a longer argument over financial issues, such as burial fees, parish assessments or tithes, or disagreement over preaching. Rather than belonging to the dregs of society, most of these speech offenders came from the otherwise-respectable mainstream. They drove their own carts, rode their own horses, and tilled their own fields. If they claimed to be able to 'make as good a sermon' as the minister and to be 'as good a man as' their parish priest they were standing up for themselves rather than pulling the clergy down. Nor were they obviously mired in the culture of reprobation. Far from being resolutely anti-clerical, the men who made their minister's life a misery often advanced an alternative view of the priestly or pastoral function. They were not so much opposed to the priesthood as exasperated by the actions or shortcomings of a particular priest. Like Zachary Some in Essex and John Whippe in Yorkshire, they wanted clergymen they could work with, men whom they could respect, rather than the 'fools' or 'asses' foisted on them by the system of clerical prefer-ment. Others, like George Catesby and Lawrence Hall in Northamptonshire, were puritan laymen who wanted a less rigorously ceremonious church. Parishioners usually had no say in the choice of their incumbent but by lan-guage and demeanour, the weapons of the weak, they let their frustrations be known.[60] If the matter went so far as to reach the court it usually ended with censure and attempts at reconciliation.

Ministers could rarely get the better of these exchanges, unless they invoked divine or episcopal authority. Usually they were resigned to endure. George Herbert advised, 'When any despises him, [the country parson] takes it either in an humble way, saying nothing at all; or else in a slighting way, showing that reproaches touch him no more than a stone thrown against heaven.' He could also, as the case required, turn revilement to pastoral advantage, offer 'a bold and impartial reproof', or refer the matter to the courts. The best defence, thought Herbert, was the minister's 'courteous carriage and winning behaviour' in the face of hostility and derision.[61] This might salve clerical dignity and personal honour, but it did not resolve the underlying clash of style and discourse, or the problem of deference and discipline. It did not help Thomas Banks in Elizabethan Yorkshire or Nicholas Darton in the Northamptonshire of Charles I.

If a priest went further than offering mild reproof it was often with words designed to re-establish social distance and to sharpen cultural boundaries. Hence we hear such terms of address as 'sirra, boy, base fellow, greasy fellow, saucy fellow, and varlet'. These were dismissive and insulting terms, with an extra sting when applied by a younger minister to an older countryman. Such language put the listener in a state of servile subjection, though it also triggered some to retaliate and give as good as they got. Ordinary insults like these could lead to a shouting match, each calling the other a 'knave'.

Sometimes we hear of churchmen whose own command of invective went well beyond anything directed against them by their parishioners, and which, if reported, could get them into trouble. Hard-line Calvinists seem to have been especially susceptible to outbursts of anger against parishioners they judged to be reprobate, but ceremonialist conformists could grow just as angry. They often drew on a bestial vocabulary, associating their opponents with farmyard animals or with vermin and sometimes implying that the trials of clerical life were akin to the biblical plagues of Egypt.

The reverend Robert Roe of Hanworth, Norfolk, in 1597 was said to be 'rude and rustical in speech and behaviour, lik[en]ing his parishioners to the spawning of a toad'.[62] The reverend Mr Baillie of Kimcot, Leicestershire, so offended parishioners with his 'wrangling and undiscreet proceedings' that in 1602 they sought relief from the Bishop of Lincoln. 'In speaking and reasoning with his neighbours', they charged, 'he giveth occasion of quarrel, by reviling them with base and railing terms, as dog, jade, stews, carrion, scurvy paremonger [*dealer in hedge-trimmings?*], scurvy companion, and such like. In sermons he calleth them swine and dogs, reprobates, bankrupts, hypocrites, etc'.[63]

An incumbent like this was very hard to remove, no matter how much hostility he showed to his flock. His resort to intemperate language could reflect the cultural alienation of the rusticated academic, as well as a Calvinist contempt for the hell-bound multitude. Sometimes the words were aimed at a particular group or faction, sometimes at everyone in sight. Often the citation for abusive language came amidst a struggle for control of the parish and implementation of a particular religious style. The parishioners who took offence at Mr Baillie's language, for example, also alleged that 'in many things he breaketh the order of the church and the Book of Common Prayer', a charge guaranteed to attract the bishop's attention. The accusations against him may have been partisan, exaggerated, or false. In this case, instead of summoning Baillie to appear before the court, the bishop ordered two neighbouring ministers to examine the matter and to restore the community to peace. Reconciliation might easily be achieved, the visitors reported, if 'Mr Baillie himself could leave wrangling and undiscreet proceeding in his ministry'.[64]

Caught between conflicting religious imperatives, and sometimes too between the Bible and the bottle, intemperate ministers of the 1630s berated their congregations with cascades of hostile speech. They gave voice to a vitriolic range of insults with socially demeaning, sexual, pathological, and animalistic connotations. In doing so they undermined their own reputations, spoiled the possibility of brotherly dealing, and diluted the honour that was essential to their priestly calling.

Cuthbert Dale, rector of Kettleborough, Suffolk, 'frequently in his pulpit upbraideth his parishioners, calling them knaves, devils, rascals, rogues and villains', according to the enemies who later secured his sequestration. Outraged by someone who put on his hat during a sermon, Dale called him 'lob, saucy goose, idiot, widgeon and cuckoo, saying he was a scabbed sheep and none of his flock'. In a similar vein Thomas Geary, the vicar of Bedingfield, Suffolk, railed at his parishioners as 'sowded pigs, bursten rams and speckled frogs'. Another Suffolk minister, Robert Shepherd of Hepworth, insulted his congregation as 'black mouthed hell hounds, limbs of the devil, fire brands of hell, plow joggers, bawling dogs, weaverly jacks, and church robbers, affirming that if he could term them worse he would'. Dr Samuel Clerke publicly reviled the churchwardens of All Saints, Northampton, as 'coxcombs' and 'giddy headed fellows' when they resisted his plans to turn the communion table altarwise.[65] Edward Layfield of All Saints, Barking, allegedly lashed out at his enemies as 'black toads, spotted toads, and venemous toads, like Jack Straw and Wat Tyler', when parishioners protested against his ceremonial innovations.[66] It is hard to imagine whether listeners shook with fear or quivered with laughter as the preachers blew their tops. Handbooks for ministers warned them to avoid 'foolish, ridiculous and . . . undecent' or 'unbefitting' terms,[67] but in times of stress it was hard to contain the anger in the breast.

Anthony Lapthorne, rector of Tretire, Herefordshire, and before that an incumbent in Somerset and Gloucester, found himself before the High Commission in 1634 for publicly insulting both laity and clergy. Lapthorne was an old-fashioned Nonconformist who was profoundly out of sympathy with the Laudian style of churchmanship. 'He reviled some of his parishioners who bowed at the name of Jesus', and referred to neighbouring ministers as 'great Rabbis . . . monsters . . . idol shepherds, dumb dogs and soul murderers'.

When told that he was to be reported to the bishop for his 'disorderly carriage' he responded, 'that he cared no more for the churchwardens' presentments than for the hissing of a goose or barking of a dog'. Incapable of reconciliation, he was suspended from the ministry and removed from his parish.[68]

Lapthorne's contemporary, Francis Abbott, of Postlingford, Suffolk, similarly lashed out from his pulpit against parishioners he deemed unteachable. At one time he told his congregation that 'if adultery, swearing, forswearing, drinking, sabbath-breaking, cosening, cheating and such-like will bring a man to heaven, then there is none of my parish but shall go thither'. Another time he addressed the women of the parish as devil-serving 'wantons, naughty plucks and whores', and then singled out 'one of the chiefest parishioners' wives' for breeding 'cuckoo's eggs' and bastards. Cautioned by Silvester Strutt, one of the churchwardens, about his 'railing, miscalling, and reviling of his parishioners', Lapthorne allegedly responded to him in the street, 'Sirra, I care no more for you than the dirt of my shoes . . . sirra, your black grandfather will come for you one of these days.' The Court of High Commission charged Lapthorne with behaving 'very scandalously and offensively', and ordered him excommunicated and suspended. It is doubtful whether they would have acted with such force if he had been a high churchman rather than some kind of puritan.[69]

Equally out of sorts with his listeners, and equally prone to abuse them as reprobates, George Burdett, the public lecturer at Great Yarmouth, faced the Laudian High Commission in 1635. A hard-line Calvinist in a Church increasingly dominated by Arminians, Burdett had preached that Christ died for the elect only, and not for the drunkards, whoremongers, swearers, and profaners who populated his Norfolk parish. As for his fellow ministers, he dismissed most of them as 'dumb dogs', observing that 'there are dogs and curs which will be snarling at the saints and servants of God' and ever licking at their vomit. Behind this intemperate language was a local dispute about order and conformity, kneeling and bowing, that mirrored divisions in the national Church, as well as arguments about inclusive versus exclusive congregations that would ultimately wreck it. Burdett might have been able to continue to conduct services that nourished Nonconformity if only he could govern his tongue. Instead, he was removed from his post and was forced to make public admission of 'his scandalous, blasphemous, erroneous, heretical and schismatical opinions'.[70]

One final case from the 1630s concerns Dr Stephen Dennison of St Katherine Creechurch, London, who 'reviled some of his parishioners, comparing them to frogs, hogs, dogs and devils, and called them the names of knaves, villains, rascals, queans, she-devils, and pillory whores'. Dennison complained 'that he was persecuted by a company of base fellows and rascals' that diverted him from his studies, and that he faced 'a damned crew' of 'cursed conspirators that were ready to thrust out their powerful minister, if all the wit in their knavish heads could do it'. His diatribes against his parishioners became a matter of episcopal concern when he derided a newly installed stained-glass representation of Abraham and Isaac as a 'whirligig, a crow's nest, and more like the swaggering hangman cutting off St John's head', to the great affront of those who 'took care for the beautifying of the church'. A dispute over language displaced an argument about ecclesiastical style and images. Though generally unwilling to prefer the complaints of laymen over clerics, the Laudian court of High Commission agreed with Dennison's enemies that he misused the pulpit, making it 'the place of revenge for his malice' and the venue for 'his personal taxations and . . . invective', and stripped him of his office.[71] The Caroline preacher Thomas Trescot may have had examples like these in mind when he warned fellow ministers against 'bitter invective' that was more like railing than reproving. 'A satire from the pulpit' would be 'unhappily repaid with a jeer at the bar', and tongues dipped in 'gall and vinegar' would bring the ministry into further contempt.[72]

Despite their many differences, puritan and orthodox clergy shared a common concern to uphold ministerial privileges, including the payment of tithes, and were equally likely to be called 'varlet' or 'fool' for their troubles. Isolated and unhappy ministers would occasionally lash back at their parishioners, though only Calvinists would dismiss entire blocks of them as reprobates rather than individual sinners. Many clergymen, by training and by temperament, were unsuited for the pastoral ministry, in the same way that some doctors of philosophy are unfit to be college teachers. Unless they found solace at a local gentleman's dinner table, or buried themselves in their books, or adapted to the ale-bench and the local culture of good fellowship, their relationship with their parishioners was subject to deterioration.

The neighbours who mocked their ministers saw the world in very different terms. Though some tormented their parson for 'sport', others were pursuing a more instructive or corrective agenda. It is clear that a good many who upbraided their priest in crude and insulting language did so to bring him down a peg, to remind him who paid the piper, and to make him dance to a different tune. Their anticlericalism, if such it may be called, was personal and circumstantial, not critically directed at the clerical calling. If parishioners grumbled over fees and tithes, resented their minister's posture of sanctimony, criticized his pastoral or liturgical performance, and generally thought him an ass, that did not necessarily turn them into anticlericalists. It was easy to fall out of charity with individual ministers without disparaging the ministry as a whole. Acknowledging the need for an established national Church with a privileged ecclesiastical hierarchy did not require extending respect to every incumbent. One could loathe the man while honouring the estate, distinguishing, as Chaucer had earlier, 'a shiten shepherde and a clene sheep'.[73]

Dramatis Personae

LAITY

William Black of Wareham, Kent
George Brysto of Stocksbury, Kent
John Pain of Medbourne, Leicestershire
John Pye of Stepney, Middlesex
Thomas Nettleton of Ratcliffe, Middlesex
Zachary Some of Sandon, Essex
John Whippe of Slaidburne, Yorkshire
John Barker of Helpringham, Lincolnshire
Thomas Massingberd of Simpson, Buckinghamshire
Edward Denston of Elford, Staffordshire
John Middleton of Anstie, Leicestershire
Christopher Blythe of Belthorpe, Norfolk
Richard Dawson of Chenies, Buckinghamshire
Richard Driver of Gargrave, Yorkshire
George Catesby of Ecton, Northamptonshire
Lawrence Hall of Kilsby, Northamptonshire
one Hodgkins, innkeeper, of Sudbury, Suffolk
George Bryan of Stepney, Middlesex

CLERGY

George Herbert of Fugglestone, Wiltshire
Richard Greenham of Dry Drayton, Cambridgeshire
Richard Baxter of Kidderminster, Worcestershire
William Attersoll of Isfield, Sussex
John Thaxter of Bridgham, Norfolk
William Harrison of Huyton, Lancashire
Ralph Cudworth of Somerset
William Hardwick of Reigate, Surrey
Anthony Anderson of Medbourne, Leicestershire, and Stepney, Middlesex
Charles Gibbon of Bury St Edmunds, Suffolk
Robert Edbrooke of St Mawgan, Cornwall
William Drake of St Just, Cornwall

Ralph Kett of Cornwall
Thomas Banks of Slaidburne, Yorkshire
John Foster of Wigtoft, Lincolnshire
Mr Dooley of Elford, Staffordshire
Richard Pole of Anstie, Leicestershire
Mr Dunn of Belthorpe, Norfolk
Mr Jay of Chenies, Buckinghamshire
William Churchman of Ecton, Northamptonshire
Nicholas Darton of Kilsby, Northamptonshire
Robert Roe of Hanworth, Norfolk
Mr Baillie of Kimcot, Leicestershire
Cuthbert Dale of Kettleborough, Suffolk
Thomas Geary of Bedingfield, Suffolk
Robert Shepherd of Hepworth, Suffolk
Samuel Clerke of Northampton
Edward Layfield of Barking, Essex
Anthony Lapthorne of Tretire, Herefordshire
Francis Abbott of Postlingfield, Suffolk
George Burdett of Great Yarmouth, Norfolk
Stephen Dennison of London

10

The Atheist's Sermon: Belief, Unbelief, and Traditionalism in the Elizabethan North

In the early spring of 1590 some of the principal inhabitants of East Drayton, Nottinghamshire, laid serious charges against their neighbour John Mynet who was under investigation by the court of High Commission. He was, they alleged, 'an atheist, heathen, or infidel who in the contempt of God and of his blessed word, hath openly and manifestly reported that there is no god, no devil, no heaven, no hell, no life after this life, no judgement to come, whereof he being persuaded as it seemeth, he thereupon rejoiceth in his sins and glorieth in his wickedness'.[1] If most parishioners had learned their creed, Mynet, it seems, had learned his backwards.

Further charges augmented this extraordinary account of village atheism. John Mynet, according to his enemies, was a greedy schemer who could 'not rest for covetousness' and could not sleep 'for devising and imagining with himself how he may join house to house, land to land, and how he may deceive his neighbour'. He was a disruptive presence, 'a brawler in the church of God and a disturber of divine service, by whom our minister hath been hindered in the exercise of his office'. He was, furthermore, 'an uncharitable contemner of our said minister . . . a slanderer, backbiter, and a common sower of dissention, discord and sedition between person and person'. And if this was not enough, they claimed that the infidel was also 'a charmer, sorcerer, enchanter, and conjuror, who taketh upon him to set down how long men shall live, and at what time they shall die, to the marvellous disquieting of the minds and consciences of the poor ignorant people'. The final charge, in this comprehensive catalogue of deviance, was that Mynet, a layman, had taken upon himself 'to preach in the church' and had preached 'false and erronious doctrine'. The presentment was subscribed by the minister, John Hutton, and by six leading parishioners of East Drayton, including the two churchwardens.[2]

If John Hutton's complaint was our sole source of information we might conclude that Mynet was that rarest of early modern phenomena, an overt and resolute atheist. His denial of the fundamental tenets of the Christian religion appears to have been comprehensive as well as 'openly and manifestly reported'. Like drunkards, scolds, and other sowers of disorder, John Mynet seems to have been a severely disruptive presence in his Nottinghamshire village. He appears as one of the reprobate, a troublemaker, a multiple transgressor, whose manners were gravely in need of reformation. But the court gave Mynet an opportunity to answer these charges, and his account, entered into the judicial record, tells a much more interesting story. The exchange between Mynet and his enemies opens another window onto parochial relations, popular culture, and the world of competing truths in early modern England.

The papers in this case, consisting of allegations and personal answers, depositions and statements of evidence before the Court of High Commission at York, shed extraordinary light on the contested world of village politics and popular religion at the end of the sixteenth century. They reveal the tension between clergy and laity, and disagreement among neighbours, over such matters as fellowship and charity, authority and deference, and perhaps also between traditional country divinity and reformed evangelical Protestantism. At stake here were issues of lay independence and community cohesion, clerical dignity and social discipline, as well as views about salvation. The case could take us in various directions, involving sorcery and atheism, popular religion and the progress of the Reformation, social and economic change and hardening divisions within communities, and the requirements and rhetoric of ecclesiastical justice. Mynet's midsummer sermon, with its 'false and erronious doctrine', provides a remarkable example of Elizabethan lay piety and may be considered a bridge between the old religion and the new.

John Mynet was a landowner in East Drayton, apparently a minor gentleman.[3] He was literate, articulate, and better educated than most of his neighbours, and this may have been part of his problem. He appears to have been quick-tempered and sharp-tongued, not one to suffer fools gladly, a man accustomed to throwing his weight around. He had little patience with the lumbering minister, and scant respect for the ecclesiastical authorities. But this does not make him an atheist, nor does it substantiate the rest of the minister's charges, though it could explain the bad blood between Mynet and his neighbours. When first summoned before the court Mynet's temper got the better of him and made matters worse. He acknowledged that when first arrested he 'did in a rage very unadvisedly say that he did not care for the Archbishop of York his grace, nor for any of the High Commissioners'. Nor did it help when he drew his dagger at the constables. He was taken to York Castle for his contempt, before being set free on bond.[4]

Mynet told the court, 'that one of his tenants paying his rent at Martinmas last . . . did desire [him] to give him 12d. back in consideration of an amercement which the said tenant had paid for him'. Mynet, as landlord, refused, 'and when the said tenant did more earnestly desire [him] to allow him the said 12d., and that for God's sake, he this respondent answered that neither for God's sake nor for the devil's sake he would pay it.' The charge of atheism seems to have rested on this uncharitable defence of his financial interests. Mynet invoked the Devil and took the Lord's name in vain, but he made no formal rebuttal of Christian beliefs. He sinned against Christian charity and Mosaic law, but no worse than scores of his contemporaries. Of course, there may have been other exchanges that Mynet would not choose to relate, but in this area his accusers alleged nothing more specific. At the core of the issue was a hot-tempered exchange between landlord and tenant, a shouting match between two laymen, rather than a fundamental reconsideration of theology. But Mynet had problems with the Church as well as with his neighbours and tenants.

Atheists, to the Elizabethan godly, were not necessarily non-believers in God. The charge was more supple and more expansive, embracing reprobates whose behaviour failed to meet the highest Christian standards and deviants whose opinions appeared to drive them away from salvation. Anthony Anderson, the Leicestershire preacher, battled against 'atheists, papists and cursed worldlings' who held back the cause of true reformation. Other clerics raged against profane 'swaggerers' and 'wicked and unrighteous people' whose atheism was evident in their actions. Simply criticizing the clergy could be a sign of atheism, if it meant that the offender turned his back on God or weakened God's ministry.[5] Principled unbelievers were extremely rare in early modern England, and the remainder of the testimony makes clear that Mynet was not of their number. There were, however, profound anxieties among England's governors that atheism might be rampant, and these concerns extended to the late Elizathan north.[6]

The charges of sorcery were neither pursued nor documented, and no other evidence survives to show whether Mynet operated as a cunning man or manipulated supernatural powers. There were several known wise men, sorcerers, or soothsayers in Nottinghamshire at this time who acted as lay counsellors and advised on the location of lost or stolen goods,[7] and it is quite possible that Mynet provided such services with some freelance astrology on the side. He was, as we shall see, attuned to traditional beliefs and customs, and may have offered local wisdom and advice of the sort that was no longer available from the university-trained clergy.

Like other Elizabethan countrymen of substance, John Mynet was a regular churchgoer. But he was not necessarily respectful, silent, and devout. He told the court that 'on a holiday in summer last Mr Hutton, vicar of East Drayton, read the Psalms of the tenth day, it being the eleventh day of the month; which this respondent noting, did tell the said Mr Hutton in friendly and quiet sort whilst he was reading that it was the eleventh day.' It was this calendar correction, called out openly in church, that led to the charges of disturbing divine service and hindering the minister in the exercise of his office. For the purpose of his defence Mynet described his intervention as 'in friendly and quiet sort' but it seems likely that he was responsible for a loud and raucous disruption. One of his accusers, Richard Pickhaven, yeoman, recalled Mynet's exact words on this occasion, 'priest thou readest wrong'. The layman's correction of the minister, even if founded in fact, could be seen as an uncharitable display of contempt, a disgracing of spiritual authority, and an occasion for 'dissension, discord, and sedition'.

Far from being an unbeliever, Mynet was active in his church, and served sometimes as a lay reader. This was an office created by the early Elizabethan Church in response to a serious shortage of clerical manpower, intended to advance, not retard, the Reformation.[8] It was ironic that Mynet used this position to promulgate a divisive and discredited doctrine. Two or three years earlier, he told the court, 'being lawfully tolerated to read in Askham chapel in East Drayton parish, [he] did openly warn the people to keep holiday upon Midsummer Day, and as for bonfires he told them they might use them or refuse them at their pleasure'. On another occasion 'he made a speech touching bonfires but what it was he now remembereth not'. Documentation introduced into the record would serve to jog his memory, furnishing a remarkable account of lay religious teaching.

The Elizabethan Church of England preserved the midsummer holiday as St John's Day, but had mixed feelings about some of the ancient attendant celebrations. Reformers in particular censured the midsummer bonfires and frowned on midsummer bell-ringing and night-time watches. A fine line divided superstition from godliness. The holiday could be marred by arguments, whether to keep up the wakes, pageant or procession, whether to light the bonfire or ring the bells, or whether to maintain the festivity at all. We do not know where Mynet's accusers stood on these issues, but his keenness to keep up traditional customs and his apparent enthusiasm for bonfires would put him at odds with puritan activists.[9]

Although Mynet's memory apparently failed him before the ecclesiastical court, his enemies supplied a digest of his controversial remarks.[10] Richard Pickhaven deposed that on St John's Day Mynet 'made a sermon in Askham chapel at which time he did declare that there was three St Johns'. This was true enough, though confusing, referring to John the Baptist, John the Apostle, and John the Divine. There were also, Mynet said, three kinds of fire—fires of bone, hence bonfires that could ward off dragons and elephants; familiar wood fires 'for people to sit and wake by'; and special fires of wood and bones. Wood fires gave light 'to be seen far off as a token that St John was a lantern of light to the people', while the bones of this third kind of fire 'betokeneth John's martyrdom, for his bones were burnt'.

Mynet's sermon also told stories of angels and holy helpers, of Zachary, Elizabeth, Mary, and the birth of St John, of Christ's baptism in the Jordan and John's death under Herod. It certainly does not sound like the work of an atheist, though its folksy naivety would not meet the standards of university-trained Protestants. Mynet's Christianity was more rooted in the traditions of medieval devotion than late sixteenth-century Calvinism. Perhaps his principal offence was to explain St John's Day to a country congregation more effectively than their ordained minister. He was clearly a person with some charisma, and the minister may have been jealous of Mynet's quick mind and easy tongue and his ability to communicate with the laity. The religious authorities were alarmed that any lay person might supplant the authority of the clergy, and they were especially troubled by lay preaching that appeared to be untouched by the Reformation.

Here are the words 'complainted against Mr Mynet, reader in Drayton parish'. (I have supplied paragraph breaks but preserved the original spelling.) It seems more likely that the text was taken from Mynet's incriminating papers than reconstructed from an auditor's notes or memory.

Deare & welbeloved frendes, ye shall understande how this feaste of St John Baptiste was firste founded & why yt is so called. It is for iiii causes.

First yt our lorde & Savyour Christe Jesus was by him baptysed in the water of flowe Jordan. Therefore to wit this feast Christian people made iii maner of fires in remembraunce yt St. John Baptised our Saviour Christe Jesus. One fire was made cleane bones & no woodd & yt is called a bonefyre: Another is cleane woodd and no bones: & yt is called a woodd fyre for people to sitt & wake by: The iii is made of woodd & bones & it is called St. Johns baptiste fyre: the first fire is of bones, as a great learned clarcke St Byllet telleth, he was in a certayne country & in that cuntry ther was so greate heate the wch caused the dragons to go together: in tokening yt St. John Baptiste died in bearing love & charity to god & man and they yt died in charity shall have p[ar]te of all good praiers. & they yt do not shall never be saved: Thenne as thes dragons flew in the ayre they fled downe to the waters & frothe of their kinde: & so venimed the waters & caused much people to take their death therby: & many diverse sikenes:

then on a time there were many greate clarkes & reede of king Alisander: how on a tyme as he should have batayled with the king of India. & this king of Inde brought wth him many Elephantes bering castles of trees on their backes as the kinde of them is to have armed knightes in that castle for the bayttle: then knew king Alisander the kind of the Elephantes that they dreade nothing more then the Jarringe of Swine. wherfore he made to geather together all the swine yt might be gotten & caused them to be dryven as nie the Eliphantes as they well might heare the iarring of the swine and then they made a pigge to cry, & when the swine harde they pigge cry anone they made a greate iarringe & as sone as they elyphantes heard that they began to flee every one. & caste downe the castles & slew the knights yt were therin: and by this meanes alizander had the victory.

also thes wise clarckes knew well yt the dragons hated nothing more then ye stinke of Burning bones: therefore they gathered as many as they might finde & burned the[m] and so wth the stinke therof they drove away the dragons & so then bonefyres were first invented for this cawse. the second fyre was made of wood yt will burne, light & wilbe seene farre. for it is the cheife of fires, to be seene farre & a tok[e]ning yt St John was a lanterne of light to the people & also the people made blases of fyre for they should be seene farre & specially in the night.

Sainct Hieromye ye prophet many a yeare or John was borne he p[ro]phecied & spake thus wth gods mouth & said (*Prinsqua te formare un utero novi te*) before thou were formed in thy mothers wombe, (*et antiqum exires de vulua sanctificavi te*) & before or thou yeldest out of thy mothers wombe I hallowed thee (*et p(ro)pheta in gentibq dedi te*) & I gave the prophete to that people. Therefor St. John should be holy or he were borne. god sent his aungell Gabriell to zachary saint Johns father, as he did sacrifice in steedd of Abia the bishoppe in the temple, & prayed to god to have a child for both he & his wife were barren & old then sayd the aingell to Zachary (*ne timeas zacharia*) dreede not zachary god hath hard thy praier   Elizabeth thy wife shall have a child & his name shalbe called John   he shall be fulfilled wth the holy ghost (*et multi in nativitate eius gaudebunt*) and many shall joy in the birthe of him for then zachary was old, he prayed the aungell to have a token for his behooffe, then sayd the aungell to him thou shalt be dombe till the child be borne, & so he was.   then conceaved Elizabeth & when she was quicke with child our lady came wth child also to speake wth Elizabeth. And assone as she spake to Elizabeth the St. John played in his mothers wombe for Joy of christes p[re]sence yt he saw in our lady, and thus our lady was wth Elizabeth unto the time yt John was borne & was midwife to Elizabeth & tooke St. John from the erthe. and when neighbours harde that elizabeth hadd a sonne they weare ioyfull and came togither as the manner was that tyme to give the child a name and called it zacharye after the father But Elizabeth badd call hym John therfore was none of the kynne of that name they asked zacharie by signes what the chyld should hight or be named. Then he wrot to them and badd call him John and therfore god losed zacharias tonge and spake readily and thancked god highlye:

thus was John holy or he was borne for he wold gyve evrie man light of grace and of good lyvinge he gave them ensample for assoone as he was of reasonable age he went into desert and was there tyll or lorde came to be Christened of hym, and there he lyved full straytlye. (*Johanis hauit vestimenta de pillis Camillox*) John had his clothes made of the heare of a Camyl and a girdle about him of the same skyne. (*Esta autem eius erat locusta et melli silvestre*) forsoothe his meat was leaves and honysockles yt hathe a wyt flower that groweth in trees and he eate all man[er] of wormes that weare noryshed in the desert amonge herbes and the wormes be as great as a mans fynger and sucked hony of flowers that be called honysuckles/ that yos people gather and frye them in oyle to their meate also John eate broord rounde leaves that growe in trees in that desert and when they be broken betwene a mans handes thei be swet as hony and he drank water of a well that was in the desert. ther was St Johns lyfe in that desert tyll that or lorde was xxx^tie wynters of age and then or lorde and he met at the water of flow Jordan, and then John told the people of Chryste and said (*ecce agnus dei*) see the lambe of god that I have told you of, that shall fulfill you in the holy ghost. Then went John into the water and there he baptized Christe and when he was baptized (*Ecce apti sunt Celi*) heaven opened (*et videt spiritum dei discendentem sicut Columba*) and he saw the holy god come downe as a dove (*et vox ale celo anorte est dicens*) and as a voyce from heaven spake thus (*ecce filius meus delectus in quo mihi bene complicavi*) This is my well beloved sonne yt pleaseth me. here learned John Baptist fyrste to know thre p(er)sons in Trinitie and all this betokeneth twoo fires.

The third fire of bones betokeneth Johns martirdom for his bones were brent. and now yo shall here we reade that kynge herode hadd a brother that was called Philip and he had a fayre woman to his wyfe and herode loved her well and held her under his wyfe where John repreved him and sayde (*non licentum est tibi here uxem fratris tui*) It is not lawefull for the to have thy brothers wyfe and therefore he put him in prison and ordeneded betwene him and his wyfe howe John might dye wthout troublinge of the people, for the comen people loved John well Then herode ordeined and made a great feaste for all the states of the countrie that thei should hold with him if yt the people had rysen. And so when the daye was come the feaste sholde be houlden & all the people were served at meate herodes wyfe as covenant was betweene them two she sent her daughter into the halle for to dannce & to tomble before the gests and that pleased her father so well yt he swore agreat oathe and sayde (*pete a me quid vis & dabo tibi*) aske of me what thou wilt & I shall give it the Then as the mother bad her saye she saide (*caput Johannis baptiste*) the hed of John Baptiste then herode feyned him wrothe & sorye yt he had made suche anothe But he was glad in his harte and then sent into pryson to Smyte of Johns head wthout anie delay or Judgmt and was brought to the damsell Then the mother bad burye it in a privie place farr from the bodye then the next after Johns disciples came & toke his boddie buried yt & there it laye tyll July and the apostea [Julian the Apostate] the Emperour came that waye then he made take up Johns bones and to burne them & windowe them in the winde hopinge that he shold never rise ['up' *crossed out*] anie to lyfe agayne thus ye may understand how holy this man was then an angell came from heaven & told zacharie of his comeinge, and was hallowed in his mothers wombe & or ladie toke him from the earthe in his birthe and an angell brought his name from heaven & after he Cristened or lorde Jesu Christe this was a holy man ye shall understande that St John ye/ Evangeliste dyed the same daye But the holy Churche maketh no mencon thereof for this daye is holden in Christmas weke therefore theis twoo Johnes be comnpted the worthiest Seynts in heaven

then there were twoo scholers of divinite thone loved John baptiste and thother John the Evangeliste and on adaye to dispute on this matter & the daye was assigned, but the nyght before ether Johnes appeared to theise schollers of divinitie and bad then leave their disputacon for thei were well accorded in heaven and made no stryfe and then on the morrowe before all the people thanked god and bothe Johnes of this fayre myracle also there were two mesell men and Lepers that loved well theis twoo Johnes and so as they were in Comminge they spake of theis two Seyncts wch were the greater in heaven and so ye one saide for that one was greater then the other and so thei begane to fyghte then there came a voyce from heaven & saide we fyght not in heaven and therefore fyght not ye on earthe for us for we be in peace & so be ye therwth thei were bothe holle of their sicknes & thancked god & both St Johnes and after woord they were both holy men and therefore let us worshipp thoes holy Sts whereby yt we maye come to ever-lastinge ['lyfe' *crossed out*] Blesse. Amen.

This is an extraordinary text for a country sermon in late sixteenth-century England. At first sight it appears to be the work of an English Menocchio, a layman who patched together his history and theology from eclectic but pious reading.[11] Its antique devotional qualities and anecdotal structure associate it with the *Golden Legend* and other popular tales of the saints, while its lore about elephants and dragons would appear to derive from ancient and medieval natural history.[12] Closer inspection, however, reveals that the text was taken almost word for word from the early fifteenth-century homilies of John Mirk (or Myrc), which were published in at least seventeen editions between 1483 and 1532.[13] Despite the turmoils of reformation and the considerable destruction of popish books, it was not improbable that a 60-year-old devotional handbook should still be in use in a late-Elizabethan northern parish. Indeed, a medieval 'gradual' or manuscript book of chants and anthems that belonged to an early Tudor vicar of East Drayton still survives, from what may have been a local devotional library.[14] When asked to read at the midsummer service in Askham chapel Mynet apparently did what he thought proper, and turned to the relevant saint's day in the book.

By 1590, however, even in north Nottinghamshire, the medieval teaching of the *Festial* and the Golden Legend was out of favour. Protestant believers in predestination and justification by faith alone would have no truck with inter-cessionary saints or holy helpers of the kind that Mynet described. Residual beliefs that saints were holy in the womb, that saints like John the Baptist gave grace, and that the worship of saints was a means to everlasting life, were anathema to Elizabethan reformers. The claim that 'they that died in charity shall have part of all good prayers, and they that do not shall never be saved', implied both the discredited theology of salvation by works and the erroneous belief in the efficacy of prayer for the dead. The devotional references to 'our lady', the exotic tales of fires, bones, and dragons, and the peppering of the text with Vulgate Latin, all hark back to a late-medieval form of piety that Protestants had sought to transform. Mynet's sermon, derived from medieval sources, was a sign that the Reformation had shallow roots. It was a demonstration, both for Elizabethan evangelists and for modern historians, of the gap between official provision and popular religion.[15] The message was neither atheism nor counter-reformation Catholicism, but it was not the kind of godly instruction that would satisfy the archbishop or dean of York.

Mynet, however, was not prosecuted for his preaching. He was not a Roman Catholic or a recusant, although he may well be fitted into the category of 'church papist' or 'parish anglican' or 'unreformed conformist'. He may even be claimed as a 'prayer-book protestant', based on his correction of the minister for failing to comply with the letter of the Book of Common Prayer.[16] From his own perspective he was merely doing his duty, and was surprised at the hostile repercussions. It must have been painful and humiliating to be taken to York prison and presented before the High Commission on charges of atheism and irreligion.

In the end Mynet bowed to the power of the Church, and confessed to his 'false and erronious doctrine'. If he had spoken offensively, he said, its was also 'unadvisedly, for the which he asketh God forgiveness'. He was a farmer, not a martyr, and was not vehemently attached to any of his alleged views. Like many men caught in the church court system, his most sensible course was to seek reconciliation. The ecclesiastical authorities for their part were willing to let him go after he admitted his error and performed public penance. If the story has winners and losers, it may be significant that the reverend John Hutton had left East Drayton by the end of 1590, while Mynet and his kinsmen continued among the principal landholders in the parish.

11

BAPTIZED BEASTS AND OTHER TRAVESTIES:
AFFRONTS TO RITES OF PASSAGE

This chapter marks another move from the mildly contentious to the flagrantly outrageous, from topics that were broadly troublesome to those that were profoundly transgressive. It focuses on violations of decorum, inversions of protocol, and travesties of religious ritual. Contemporaries found these incidents to be profane and offensive, the work of reprobates and ruffians, but historians may judge them to have been subversive or insubordinate, ludic or carnivalesque. I shall begin with an incident from the 1640s which suggests that even the grossest affrontery was governed by latent protocols and traditions.

In the summer of 1644, writes the presbyterian chronicler Thomas Edwards,

Captain Beaumont and his company being quartered at Yaxley in Huntingdonshire, there being a child of the town to be baptised, some of the soldiers would not suffer the child to be carried to church to be baptised, and the lieutenant of the troop drew out a part of the troop to hinder it, guarding the church that they should not bring the child to be baptised; and instead of the child being baptised, in contempt of baptism, some of the soldiers got into the church, pissed in the font, and went to a gentleman's stable in the town, and took out a horse and brought it to the church, and there baptised it.

The villagers of Yaxley, like readers of Edwards's *Gangraena*, were expected to react with horror. Here was friction between soldiers and civilians that bode ill for the parliamentary polity; here was thwarting of a customary social ritual that family and kinsfolk normally cherished; here was interference with a fundamental rite of passage that all but anabaptists deemed holy; and here, most transgressive of all, was derision of the sacrament and profanation of the church. The soldiers' urine and the gentleman's horse were instruments of pollution, their conjunction at the font a sign of the world turned upside down.[1]

There were several ways to understand this troubling incident. It can be seen as part of a pattern of irreligious or mock-religious behaviour that reflected the continuing conflict between popular and official culture. It set licentiousness against decorum, profanity against respect for the traditions of the Church. It can also be interpreted as a breach of discipline, an act of revolt, and a form of social drama enacting and defaming the sacramental performance of the priest. Contemporary guardians of order found it strange and disturbing, but this was neither the first nor the last time that an animal would be offered the baptismal sacrament of salvation.

Edwards framed his report with reference to the reliability of his sources. His problem, like ours, was to probe for deeper significance and to gauge if the story was true. Like earlier accounts of miracles and monstrous births, reports of travesties of the sacraments might be cries in the wind unless rooted in credible report. 'Two citizens, honest men, related to me this story in the hearing of another minister, and that with a great degree of confidence,' Edwards began. 'Yet because I well know that reports will fly variously, and many mistakes may arise in relations, and because this was so sad a story and such a desperate profanation and contempt of God's ordinance of baptism, I therefore entreated the citizens for my satisfaction, and for the credit of the story to others,' to furnish an account of it in writing, signed or certified by witnesses. Edwards then printed an elaborated retelling of the outrage at Yaxley, drawn up more than two years after the incident, with the signatures of six men and the mark of another, as if that would clinch the matter.[2]

In this version we learn,

that Captain Beaumont was quartered at Yaxley in the county of Huntingdon about 2 June 1644, and preached on the Lord's day in the parochial church; and in the time of his quarter there, his soldiers fetched a bald horse of the captain's out of Mr Finmore's stable where he was quartered, and in the church at the font, having pissed in it, did sprinkle it on the horse, and call him Bald Esau (because he was hairy) and crossed him in the forehead. They had soldiers [as] godfathers, and one widow Shropshire, a soldier so-nick named, was the godmother. This the lieutenant, Brayfield by name, reported to the captain, and they all glorified in it at Mr Finmore's, and the other soldiers immediately reported the same to be done in many houses where they were quartered . . . Robert Rayner, corporal, was the man that acted the part of the minister; Bartly Ward by name was the godmother; Lawrence Dodds, Lieutenant Brayfield's man, was he that fetched the horse out of the stable.

Furthermore, the minister added, he could report 'many other misdemeanours of some of the same sectarian soldiers . . . as the baptising of a pig, and other strange exploits'.[3]

The exploit at Yaxley could be explained in terms of the disruption of war, when a radicalized but ill-disciplined fighting force had too much time on its hands and too much beer in its belly. It could be taken as a symptom of irreverence and irreligion, to which the young and the reprobate were ever prone. It could also be attributed to sectarian teaching that disparaged the baptismal ceremonies of mainstream Protestants. This was Edwards's view, which blamed derision of the sacrament on the anabaptist preachers and sectarian agitators who sometimes accompanied the troops, as well as the malicious high spirits of Captain Beaumont's company.

Anabaptists, according to Edwards, insisted that "tis as lawful to baptise a cat, or a dog, or a chicken, as to baptise the infant of believers'. To drive their point home, 'they have done and practiced many strange things in reference to baptism of children, dressing up a cat like a child for to be baptised, inviting many people both men and women as to baptising of a child, and then when neighbours were come, having one to preach against baptism of children'.[4] Travesties of the sacraments, then, were crude theatrical enactments of a deviant theological position, and the Huntingdonshire incident belonged to this vein. Indeed, as a concrete illustration of previously undocumented charges it was almost too good to be true.

Stories of mock baptisms and 'other strange exploits' spread rapidly in the news-hungry culture of civil war England. It was difficult, as Edwards recognized, to differentiate reliable information from propaganda and gossip. The militarization of society increased the chances of vandalism and religious profanation, as huge numbers of young men were removed from their homes, given weapons and companionship, and placed in circumstances where discipline might fail. Commanders and chaplains worked hard to secure order, but occasionally things got out of hand. At the same time the expansion of printing made it possible for outrageous acts to gain national attention. If soldiers were involved in the soiling of a church, pulling down altar rails, chipping at images, or parodying the sacraments, their exploits would quickly be memorialized in print.[5]

In the same year as the mock-baptism of a horse at Yaxley, the royalist propaganda sheet, *Mercurius Aulicus*, reported from another front: 'the highest, boldest blasphemy and treason we have ever yet told you of, against God or his sacred majesty: viz. When the Earl of Essex was at Lostwithiel in Cornwall, one of the rebels brought a horse into that church, led him up to the font, made another hold him while himself took water and sprinkled it on the horse's head and said, "Charles, I baptise thee in the name of the Father, etc.," then crossed his forehead and said, "I sign thee with the sign of the cross, in token thou shalt not be ashamed to fight against the Roundheads at London," with a deal more such horrid blasphemy as no modest Christian is willing to repeat.'[6] The royalist Richard Symonds, a veteran of the western campaign, incorporated this story into his diary, claiming, 'in contempt of Christianity, religion and the church, they brought a horse to the font in the church, and there with their kind of ceremonies did as they called it Christian the horse, and called him by the name of Charles, in contempt of his sacred majesty'.[7] The story spread across the country from the likes of Robert Tite, a

Norwich minister recently returned from Cornwall, who told it to his East Anglian congregation.[8]

Though incidents of this sort were rare, they fed a legend about the iconoclastic irreverence of the parliamentary forces and their sectarian allies. It seemed always to be parliamentary soldiers who offended by parodying the sacraments or profaning the church.[9] (Royalists, by contrast, were renowned for debauchery and plunder.) If Cromwellian soldiers were not smashing fonts with hammers they would appear to have been filling them with urine to baptize their beasts. It was as if they had taken to extremes the notion of 'the priesthood of all believers' against a monarchy and a religious establishment they deemed utterly devoid of divinity. By offering the laver of salvation to cats, dogs, pigs, and horses, the soldiers added insult and mockery to a sacramental regime that was already experiencing theological and liturgical attack.[10] Looking back on these years of excess and disturbance, the London puritan Nehemiah Wallington recalled an anabaptist 'that did deride and mock of the ordinance of baptism in the baptising of a cat', and who subsequently suffered the judgement of God.[11] William Dugdale expressed outrage at the parliamentary soldiers at Lichfield cathedral who 'brought a calf into it wrapped in linen, carried it to the font, sprinkled it with water, and gave it a name in scorn and derision of that holy sacrament of baptism'.[12] A London woman was questioned in 1644 for accusing another of 'baptising a cat, and speaking words of defamation against the sacrament of baptism'.[13]

What should we make of these various fragments? Do they belong to the history of riot or the history of religion? What did the actors themselves think they were doing, and why were the chroniclers so deeply offended? Whose interest governs the narrative and whose viewpoint should we adopt? What part did alcohol play in these mock ceremonies, and what was the role of radical sectarianism and crowd dynamics? Were those involved spontaneously creating an original piece of theatre, or were they reproducing a ritual, or counter-ritual, with a scripted tradition of its own? Were these incidents symptoms of social or spiritual disorder, or relatively harmless outbreaks of high spirits? Above all, what light can they throw on the social and cultural history of early modern England? Baptisms of beasts are puzzling phenomena, and it is by no means clear how they fit into our larger understanding of history.

We can find examples of mock baptisms and other travesties of religious ritual in each of the reigns of the Tudors and Stuarts, with different weight or significance according to the religious climate of the time. Some of the evidence comes from diaries and correspondence, but most is drawn from the records of ecclesiastical courts. Usually we have no more than the citation, a statement of the presentment or charge, but occasionally witnesses told in detail what was said and done. Unlike the reports from the civil war period, these accounts were buried in manuscripts, not published in print, though news might spread through oral networks. The following discussion examines a variety of these 'strange exploits', most of them involving the sacrament of baptism.

John Stokesly (1475–1539), principal of Magdalen Hall, Oxford, and later Bishop of London, was charged in 1506 with baptizing a cat in the course of a conjuring ritual to discover buried treasure in his home parish of Collyweston, Northamptonshire. He was defamed 'de baptisatione mureligi et conjuratione illicita pro thesauro inveniendo', and was summoned before the council of Margaret Tudor, Countess of Richmond, the queen mother, who had jurisdiction over the manor of Collyweston. The charge of baptizing the cat was revived at a college visitation in 1507, compounded by complaints of Stokesly's alleged unchastity, adultery, heresy, and receipt of stolen goods. No evidence was introduced to support any of these charges, and Stokesly was able to clear his name. Six compurgators made oaths in his favour, and he was formally reconciled by the visitor, a commissary of Bishop Richard Foxe. Nothing more can be learned about the incident with the cat, but if it happened at all it seems more likely to have belonged to a quasi-occult practice than to the drunken disorder of other travesties of the sacraments. Perhaps his former neighbours looked on their Oxford priest as a kind of academic cunning man, and Stokesly obliged them with some kind of supernatural religious business involving the christening of a cat. The incident came back to haunt him in the early years of the Reformation, as Stokesly, a heretic-hunter, was derided as 'bloody bishop christen-cat'.[14]

Cats were in the news again, in mockery of the mass rather than baptism, at a later stage in the Reformation. In April 1554, within a week of the consecration of six new Catholic bishops in London, somebody hung up a cat, gibbet style, on the gallows next to Cheapside Cross in the commercial heart of the city. The party responsible remains unknown, but was evidently someone with a cruel wit and ingenuity as well as hatred for the Marian religious regime. The cat was 'habited in a garment like to that the priest wore that said mass; she had a shaven crown, and in her fore feet held a piece of paper made round, representing the wafer'. Within days a proclamation was made offering twenty marks (£6 13s. 4d.) to anyone 'that could bring him forth that did hang the cat on the gallows' but none appeared to claim this hefty reward.[15]

Half a century later, when England was officially Protestant, opponents of godly order again resorted to the theatrics of religious travesty. William Cotton, Bishop of Exeter, complained in 1600 about the 'profane atheists' who were undermining the work of reform in south-west England. Among many outrages, 'there was a ridiculous and profane marriage of a goose and a gander; a cat having an apron, and a partlet, brought to the church to be baptised; a horse head at Launceston lately lapped in a mantle and brought to the church to baptism, and afterwards the bell tolled and rung out for the death of his head; a dead horse brought to the communion table with his feet spread upon it, as being prepared to receive the sacrament; a young youth of sixteen years baptised by the name of Gurlypot, at which time the font was overthrown, libels made upon every sermon almost in every town.'[16] The dead and decapitated horses were especially horrific, as props in a grossly profane parody of the two remaining sacraments.

Similar episodes offended religious sensibilities in eastern and southern England. The devout Lady Margaret Hoby recorded a 'judgement . . . worth noting' when one of her reprobate neighbours, young Farley, was murdered in 1601. 'This young man being extraordinary profane, as once causing a horse to be brought into the church of God, and there christening him with a name, which horrible blasphemy the lord did not leave unrevenged.' Though Farley's death had other causes, Lady Margaret associated it with his mockery of the sacrament of baptism.[17] With less of a sense of providential retribution, an archdeaconry court in Sussex cited Peter Simons of Udimore 'for baptizing a cat' in 1603. Simons denied his involvement, and at the next court session the same charge of 'baptising a cat' was levelled at Joan Golding of Winchelsea.[18]

Mock baptisms did not have to involve animals to violate godly order, for mockery and profanity of any sort were deeply offensive to committed Christians. Officials of the archdeaconry of St Albans appeared to be embarrassed in 1616 when they reported to the Bishop of London 'a notorious and wicked misdemeanour, whereby the holy sacrament of baptism was by certain lewd persons profaned'.[19] In this case there was an abundance of testimony explaining who did what to whom.

Fifteen-year-old Thomas Bennet of Watford, Hertfordshire, servant to William Edlyn, recounted the abuse he had suffered at the hands of neighbourhood bullies who were also the parish bell-ringers. Here as elsewhere, the bell-ringers formed an informal fraternity who enjoyed privileged access to the church, but were more renowned for their strong arms and capacious bellies than for their piety or decorum. (As at Holton, Oxfordshire, the ringers were single young men who formed a close-knit community within the parish.) Appearing on oath before the archdeaconry court, in the presence of the mayor of St Albans, Bennet testified that upon an holiday in Easter week was twelve months last past, between one and two of the clock in the afternoon, divers young men being then ringing of the bells in Watford church, he and divers other boys being at play in the church, the ring being ended, one William Haydon beat him with a rope to cause him to depart the church, whereupon the rest of the boys came out of the church. He made haste also to be gone, but Roger and William Haydon laid hold of him, and William wished to have him to the font, and thither the two did draw him, demanding of him what his name should be, until Ralph Stretton . . . answered, 'Hodge of the town's end', and till the said Stretton had most profanely and wickedly taken water out of the font with his hand and cast it upon his face, and said, 'I baptise thee in the name of the Father, and of the Son, and of the Holy Ghost': Whereto Thomas Hoddesdon standing by said 'Amen'. Then he ran away, having got loose from them, but William and Roger Haydon, Stretton and Hoddesdon ran after him again, saying they had forgotten to sign him with the cross; but they could not take him for that he ran apace.

It did not take long for the bullies to regret their prank. As bell-ringers they would have been liberally supplied with beer, and their refreshment had most likely weakened their judgement. But they continued to be busy on festive and sacred occasions. Meeting Thomas Bennet in church a few months later, William Haydon offered him twelve pence to keep quiet about the incident, but word had already spread. 'Goodman Peter's son was in the bell loft where they ring' and heard the whole exchange. Joseph Potter asked about the noise in the church and was told that 'the boys have christened a boy, and have named him Hodge of the town's end'. Edward Berry, wheelwright, found young Bennet in the church porch, 'wiping his face with his hat, and his face was all wet, and he cried . . . and he said, they have christened me'. The wheelwright 'went into church and told them it was no place to play the knave in', but he would not inform against the ringers. There seems to have been some intimidation of witnesses, but attempts to halt the judicial proceedings were ineffective. Thomas Bennet may have been an outsider in the community, since his father lived not in Watford but in Bushey. The derisory name given him, 'Hodge of the town's end', implies rustic poverty and simple-mindedness, but it may have been an inverted insult for someone who actually had pretensions to quality. But there was nothing to excuse such violence or disorder in church, mimicry of the minister, mockery of the sacrament, and misuse of baptismal water. When last heard of the Haydon brothers and Ralph Stretton were in prison awaiting questioning before the High Commission, and Thomas Hoddesdon had run away, to be followed by a warrant for his arrest.[20]

One of John Cosin's correspondents, Oliver Naylor of Tavistock, Devon, wrote in March 1617 of a mock baptism involving not an animal or a servant

but a pot of ale. The offender staged a derisive parody of the religious ceremony, whose words and procedures he evidently knew by heart. 'There's one
Allen in a town called South Moulton, not far from us, that hath christened a
pot of ale lately, with all the ceremonies belonging to a christening. His bell was
a candle stick, his font a salt cellar, two double jugs the gossips, and a dozen jugs
more the witnesses. He used the very words of our liturgy and, lest any thing
should be wanting, he had gossips' feasts when he had done. He is thought to
have done it in derision of our ceremonies and religion.' Though this particular
offence involved no profane misuse of the church, no actual mockery at the
font, and nothing that might be thought of as riotous, Cosin's circle of fastidious ceremonialists could cite it as an instance of unruly irreverence that both
puritans and prelates sought to reform.[21]

Drunken disorder led to the mock christening of a dog at East Brent, Somerset, in 1620 'to the great profanation of the holy sacrament of baptism'. May-tide
revellers at the Red Lion inn forced beer into the animal, dressed it in a black
coat to represent a clergyman, and named it Cutty Hill 'in derison of the minister, Mr Hill'. Richard Dodd, the ring-leader, 'pouring some of the drink before
them upon the dog's head, made the sign of the cross over him' and named two
drinking companions as godfathers. Church and State were both outraged
by this irreverence, and examined the offenders before both the ecclesiastical
court and the Quarter Sessions.[22] A few years later the Somerset authorities
dealt with more drunken revellers, this time Christmas bell-ringers, who
thought it amusing to dunk a dog in the baptismal font at Crewkerne.[23]

The next few examples have more in common with the bestial baptisms of
the 1640s. In 1618 John Prowse of Brixham, Devon, was committed by local
magistrates and sent up to the archbishop in London for 'riding on horseback
into church, offering to have his horse christened'. No bestial christening
occurred, perhaps because Prowse was too drunk to follow through on his
threat, but the sacrament and the sacred space were profaned. Though himself
a gentleman and a justice of the peace in Exeter, Prowse had evidently parted
with all sense of propriety. He was cited 'for profaning the church' and for using
'contemptuous and menacing language' against the authorities who attempted
to restrain him.[24] Thomas Easton of Loughton, Buckinghamshire, was likewise
cited 'for leading a horse into the church upon the 7th day of November [1636]'
though whether he intended to baptize it is unclear.[25] A decade later Isaac
Antrobus, the 'malignant' parson of Egremont, Cumberland, was ejected from
his living because, among other offences, he 'baptized a cock, and called him
Peter'.[26] There is no further information to expand this strange fragment, but it
seems to involve a muddled reference to the cock that crowed after St Peter's
denial of Christ.

In the early 1630s a dispute between factions in the Essex seaport of Harwich led to a temporary chill in relations between the secular and ecclesiastical arms of the government of Charles I. At the heart of the dispute was the claim by William Innes, the minister of Harwich, that Sara Peck, the wife of a mariner, had led other parishioners in 'the profane christening of a dog', giving it 'the name of Jeffery', and that Mr Bishop and Mr Taylor served as 'godgaffers'. If this was true it was multiply transgressive; it brought a polluting beast into the holy sanctum, mocked the Christian sacrament of baptism, subverted the authority of the parish priest, and placed a woman in the jesting role of ceremonial offi- ciant. Innes complained to the ecclesiastical authorities and eventually in 1631, 'upon a judicial and public hearing' before the Court of High Commission, Sara Peck 'was adjudged guilty and condemned for the same'.[27]

Sara's friends and the minister's enemies were not about to let the matter rest, and used alternative chains of influence to get the judgement reversed. In September 1631 the mayor of Harwich listed grievances against the minister, invoked the assistance of the puritan Earl of Warwick, and petitioned the king for redress. Lord Rivers, Sir Harbottle Grimstone, Sir John Barker, and Sir Thomas Bowes took up the case and persuaded the Council to overthrow the decision of the ecclesiastical court. Regarding the baptism of the dog, the coun- cillors pronounced, 'there was never any such act done or committed either by the said Sarah or any other in the town of Harwich, but was a mere fiction raised as may appear by the manner of Mr Innes's proofs'. Conflicting strands of evidence offset each other, and this most disturbing incident of profanity and disorder was determined not to have taken place. This was an extraordi- nary rebuff for the clerics of the High Commission, who expressed their resent- ment against 'the strangeness, insolency, and ill consequence of this proceeding by private men against the highest ecclesiastical court in England'.[28] In future, if anyone complained against travesties of the sacraments they would have to get their stories straight.

Other ecclesiastical rituals besides baptism came in for their share of profa- nation, and alcohol seems to have gone hand in hand with irreligion. Writing in 1635 Nehemiah Wallington pondered 'a memorial of God's judgements upon drunkards in Derbyshire', after four villagers parodied the ceremony of thanks- giving for women after childbirth by conducting the mock churching of a cow. Wallington notes, 'I did hear very credibly, that at a place called Eyam in Der- byshire that there were four drunken fellows which met at an alehouse to drink a barrel of ale; and when they were inflamed with liquor they would needs do something to be talked on; going through the church yard, the church door being open, they drove a cow into the church; and that which is appointed for churching of women they read it for the cow, and led her about the font: a

wicked and horrible fact, but it was strangely and fearfully punished.' Soon
after this infamous feat the actors suffered terrible afflictions. One became
dumb, one blind, another mad, and the fourth suffered a broken neck. Wallington comments, 'this was done near thirty years ago [i.e. early in the reign of
James I] but it is still fresh in memories there'. Keith Thomas cites this churching of the cow as part of the desanctification of religious ritual in the wake of
popular Protestantism, but from Wallington's point of view it pointed more to
the sifting of the godly from the reprobate in the unending struggle for the
reformation of manners.[29]

Revellers occasionally came before the church courts for drunken mockery
of the solemnities of death and for parodying of the rituals of funerals and
weddings. Pranksters were presented for such crimes as 'carrying William
Goodin upon the old hearse into the churchyard' and having the bells rung
for his funeral when he was not dead but dead drunk; for tolling the bells
'for Collins, a dead drunkard, to the disturbance of the whole parish'; and 'for
causing the bell to be tolled for a dead horse'.[30] These were minor incidents,
more quirks and curiosities than challenges to the established order. They
involved violations of social protocols and godly decorum, and sometimes
invited disorder. But none of them turned the world upside down for more
than a few noisy minutes.

An alehouse joke that went too far began in the Hallowe'en revels in 1637
when a group of Oxfordshire villagers, 'being merry and drinking together',
persuaded old Elizabeth Bullock, 'aged about 100 years and a weak woman of
sense and understanding', to claim marriage to William Allen of Stanton Har-
court. They 'persuaded her to report that she was with child, and put a cushion
under her petticoat, which she consented to out of her weakness and dotage'.
One of them then 'did draw a form of banns to be published between them,
which she carried to the curate'. Though obviously intended as a jest, this
parody of marriage-making was sufficiently offensive to be brought before the
archdeaconry court. It mocked the serious matter of matrimonial contracting
and sexual discipline that gave so much business to the ecclesiastical courts,
and it mocked the solemnities of banns of matrimony that ministers published
in church. William Allen was defamed by being named as the lover of the
ancient Elizabeth Bullock and for allegedly fathering her child. One of the perpetrators, John Wood, was also a churchwarden, who should have known
better, and he regretted his involvement in the incident when he presented his
information to the court. The matter seems to have been resolved by the
offenders apologizing and promising not to do it again.[31]

*

What by now may be considered the standard features of the genre recurred in two final cases from the reign of Charles II. Each involved young men carrying or leading animals to the font, sprinkling them with water in parody of the action of the minister, and naming them like Christians. In one case the authorities accepted that the action resulted from the 'indiscreet wantonness' of the perpetrators rather than their 'intention to deprave the holy sacrament'. The other they simply judged 'blasphemous'. After the turmoil of the revolution, in which the traditional ritual of baptism had been abolished, it was hard to secure reverence for the restored Prayer Book ceremonies. The revived church courts attempted to rebuild a religious culture of discipline and decorum while facing the perennial problem of youthful folly.

Five young bell-ringers were responsible for the profane baptism of a cat at Henley, Oxfordshire, in the early years of the Restoration. 'Meeting at Henley church in the evening' on 21 November 1662, they confessed, 'one Isaac Keene brought a cat with him into the church and made him fast in the church till they had rung the eight o'clock bell, and after the bell was rung they carried the cat to the font, and one of them taking up the cover of the font, Benjamin Wooldridge took out water out of the font and sprinkled the cat, which Thomas Talent had in his arms, and named the cat Tom, and appointed Isaac Keene and Thomas Wheeler to be gossips.' Pressed to explain this irreverence, with an opportunity to lessen the charges against them, 'they say they did not use the word "christen" or "baptise" but did this out of indiscreet wantonness, and not out of intention to deprave the holy sacrament of baptism.' Satisfied with this confession, the court ordered the offenders to perform public penance in the very church where they had sprinkled the cat.[32]

Two parishioners of Radcliffe, Lancashire, were responsible for a much more serious breach of discipline when they brought a horse to be baptized in church in 1662. Their offence, so far as it can be reconstructed, was a calculated comment on the restored Church of England rather than a mindless juvenile prank. John Angier, the curate of Ringley chapel, set out to discover and report the details of the offence, but was thwarted by uncooperative witnesses. John Lowe, the sexton of Radcliffe, was 'somewhat unwilling to give home a full and true relation of the whole manner, though he was present'. None the less, the following story emerged. On 5 November 1662, the anniversary of the gunpowder treason and a day of anti-popish festivity, Otto Holland and Peter Walker took advantage of the church being open 'to ring the bells for the solemnity of that day', and entered with their horse. Apparently, the sexton 'did not mind it, for he turned from them and went into the belfry'. The young men then led the horse to kneel near the communion table, and 'gave him a piece of bread, with some blasphemous expressions', and said 'that he was as good an episcopalian as any of them, for he had bowed to the altar'. After this profane parody of the holy communion they led the horse to the font, removed its cover, and 'sprinkled water on [the horse] and called him Surly Boy'.[33] The incident evoked memories of earlier disputes over altars and communion tables, fonts and font covers, and contentious liturgical gestures like kneeling and bowing, and echoed the actions of civil war soldiers. Surly Boy, if he did not foul the chancel floor, did all that was intended of him to outrage the ecclesiastical authorities.

Though isolated and unusual, these mock baptisms from different periods had several points in common. They brought together, in an incongruous and insulting manner, common domesticated animals and the holiest rituals of the Church. By sprinkling the horses and cats with water and giving them names in parody of the ritual by which babies became Christians, they profaned the sacred ceremony and blurred the boundary between humans and beasts. Baptism saved souls, animals had no souls, and the young men (for the most part) who staged these travesties imperilled their own salvation, so pastoral counsellors might argue.

The sacrament of baptism and the font where it was performed were controversial features of English Protestant culture. 'Baptism is an action in part moral, in part ecclesiastical, and in part mystical: moral, in being a duty which men perform towards God; ecclesiastical, in that it belongeth unto God's church as a public duty; finally mystical, if we respect what God doth thereby intend to work', claimed the influential Richard Hooker.[34] It was 'that universal, plain and easy rite . . . exceeding proper, and very innocent,' according to the Restoration churchman Thomas Comber.[35] Every English Christian was supposed to be baptized. The font, in most parishes, was sanctified equipment that belonged, with the altar, as the fulcrum of reverence and devotion. To sully it with urine, to soil it with animals, to allow drunken soldiers, bell-ringers, or other roisterers to subject it to ridicule, was not just profanation of the church but an act of dishonour to God.

At the same time, however, there were reformers who challenged the manner of Prayer Book baptism and disparaged the liturgical equipment with which it was performed. Puritans were more inclined to construe baptism as a ceremony of initiation than a sacrament of salvation, and some thought the font a leftover popish invention. Theologians disputed the efficacy and meaning of baptism, and there were countless parish squabbles over such accessories as the sign of the cross, the presence of godparents, and the application of water from the font. Most of these discussions were conducted with civility, but occasional outrageous travesties of the kind cited here could be seen as disorderly comments on the debate.[36] The young men responsible for these provocative 'strange exploits' knew the words and knew the rules of the rituals they were working to subvert. It is striking how closely they parodied the rubric, appointing 'godgaffers', mimicking the priest, and making a point of signing with the cross. Like the soldiers at Yaxley, the blasphemers at Radcliffe were engaged in a rowdy argument about baptism in the Church of England as well as a dramatic exploit with a horse.

It would be wrong, however, to recruit all these bravadoes to the cause of radical reform, to associate them with religious iconoclasm, or to claim for them an articulate sectarian agenda. Ecclesiastical sources insist that the offenders were 'profane' or 'blasphemous' in their behaviour, and that they acted 'to deprave the holy sacrament' or 'in derision of our ceremonies and religion'. But it might also be argued that their antics were driven by boredom, anger, or alcohol, by larrikin daredevilry or 'indiscreet wantonness', rather than hostility to the ritual and fabric of the Church of England. Their parodies of the sacrament could then be understood in terms of youthful mischief and reckless high spirits which only came to official notice because it crossed religious boundaries. Alehouse culture and Christian devotion were not necessarily incompatible, and most people knew the difference between what was expected during worship and what was permissible in one's cups. There was no harm in naming a dog Jeffery or calling a teenager Gurlypot, so long as it was not mixed up with the sacrament of baptism. If Thomas Bennet had been ducked at the village pump instead of in Watford church font the High Commission would never have been interested.

This takes us very close to interpreting the baptism of beasts in terms of festive misrule—skylarking, jesting, *homo ludens* playing the fool—in which the cherished rituals of mainstream culture are subjected to symbolic inversion. Besmirching the sacred, provoking the authorities, and advancing the interests of topsy-turvydom are familiar features of the carnivalesque. The groups of bell-ringers and other young men responsible for these acts are as close as one comes in England to the youth 'abbeys' or lords of misrule of early modern France.[37] Their mockery of the sacrament may then be seen as a transgressive interrogation of a familiar ritual, but one that did little real damage. The fact that they did not attempt to smash the font, but only to borrow it for a moment of roistering profanity, suggests the fundamental innocency of their action. If their crime was irreligion, it was irreligion with a curiously muted ring.

An entirely different explanation has been offered, from another anthropological perspective, proposing that the baptism of beasts was intended to secure them benefits. The men who took their animals to the font, had them churched, or rang church bells when they were dying, could then be viewed in terms of a tradition of folk magic, charms, and curative practices associated with unreformed Roman Catholicism. Keith Thomas suggests that 'it is possible that some of the numerous cases recorded in the sixteenth and seventeenth centuries of attempts to baptise dogs, cats, sheep, and horses may not have arisen from drunkenness or puritan mockery of anglican ceremonies, but have reflected the old superstition that the ritual had about it a physical efficacy which could be directed to any living creature'.[38] But this is more ingenious than persuasive; none of the evidence points in that direction. Large animals were valuable properties, and there was no shortage of horsemen and farmers to take care of them with conventional cures and wisdom. Cats, by contrast, were lowly beasts—Thomas Edwards thought them a 'vile, mean creature'[39]— and it would hardly have been worth the effort to give them the benefits of baptism. Household pets were more likely to thrive on fondling than sprinkling, and witches' familiars would surely have been averse to holy water. There is simply no trace of the supernatural in any of the mock baptisms we have covered, but abundant evidence that they had their origin in horseplay.

Nor can it be argued that travesties of the sacrament were signs of a disorderly society, ready to break out in revolt. The onlookers, so far as we know, disapproved of the action, and none was persuaded to join in. Unlike the battles over altar rails, that broke out in some churches at the beginning of the English revolution, the baptisms of beasts were minor scandals, soon suppressed though often remembered. They were provocations to outrage and affronts to religious decorum, but hardly acts of resistance or incitements to riot.

Dramatis Personae

Captain Beaumont at Yaxley, Huntingdonshire
Robert Rayner, corporal
Bartholemew Ward, soldier
Lawrence Dodds, soldier
John Stokesly, cleric of Oxford
Peter Simons of Udimore, Sussex
Joan Golding of Winchelsea, Sussex
Thomas Bennet of Watford, Hertfordshire
William Haydon of St Albans, Hertfordshire
Roger Haydon of St Albans, Hertfordshire
Ralph Stretton of St Albans, Hertfordshire
Thomas Hoddesdon of St Albans, Hertfordshire
Oliver Naylor of Tavistock, Devon, clerk
one Allen of South Moulton, Devon

Richard Dodd of East Brent, Somerset
John Prowse of Brixham, Devon
Thomas Easton of Loughton, Buckinghamshire
Isaac Antrobus of Egremont, Cumberland, clerk
Sara Peck of Harwich, Essex
William Innes of Harwich, Essex, clerk
Isaac Keene of Henley, Oxfordshire
Benjamin Wooldridge of Henley, Oxfordshire
Thomas Talent of Henley, Oxfordshire
Thomas Wheeler of Henley, Oxfordshire
John Angier of Radcliffe, Lancashire, clerk
John Lowe of Radcliffe, Lancashire
Otto Holland of Radcliffe, Lancashire
Peter Walker of Radcliffe, Lancashire

12

THE BATTLE OF THE ALTARS:
TURNING THE TABLES AND BREAKING THE RAILS

Charles I's reign proved yet again that one man's godly devotion could be another's blasphemous transgression. In the cultural wars of Caroline England, preceding the actual fighting of the 1640s, few topics were potentially as divisive as the positioning and treatment of the furnishings for holy communion. Tables and altar rails—in themselves innocent adiaphora—stirred some people to veneration while incensing others to violence. Liturgical trappings and equipment came to encode alternative visions of community, worship, and godly devotion.

Though disagreements about the architectural and material arrangements for the sacrament dated back to the sixteenth-century origins of the Church of England, they grew more acute in the period of Laudian ascendancy in the 1630s. The collapse of Archbishop Laud's power at the end of 1640 allowed local activists and parliamentary puritans to reverse the process of ceremonial innovation and to push for liturgical changes of their own. The eucharist itself was rarely parodied or profaned in these disputes (unlike the contemporary battles over fonts and baptism), but the energies released in eucharistic protest were sometimes shunted into scuffles around the threshold of the holy table.

This chapter is concerned with the contentious conversion of tables into altars, the controversial erection of communion rails, and their violent taking down. It focuses on the reign of Charles I, when these issues were most acute. Local disputes about church furnishings and liturgy, like the contemporary battles over rites of passage, provide another point of entry into the divisive religious culture of early modern England. Rather than focusing on the theology, policy, and churchmanship of the Caroline regime, where recent scholarship in this areas is centred, I propose to examine the consequences of official action. My focus is once again on lay–clerical interactions at the regional and parochial level.[1] An episode from late Caroline London provides a useful place to begin.

When parishioners gathered to subscribe the national Protestation in the London church of St Thomas the Apostle on 11 June 1641, one of them, John

Blackwell, grocer to the king, urged his neighbours to action: 'Gentlemen, we have here made a Protestation before almighty God against all popery and popish innovations, and these rails (laying his hand upon the rails about the communion table) are popish innovations, and therefore it is fit they be pulled down, and shall be pulled down.' The Protestation, drawn up in parliament in May 1641, was intended to unite the political nation in defence of the reformed Church of England. It was designed to solidify opposition to popery and Arminianism at a time when both appeared to be dangerously ascendant. But it could also be used more radically to decry those aspects of Laudian church-manship that puritans found offensive. In the parish of St Thomas, which was one of the first to subscribe the Protestation (which was not extended nation-wide until the following January), the occasion served as a licence and a catalyst for direct violent action.[2]

Parish zealots agreed with Blackwell that the communion rails were popish innovations, while conformists defended the rails and resisted efforts to break them down. A tussle ensued in the church, in which the churchwardens were knocked about and forced to retreat. According to a complaint addressed to the House of Lords, Blackwell's associates then 'with great insolency pulled down the rails' and bore them triumphantly out of the church saying, 'that Dagon being now down they would burn him'. Likened to Dagon, the idol-god of the Philistines which was shattered by the power of the ark of God, the rails were quickly reduced to ashes. A few enthusiasts threatened to burn the minister's surplice, and perhaps the minister too if he opposed them, in the same cleans-ing fire. In earlier times, in the face of such sacrilegious disorder, parish conser-vatives might have turned to the ecclesiastical courts for disciplinary redress; but now, with the courts in disarray and episcopacy itself in trouble, their only hope was that parliament might punish Blackwell and his fellow offenders. Their petition to the Lords, bewailing the violence and misrule with which the rails were removed, was signed by the rector and eight parishioners including one of the churchwardens.

Clearly the parish was polarized, as was much of the country, in this over-heated revolutionary summer. Activists in dozens of parishes sought the removal of altar rails at this time, anticipating by a year or more the official order to pull them down. Scenes as wild as that reported at St Thomas's were unusual, but all over England there were arguments about altars, tables, rails, and the conduct of holy communion. Local religious animosities focused on such seemingly trivial items as church furnishings because they were immedi-ate and familiar as well as controversial, and because they stood for larger prob-lems of theology, liturgy, and discipline.

In an attempt to assure parliament of their respectable godly intentions,

Blackwell's faction addressed a counter-petition to the House of Commons, who they rightly assumed would be more sympathetic than the Lords. This petition, subscribed by more than forty parishioners including the other churchwarden, asked that 'peace and quietness may be settled in the parish'. The petitioners did not dispute that a violent and irreverent episode had taken place, but in their version of recent events the responsibility for dissension lay with the party that had installed the controversial rails, not those who had pulled them down. Unlike the wilder sectarians who were beginning to break away from parochial discipline, these solid Londoners sought to reform their part of the Church of England and to join together in a purified parish communion.

St Thomas's parish, it emerged, had never fully complied with the Laudian altar policy, 'the table neither standing altarwise nor at the east end of the chancel, but in the usual place where it hath stood time beyond memory of man'. It probably stood, as did many an Elizabethan and Jacobean communion table, between the chancel and the nave, providing convenient access for all. The controversial rails, the petitioners explained, had only been installed in 1638, 'we know not by whose authority'. Though the minister said they were added 'for decency', and that people were not 'pressed' to come up to the rails to receive the sacrament, the local puritans claimed that the rails were 'offensive to the parish', an intrusive innovation, and 'a cause of very much trouble, grief and dissension'. Indeed, so burdensome was the innovation of kneeling at the rails to take communion that one 'grave pious matron' blamed her illness and impending death on the change of sacramental practice. Here as elsewhere, the rails represented the officious high ceremonialism associated with Archbishop Laud. They also stood as an obstacle among neighbours, a barrier between priest and parishioners, and a physical reminder of worrisome changes that seemed to be leading the Church of England to Rome.

Having taken parliament's Protestation against 'all popery and popish innovations', the petitioners continued, some parishioners asked 'to take away the rails', but wished it done 'in an orderly way'. Presumably if both churchwardens had been in agreement and if the minister had been willing to bend, that is what would have happened. Unfortunately, however, 'in the interim some youths in the place . . . pulled down the rails presently', provoking 'great division in the parish and most threatening speeches . . . from the rector'. All blame for the violent and disorderly attack on the rails was deflected onto these unnamed 'youths', while the godly petitioners assumed an air of righteousness against 'innovations' they deemed to be 'offensive'. John Blackwell, previously identified as a ringleader, played no part in this alternative narrative, though he was one of the most prominent signatories to the petition and possibly its author. Well-known as a puritan activist, Blackwell would soon become more prominent in his support for the parliamentary cause.[3]

The episode in this London parish, though by no means extraordinary, touches on several contentious topics. It exposes strains in lay–clerical relations and fractures within the parochial community that intensified from the mid-1630s to the threshold of civil war. It points to variant views on holy communion and changing attitudes to ecclesiastical furnishings that affected the local micro-environment of worship and devotion. The tussle at St Thomas's reflects the sometimes-volatile struggle over different devotional styles and different scales of uniformity within the early Stuart Church. It shows that there were orderly and disorderly ways of effecting change, as well as different ways of telling a story. Each side laid claim to a particular memory of liturgical arrangements, and each blamed the other for changes that fomented disorder. Here as elsewhere the conduct of the sacrament, the placement of the table, and the presence or absence of communion rails served as indicators of religious discipline and devotional style. The episode provides another point of entry for examining the contested cultural history of early modern England.

Disagreement about the meaning and significance of the mass, the eucharist, the Lord's supper, or holy communion stirred one of the fiercest theological controversies of the age of the Reformation. It split Catholics from Protestants, and left reformers arguing amongst themselves. The variety of names for this central sacrament indicates some of the sensitivity and controversy surrounding it. So do the competing terms of altar, table, and board. Bound up in this sacramental ensemble were aesthetic, architectural, liturgical, and theological issues of continuing weight and moment. The early Church of England emphasized the commemorative aspect of communion, allowed the laity to take both bread and wine, and left somewhat ambiguous the relation of the consecrated elements to the body and blood of Christ. Anti-ceremonial Calvinists sought relative simplicity and severity, while seventeenth-century Arminians laid more stress on the eucharistic miracle and a few veered back towards the doctrine of transubstantiation.[4] The sacrament involved the deepest mysteries of faith, though moderates might argue that what one took into one's mouth mattered less than what one took into one's heart.

While Protestant divines largely resolved the theological issues of transubstantiation and consubstantiation, discerning not the fleshly but the spiritual presence of Christ in the consecrated wine and bread, the practical consequences of their discussion continued to reverberate in parish life. It would never be clear, from an ordinary lay point of view, whether communion was something you took or something you received, whether the experience was primarily physical or spiritual, whether it should be construed as a miracle, a mystery, a sacrifice, or a commemoration, and whether it should be approached in humility or joy. In practice the holiness of holy communion varied with its solemnity and setting, and its performance took on different registers according to how the minister officiated, where in the church people communicated, and whether they did so standing, sitting, or meekly kneeling upon their knees.

The official position of the Church of England, set forth in the Thirty-Nine Articles (1563), treated the sacrament as a social drama binding neighbour to neighbour and priest to parishioners, as well as Christians to their God. 'The Lord's Supper' was intended as 'a sign of the love that Christians ought to have among themselves, one to another', as well as a partaking, for true believers, in the body and blood of Christ.[5]

The Book of Common Prayer (1552 and 1559) reinforced this notion of communion as a love-feast by denying the sacrament to any 'open and notorious evil liver' and to those among whom 'malice and hatred . . . reign'. Only the faithful, charitable, and reverent should approach God's holy board. We are reminded that communion was a ritual of inclusion, of membership and belonging, and that separation from its benefits (as occurred in the Caroline altar dispute) spoke of social isolation as well as estrangement from God. The communion table (no longer officially called an altar after 1552) was to stand 'in the body of the church or in the chancel, where morning prayer and evening prayer be appointed to be said', and the priest was to stand at the north side of the table to read the service. These arrangements made it easy for all to see and hear, and easier for parishioners to approach or gather round. Communicants were supposed to receive the sacrament kneeling, but the rubric said nothing about exactly where they should position themselves within the intimate geography of the church. Nor was there anything in the Prayer Book or Articles to indicate that the table should be protected, elevated, or offset by rails.[6]

So varied were local liturgical practices, even within the well-run diocese of London, according to a report in Lord Burghley's papers, that 'the table standeth in the body of the church in some places, in others it standeth in the chancel; in some places the table standeth altarwise, distant from the wall a yard, in some others in the middle of the chancel, north and south; in some places the table is joined, in others it standeth upon trestles; in some places the table hath a carpet, in others it hath not . . . some receive kneeling, others standing, others sitting'.[7] Though senior Elizabethan clerics might regret this diversity, none worked single-mindedly on behalf of uniform practice.

The Jacobean canons of 1604 repeated and amplified the Tudor requirements. Every church was required to maintain 'a decent communion table', to be 'placed in so good sort within the church or chancel, as thereby the minister may be more conveniently heard of the communicants in his prayer and minis-tration, and the communicants also more conveniently, and in more number, may communicate with the said minister'. Typically, the Jacobean canons left the placement of the table to local convenience, saying nothing about rails, steps, orientation, or positioning towards the east. The only thing required in the east end of the church was a copy of the Ten Commandments, so that the prohibitive word of the Father would overshadow the liberating sacrifice of the Son.[8]

Though wedded in principle to uniformity, the Jacobean Church counte-nanced a wide variety of liturgical expression and contingent material organi-zation. It remained, in practice, a matter of local preference whether the table stood at the east end of the chancel or out in the body of the church, or whether it was moved back and forth in preparation for worship. Jacobean visitation articles followed the formulae of the canons, typically inquiring whether the communion table was 'conveniently placed' within the chancel or church where the minister could best be heard and where the greatest number could communicate.[9] Customary arrangements varied in practice, so that communi-cants in some parishes approached the table at the east end and knelt in rever-ence at communion rails, while elsewhere they received the bread and the wine while standing at a table in the body of the church or even seated in their pews. A favoured Jacobean arrangement was for communicants to sit around the table in the chancel, as we might sit for a seminar, or in seats that later became choir stalls.[10] When not in use for the sacrament the table might serve for a desk top or counting board, like any other useful piece of furniture. The ecclesiasti-cal authorities, for the most part, were content to wink at many things, and they generally thought it better for communion to be administered irregularly but quietly than to make it a focus of contention. This policy might be described as irenical or Laodicean (peace-loving or lukewarm), but it met the needs of a diversified national Church.[11]

The reign of Charles I, by contrast, saw a drive toward religious conformity as Arminian and ceremonialist clerics enjoyed preferment and began to assert their power. The Jacobean notion of 'convenience' gave way to Caroline ideals of 'decency' and 'order', as high-church ministers indulged their taste for orna-mentation and hard-line prelates pressed for tighter parish discipline. Thou-sands of communion tables were moved altarwise to the far east end, hundreds of sets of rails were erected to enclose them, and an untold number of steps were built to offset chancels from naves. The result, in many dioceses, was a dramatic rearrangement of sacramental space and a controversial redirection of liturgical style. Though high churchmen were deeply gratified by the changes, many ordinary communicants found them disquieting. The ceremonialists sought to raise devotional standards and to secure religious conformity. Instead they spread discord and dissension. Though their intentions were benign, in pursuit of decency and order, their programme proved disastrously counter-productive and undermined the peace of the Church. The Stuart historian Thomas Fuller, writing soon after the event, astutely attributed the troubles of Charles I's reign to the failure of accommodation and moderation in such matters.[12]

Though never entirely uniform or consistent in application, the new altar policy emerged in the mid-1630s during the ascendancy of Archbishop William Laud. The religious programme of this period is often described as 'Laudian', though 'Caroline' might be a better term because the archbishop himself was not necessarily its most vigorous champion. Richard Neile at York, Matthew Wren at Hereford, Norwich, and Ely, and Richard Montague successively at Chichester and Norwich, were among the bishops who were most adamant about turning tables into altars and protecting them with rails. Laud and Neile had earlier been responsible for moving the tables at Durham and Gloucester cathedrals, and a few precocious ministers set their tables altarwise in Hertfordshire and Lincolnshire in the early years of Charles's reign. In 1633, just two months after Laud's elevation to Canterbury, Charles himself ruled in the celebrated case of St Gregory's church, London, that parishes should be guided by their mother cathedrals in this regard.[13]

During the remainder of the 1630s Caroline churchmen used the machinery of ecclesiastical administration to advance their vision of the altar and to promote the new liturgical regime. Some incumbents anticipated instructions by eagerly implementing the innovations,[14] while others responded sluggishly to pressure from above. By the late 1630s a preponderance of parishes had come into line.

John Williams of Lincoln, a Jacobean appointee, was one of the few bishops to battle against Laudian officialdom. Though his own ceremonial preference may have been for tables offset by 'steps or ascents, in the upper end' of the church, he allowed the placement of the table at Leicester to be governed by local concerns about harmony and convenience, and earlier he had enjoined the vicar of Grantham against constructing an altar that parishioners thought offensive.[15] Williams's treatise *Holy Table, Name and Thing,* which argued vociferously against the imposition of altars, triggered a vigorous response from the ceremonialist avant-garde, after its manuscript circulation in 1633 and its publication in print in 1637. It was a sign of the times that Williams's old-fashioned plea for 'Christian charity' was scathingly countered by Laudians who questioned the bishop's 'zeal to the truth'. Not surprisingly, Williams's career was ruined.[16]

More typical, perhaps, was the response of Richard Corbet, bishop of Norwich, not otherwise renowned as a stickler for discipline. Late in 1633, after Lambeth and Whitehall had spoken, Corbet admonished several parishes in his diocese for not repositioning their communion tables against the eastern wall or below the eastern window of the church. The parishes of Pentney, Crostwick, Fordham, and Hoo were among those cited as delinquent, but each soon conformed and the clerk was able to record that their tables were satisfactorily moved. Only at Morningthorpe was the table not relocated beneath the east window because, the rector explained, 'the grave of Elizabeth Garmish was made and she interred nigh unto the same window a year since', thereby pre-empting the space. Corbet made no mention of rails, the next refinement on the ceremonialist agenda, but his successors would press hard in that regard.[17]

In 1634 Archbishop Laud issued a metropolitical order, strongly supported by the king, requiring officials throughout the province of Canterbury to turn communion tables altarwise and offset them with rails. An increasing number of bishops issued their own orders to that effect, and Wren, Dee, and Towers showed exceptional determination in having them carried out in East Anglia and the east Midlands. William Piers began to implement the policy in the diocese of Bath and Wells in 1634, though two years later two thirds of his parishes had yet to comply.[18] In the diocese of London the bishop's chancellor, Dr Arthur Duck, and the vicar-general of Canterbury, Sir Nathaniel Brent, issued instructions at episcopal and metropolitan visitations that encouraged local Laudians to take a hard line on altar rails.[19] In the north Archbishop Neile sought compliance from local parishes, and the archdeacon of York inquired in 1635 whether each communion table was 'rightly placed, and encompassed within a decent rail . . . according to the instructions and order lately given by this court'.[20]

Following his visitation of the diocese of York in 1636, Archbishop Neile rebuked the parish of Hosforth because 'the communion table is not railed', and issued specific instructions to bring about conformity. At Bolam 'there wanteth a decent rail before the communion table', a deficiency that was quickly remedied. At North Wheatley he ordered the churchwardens 'to cause the communion table to be set close up in the chancel . . . and to be railed'. Several other parishes were similarly censured. Keyworth was in default because 'the communion table standeth a yard and a half from the wall', and Bulcote 'for not providing a cloth nor carpet for the communion table'.[21] Episcopal records suggest that most parishes accommodated themselves to the new ceremonialist policy, and those who were reluctant to move and rail their tables eventually conformed with a little prompting. Only a parish-by-parish examination of churchwardens' accounts would reveal the actual timing and cost of these changes.[22]

The Caroline altar policy was driven by a heightened sense of religious propriety. It was designed to secure greater reverence for the sacrament of communion and to protect the table or altar from profane uses. Archbishop Laud himself called the altar 'the greatest place of God's residence upon earth . . . for there 'tis *Hoc est corpum meum*'. Laud's acolyte John Pocklington called it 'the most holy place of all others under the cope of heaven'.[23] Such a numinous place warranted the highest security and respect. To conform in full to these demands a parish would position its communion table in a north–south alignment against the far east wall of the church, in the place once occupied by the Roman Catholic altar. The chancel would be raised by two or three steps closer to heaven, and this sanctuary would be separated from the less sacred part of the church by a barrier or rail. Lay access to the holy table would be restricted, fine fabrics would protect its surfaces, and parishioners who refused to kneel at the rail to communicate would be punished. Communion then became less an exercise of religious community among neighbours and more a ritual centred on the priest. It was easier in this setting to imagine the sacrificial elements as blood and flesh, and tempting for the priest to approach the altar with the bows and obeisances formerly associated with the Roman Catholic host.[24] It was equally easy for anyone who feared that the Church of England was headed toward Rome to find confirmation of this trend in the Laudian veneration of altars and in the ceremonialist conduct of the sacrament.

The rehabilitation of the word 'altar', with all its popish connotations, was an especially controversial feature of the new devotional ethos. Ceremonialist and Arminian clergy made deliberate use of the term, which they must have known would upset their more staunchly Calvinist neighbours. 'He speaks for altars—altar! altar! altar! altar!—just like his fellow monks of his acquaintance,' complained a fellow minister of Archbishop Laud in 1637.[25] Richard Montague was especially keen to call the communion table an altar, despite his awareness that this usage 'offendeth many'. He instructed his diocesan officials at Norwich, in order to 'follow the course and practice of the ancient, primitive, apostolical church, we ought not to be offended at the name, thing, or use of altar, whereat manifold sacrifice is offered to God'. The provocative Laudian canons of 1640 declared that although the table was not 'a true and proper altar, wherein Christ is again sacrificed . . . it is and may be called an altar by us in that sense in which the primitive church called it an altar and no other'.[26]

In keeping with Caroline respect for the beauty of holiness, the table or altar was to be guarded against all profane usage, from storage of hats and placing of feet to pollution by children and dogs. If it were not railed in at the eastern end of the chancel, warned Laud in 1634, 'churchwardens will keep their accounts at the Lord's table, parishioners will sit round it and talk of parish businesses . . . schoolmasters will teach their boys to write upon this table, and boys will lay their hats, satchels and books upon it, and in their master's absence sit upon the same; and many will sit or lean irreverently against the Lord's table in sermon time; glaziers will knock it full of nail holes . . . and dogs will defile the Lord's table'.[27] This was an appeal to practical seemliness that masked a fundamental reordering of sacramental priorities and a shift in eucharistic theology.

Local Laudians took up the refrain. Having railed his table at Grantham, Lincolnshire, the minister expressed satisfaction that it was 'now much better than before for edifying the communicants and for avoiding profane usage of it by the boys and others in sermon time, in sitting under it, playing or sleeping and standing leaning the elbows on it, in most irreverent manner whilst prating, to the offence of the congregation'. Parishioners who found fault with the new arrangement were clearly uncouth and irreverent, and had only themselves to blame if they were excommunicated for refusing to come up to the rails. There could be no concession to any who found the new proto-cols idolatrous. Richard Drake of Radwinter, Essex, claimed similarly that his newly moved communion table, with its ensemble of chancel rail, screen, and steps, was set forth only 'for beauty and comeliness' and 'for the more decent performance of the divine service'. The Laudian Canons of 1640 reiterated this point, justifying rails as a remedy for irreverent leaning or the casting of hats.[28] Insistence on practical seemliness diverted attention from the far more complex theological issues of altar placement, which reopened the doors to transubstantiation and appeared to give passage to the Counter-Reformation.

Apologists for the new policy repeatedly drew attention to acts of sacrilege associated with unprotected tables. They took deep offence, on behalf of God's honour, when a Wolverhampton woman used an altar napkin instead of a veil to cover her head at her churching in 1637, and again in 1640 when a Yorkshire man was seen 'wiping his face, being sweaty, with the cloth of the communion table'. They were distressed by a Leicestershire parishioner who leaned his back against the communion table and helped himself to the leftover wine and invited fellow communicants to do likewise. They were apoplectic in 1638 when a Cambridgeshire communion had to be abandoned when a parishioner's dog ran up to an unrailed table and took the consecrated bread.[29]

Benjamin Spencer, the minister of St Thomas, Southwark, had only harsh words for 'those who set their tails where we set the sacrament, when there is room enough to sit elsewhere'.[30] Ephraim Udall of St Austin's, London, worried about schoolboys who 'do write on the communion table . . . fouling and spotting the linen and table at the same time with ink', and about communicants who might jog or crowd the table. But this was nothing beside the threat of someone 'infected with the plague, or having a plague sore on him, which is no rare thing in our churches of London', indiscriminately infecting others by breathing over the unprotected bread and wine.[31] Even more shocking was the 'pollution' Thomas Cheshire witnessed at St Sepulchre's church in London, which, he gauged, 'would have made the good primitive Christians to have trembled themselves out of joint'. Cheshire reported seeing 'a woman dandling and dancing her child upon the Lord's holy table; when she was gone I drew near and saw a great deal of water upon the table; I verily think they were not tears of devotion, it was well it was no worse.'[32] Intrusions of this sort were intolerable, but they might be prevented by the erection and maintenance of rails.

Supporters of the ceremonialist programme were eloquent in its favour, and could only explain resistance as the products of malice or irreligion. The moving and railing of tables, they insisted, was improvement, not innovation, and the change was pleasing to God. Words like 'fairer', 'seemly', 'orderly', and 'decent' were employed to applaud the alterations. Bishop Matthew Wren, in one of the fullest formulations of the Caroline altar policy, insisted that the furnishings for holy communion be 'comely' and 'handsomely' arranged. These words—along with 'decently', 'devoutly', and 'reverently'—were code words for the ceremonialist 'beauty of holiness' and alarm signals to local puritans.[33]

In his visitation articles at Norwich in 1636 and Ely in 1638, Wren instructed parishes in the new arrangements. Each was to furnish 'a decent rail . . . near one yard high', tightly constructed so 'that dogs may not anywhere get in'. Beyond the rail, in an area reserved for the clergy, would be the holy table, 'placed conveniently . . . at the east end of the chancel where the altar in former times stood, the ends being placed north and south'. There the communicants would kneel to attention, and the sacrament would be denied to any 'that did unreverently either sit, stand or lean, or that did not devoutly and humbly kneel upon their knees'.[34] Richard Montague, Wren's successor at Norwich, specified that the chancel should be divided from the nave 'with a partition of stone, boards, wainscot, grates, or otherwise', with steps or 'ascents up into the altar'. The table or altar should be 'fixedly set ... at the east end of the chancel, close unto the wall, upon an ascent or higher ground', it was not to be 'removed down at any time, either for or without communion, into the lower part of the chancel or body of the church', and it should be 'enclosed and ranged about with a rail of joiner's and turner's work, closely enough to keep out little dogs or cats from going in and profaning that holy place, from pissing against it or worse'. Communicants were to approach in reverence, of course, and none was to receive the sacrament unless 'meekly kneeling upon his knees'.[35]

Philip Parsons, the vicar of Great Finsborough, Suffolk, was among the dozens of ceremonial enthusiasts who put these policies into practice. He completed his reforms by building three steps before the altar, and 'named the first step the father, the second the son, and the third step the holy ghost, and bowed to them, all severally', according to opponents who later secured his ejection.[36] Archbishop Laud's chaplain, William Heywood, the rector of the parish of St Giles in the Fields, Middlesex, similarly officiated in a radically transformed church. A large decorated screen, 'set above with winged cherubims and beneath supported by lions', provided a theatrical setting for the sacramental enclosure, separated from the congregation by three chancel steps and a wall-to-wall rail. Here, according to disgusted local puritans, the minister prepared the holy sacrament with 'antic gestures of cringings and bowings' which they considered 'impious, ungodly, and abominable to behold'.[37] Most of the complaints against the Laudian innovations cite the priest's superstitious cringing and bowing as well as his forcing communicants to kneel at the rail.

The Laudian altar policy culminated in the 1640 'Constitutions and Canons Ecclesiastical', which attempted to codify for national use the arrangements that ceremonialist clerics had already imposed in various dioceses. Promulgated at a time when these policies were already under attack, the Canons of 1640 mandated that tables or altars stand sideways under the east window of every chancel or chapel, insisted that they be railed to protect them from abuses, legitimized reference to communion tables as 'altars', and required communicants to 'approach to the holy table, there to receive the divine mysteries' on their knees.[38] Adopted, so their authors said, to secure 'unity of practice in the outward worship and service of God', the new Canons triggered a backlash that helped to destroy the Church. To critics who charged them with 'innovation' the Laudians answered ingenuously that they were merely reviving an 'ancient and laudable custom'. Laud and his fellow bishops must have known that the new Canons were explosive, yet they persisted in expounding their policy at length. Though they acknowledged that the position of the table was 'in its own nature indifferent', they continued to demand conformity to arrangements that many of their countrymen found offensive.[39]

Bishop William Juxon invoked the authority of the recent canons, as well as the questionable mantle of Queen Elizabeth, when he insisted late in 1640 that all parishes in the diocese of London should have 'a comely partition betwixt your chancel and the body of the church', an 'ascent or steps' before the holy table, and the table itself to be 'set as is directed in the queen's Injunctions [of 1561] and as appointed by the Canon made in the Synod held at London, anno 1640'.[40] History was once again deployed to legitimate as traditional a practice that would otherwise appear to be innovation. In the event, in the crisis of 1640–2, the visitation for which these articles were drawn was never conducted.

Puritans were naturally alarmed by the rehabilitation of popish altars and the promotion of popish ceremony that appeared to reverse the Reformation.[41] But conservative lay parishioners could also take offence at the Laudian 'innovations' because they represented change. Between 1633 and 1640 they had seen a significant redirection of liturgical policy that intruded on local custom, rearranged church furnishings in a popish or superstitious manner, distanced the table from communicants, and tapped into parish funds to pay for the work. English religious culture had taken a new direction and it seemed to be heading towards Rome. At stake were community, custom, and convenience as well as variant views on religion. It was especially distressing that a policy designed to enhance communion led to some people being denied it, and to others being excommunicated, because they would not conform to the ritual of the rails.

'See the practice of these times,' wrote Charles Chauncey, who quit his ministry in Hertfordshire to go to New England in 1637. 'They will have priests not ministers, altars not communion tables, sacrifices not sacraments; they will bow and cringe to and before their altars, yea, they will not endure any man to enquire after what manner of Christ is in the sacrament, whether by way of consubstantiation, or transubstantiation, or in a spiritual manner; yea, they will have tapers, and books never used, empty basins and chalices there, what is this but the mass itself, for here is all the furniture of it.'[42]

William Prynne, in *A Breviate of the Prelates Intolerable Usurpations* (printed privately in Amsterdam in 1637), charged the bishops with acting illegally by 'turning communion tables into altars, railing them close prisoners against the east wall of the church', and forcing people to communicate at the rail, 'contrary to the usage ever since reformation first brought in'. The recklessly hostile

Newes from Ipswich (1637, reprinted 1641) repeated the charge that the bishops were acting tyrannically as well as popishly by 'railing in the communion table altarwise, and causing the communicants to come up to the rail to receive in a new unaccustomed manner'.[43]

Rumours abounded to the effect that Laud and his associates were 'setting up the mass and maintaining idolatry'.[44] Henry Tailor of Hardingham, Norfolk, was charged in 1637 with putting it about that the Archbishop of Canterbury was 'a favourer of popery' who wanted 'real adoration, worship, and reverence to the very communion table'.[45] Even moderate conformists were alarmed, such as John Ley, the pastor of Great Budworth, who was troubled by the erection of an altar in Chester cathedral. The Church, he thought, had been hijacked by innovating prelates, and 'the communion table hath lately gained a new name, a new nature, a new posture, and a new worship'.[46]

The relocated tables provoked hundreds of parish disputes and ripples of local disagreement that swelled into tides of anger and recrimination. But the problem was not just about religion, which may have been too 'deep' and difficult for many laymen. Crises also developed over custom and convenience, seating and precedence, and the sight-lines and earshot within the performance space of the church. Arguments about altars became entwined with other troublesome issues, from pew assignments to tithe assessments, from personal conflicts to matters of liturgical style.

When Thomas Wolrych, esquire, attempted to take communion in his customary manner at Cowling, Suffolk, in 1638, kneeling by his seat in the chancel, the minister refused him unless he would move 'unto the rails near the communion table of late years removed into a new place at the upper end of the chancel'. Wolrych was no puritan and was perfectly content to kneel in his usual place, but he was adamantly opposed, he said, 'to the alteration of old customs'. Adding further insult to the public humiliation of refusing him the sacrament, the Church then had Wolrych excommunicated for not receiving the communion at the rails. The ecclesiastical authorities, in Wolrych's view, had acted with questionable legality, and proceeded contrary to the word of God and to Christian charity.[47] Anyone who wonders at the wave of hostility that broke against the Laudian Church as soon as Charles I called a parliament in 1640 has only to look at cases like these.

Similar contests between traditionalists and innovators were played out in hundred of parishes where Laudians had gained control. Ecclesiastical court records of the later 1630s are sprinkled with cases of laymen who resisted the sanctification of altars or who spoke against the ceremonialist innovations. Not all of them were puritans, but most accumulated a grudge against the Laudian regime. Parliamentary petitions and inquiries of the early 1640s tell more of the story, often from the other side, as an alternative forum opened for the airing of parochial disputes. A selection of these cases shows how the battle of the altars built up layers of distrust and frustration that affected the national mood.

In a landmark case at Beckington, Somerset, the churchwardens were excommunicated and eventually imprisoned for refusing to move their communion table. The table had stood on its 'mount' in the chancel since the middle of Elizabeth's reign, 'with a very decent wainscot border and a door, with seats for the communicants to receive in round about it'. But in the changed religious climate of the 1630s this antique arrangement no longer satisfied the ceremonialist avant-garde. One of the problems with the Beckington ensemble, according to the Laudian rector Alexander Huish, was that it was difficult to see whether communicants were actually kneeling on their knees; another was that the table took up too much of the chancel and so limited the parson's opportunity to profit from burials in that sanctified area. The battle 'to remove the table to the east end and place a decent rail before it'—a battle that lasted from 1634 to 1638—pitched minister, bishop, and archbishop against an outraged local community. And the community itself was deeply divided. The churchwardens were backed by the lord of the manor, and by a petition with one hundred subscriptions, but the episcopal authorities used heavy weapons to crush this local dissent. In 1637 a riot broke out in the churchyard and parishioners were indicted at the Somerset assizes. The battle of Beckington was an important test case for, as Bishop Piers wrote to Laud, 'if the parishioners in every parish be left unto their own wills, in some places they will have the communion table railed in the midst of the chancel, in other places above the steps; in some places they will have it stand upon a mount, in other places they will make all the ground of the chancel level; and so they will follow their own fancies, which is the thing they desire'. This was explicitly a battle about the crushing of 'wills', the reining in of local 'fancies', and the imposition of centralized episcopal power.[48]

In another Somerset conflict, after the parishioners of Stretton resisted the Laudian innovation and brought their table 'down again in his former place', Bishop Piers instructed the minister 'not to administer the communion until the table was again set up altarwise', and the 1637 Easter communion was abandoned. Piers's hard line prompted the following attack charge from his enemies: 'O monstrous superstition, sacrilege and impiety, to deprive the people of the sacrament, because the table stood not after his new fancy.'[49]

Laudian officials precipitated a similar crisis at Market Harborough, Leicestershire, in 1636 when they insisted that the communion table be set altarwise and railed in, and that none should communicate except at the rails. 'Divers refused to come to the rails, desiring to receive the communion in the accustomed place', and were cited to the court for their pains. At this point most of the parishioners agreed to conform, except for Christian, the wife of John Harper, who 'refused to obey, and was excommunicated', and continued so about four years, 'notwithstanding divers demands for absolution'.[50]

Excommunication was a relatively heavy weapon—a sanction with social, spiritual, and financial consequences—which seems to have been used more commonly by the Caroline episcopal regime. One of the mistakes of the Laudian Church was to use this weapon against prominent parishioners, upright members of the local community rather than obvious deviants, whose conformity and humility they judged incomplete. John Hocker, a Colchester churchwarden and businessman, was 'excommunicated from participation in divine ordinances and commerce and trade' after refusing to rail—in the communion table in 1635.[51] Andrew Keate, a churchwarden at Great Wratting, Suffolk, was among those excommunicated in 1636 because he failed to follow orders to construct the newly commissioned altar rails. After another churchwarden finished the job a year later Keate's wife, though 'very sick near unto death', was also excommunicated 'for not going to receive the communion at the rails'. The couple's excommunication continued until 1641, when Keate took his case to Westminster.[52] The churchwardens of Upton, Northamptonshire, were also excommunicated because they would not disburse parish funds when the minister 'caused the communion table . . . to be removed, altered and cancelled [railed], and set in the east end of the church from the ancient place where time out of mind it hath usually stood'. A sympathetic House of Commons took up their case in December 1640 and ordered the minister 'at his own cost and charges' to return the table 'to the place where it hath formerly stood'.[53]

'Innovation' and 'convenience' were also at loggerheads in the parish of All Saints, Northampton. Until late in the 1630s, claimed two former churchwardens, the communion table at All Saints stood 'in the middle of the chancel . . . according to the rubric, as in the most visible and convenient place'. At some time—presumably under King James—it had been railed and set about with 'convenient seats', in accordance with orders from the bishop's chancellor and at a cost to the parish of about two marks. But in recent years, 'innovations daily dripping into the church', Dr Samuel Clark, an official of the ecclesiastical court, ordered them 'to take away the old rails . . . and to pluck up the seats . . . and to place the said table at the upper end of the said chancel under the east window altarwise, and there to rail it in'. This, the churchwardens protested, would remove the minister to a place where 'a third part of the congregation could neither hear nor see him', and would therefore offend

against the Jacobean canons. When the churchwardens delayed in their execution of the order they too were excommunicated, and the parish was eventually
forced 'to remove the communion table and set it altarwise' as the authorities
insisted.[54]

Nor was this the end of the matter, for a Mr Ramsdell, a local supporter of
ceremonial discipline, complained to the Council about irregular goingson
in the parish. Despite their apparent compliance with physical arrangements,
the minister of All Saints and his allies showed ingenuity in flouting the spirit
of the Laudian reforms. 'Though the communion table is set altar-wise at
the end of the chancel, and railed in, yet ordinary townsmen follow the
priest within the rails with the consecrated bread and wine.' The case was
still before the High Commission in 1641 when the aggrieved churchwardens
complained to parliament, and when that prerogative court came to an
end.[55]

Excommunications soured the air at Aldeburgh, Suffolk, where parishioners
complained that the repositioned table was 'so far remote from the body of the
church', and was so obstructed by arches, 'as not the one half of the people can
either see or hear' the ministration. 'Convenience' had given way to a blind
uniformity.[56] The parishioners of St Peter's, Nottingham, also complained that
with the table turned altarwise, they 'could not see and hear the consecration',
and they 'could not have it as [they] used to receive it'. Forty-five of them were
cited in 1638 for not receiving the communion at Easter when they objected to
kneeling at the rails.[57]

A similar small-scale revolt broke out at Epping, Essex, in 1639 when half a
dozen parishioners, including one of the churchwardens, 'refused to come up
to the communion table to receive the communion there'. Samuel Greygoose,
the churchwarden, was further cited before the London commissary court 'for
attempting to take the communion table out of the rail, saying the rail is an
idol'.[58] Dagon would remain for as long as the ceremonialists held sway, but as
soon as they faltered the idol would come down. Few places were as accommodating as the unnamed Midland parish under the patronage of Sir Thomas
Temple where, despite the establishment of an altar and the erection of rails,
communicants could 'for money' dispense with the need to come up to the
rails, and where the priest turned a blind eye to the restoration of the table to
the chancel on occasions when a neighbouring minister officiated.[59]

At Radwinter, Essex, the Laudian minister Richard Drake took pride in his
railed chancel and ornate new screen which he described as 'a tribute of my
devotion and thankfulness to God'. Certain parishioners, whom Drake
described as 'unthankful men', took a different view, characterizing the changes
as popish innovations. The deep divisions in the community became apparent

one Easter when Drake refused communion to 'at least a hundred' who 'would not come up to the rail, although they all presented themselves kneeling in the chancel or near it'. Resolving to 'give the water no passage, no not a little, fearing lest the yielding to one omission or alteration might be an inlet to many to follow', the minister succeeded in mobilizing a substantial section of his moderately devout congregation against both himself and the Laudian regime. Parishioners who came diligently to church and who were ready to kneel for communion were hard to brand as puritans, but Drake facilitated their conversion.[60]

Radwinter was already in turmoil at the end of the 1630s and the situation only got worse. As a strict disciplinarian and devout ceremonialist, Drake was increasingly at odds with the good-fellows as well as the godly in his parish. His opponents jangled the bells during worship, mocked his liturgical gestures, and complained of his devotional style. It was little wonder that a fracas should occur over church ornaments at Radwinter in July 1640, that Drake should be called before the parliamentary committee for religion in January 1641, and that an antagonistic churchwarden should take back the communion table 'and set it below the steps' as soon as opportunity offered in September 1641. Drake was eventually driven from his parish by threats of violence in the course of the civil wars.[61]

Beginning in some parishes in 1640, and quickening with the attack on episcopacy in 1641, the tables were literally turned. Just as the conversion of tables to altars had relied on a mixture of individual initiative and episcopal instruction, so the reversal of that process involved both parliamentary ordinances and freelance reform and iconoclasm. In most places cautious officials waited until instructed by authority, but a few zealous souls, like those at St Thomas the Apostle, took matters into their own hands.

It was during the summer of 1640 that reports first appeared of the violent destruction of communion rails and unlicensed attacks on other liturgical furnishings. These were clear signs that the Laudian ascendancy was in trouble. The dissolution of the Short Parliament in May 1640 stalled hopes of a political settlement, while the promulgation of the new church canons raised fresh fears of a popishly inclined religious hierarchy. The military situation was unstable, with the Scots menacing Newcastle and the troops pressed for service threatening to get out of control.

In July 1640 persons unknown (supposedly a faction in the parish) broke into the church at Esher, Surrey, late at night, and destroyed their controversial altar rails.[62] A rash of similar attacks followed, mostly in eastern and central England. Many of the assaults were blamed on unruly soldiers. The Earl of

The Souldiers in their passage to York turn unto reformers pull down Popish pictures, break down rayles, turn altars into Tables

5. The destruction of altar rails, 1641

Warwick wrote to Secretary Vane on 27 July 1640 about the insolencies of Captain Rolleston's company in Essex, 'caused by a barrel of beer and fifty shillings in money sent them by Dr Barkham, parson of Bocking, of whose kindness it seems they took too much; for I found them much disordered by drink that day, and they went to his church and pulled up the rails about the communion table, and burnt them before their captain's lodgings.' A similar fate befell the communion rails at Braintree as well as the rails and religious ornaments in Richard Drake's church at Radwinter. One of the soldiers pulling down the rails in the Stour valley adopted the nom de guerre of 'Bishop Wren'.[63]

These actions were evidently contagious, for two weeks later the Earl of Salisbury reported from Hatfield, 'the soldiers here begin to follow the example of those of Essex in pulling down communion rails, and at Hadham in Hertfordshire, where Dr Pashe [Thomas Paske] is incumbent, they have pulled down a window lately built by him . . . It is very likely the people of the town set them on.'[64] Urged on by radical puritans, fuelled by drink, and excited, perhaps, by the pleasure of smashing things, the iconoclasts tore down the rails in at least seventeen churches in Hertfordshire. The season was memorialized in later chronicles as the time when 'the soldiers in their passage to York turn reformers, pull down popish pictures, break down rails, turn altars into tables'.[65]

Pressured by the Council in London, local magistrates attempted to stem these disorders and to punish those responsible. Edward Aylee of Bishop's Stortford, glazier, a local man impressed for military service, was identified as the ringleader in pulling down the altar rails at Rickmansworth after the Sunday morning service. Aylee confessed his crime, and also acknowledged defacing the cover of the font, but insisted 'that he was not hired nor entreated by any body to do the same'. When further charged with speaking in favour of the Scots, against whom he was supposed to march as a soldier, he said 'that if he did speak any such words it was in heat of drink, and not out of any ill purpose or intent'. Local juries empanelled to investigate the charges were inclined to downplay the business. Regarding the destruction of the rails in five churches in Broadwater Hundred, they affirmed on oath that they could not discover the names or dwellings of any of the rioters. Furthermore, they were by no means certain that any true riot had taken place. The perpetrators, usually no more than five persons, had secured entry to the church by finding the door open or by procuring the key.[66] Though local people were suspected, they seemed to enjoy a measure of protection and their involvement in attacks on the communion rails was difficult to prove.

Local men as well as travelling soldiers took part in the defacement of the chancel at Much Hadham. Examined by the Hertfordshire Quarter Sessions, Richard Mose, blacksmith, confessed that he only joined in the attack after several other men promised him money and urged him on. A few weeks later the incumbent, Thomas Paske, wrote magnanimously from Cambridge to say that he had 'discovered the actors and abettors' in 'that barbarous and most impious fact lately committed' in his church, but offered that 'if they will willingly repair the breaches they made and set them in their former state, all proceedings against them may be suspended'.[67]

The worst outrage occurred at King's Walden, in Hitchin half-hundred, where two dozen soldiers entered one Sunday during service. They 'sat in the chancel till the sermon was ended, and then, before all the congregation, they tore down the rails and defaced the wainscot which adorned the chancel, invited themselves to the churchwardens to dinner, exacted money from the minister, brought an excommunicated person into the church and forced the minister to read evening prayer in his presence'. They seem to have behaved more like vigilantes than a disorderly mob, driven more by a corrective religious agenda than an appetite for destruction. Again, their anonymity was preserved. They could not be identified among the local impressed 'servants, labourers and tradesmen' who 'after their disbandment returned immediately to their homes and callings', but rather were thought to be 'vagabonds . . . whom neither the house of correction nor any other punishment will reform of their roguish life'. It is not clear whether the jurymen were collusive with those who pulled down the rails, or sympathetic with their action, or whether the offenders were truly outsiders whose identities could not be learned. The Council demanded the names of the 'countenancers and abbettors' of the rioters, but Hertfordshire assured them that the problem had gone away.[68]

Perhaps it had gone to Suffolk, where at Sudbury in October 1640 'a rout of apprentices, saye-weavers and other poor rascals' entered the church during sermon time, and when the preacher was finished they tore up the communion rails and armed themselves with the pieces. More rails fell at Ipswich, Suffolk, and at Marlow, Buckinghamshire, before parliament assembled in November.[69]

An incident at Latton, Essex, combined puritan reform with festive misrule, with some rioters citing provisions against iconoclasm in Exodus and others braying for beer. The attack on the altar rails began on New Year morning, 1641, when some of the bell-ringers, well lubricated and well exercised, decided to set the table in the chancel 'as it had formerly stood' and to pull down the hated rails. This was a defiant and decisive rejection of the Laudian altar policy, carried out by the same kind of young men who had apparently buried Mrs Horseman at Holton. Excitement grew as the rails were tossed over the church-yard wall, broken into manageable pieces, and then carried 'to the whipping post' at the centre of the village where they were set on fire. A kilderkin of beer appeared from the Black Lion inn, purchased by subscription, and when the rails were reduced to ashes the celebrants took the remains of the beer back to the church where they resumed their ringing of the bells. 'The chief actor', a servant named Jeremy Reeve, led the assault with an axe, but the rest of the crowd, mostly servants and apprentices, insisted that they had only used their hands. More substantial members of the community were said to have lent their vocal encouragement and support. By the time the magistrates got round to examining the affair ten days later Reeve was not to be found and was believed to have gone to London. The magistrates described the affair as an 'insolency' but were remarkably lenient in their treatment of offenders. It was enough if the rail-breakers said they were sorry and confessed 'it was most unadvisedly done'. One of the rioters explained that the rails 'gave great offence to his conscience' and said 'that the placing of them was against God's laws, and the kings, as appeared by the 20th chapter of Exodus, about the 20th verse'. Others excused their action 'because the rails had been pulled down in other places without punishment therefore'.[70]

Reports of profanations of churches were more common in the south, where troops were recruited, than in the north, where they awaited the possibility of military action against the Scots. Sir John Conyers wrote from York in February 1641 that 'the insolencies in the army daily increase', but the problem stemmed from idleness, indiscipline, and lack of money rather than sectarian violence or profanity. Troopers in some companies were on the brink of mutiny, and reportedly went in for intimidation, extortion, and highway robbery, but they did not direct their anger against Yorkshire churches or communion rails.[71] This may, in part, reflect the survival of evidence for Archbishop Neile had made sure that there were no fewer ceremonialist innovations in the northern province and rails were no less common or controversial.[72]

With the sitting of the Long Parliament there was open season on Laudian priests. The new parliamentary committee on religion, established in November 1640, was as hostile to rails and chancel steps as the Laudian regime had been favourable, and it took to reversing parochial and episcopal decisions. Aggrieved parties, especially those subjected to excommunication, at last had a forum to expose their grievances and an opportunity to seek revenge.[73] The effect was a flurry of acrimonious paper as well as more work for the parish carpenters. Hundreds of letters and petitions poured in, relating every kind of grudge and grievance, some of which we have already sampled. Especially notorious cases were trumpeted through the press.

Many of the arch-conformists who became the targets of parliamentary petitioning in the early 1640s, and many of those priests charged with 'malignancy' later in the decade, were cited for railing and repositioning their communion tables and with reverencing them in accord with the prevailing Laudian orthodoxy. It was a common complaint that the minister had 'set up their communion table altarwise' behind rails, had worshipped it as a 'great idol' with 'unreasonable bowings', and 'would not administer the holy sacrament to those which would not come up unto the rails and bow thereunto with humble adoration'.[74] But hovering behind these claims was resentment at the ministers lording it over the laity, and damage they had done to custom, convenience, and community cohesion.

As the attack on episcopacy intensified, Laudianism further retreated, the church courts ceased to function, and the new political climate encouraged the reversal of ceremonial innovations. The parishioners of St Saviour's church, Southwark, previously cited for pulling down their altar rails, felt confident in July 1641 in petitioning parliament for discharge.[75] The puritan faction at St Thomas the Apostle judged correctly that parliament would treat them leniently for their haste in pulling down the rails.[76] At Isleworth, Middlesex, the hated rails 'were riotously broken down by a tumultuous company' under the command of a reputable local attorney.[77] Godly parishioners in Herefordshire, allied to Sir Robert Harley, used news of parliamentary proceedings to bring about the relocation of tables and the dismantling of rails.[78] Many parishes quietly reversed the Laudian reforms, and most now looked to Westminster (rather than to Canterbury) for official instruction. Alarmed conservatives wrote of parishes where 'half refuse to receive the blessed sacrament, unless they may receive it in what posture they please'.[79] Purveyors of scandal included the 'rending the rails from before the communion table, and then chopping them in pieces and burning them in the church yard, and this to be riotously done without authority, commission or order', among the 'violent outrages and sacrilegious disorders' of the times.[80]

The Lords and the Commons pursued different policies, but both sent clear signals that the Laudian revolution was finished. In November 1640, before taking the sacrament at St Margaret's, Westminster, the members made sure that 'the rails were pulled down and the communion table was removed into the middle of the chancel'.[81] In January 1641 the Lords passed an order forbidding religious 'rites and ceremonies that may give offence', and they followed this in March with instructions that every communion table should 'stand decently in the ancient place where it ought to do by law, and as it hath done for the greater part of these three-score years last past'.[82] The liturgical clock would be put back to the late sixteenth century, ideally erasing Jacobean irregularities as well as Laudian innovations.

In September 1641 the House of Commons passed an ordinance requiring the churchwardens of every parish 'forthwith' to 'remove the communion table from the east end of the church, chapel or chancel, into some other convenient place, and that they take away the rails, and level the chancels, as heretofore they were before the late innovations'. Henry Cogan, writing to Sir John Pennington, described this as an ordinance 'for the removing of superstition', and for 'placing the communion tables as they were in Queen Elizabeth's time'. Though other interpretations were possible, some more radical than conservative, the action was generally aimed at restoring the Jacobean status quo.[83]

The parliamentary work coincided with a spate of publications on 'the altar dispute', most arguing against the Laudian innovations, but some expressing alarm at the 'rash and misguided people' who pulled down communion rails in a spirit of mutiny or rebellion.[84] Henceforth the removal of rails could be done by authority, under the supervision of churchwardens, rather than irregularly and violently by lawless soldiers or routs of rascals and radicals. The House of Commons absorbed and legitimized the iconoclasm, as they would two years later when they pulled down Cheapside Cross.

Bishop John Williams of Lincoln, who had earlier burned his hands in the altar controversy, and whose fortunes rose briefly as those of Archbishop Laud plummeted, attempted a rearguard action on behalf of episcopal discipline when he insisted on visiting his diocese in September 1641. Altar-wise placement of communion tables was now forbidden, chancel steps were to be levelled, and citations to be issued against any minister who refused communion to 'any that will not come up and receive it at the rails'. Not since the Reformation had a bishop so explicitly rejected the policies of his superiors and colleagues, but it was too late to save the traditional Church of England. 'Anabaptists, Libertines, Brownists' and other schismatics were on the rise, some of them energized by the dismantling of the Laudian-Caroline Church, and parishes were increasingly detached from episcopal authority.[85]

Thwarted ceremonialists often became sullen and uncooperative when their rails were removed and their tables moved closer to the congregation. William Heywood, who was already under investigation at St Giles in the Fields, refused to allow the House of Commons order 'concerning the pulling down of the rails about the communion table' to be read in his church, and in October 1641 was summoned to appear before the House to answer charges.[86] Benjamin Spencer, the vicar of St Thomas, Southwark, asserted that he would continue to bow to the holy table, 'whether the railes be taken away or not'.[87] Despite decisions taken at Westminster, many country churches maintained the arrangement that they had only recently implemented.[88]

In Suffolk, when parliament ordered the communion table to be moved away from the east window at Melton, William Pratt the rector 'commanded it to be set there again'. After the table was 'brought down into the usual place' at Grundisburgh, Edward Barton the rector 'refused to administer the sacrament'. At Debenham, 'at the taking down the communion table from the east end', the vicar, Thomas Bond, was 'much offended' and warned 'that we should be so scrupulous now of superstition that we should fall to plain prophaneness'. William Proctor, the ceremonialist rector of Stradishall, observed the letter but defied the spirit of the newly approved arrangement, for 'after the rails were taken away' he substituted forms or benches and made the communicants kneel there instead.[89]

Few reacted so wildly as Andrew Sandiland, the minister of Waldringfield, Suffolk, a man 'given to superstitious and vain gestures in the church' including 'bowing towards the communion table'. On the day that the rails were pulled down he was so angry that 'he came into the church porch with his pistol charged . . . and threatened to dispatch the first that came out of the church'. Even after the rails had gone, he refused to administer the sacrament unless communicants knelt at their former place at the chancel steps, 'whereby some were grieven, and would not come unto the communion'.[90]

Others, like the perennial vicar of Bray, changed with the tenor of the times.

One curate complained of an incumbent whose views on ceremony changed like a weathercock in the wind. 'He hath made a terrible combustion where and how to place the Lords table. It stood in the church, anon it must be advanced into the choir; then it must be east and west, and presently after north and south, covered, uncovered, railed, without rails, of this fashion, of that, of this wood, of another; nay, he himself who was the first that altered it, hath now, within this month or two, altered his opinion, and placed it again in the body of the church.' Another of this ilk, John Hill, the incumbent of Holdenby, Northamptonshire, was formerly considered 'the greatest conformist to the church discipline', but by August 1641 he was reportedly 'so indifferent that he cares not if the communion table stand in the belfry'.[91]

When war broke out in 1642 the iconoclastic violence resumed, although by this time many rails had already been removed. Soldiers were on the march again, in greater numbers and with tighter discipline than in the summer of 1640, but those who fought for parliament were just as willing to destroy religious imagery of which they disapproved. Passing through Middlesex in August 1642, detachments of the Earl of Essex's army smashed glass, shredded surplices, and 'burned the holy rails' at Acton, Chiswick, and Uxbridge. They did the same, almost as a matter of course, as they pressed on towards the Midlands.[92] Passing through Marsworth, Buckinghamshire, 'a certain number of soldiers calling themselves by the name of London Apprentices' demanded the keys to the church 'and broke down the rails at the upper end of the chancel, where formerly the communion table stood'. They also smashed the painted windows, shredded two copies of the Book of Common Prayer, and marched away derisively parading the minister's surplice. Conformists would say that the church was grossly defiled, but iconoclasts could claim that it was forcefully cleansed of its superstitious and ceremonial trimmings.[93]

Parliamentary soldiers similarly spent their fury in southern cathedrals, sometimes smashing communion tables as well as the remaining rails. At Canterbury they 'overthrew the communion table, tore the velvet cloth from before it, defaced the goodly screen' and 'brake down the ancient rails'. At Rochester they pointedly 'brake down the rail' and 'removed the table itself into a lower place of the church', as if they were enacting liturgical reform.[94]

Alarmed conformists wrote as if the soldiers had gone berserk, but in fact the iconoclastic violence of the early 1640s was rarely indiscriminate. Nor, besides a few notorious incidents involving horses, was it accompanied by travesties of the sacraments or wilder acts of irreligion. When soldiers smashed windows and organs, broke down altar rails, dressed in the remnants of copes or surplices, and paraded with pages of the Book of Common Prayer on their pikes, they were effectively implementing by force the forward edge of the puritan agenda. They were performing by violence and embodying in action the programme of cleansing and reform that many of their religious leaders had pressed for. Indeed, what stands out in these incidents is not the wild tumult of disorder in church but rather the precision with which the enemies of altar rails acted.

The Parliamentary ordinance of August 1643 requiring the removal of all fixed altars, rails, and chancel steps, took the iconoclasm out of unlicensed hands, and put it on a civil rather than a military footing, obliging churchwardens in parliamentary areas to undertake the task of destruction.[95] William Dowsing's team, who followed this up in East Anglia with a commission from the Earl of Manchester, found only three remaining sets of rails to break down in 147 Suffolk parishes. Most of the furnishings associated with Wren's and Montague's innovations had already been removed, although there were still dozens of chancel steps remaining to be 'digged up' or 'levelled'.[96]

Parliament, however, was no more successful than Convocation in bringing order and conformity to the parishes. The religious complexion of revolutionary England was beyond anyone's control. Soon it would no longer matter whether parishioners took communion at an altar or table, or knelt at the rails. Rather, the issue became whether they would worship together as a community at all, or would fragment into schisms and sects. The fear of conservatives and the hope of some radicals—fears and hopes that echoed from the earliest years of the Church of England—was not that people would disagree how to interpret the Book of Common Prayer, but that they might reject it altogether. The presence and position of rails and tables would be not just adiaphora—theologically indifferent—but completely irrelevant if people could find the Lord where they list and worship him as they pleased.

Dramatis Personae

LAITY

John Blackwell, grocer, of London
Henry Tailor of Hardingham, Norfolk
Thomas Wolrych, esquire, of Cowling, Suffolk
Christian Harper of Harborough, Leicestershire
John Hocker, churchwarden, of Colchester, Essex
Andrew Keate, churchwarden, of Great Wratting, Suffolk
Samuel Greygoose, churchwarden, of Epping, Essex
Edward Aylee, glazier, of Bishop's Stortford, Hertfordshire
Richard Mose, blacksmith, of Much Hadham, Hertfordshire

Jeremy Reeve, servant, of Latton, Essex
Sir Nathaniel Brent
Sir John Conyers
Sir Robert Harley
William Prynne

CLERGY

William Laud, Archbishop of Canterbury
Richard Neile, bishop
Matthew Wren, bishop
Richard Montague, bishop
John Williams, bishop
Richard Corbet, bishop
William Piers, bishop
William Juxon, bishop
Dr Arthur Duck
John Pocklington
Richard Drake of Radwinter, Essex
Benjamin Spencer of Southwark, Surrey
Ephraim Udall of London
Thomas Cheshire of London
Philip Parsons of Great Finsborough, Suffolk
William Heywood of St Giles, Middlesex
Charles Chauncey of Hertfordshire
John Ley of Great Budworth, Cheshire
Alexander Huish of Beckington, Somerset
Dr Barkham of Bocking, Essex
Thomas Paske of Hadham, Hertfordshire
William Pratt of Melton, Suffolk
Edward Barton of Grundisburgh, Suffolk
Thomas Bond of Debenham, Suffolk
William Proctor of Stradishall, Suffolk
Andrew Sandiland of Waldringfield, Suffolk
John Hill of Holdenby, Northamptonshire

13

The Portraiture of Prynne's Pictu.
Performance on the Public Stage

Addressing his readers in the revolutionary ferment of 1641, William Prynne offered to present 'a late tragical history' with 'such a spectacle, both to men and angels, no age ever saw before'. The central player in this spectacle was Prynne himself, and his adversaries were Charles I's bishops, 'metamorphosed into ravenous wolves'. Prynne's *New Discovery of the Prelates Tyranny* recapitulated his conflict with the authorities over the previous decade, and ended with the sufferer's famous vindication and the concomitant downfall of his enemies.[1] *A New Discovery* is prolix and partisan, like all of Prynne's output, but it is singularly useful in gathering together many of the documents and letters that related to the author's ordeal. By the spring of 1641 Prynne had possession of many of Laud's papers, episcopal correspondence, and records of the courts of Star Chamber and High Commission. He would use them to illustrate his account of his recent sufferings, and to call for revenge against the cruel archbishop.

William Prynne would have made an effective theatrical director or actor-manager. He knew the importance of putting on a show. Notwithstanding Prynne's protestation against the theatre, expressed at tendentious length in *Histrio-Mastix* (1633), the puritan lawyer and ecclesiastical historian played to the gallery through most of his public career. In his greatest role, as the persistent opponent to the villainous Archbishop Laud, he took the part of the heroic 'Mr. Prynne'. Though drawn to a career in scholarship and law, he accepted the role of plaintiff, sufferer, and symbol. From his first eruption onto the public stage in the early 1630s, Prynne looked past his enemies and accusers to a cheering and adoring crowd. He exploited the Laudian machinery of justice for its set, script, and props, made effective use of the licit and illicit press, and published his own publicity with his own most favourable reviews. The author of more than a hundred books from the 1620s to the 1660s, Prynne was more a professional polemicist than an original thinker. He practised the rhetoric of provocation and revelled in the role of victimhood. Both he and his tormentors were players in a spectacle of power and propaganda, and each made effective use of the symbolic resources at their disposal. They understood the

.ance of propaganda and symbolism, and turned the suffering of the ody and the manipulation of text into a fine political art.

Prynne's career is well known to students of early modern England. His life and work have been the subject of several important books.[2] He is usually depicted as a humourless lawyer, a prolix author, and a tedious puritan activist who brought his misfortunes upon himself. Born in 1600, he was educated at Bath Grammar School and Oriel College Oxford, earning his first degree in 1621. Like many ambitious gentlemen he then studied law in London, a member of Lincoln's Inn, and was called to the bar in 1628. He spent the rest of his career as a gadfly, attacking the moral and religious failings of successive authoritarian regimes, until dying in 1669. In this chapter, instead of addressing Prynne's work through his writings I focus on the part he played in the judicial and political theatre of Caroline England. I am interested in Prynne's engagement with his audience as well as his audience's response to his troubles.

Prynne's most important performances belonged to a cluster of incidents between 1633 and 1641 in which he starred as dramaturge, protagonist, celebrity, and martyr. The first was his trial and punishment following the publication of *Histrio-Mastix*, when Prynne gained notoriety and some sympathy for his ordeal in the pillory, the lopping off of his ears, and the public burning of his book. The second involved the government's further attack on Prynne in 1637 for his authorship of *News from Ipswich*, and his condemnation, along with Burton the minister and Bastwick the physician, to further humiliation and violent disfigurement. It was at this time that the authorities branded Prynne's cheeks with 'S. L.' for 'seditious libel', which Prynne proudly reinterpreted as 'stigma of Laud'. The third incident, which is the least well known, centred on the extraordinary events at Chester at the end of 1637 where Prynne was first received like a hero or prophet, and was then so excoriated that all traces of his image were ritually destroyed. The final episode in this cluster was Prynne's triumphal entry into London in November 1640, his day of hosannas, when the return of the martyrs signalled the downfall of the Laudian regime.

A review of these episodes, paying attention to audience reactions as well as the principal protagonists, may be helpful in enhancing our understanding of the society, culture, and politics of early modern England. Prynne's evolution from moral critic to public enemy, from godly polemicist to hammer of the Laudian regime, parallels the rising tensions and changing fortunes of the years from 1633 to 1641. Prynne's experience, and the contest among contemporaries to control and interpret it, undermines any notion that the personal rule of Charles I was an era of order, consensus, and moderation.[3] Prynne's collisions with the authorities point to a rising political temperature, an escalation of vituperative rhetoric, and a sharpening of cultural divisions. They also

Mr. William Prynne, for writing a booke
against Stage-players called Histrio-mastix
was first confured in the Starr-Chamber to looſe both his eares in the pillorie, fined 5000ℓ. & perpetuall imprifonment in the Towre of London
After this, on a meer fufpition of writing other
bookes, but nothing at all proved against him,
hee was again confured in the Starr-chamber to
loofe the ſmall remainder of both his eares in
the pillorie, to be Stigmatized on both his Cheekes
with a firey-iron, was fined again 5000ℓ and baniſhed into yᵉ Iſle of Ierſey, there to ſuffer perpetuall-Cloſe-imprifonmᵗ no freinds being permitted to fee him, on pain of imprifonment.

P. 122/

6. Portrait of William Prynne, *c*.1641

demonstrate that the power of the state was far from monolithic, and that attempts by the regime to impose discipline and punishment permitted counter-gestures and responses that subverted or challenged its authority.[4]

Act 1. 1633–4

It was ironic, perhaps deliberately ironic, that Prynne's massive attack on the theatre was divided into 'acts' and 'scenes', like the printed editions of early modern plays. This was an extremely unusual arrangement for works of polemical prose. *Histrio-Mastix. The Players Scourge, or Actors Tragedie* was arranged in two parts. Part one opened with a 'Prologue', proceeded from 'Actus 1, Scaena Prima' to 'Actus 8, Scena Sexta', and concluded with a 'Chorus'. Part two moved more briskly from 'Actus Primus' to 'Actus Quintus' and ended with a 'Catastrophe' or final dramatic denouement.[5] What saved it from condemnation, from the viewpoint of the scourge of players, was that Prynne's tragedy was 'penned only to be read, not acted', and involved none of the theatrical sins of representation.[6] Its title echoed another *Histrio-Mastix*, a late Elizabethan play in six acts attributed to John Marston, though its message entirely opposed that of the earlier work.[7]

At the outset Prynne promised 'a fatal, if not final overthrow or catastrophe to plays and actors, whose dismal tragedy doth now begin'. A thousand pages later he was still fulminating against all popular, festive, and dramatic entertainments that furthered the work of the Devil. The chorus recapitulated Prynne's central message, 'that all popular and common stage-plays, whether comical, tragical, satirical, mimical, or mixed of either, especially as they are now compiled and personated among us, are such sinful, hurtful, pernicious recreations, as are altogether unseemly, yea unlawful unto Christians'.[8] It was as if Prynne had taken Polonius's commendation of 'the best actors in the world' and cast them all as reprobates.[9]

Histrio-Mastix bore the imprint of 1633, but copies became available at the end of 1632.[10] They immediately got Prynne into trouble. Although the book was openly published, with approval from an official licenser, the authorities treated it as a libellous and subversive publication. Although the work had taken many years to complete, they chose to interpret it as a deliberate insult to Queen Henrietta Maria, who took part in theatrical entertainments at court six weeks after the book's first appearance. William Laud, at this time still bishop of London, and still smarting from Prynne's earlier attack on Arminianism,[11] was determined to make the writer suffer. Although Prynne borrowed heavily from earlier authors, including classical, biblical, and early Christian sources, Laud's

HISTRIO-MASTIX.

THE

PLAYERS SCOVRGE,
OR,

ACTORS TRAGÆDIE,

Divided into Two Parts.

Wherein it is largely evidenced, by divers *Arguments,* by the concurring Authorities and Resolutions of *sundry texts of Scripture;* of the *whole Primitive Church,* both under the *Law and Gospell;* of 55 *Synodes and Councels;* of 71 *Fathers and Christian Writers,* before the yeare of our Lord 1200; of above 150 *foraigne and domestique Protestant and Popish Authors,* since; of 40 *Heathen Philosophers, Historians, Poets;* of many *Heathen,* many *Christian Nations, Republiques, Emperors, Princes, Magistrates;* of sundry *Apostolicall, Canonicall, Imperiall Constitutions;* and of our owne *English Statutes, Magistrates, Vniversities, Writers, Preachers.*

That popular Stage-playes (the very Pompes of the Divell which we renounce in Baptisme, if we beleeve the Fathers) *are sinfull, heathenish, lewde, ungodly Spectacles, and most pernicious Corruptions; condemned in all ages, as intolerable Mischiefes to Churches, to Republickes, to the manners, mindes, and soules of men. And that the Trofession of Play-poets, of Stage-players; together with the penning, acting, and frequenting of Stage-playes, are unlawfull, infamous and misbeseeming Christians.* All pretences to the contrary are here likewise fully answered; and the unlawfulnes of acting, of beholding Academicall Enterludes, briefly discussed; besides sundry other particulars concerning *Dancing, Dicing, Healtho-drinking, &c.* of which the Table will informe you.

By WILLIAM PRYNNE, *an Vtter-Barrester of* Lincolnes Inne.

Cyprian, De Spectaculis lib. p. 244.
Fugienda sunt ista Christianis fidelibus, ut iam frequenter diximus, tam vana, tam perniciosa, tam sacrilega Spectacula: quæ, etsi non haberent crimen, habent in se et maximam et parum congruentē fidelibus vanitatē.
Lactantius de Verò Cultu cap. 20.
Vitanda ergo Spectacula omnia, non solum ne quid vitiorum pectoribus insideat, &c. sed ne eius nos voluptatis consuetudo delineat, atque à Deo et à bonis operibus avertat.
Chrysost. Hom. 38. in Matth. Tom. 2. Col. 399. B & Hom. 8. De Pœnitentia, Tom. 5. Col. 750.
Immo verò, hic Theatralibus ludis ruersis, non leges, sed iniquitatem evertetis, ac omnem civitatis pesiem extinguetis. Etenim Theatrum, communis luxuriæ officina, publicum incontinentiæ gymnasium, cathedra pestilentiæ; peffimum locus; plurimarumque morborum plena Babylonica fornax, &c.
Augustinus De Civit. Dei, l. 4 c. 1.
Si tantummodo boni et honesti homines in civitate essent, nec in rebus humanis Ludi scenici esse debuissent.

LONDON.

Printed by *E. A.* and *W. I.* for *Michael Sparke,* and are to be sold at the blue Bible, in Greene Arbour, in little Old Bayly. 1633.

7. Title-page of Prynne's *Histrio-Mastix,* 1633

agents scrutinized every passage to see if it could be construed as seditious. Prynne made explicit rebuttal of the charge 'that puritans and precisians are seditious, factious, troublesome, rebellious persons, and enemies both to state and government', but this was exactly what his work was taken to prove.[12] Readers who expressed approval for Prynne were themselves in turn in trouble, and one Yorkshire minister, William Brearcliffe, who commended Prynne's book for its 'show of much reading and multiplicity of quotations', soon found himself under investigation for nonconformity.[13]

After an initial examination on 31 January 1633 Prynne was confined to the Tower. A whole year would pass before he was brought to trial, during which time the government developed charges against Michael Sparkes the publisher and Thomas Buckner the unfortunate cleric who had approved the book for the press. The king himself was initially reluctant to proceed, but Laud was determined to bring the libeller down.[14] Prynne, throughout this time, maintained contact with puritan supporters and worked to prepare his defence. The trial took place in Star Chamber in the first half of February, in a rigidly hostile environment, and sentence was pronounced on 17 February 1634.[15]

The judicial vengeance that fell on William Prynne may be considered an extreme application of reader response. His thousand-page treatise may have looked like an unwieldy mélange of history, scripture, and law, but it was taken to threaten the security of the realm. Although Prynne's book represented seven years of research and writing, and recapitulated dozens of ancient arguments, it was treated as a timely and poignant commentary on contemporary conditions at court. According to William Noy, the Attorney General, 'he hath therein written divers incitements to stir up the people to discontent, as if there were just cause to lay violent hands upon their prince . . . He hath cast an aspersion upon her majesty the queen, and railing and uncharitable censures against all Christian people. He hath commended all those that are factious persons, that have vented anything in any book against the state,' and he had 'deeply wounded' the Church.[16]

The Attorney General listed Prynne's many offences. He had written against 'plays, masques, dancings, etc . . . although he knew well that his majesty's royal queen, lords of the council, etc., were in their public festivals, and other times, present spectators of some masques and dances'. He had criticized 'many recreations that were tolerable, and in themselves sinless' (according to King James's 'book of sports' which King Charles republished while Prynne was languishing in the Tower). He had 'railed, not only against stage plays, comedies and dancings, and all other exercises of the people, and against all who such as behold them, but further and particular against hunting, public festivals, Christmas-keeping, bonfires and maypoles', and even 'against the dressing up of a house with green ivy'. Prynne's book, then, could be construed as an attack on the honour of those closest to the king, as a challenge to royal authority, and an assault on the entire public, festive, celebratory, and recreational life of the country and the court. It mattered little that there was nothing new in *Histrio-Mastix*, that it was a turgid and intemperate compilation of precedents and injunctions, or that it had actually been licensed for the press. What mattered most to Prynne's enemies at Whitehall was that the book exposed their sensitivities, touched their nerves, and provided an opportunity to punish an outspoken puritan author. Prynne may have been taken by surprise at the ferocity of the assault but he rose courageously to the occasion.

In his defence, Prynne reiterated that his work had taken more than seven years in the making and was not intended as a commentary on current events. It was, rather, a compendium of 'arguments and authorities against stage plays', which he had taken through the normal channels of approval for publication. 'As for the encouraging of others to be factious or seditious, he saith upon his oath, that he was so far from disloyalty, schism, or sedition, or neglect of the king, state, or government that he hath with much joy, cheerfulness and thankfulness to God ever acknowledged his, and the rest of the king's subjects happiness, by the peace we have under his majesty's happy government.' He willingly withdrew anything that mistakenly caused offence, and was now ready to 'prostrate himself at his majesty's royal feet, and crave pardon and grace'.[17]

If Prynne thought that he was playing according to a script of judicial leniency and moderation it rapidly became clear that the rules had changed and he would receive no 'pardon and grace' from the Laudian–Caroline regime. This was a show trial, and his enemies wanted a show. The judges lined up to pour venom on the defendant for his 'monstrosity', 'malice', and 'spleen'. Lord Justice Richardson identified *Histrio-Mastix* as 'a monster, *monstrum horrendum, informe, ingens* . . . eye never saw, nor ear never heard of such a scandalous and mis-shapen thing as this monster is'.[18] One would think the author had given birth to a misshapen beast rather than a plump squat book. The Earl of Dorset mocked Prynne's scruples as the zealousness of a 'brittle conscience brother', and turned puritan preaching against him by identifying Prynne as 'this Achan' whose impieties need to be purged.[19] The judicial tenor was intemperate and vituperative, but few outside the court were prepared for the violence (and theatricality) of the Star Chamber judgements of February 1634.

So monstrous was Prynne's offence, so transgressive his textual crime, from the government point of view, that ordinary censorship and punishment would be insufficient. Chancellor of the Exchequer Francis Cottington led the judges in sentencing *Histrio-Mastix* to a self-consciously innovative destruction. 'I condemn it to be burnt, in the most public manner that can be. The manner in other countries is . . . to be burnt by the hangman, though not used in England. Yet I wish it may, in respect of the strangeness and heinousness of the matter contained in it, to have a strange manner of burning; therefore I shall desire it may be so burnt by the hand of the hangman.' The rest of the Star Chamber judges endorsed this innovation. They further committed Prynne to 'perpetual imprisonment', fined him a massive five thousand pounds, expelled him from Lincoln's Inn and from the practice of law, and stripped him of his degrees from the University of Oxford.[20]

This was harsh, perhaps excessive, but only the beginning of Prynne's ordeal. Fining, imprisoning, disbarring, and degrading were indoor judgements— office procedures appropriate for a lawyer and gentleman—but Prynne was also to star in a more humiliating and painful outdoor spectacle that was staged to express the government's anger and contempt. The sentence continued, 'that he be set in the pillory at Westminster, with a paper on his head declaring the nature of his offence, and have one of his ears there cut off; and at another time be set in the pillory in Cheapside, with a paper as aforesaid, and there have his other ear cut off; and that a fire shall be made before the said pillory, and the hangman being there ready for that purpose, shall publicly in disgraceful manner cast all the said books which could be produced into the fire to be burnt, as unfit to be seen by any hereafter.'[21]

Some of the judges outbid each other in suggesting refinements or additions to Prynne's punishment. Lord Dorset urged greater violence against Prynne's body, to have him 'branded in the forehead, slit in the nose, and his ears cropped too', so that he could not hide his disfigurement with a periwig. Others suggested that the author and printer should be pilloried in St Paul's church-yard, as a warning to the London book trade, but Archbishop Laud vetoed this as misuse of a consecrated place.[22]

Justice (or vengeance) would be seen to be done. Prynne would be on view, displayed in the pillory and publicly mutilated in the streets of London and Westminster, in the places of greatest concourse. His literary offence would be countered by a written declaration; and the offending books would be burnt before their author's eyes in a fire fuelled by the common hangman. The punishment was clearly theatrical in its staging, with set, script, actors, audi-ence, and props, and particularly appropriate for one who had written against dramatic representation. Prynne was not a heretic to be burned, nor were his cropped ears (or other members) roasted in front of him; but the possibilities of greater violence hung over the occasion. The hangman's usual business was with ropes, not books; and Cheapside was the site of earlier bonfires, associated with the Marian martyrs and the annual commemoration of 5 November.

Henceforth the hangman was de rigueur for the public
The parliamentary regime of the 1640s appointed the co
burn such offensive items as the Book of Sports, and th
Charles II used the hangman to destroy the detested
Covenant. London crowds became used to such spectacles
such as Cheapside, Cornhill, Smithfield, Paul's Cross, and Westminster
Yard.[23]

Prynne's last hope was an appeal to the Privy Council, to whom he offered 'all humble submission'. He wrote that he regretted those 'passages inconsiderately fallen from his pen' and sought 'mitigation and pardon of his fine and corporal punishment'.[24] Not surprisingly, given the overlap between the membership of the Privy Council and the Star Chamber judges, the appeal was rejected. Prynne stood in the pillory on 7 and 10 May 1634, his books were burned and his ears were duly cropped. According to one reporter the books 'were burnt under his nose, which had almost suffocated him'. At least a thousand copies of *Histrio-Mastix* had been printed, but most escaped the government's efforts to call them in.[25]

Reactions to Prynne's punishment followed the cultural and political divide that was widening in Caroline England. It is simply not true, as has recently been suggested, that Prynne's case attracted 'little public attention or sympathy'.[26] Some observers were delighted by Prynne's come-uppance, others were appalled by the savagery of his mistreatment. Thomas Windebank, the courtier politician, wrote gleefully in the spring of 1634 'that Mr. Prynne, the enemy of dancing, had become so enamoured of it, that he was to dance a galliard on the loss of his ears, and after that to make a pilgrimage to the prison, where he would pass the time in waiting till the king should make him dance the brawl *De Sortie*'.[27] Archbishop Laud thought Prynne had not been punished enough, and initiated further proceedings against him in the Court of High Commission. King Charles, it seems, was content with Prynne's treatment, though Henrietta Maria had made some intercessions for mercy and pardon.[28] William Noy, the Attorney General, was said to have laughed so hard while Prynne was suffering on the pillory that he was 'struck with an issue of blood in his privy part, which by all art of man could never be stopped unto the day of his death, which was not long after'. Prynne could not later resist telling this story, which could be read as a providential judgement of the sort anthologized in Henry Burton's *Divine Tragedy*.[29]

Supporters commended Prynne's courage as well as his cause, making his heroic endurance of his penalty the stuff of puritan legend. 'The gentleman like an harmless lamb took all with such patience, that he not so much as once opened his mouth to let fall any one word of discontent,' wrote the London

.ster Henry Burton, who may have been influenced as much by his reading Foxe's *Book of Martyrs* as by his witnessing of the scene at Westminster.[30] The London artisan Nehemiah Wallington also compared Prynne's demeanour on the pillory to that of 'a harmless lamb', while the Dorset diarist William Whiteway likewise memorialized Prynne's courage.[31] The lawyer William Drake (later MP for Amersham) remarked on Prynne's punishment in his commonplace book, 'he took his punishment patiently, and was generally pitied of all sorts'.[32]

While nursing his wounds in the Tower, and not yet deprived of writing materials, Prynne composed an extraordinary letter to Archbishop Laud. At one level this was an appeal for justice, at another a recapitulation of the main points of *Histrio-Mastix*, above all a daring attack on the most powerful person in England under the king. At one point Prynne likened himself to St Paul, who had also been charged with sedition, and later he observed that he was 'not above thirty-three years old', which was Jesus's age at the time of his ministry. In a blistering personal attack upon his tormentor, Prynne accused Laud of everything from bad law to bad logic, from favouring of Jesuits to being raised to his present eminence 'almost from the very dunghill'. Repeated sarcastic comments about 'your lordship's charitable agents', 'your lordship's arch-charity, piety, clemency, or justice', and the archbishop's 'episcopal candor', 'pity' and 'grace' did nothing to improve the petitioner's case. Prynne berated the bishops for their 'cruelty, insolency, violence, malice [and] pride', and accused Laud directly of proceeding from enmity, malignancy, and spleen. Prynne could not know that within a decade the tables would be turned, but he warned Archbishop Laud that he too had enemies, and that his career might end in 'misery, ruin, if not hell itself'.[33]

The letter was a remarkable performance, vintage Prynne, and of course it only made matters worse. It was sent to the archbishop on 11 June 1634, and duly copied. When confronted with the original a few days later, and asked by the Attorney General whether it was in his hand, Prynne replied that 'he could not tell unless he might read it'. He then ripped the letter into pieces and threw the shreds out the window, saying 'that should never rise in judgement against him'. This minor *coup de théâtre* had a small audience and no ameliorative effect, though news of it went the round of the newsletters.[34] Prynne remained imprisoned for the next three years.

Act 2. 1637, London

By 1637 Prynne was in trouble again and was condemned, along with Burton and Bastwick, for writing the pamphlet *News from Ipswich*. Again he was pilloried, mutilated, and humiliated, and copies of the offending texts were destroyed. This time the authorities were determined to silence him, and to impose the harshest penalties permissible by law, but Prynne once again turned his suffering into a performance of celebrity and reproach.

Prynne had remained in the Tower since February 1633 (with a few removals to the Fleet prison), but was not deprived of news, company, or writing materials. He managed to write several inflammatory pamphlets including *A Breviate of the Prelates Intollerable Usurpations*, *The Unbishoping of Timothy and Titus*, and *Briefe Instructions for Churchwardens*. None of these carried their author's name, each was printed secretly or abroad, and each continued Prynne's campaign against the Laudian bishops. *News from Ipswich*, which appeared in three editions in 1636, claimed to be written by one Matthew White and printed in Ipswich, but this too was Prynne's work, most likely printed in Scotland.[35]

Much more intemperate than *Histrio-Mastix*, *News from Ipswich* was a recklessly hostile attack on the 'detestable practices of some domineering lordly prelates' in the dioceses of London and Norwich. It accused the bishops, in particular Laud and Wren, of suppressing godly preachers and advancing popish innovations, of setting up altars while pulling down lectures, of murdering people's souls while 'tyrannizing' over 'bawdy theivish court[s]'. At issue now, in Prynne's view, was not just the sinfulness of dramatic entertainments but the threat of 'backsliding to popery' and the 'sudden alteration of our religion'. England had not only turned away from God but had permitted a pack of lordly popish prelates to gain control of the Church.[36] A cluster of similar unlicensed publications including *A Divine Tragedy* (once attributed to Prynne but now identified as the work of Henry Burton)[37] provoked the authorities into action.

Informed parties knew by March 1637 that the regime was preparing to proceed against Prynne and some others, 'all for books and pamphlets against the present government of the church'.[38] The blow fell in April when the authorities seized Prynne's papers on the grounds that they contained printed sheets 'which, if dispersed and published, might tend much to the prejudice of the state'. Along with other suspected authors, John Bastwick and Henry Burton, Prynne then became the subject of renewed Star Chamber investigations 'for the publication of various libellous books with intent to move the king's people against the king's ecclesiastical government'.[39]

The sentence of the court, announced on 14 June 1637, repeated some of the punishments of 1634. All three men were to be fined and pilloried and to lose their ears. In Prynne's case the court examined whether he had any ears left, before ordering that the remaining stumps be cut off.[40] This time the offenders were to be firmly muzzled, to be deprived of 'pen, ink or paper', and to have no

other books than the Bible, the Prayer Book, and conformable books of devotion. They were to be radically isolated from their puritan supporters, removed into perpetual imprisonment in such distant locations as Cornwall,
Lancashire, and North Wales (and eventually further exile in the remote
Channel Islands and Isles of Scilly).[41]

Prynne, as a repeat offender, was singled out for harsher treatment. His
cheek was branded with the letters 'S. L.' for seditious libel. A textual coding was
imprinted on the author's flesh. But Prynne boasted that the letters stood for
stigmata Laudis. Here again the sign was ambiguous, laden with contradictory
meanings. The state showed its power by imposing pain and disfigurement,
but the subject turned his punishment into a triumph of propaganda. As the
chronicler Thomas Fuller recalled, 'so various were men's fancies in reading the
same letters, imprinted in his face, that some made them to spell the guiltiness
of the sufferer, but others the cruelty of the imposer'.[42] Prynne himself made
verses on the occasion, which circulated rapidly around the country in manuscript newsletters.

> Triumphant I return, my face discryes
> Laud's scorching scars.
> God's grateful sacrifice.
> S. L. Stigmata Laudis.
> Stigmata maxellis baiulans insignia Laudis
> Exultans remeo victima grata Deo.[43]

Although the press was closed to Prynne's supporters, other avenues
remained open for criticism and comment. The case of 'the three delinquents',
or as they became known in puritan circles 'the three martyrs', became a lively
topic of conversation and correspondence. Even before the sentence was
pronounced, Laud's informants in Northamptonshire reported that 'the whole
tribe of Gad', a mocking label for the local godly, had gathered for a fast day 'to
join in prayer that God would deliver his servants from persecution, whom we
conceive to be Bastwick, Prynne, and Burton'.[44]

Even observers who agreed that Prynne and his fellows should be punished
commented on the courage and fortitude with which that punishment was
endured. Writing to the Earl of Leicester in June 1637, William Hawkins
described Bastwick, Burton, and Prynne as 'the most undaunted men that
ever were seen', and a few weeks later he wrote that they received the 'execution'
done upon them 'with the most undauntedness that hath been seen, though it
were done with an austere hand'.[45] The Dorset draper Dennis Bond observed
that 'they were wonderfully patient and carried themselves so meekly and resolutely that all beholders except some ruffians . . . shed many tears'.[46] A London

lawyer remarked that 'when Prynne suffered condign punishment . . . he took it patiently and joyfully, whereas his adversaries might have quaking hearts'.[47]

The most complete account of the martyrs' punishment comes from the London writer Edward Rossingham, who reconstructed the drama for subscribers to his manuscript newsletters:

Friday last [30 June] Dr. Bastwick, Mr. Burton, and Mr. Prynne stood in the pillory in the palace of Westminster. As Dr. Bastwick came from the gate-house towards the palace the light common people strewed herbs and flowers before him. Prynne and he stood upon one scaffold and Mr. Burton upon another by himself. They all three talked to the people. Bastwick said they had collar days in the king's court, and this was his collar day in the king's palace; he was pleasant and witty all the time. Prynne protested his innocency to the people of what was laid to his charge. Mr. Burton said it was the happiest pulpit he had ever preached in. After two hours the hangman began to cut off their ears; he began with Mr. Burton's. There were very many people; they wept and grieved for Mr. Burton, and at the cutting of each ear there was such a roaring as if every one of them had at the same instant lost an ear. Bastwick gave the hangman a knife, and taught him to cut off his ears quickly and very close, that he might come there no more. The hangman burnt Prynne in both cheeks and, as I hear, because he burnt one cheek with a letter the wrong way he burnt that again. Presently a surgeon clapped on a plaster to take out the fire. The hangman hewed off Prynne's ears very scurvily, which put him to much pain, and after he stood long in the pillory before his head could be got out, but that was a chance. The reason why Prynne was so ill used by the hangman was he promised him five pieces to use him kindly the time before, which he did, and Prynne had given him but half a crown, in five sixpences. But now the hangman was quit with him, for it is said that Prynne fainted in the pillory after the execution; the cause was his standing in the pillory so long after. The humours of the people were various, some wept, some laughed, and some were very reserved. . . . Saturday all the town was full of it that Mr. Prynne was dead, found dead upon his knees with his hands lift[ed] up to heaven, but there was no such thing, for I hear he was not sick.[48]

Reactions to the sentence again reflected England's cultural and religious divisions. A few high conformists thought the judgement too light, and wished 'the pillory had been changed into a gallows'. More moderate men thought the censure 'too sharp, too base and ignominious for gentlemen of their ingenuous vocation'.[49] The Catholic courtier Sir Kenelm Digby, writing to Viscount Conway, remarked sarcastically on the 'venerations' of the 'puritans', who 'keep the bloody sponges and handkerchiefs that did the hangman service in the cutting off their ears. You may see how nature leads men to respect relics of martyrs.' Another of Conway's correspondents referred dismissively to Burton, Bastwick, and Prynne as 'the cropped libellers'.[50] Others of a different persuasion used 'slanderous and censorious' words against the judgement in Star Chamber. Some likened the martyrdom to 'a glorious wedding day', and someone displayed a placard in Cheapside threatening Laud himself with 'a pillory of ink'.[51]

According to the news-writer Rossingham, 'the minister of Shoreditch, observing the humours of the people so much to compassionate these three delinquents', preached 'that they all incurred damnation which thought well of those three, who had been justly punished for their demerits'.[52] Elsewhere in London, in the parish of St Clement's, drinkers at the Castle tavern almost came to blows over the treatment of the prisoners in Westminster palace yard. Philip Thomas thought the punishment 'not more than they deserved', but Joseph Hutchinson asserted that Burton, Bastwick, and Prynne were 'as honest men and as good subjects as any the king has'. It was a sign of the political sensitivity of these issues that remarks of this nature should immediately be reported to the Council.[53]

When news of the sentence reached Sion College it prompted an angry outburst from Mr Shepard, 'a silenced minister', that led to his own investigation for sedition.[54] George Catesby, a Northamptonshire gentleman, let out that 'he disliked the justice executed upon Mr Prynne, taxing it of rigour'.[55] A Northamptonshire minister, Miles Burkitt of Patishall, drew the authorities' attention 'for exhorting his parishioners to contribute to the necessities of the saints in want, meaning Burton and Prynne', and found himself under investigation by the Court of High Commission. Burkitt had been one of the 'tribe of gad' attending the fast for the saints' deliverance, and after Prynne's punishment he preached that 'though the faithful were molested, persecuted and cropped, yet they would continue faithful still'.[56] Nehemiah Wallington referred to the sufferers as 'those three renowned soldiers and servants of Jesus Christ', a usage he borrowed from Prynne himself.[57]

Act 3. 1637, Chester

When Prynne and the others left London at the beginning of July 1637, on their way to their several prisons, they enjoyed a tearful and buoyant send-off. Burton's report that 'forty thousand' gathered to cheer him from London seems excessive, but the estimate is attributed to the keeper of the Fleet.[58] William Hawkins reported to the Earl of Leicester that they 'were mightly courted by the people at their departure and on the way, one of them being met, as I was told, with sixty horse accompanying him on the way'.[59] Sir Kenelm Digby mockingly referred to their journey as a 'pilgrimage', attended by 'great flocking of the people'.[60] Others reported that the libellers enjoyed popular prayers and expressions of sympathy and goodwill all along their route. So troubled was the Privy Council by the 'great concourse of people' that flocked around Burton and Prynne that they initiated an inquiry into 'what persons did accompany, converse with, or entertain either of them in their said passage, what money was given to them, or either of them, or other remarkable expressions of courtesy or encouragement'.[61] The spectacle of the trial and punishment had been intended to secure respect for the Laudian regime, but its effects were counter-productive. Competition for interpretative control extended from London to Chester, as the script of Prynne's drama unfolded in unexpected ways.

Prynne's journey from London to North Wales in the summer of 1637 took on some of the attributes of a defiant progress attended by knots of supporters. 'Divers persons resorted to Prynne in the streets and highways as they went, and some prayed for him', reported John Maynard, yeoman. The crowds cried 'God be with you' and 'God bless you', and shook him by the hand, reported the deputy warden of the Fleet. At every place he stopped there were supporters offering him comfort, food, and support.[62]

When Prynne reached Chester at the end of July he was rapturously received by puritan well-wishers. He was lodged in 'the best inn in Chester', Sheriff Calvin Bruen entertained the prisoner at his house, gentlemen 'feasted and defrayed him', and for forty-eight hours Prynne was the centre of local attention.[63] Someone commissioned a local artist—Thomas Pulford, limner—to paint Prynne's portrait, and several copies of this likeness circulated as cherished tokens. What followed is further revealing of the power of the image, and the elaborate pains taken by the authorities to counteract it. The government had not exhausted its repertoire of symbolic action, and was prepared to do battle to extinguish unlicensed imagery and forcefully to reassert its own.

Bishop John Bridgeman, who was absent from Chester at the time of Prynne's visit, was furious that the city was 'much defamed by having entertained notorious and factious schismatics'.[64] He determined, he said, 'to cast water on that fire which is already kindled, or leastwise that none may get a stick from this place to increase the flame'.[65] Later he decided to fight fire with fire. A process of cleansing and purgation was initiated, which ended with a remarkable display of officially sponsored iconoclasm. As Prynne himself, the target of this attack, later reported, the commissioners, 'hearing that there were pictures of Mr. Prynne's portraiture in Chester, persecuted the poor painter . . . for drawing them, and made two orders in court, first to deface and then to burn them publicly at the cross in Chester'.[66] It is another irony of the story that Prynne, the enemy of images and representations, should himself be treated like a patron saint.

Puritan activists were summoned to York to face charges before the High Commission, while episcopal officials in Chester took action against the souvenirs of Prynne's embarrassing visit. On 10 November 1637 Bridgeman wrote to the Archbishop of York, 'may it please your Grace, I have seized on five pictures of Prynne, drawn by the painter Pulford . . . and I now desire your Grace's pleasure for the disposal of them.' (The painter was already in prison for his pains.) Should they be sent to York or, rather, be 'sacrificed here to Vulcan, either publicly in the market, or privately before some good witnesses'?[67] (The bishop's flippant invocation of classical divinity and pagan sacrifice was just the sort of thing that serious Protestants like Prynne found so offensive.)

Archbishop Neile responded on behalf of the northern High Commission, instructing the Chester officials to 'spoil and deface, or else cause to be spoiled and defaced, the aforesaid pictures', and to return their frames to the artist. On 15 November Bridgeman's Vicar General, Mainwaring, reported to the archbishop, 'I caused the pictures . . . to be defaced before my Lord of Chester, and in the presence of a public notary.' The deed was done in private, before solemn witnesses, using procedures similar to those traditionally employed for the burning of books. But by this time the High Commissioners had changed their minds, and now desired that the pictures, like Prynne's books, should be publicly burned. Word reached Chester too late. The Vicar General apologized, 'I am sorry that my zeal and duty to obedience hath anticipated your late resolutions. But,' he added helpfully, 'I have the frames still.'[68] The public retribution that was to be unleashed against the portrait (itself a substitution for the living Prynne) might now be visited on their frames (which were contaminated by association or contagion). Whether symbolic violence or sympathetic magic, the business of Prynne's pictures and their frames would occupy the authorities in Chester for several more weeks. To make up for their earlier slackness, the civic and episcopal authorities put on a show of loyal diligence and dedication. Bishop Bridgeman was a Jacobean hold-over who had been appointed in 1619,[69] but now he was bustling to support the Laudian regime.

Finally, Vicar General Mainwaring could certify to the High Commissioners, 'that upon Tuesday last, being the 12 day of this instant December, I delivered the five frames containing of late the portraiture of Prynne's pictures to Mr. Blancherd, who caused the same to be publicly burnt at the High Cross in Chester, in the presence of the mayor and aldermen, and other citizens and persons to the number of a thousand, as was conceived according to the tenor of your late warrant; which was performed with the public acclamation of the people, crying out, "burn them, burn them", thereby attesting their hatred of Prynne's person, and his proceedings.'[70]

Prynne later collected these letters and warrants and published them to publicize his cause. Of the large and vocal crowd at the burning of the picture frames, Prynne explained, 'the pursuivant standing there in his coat of arms bid them thus cry in the king's name, and commanded the mayor and aldermen to be present at this bonfire'. The frail sticks of the picture frames that represented seditious libel and puritan defiance were no match for the costume of lions and fleurs-de-lis that stood for the king. The government orchestrated the occasion, using an intimidating display of royal emblems and the ritual vocabulary of fire to exorcise Chester's previous support for the troublesome lawyer. Chester enjoyed a rich civic history and was used to politicized pageantry.[71] Now the citizens were treated to a winter bonfire (itself a potent symbol), with costumed representatives of civic, episcopal, and royal authority to witness and complete the purgation.

As Prynne himself put it, 'these High Commissioners not satisfied with the defacing of the pictures, would needs proceed to burn them for heretics; and since they could not burn Mr. Prynne in person as they desired, being then on the sea sailing to Jersey, they would do it at least by effigy; and to show the extravagance of their unlimited malice, not only the pictures but the very frames wherein they stood (poor innocents) must to the fire'.[72] Prynne himself certainly understood the symbolic significance of the affair, and his sympathizers could feel that he was violated by this attack on his portrait almost as much as by the savage attack on his person. Indeed, Prynne later protested, 'to burn the picture of a living man . . . is well nigh as great a crime as to burn this dead gentleman's corpse'.[73] Thus was completed a metonymic chain, in which Prynne represented the enemies of Laudianism, the portrait stood for Prynne, and the paintings were represented by their frames. One finds little mention of this episode in the books about Prynne, or in studies of Chester on the eve of the civil war. But it is richly revealing of cultural and political communications and the fighting of fire with fire among the subjects of Charles I.

Act 4. 1640

The parliament that opened on 3 November 1640 provided an opportunity to redress old wrongs and for Burton, Bastwick, and Prynne to receive a fresh hearing. One of the first orders of the House of Commons, dated 7 November, was for the exiles to be released from prison and to be brought back to Westminster to restate their case.[74] Radical London rallied to their side, and Prynne, the puritan who had written against health-drinking, became the toast of the town.[75] Versifiers celebrated 'the three holy martyrs' who had endured and exposed the cruelty of the prelates, and several referred to them satirically as 'Saints Burton, Prynne and Bastwick'.[76]

Prynne and Burton had left London together as prisoners in 1637, and three years later they were reunited in a triumphant return. Their journey from the south coast took on the character of a joyous pilgrimage or progress in which they were honoured with every element in the vocabulary of celebration. Bonfires and bells, rosemary and bays, accompanied them on their way. Even the weather showed them favour, with a warm November sun pushing back the clouds and mists as if to symbolize the lifting of the Laudian gloom.[77] No bishop ever entered his see with such attendance, and no group of actors ever came to court with such carnival clamour. Observers might be forgiven for making mental comparisons to the king's return from Scotland or Christ's entry into Jerusalem. Several commentators noted the return of the martyrs as the most memorable event of a remarkable political season. Bastwick came home a week or so later to similar crowds and acclaim.[78]

When Prynne and his party stopped for dinner at Brentford on the outskirts of London they were greeted by hordes more well-wishers, a throng of pedestrians, horsemen and coaches, who escorted them into the City. So thick was the crowd, so heavy the traffic, that their progress was reduced to one mile an hour. Viscount Montague, a Catholic recusant and no friend to the puritans, noted in his journal for 28 November 1640, 'This day Burton and Prynne came to town, met upon the way with a number of coaches, and multitudes of people on horseback, with rosemary branches, and the streets and windows full of people to see them coming in.'[79] Robert Woodford, the puritan diarist of Northampton, wrote more rapturously, 'Oh blessed be the Lord for this day, for this day those holy living martyrs Mr. Burton and Mr. Prynne came to town, and the Lord's providence brought me out of the Temple to see them. My heart rejoiceth in the Lord for this day; it is even like the return of the captivity from Babylon.'[80] William Hawkins wrote to the Earl of Leicester about this 'strange' turn of events, while others in London related the puritan triumph to their correspondents and constituents in the country.[81]

Most accounts of Prynne's entry into London emphasize the large numbers and reputable quality of the people who accompanied the returning martyrs. Exact numbers remain elusive, but everyone refers to a multitude. Writing just a few days after the event, the Scottish commissioner Robert Baillie cited estimates of from one hundred to three hundred coaches, and from one thousand to four thousand horse, as well as 'a world of foot, everyone with their rosemary branch'. By Robert Woodford's estimate there were about 100 coaches and 1,500 to 2,000 horsemen among the rejoicing London crowd.[82] This was Prynne's best audience, and all he had to do to win applause was to allow himself to be carried to Westminster.

Robert Baillie reported the spectacle to his presbyterian colleagues in Scotland, observing that there had never been 'such a like show'. He added, with some satisfaction, that it 'galled the bishops exceedingly'.[83] The Venetian ambassador also reported the return of the martyrs, correctly interpreting their homecoming as an ill omen for the Laudian regime. Prynne and Burton entered London, he said, 'accompanied by 300 horse and met by a hundred coaches and countless number of the common people, not without grave scandal to right-minded men and increased peril to the archbishop'.[84] Conservative defenders of the Caroline regime expressed alarm at the 'audacious riots and tumults attending their return', and mockingly labelled the returners as the 'three champions and puritan beautifews'.[85] They arrived, wrote Thomas Hobbes, 'as if they had been let down from heaven'.[86] Edward Hyde (Earl of Clarendon) recalled 'a marvellous conflux of company' and 'wonderful acclamations of joy' when Burton and Prynne approached London, and he correctly interpreted this 'extraordinary demonstration' as an early sign of 'insurrection'.[87] The massed reception for the returning martyrs was the first major crowd event of the English revolution.

On 30 November Prynne appeared in the gallery of the House of Commons, all eyes upon him. On 3 December he presented his petition for redress, assured of a favourable hearing. Significantly, the committee convened to review the returners' petitions met in Star Chamber, 'the place where the petitioners were censured'.[88] Prynne's prescient warning to Archbishop Laud, that his own career could end in misery and ruin, was about to be spectacularly fulfilled. On 18 December 1640, while the former martyr was basking in the attention of his supporters, the Commons charged Laud with high treason. When Laud was removed to the Tower in the spring of 1641, Prynne gained entry to his study and used the archbishop's papers to prove his claims about the prelates' tyranny. By April 1641 Prynne had possession of thirty-seven parcels of documents relating to proceedings against him and Burton and Bastwick, many of which he made public with his own distinctive gloss.[89] By May he was fully vindicated, restored to his privileges as a bencher of Lincoln's Inn, and restored to his university degrees.[90]

Prynne's public career between 1633 and 1641 followed the rise and fall of the Laudian regime. It climaxed in a spectacular reversal of fortune, in which Laud went down as Prynne went up. Prynne's own well-publicized suffering, and the violence inflicted on his body, helped make the case that the regime had succumbed to bestial cruelty and now deserved to be punished. The prelates, Prynne wrote, had degenerated into 'wolves and tigers', abandoning 'all charity, pity, and common humanity'.[91] By casting the bishops as 'ravenous wolves' and himself as a soldier of Christ, Prynne hastened the collapse of Laudian episcopacy. By characterizing the prelates as cruel and venomous 'furies' (using imagery associated with mythological creatures, wild beasts, and snakes), he helped to raise the temperature of the debate and to move it from reform to revolution. The Prynne of 1633 was a conforming member of the Church of England, alarmed by Arminianism, aggrieved by England's sins, a proponent of the reformation of manners. By 1637 he was sounding the alarm against popish innovations and exposing the pride and oppression of the bishops. In 1641 he was leading the call for revenge against the archbishop of Canterbury and participating in the assault on episcopacy. Prynne still had a part to play in William Laud's trial, and several more books to write. But by 1642 his time in the spotlight had passed, as the country became occupied with a drama of greater epic proportions.

Dramatis Personae

William Prynne, lawyer
Thomas Buckner, clerk, licenser
Michael Sparkes, publisher
Henry Burton, clerk
John Bastwick, physician
William Brearcliffe, clerk
Nehemiah Wallington, wood turner
William Whiteway of Dorchester
William Drake, lawyer
William Hawkins, correspondent
Edward Rossingham, journalist
Miles Burkitt, clerk
Calvin Bruen, sheriff of Chester
Thomas Pulford, limner
Robert Woodford, steward of Northampton
Robert Baillie, Scots commissioner

THE REGIME
Charles I, king
Henrietta Maria, queen
William Laud, Archbishop of Canterbury
Richard Neile, Archbishop of York
John Bridgeman, Bishop of Chester

William Noy, Attorney General
Lord Justice Richardson
Earl of Dorset
Francis Cottington, Chancellor of the Exchequer
Thomas Windebank, courtier
Sir Kenelm Digby, courtier
the hangman

SUPPORTING CAST

Philip Thomas; Joseph Hutchinson; Mr Shepard; George Catesby, gent.; John Maynard, yeoman; vicar general Mainwaring; Mr Blancherd; Viscount Montague; Thomas Hobbes; Edward Hyde; thousands of Londoners

14

The Downfall of Cheapside Cross:
Vandalism, Ridicule, and Iconoclasm

'Down with all universities, colleges and schools, they do but maintain learning, an enemy to us. Down with churches, hospitals and alms-houses, they do but help the widows, fatherless, blind, sick and lame, these were most of them founded by papists. Down with all these crosses in general, especially that idolatrous cross in Cheapside.' Thus Richard Carter mimicked the destructive religious fanatics of late 1641 who sought to turn the world upside down. Carter's characterization of the schismatic voice exactly captures the alarmed indignation of respectable London at the frenzy and folly that led to 'rebellion, schism and faction'. Alongside the principled contest between king and parliament, the revolutionary ferment of the early 1640s produced a 'rout and rabble' of 'brain-sick' radicals who focused their hatred of all things popish on London's Cheapside Cross.[1] Until it was finally destroyed in 1643 in the midst of the civil war, the Cross was a lightning rod that attracted hyperbolic language and iconoclastic action.

Cheapside Cross had endured repeated assaults since the beginning of the Reformation. Hammer-wielding activists had attacked it at various times under Mary, Elizabeth, and James. The Cross was threatened again in the revolutionary crisis of 1641. Radicals saw it as a symbol of the unreformed religion, conservatives as a venerable ornament of the city. Within a month of the publication of Carter's pamphlet Cheapside Cross was once again wounded, losing some of its decorative extremities in a night-time attack in January 1642. Within a year and a half, in May 1643, the structure was ceremoniously executed and levelled to the ground.

This chapter examines the furore surrounding the final days of Cheapside Cross. Its main purpose is to show how an agitated popular press brought life and death to an inanimate historical monument, until the structure was reduced to rubble. It follows the invective launched against the Cross, commentary on its condition, and arguments used in its defence, to situate Cheapside Cross in the turbulent discourse of the early 1640s. Protestant enthusiasts urged the downfall of this Dagon as a work of godly cleansing; but more moderate and traditional minds saw the martyrdom of Cheapside Cross as the consequence of blindness, zealotry, and folly. Authors and audiences ranged themselves on every side of the issue, projecting their own opinions and lambasting those of their opponents. The Cross, one author claimed, was a 'stalking horse' for the malice of the multitude.[2] It was also a laughing-stock, a topic for humour, a source of amusement in times of darkness and distraction. While zealous brothers egged their readers on to remove the idol in their midst, cavalier satirists treated the matter more lightly with wry amusement and hostile wit.

Pamphleteers repeatedly wrote of the Cross as a sentient being, as if it had a voice and social identity of its own. According to the needs of their polemic they reconstructed the Cross as a heathen idol, a popish monument, a foolish Catholic, and a sturdy citizen. Commonly, in satirical and polemical discourse of the revolutionary era, the Cross was gendered as female and tied to the 'womanish' faith of Roman Catholicism. Attacks on Cheapside Cross therefore had elements of a sexual assault, made legitimate because the victim represented the Whore of Rome or the Whore of Babylon. The Cross could also be male or androgynous, depending on the needs of the writer, addressed as 'sister' in one pamphlet, 'Jasper' in another, even rendered phallic in a third.

Cheapside Cross dominated the commercial centre of pre-civil war London. Generations of citizens had enjoyed its presence and contributed to the cost of its maintenance. For more than three hundred years market-goers conducted their business in the shadow of the Cross and gathered near by for civic and regal spectacles. The Cross was a well-known landmark, a familiar companion to the capital's ceremony and commerce. It was one of the places where monarchs were proclaimed and where malefactors were punished. Royal entries and mayoral processions passed by the Cross or paused there for speeches and entertainment. The shaven cat that mocked the Marian bishops was hung on the gallows at Cheapside Cross ensuring maximum attention.[3] It was one of the places where William Prynne was pilloried, the site where he lost one of his ears. Heretical books had been burned there in the sixteenth century, seditious books in the seventeenth. The Elizabethan preacher Edward Dering identified the Cross as 'a gorgeous idol, a fit stake' for burning godless and licentious books.[4] It marked a nodal point in the symbolic geography of the city, associated with the majesty as well as the ferocity of the state. The depiction of Cheapside Cross in contemporary illustrations of state occasions testifies to its significance in affairs of the kingdom as well as those of the metropolis. As a monument of medieval piety it survived the Reformation with civic, public, royal, religious, and historical connotations.

Originally erected at the end of the thirteenth century, one of the so-called

Eleanor crosses commemorating the wife of Edward I, Cheapside Cross had ancientry on its side. It was substantially rebuilt in the reign of Henry VI, and was several times remodelled or refurbished before the seventeenth century. Several of the pamphlets describing attacks on the Cross in the early 1640s cited earlier occasions when governments had contributed to its beautification. Edification preceded destruction; the Cross had to be set up before it could be pulled down.

In its Tudor splendour, Cheapside Cross rose twelve yards high in three tiers of stone, with niches and ornaments representing the Virgin and child and other religious figures. It was surmounted by a large gilded cross and a dove representing the Holy Ghost. The ensemble was renovated for Henry VII in 1486, regilded for Henry VIII in 1522 and for his new queen in 1533, refurbished for Queen Mary in 1553, and again regilded in 1554 in preparation for the arrival of King Philip. In that year, in response to anti-Spanish and anti-Catholic violence, the city authorities paid for 'a handsome pale to be made about the cross . . . for the defence thereof'. By the accession of Queen Elizabeth the threat appeared to have subsided and in 1560 the protective fence was removed.

On Midsummer night, 21 June 1581, the Cross suffered one of its periodic attacks. 'Certain young men, drawing ropes thwart the street, on both sides the Cross in Cheap, to stop the passage, did then fasten ropes about the lowest images of the said Cross, attempting by force to have plucked them down; which when they could not do, they plucked the picture of Christ out of his mother's lap, whereon he sat, and otherwise defaced her and the other images by striking off their arms.'[5] A later pamphlet imagines the Cross remembering this assault: 'my lower statues were in the night with ropes pulled and rent down, as the resurrection of Christ, the image of the Virgin Mary, Edward the confessor, and the rest'.[6] The perpetrators were never identified, despite the offer of forty crowns by way of reward. The attack could have been a case of urban vandalism or youthful folly, an outbreak of midsummer madness. But the specific targetting of sensitive religious imagery and the elaborate engineering with ropes suggests the work of determined Protestant iconoclasts.

The Cross needed substantial repair in 1581, and further work in 1595. The Lord Mayor inquired of the Council to know the queen's pleasure, after some 'light persons' had defaced the statuary and pilfered what lead they could reach. It was perhaps in response to this exchange that the controversial figure of the Virgin Mary, which had suffered repeated assaults, was replaced by the classical goddess Diana, with water from the Thames 'prilling through her naked breasts'.[7] The structure was adapted to serve as a public fountain, and its sculp-

8. Attacks on Cheapside Cross

ture made reference to the virgin queen Elizabeth who was herself sometimes likened to the celibate goddess of the chase.

The Cross was remodelled again in 1600 and 1601. The rotted wooden cross at the top was renewed, but not without argument. The figure of the Virgin Mary was restored, and the statues of apostles, kings, and bishops were beautified with new coats of lead and gilt. The whole ensemble was now ringed with railings, to separate it from the press of commerce and to protect it from would-be attackers.[8] Some godly citizens argued at this time that the whole Cross should be demolished rather than restored, claiming that its removal would leave more room for traffic as well as less temptation to superstition. The universities were asked for advice and George Abbot, vice-chancellor of Oxford (later archbishop of Canterbury), prepared an extensive consultant's report, which was reprinted amidst renewed interest in the Cross in 1641.

Abbot recommended that Cheapside Cross should remain, but that it should be purged of its most offensive imagery. He was particularly opposed to 'the image of the Dove for the Holy Ghost', which he held to be 'one of the highest points of popery'. Abbot was less sure that the surmounting cross or 'crucifix' was unlawful, but because it attracted 'adoration and worship' and induced the ignorant to credulity and superstition, he warranted the magistrates 'to remove it away'. These ornaments, he concluded, had no place in a reformed Church, 'lest we should seem to persist in that palpable darkness of Egypt'. It seems odd then, in light of the Egyptian reference, that Abbot should recommend that the authorities erect a pyramid in place of the crucifix, in hope that in time people would cease to refer to the monument as 'the Cross in Cheap'.[9] Abbot was adamantly opposed to anyone acting 'rashly nor tumultuously' on their own against the Cross. Only the magistrates were empowered 'to redress such enormities'. If anyone was 'to rend, break and tear' they were to do it 'decently and in order' with 'the advice and consent of superior powers'. It was work for a Hezekiah, not for midnight hammer-men or unruly mobs.[10]

Abbot's report was largely ignored, not least because the queen herself and Bishop Bancroft of London cherished it as 'an ancient ensign of Christianity'. Within two weeks of the completion of the restoration in January 1601 somebody attacked it again, once more defacing the statue of the Virgin Mary, plucking off her crown, and stabbing her image in the breast. The Cross continued to attract opposition as well as approbation, but Abbot himself later moderated his opinion, judiciously praising Bancroft's restoration of the Cross just before he became archbishop in 1611.[11]

Cheapside Cross remained as an ornament of the city under the early Stuarts, although zealous reformers still took offence at its gilded cross and figures of saints and pilgrims. It was 'marvellously beautified and adorned against the coming in of King James' in 1603, regilded for the Lord Mayor's procession in 1612, and periodically maintained and re-edified under Charles I. In 1626 Sir Robert Harley supported a motion in parliament to pull down Cheapside Cross 'for fear of idolatry',[12] but city officials instead commissioned a new iron grate 'for the better preservation of the same', which was installed the following year.[13] A ballad appeared about this time to celebrate the 'shining beauty' of the city's regilded gem, comparing it favourably to the deteriorated Charing Cross.[14]

By the time of the Long Parliament Cheapside Cross was an ancient monument, its gilding somewhat darkened by soot[15] but otherwise none the worse for its long history of wounds and scars. Most people accepted it as part of the urban environment, though a few critics grumbled that the Cross was a traffic hazard, an 'encumbrance of the street and hindering of carts and carriages'.[16] Writing from London in the year of its final fall, the Venetian ambassador described Cheapside Cross as 'a most beautiful pyramidal cross surrounded with figures of saints of exquisite workmanship'. It was, he continued, 'the most conspicuous ornament of the principal street of this city'. 'It was ever held a graceful fabric to London, till of late years', remarked another commentator in 1643 who was sad to see it disappear.[17]

The principal case against Cheapside Cross was that it remained as a relic of the old religion. Although shrines and other traditional devotional attractions had been desecrated or removed under godly reformist monarchs, Cheapside Cross remained as an insult and irritant to the iconophobic culture of Protestant England. Roman Catholics, traditionalists, and people of superstitious inclination continued to pay devotional respect to the Cross, as they might to any altar or figure of a saint. When the Jesuit Edmund Campion was captured in 1581 he was taken through London to the Tower, tied to his horse 'with a sign in large letters reading "Campion the seditious Jesuit" stuck in his hat, but he still managed a deep bow to the Cross in Cheapside'.[18] This act of defiance further identified the Cross as a popish symbol and it was cited from time to time in arguments for removing the religious imagery from the cross or for demolishing it altogether. The Lord Mayor's letter of 1595 reported that 'strangers and other superstitious people . . . passing by the Cross . . . daily give idolatrous worship thereunto . . . to the offence of God, and to the contempt of the laws and orders of the church'.[19]

Abbot's report in 1601 recalled Campion's gesture of twenty years earlier, and identified the Cross as a magnet for devotees of the old religion. 'The Cross in Cheapside hath many in the twilight and morning early which do reverence before it,' observed the vice-chancellor, and women in particular, the weaker sex, were attracted to 'adoration and worship' before its enticing images.[20] 'This outward and material sign of the cross hath been and is abused to idolatry and superstition,' wrote a group of Abbot's Oxford colleagues. A Jacobean preacher warned a few years later that the Cross was 'a snare unto the ignorant people' and an idol for those 'popishly affected amongst us'.[21] Tales of popular popish devotion in the face of Cheapside Cross became standard fare in pamphlets hostile to the monument, although actual evidence of such behaviour was hard to find.

Strict Protestants were scandalized again in the reign of Charles I when people were seen surreptitiously nodding to the cross and making other covert gestures of Catholic devotion in its direction. Pamphleteers of the early 1640s claimed that it was common knowledge that papists approached the Cross with their 'daily adorations'[22] and that foolish people were drawn there to 'commit spiritual fornication . . . with the said idol'.[23] 'Men and women both have been observed to bow there, and to patter out we known not what, nor themselves neither,' remarked one publication.[24] Another claimed more specifically that 'sundry sorts of people have by three o'clock in the morning come barefoot to the Cross, and have kneeled down, and said something to themselves, crossed their forehead and their breast, and so risen and making obeisance went away . . . Likewise that hundreds of people have been publicly seen, and in the midst of the day, bend their bodies to it, and put off their hats to it, and cross themselves'. The 'honest, ancient and good inhabitants' of Cheapside who supplied this information also said that people on horseback and passengers in coaches had doffed their hats 'and done reverence to it.' Popish fanatics were said to be plotting to 'make all England of that religion . . . to pray for and towards Cheapside Cross'.[25] The Cross was therefore denounced as an idol in the midst of the city and as a stimulus to Roman Catholicism. Interest in the Cross rose with every wave of anti-popery that swept across Protestant England, and claims of Catholic devotion in its presence were cited as evidence of the popish threat. It was hardly surprising that the Cross should become a target for iconoclasm when it suffered such a barrage of hostility and abuse.

Following the common post-Reformation convention of attaching Old Testament names to contemporary issues and figures, critics of Cheapside Cross used familiar biblical references to call for its suppression. George Abbot had likened some of the ornaments at Cheapside to the 'brazen serpent' of the Israelites, and urged the Elizabethan authorities to adopt the iconoclastic role of Hezekiah. Others reminded readers of the unhappy example of Gideon, whose people lost God's favour when they worshipped before the Ephod. The Cross was described as Baal's image or as Dagon, the filthy god of the Philistines. It was the whore of Rome or the whore of Antichrist and one of the abominations of Babylon. It was, wrote one inspired commentator, like Priapus, 'a filthy god indeed'. Puritans agreed that the Cross was dangerous and offensive, like the 'accursed thing' retained by the Israelite Achan. As a permanent structure erected against heaven it was worse than the seasonal maypoles. As a popish monument in the heart of the City it was 'a trap and a snare . . . to God's own people'.[26]

John Archer, who preached against the Cross in 1606, regarded it as 'one of the special plague tokens of God's anger', like 'images of Baal' and other strange gods. England would surely suffer for building it up rather than pulling it down. 'Witness the Cross in Cheapside, that is lately beautified by you: I am troubled to think how God expressly hath been provoked, and wrath I fear will

9. London's Dagon, Cheapside Cross

be poured out upon you.' The presence of the Cross was a betrayal of the covenant and a mockery of the Reformation; its restoration encouraged papists to hope for the return of Roman Catholicism. 'Oh, this Cross is one of the jewels of the whore of Rome, and is left and kept here as a love token, and gives them hope, one day, that they shall enjoy it and us again.'[27]

By 1641, by all accounts, the Cross had more enemies than friends. Henry Burton preached before parliament in June 1641 and called on the members to 'cast down all these abominations' and to 'begin with the golden idol in Cheapside'.[28] Mock sermons in popular pamphlets echoed the refrain. In *The Brownists Conventicle* of July 1641 the preacher, 'a learned felt-maker', associates the

Cross with the superstitions, ceremonies, traditions, and hierarchy of the Church of England. 'My dear brethren,' he warns, 'there is another cross which stands in our way, and it is an eyesore to our uprightness: that gilded, idolatrous cross in Cheapside, which so many adore and reverence when they pass by it.'[29] In another mock sermon of 1641, allegedly delivered to an Adamite congregation in Marylebone park, the preacher, 'a grave weaver', declaims: 'I will prophecy the destruction of these crosses. Thou, cross in Cheapside, shall be deprived of thy head, for thou art a traitor. Thou art like the image that Nebuchadnezzar set up, thou hast a head of gold. Thy bars about thee shall not defend thee, thou shalt down, and the idols which thou bearest about thee shall down also. Thou shalt be like thy idolatrous sister in the Strand [Charing Cross], then shalt be robbed of thy riches, have thy head cut off, and be made a by-word to the brethren.'[30] Nor were the iconoclasts immune from reckoning the material value of the Cross in baubles, stone, and metal. One commentator remarked 'that there are certain men amongst them who, under presence of zeal, weigh not altogether so much the idolatry of the form as the ponderous substance of the lead'.[31]

By common conceit the Cross was personified, with the weakness of a woman, ears to listen, parts to suffer pain, a dignity to be dishonoured, and wealth to be dispossessed. Her trappings and baubles were likened to the corrupt allurements of a popish temptress, to be shunned if they could not be stripped. The pamphlets also gave the Cross a voice, enabling her to participate, satirically, in discussions about her destruction. 'I am accused for a papist, and not thought fit to have an abiding in the heart of the city. I am called and preached against by the name of the city idol. The Brownists spit at me as they come along, the Familists hide their eyes with their fingers, the Anabaptist wishes me knocked into a thousand pieces, the sisters of the fraternity will not come near me, but go about by Watling Street and come in again by Bow Lane to buy their markets of the country women.' Indeed, 'so extremely they hate the Cross, that they abhor everything that maketh a show or carrieth but the resemblance of a cross.'[32]

The target of most of these pamphlets was not directly Cheapside Cross itself but rather the radical schismatics who made such a fuss about her. Satirists played on the puritan obsession with crosses, pushing their aversion to such extremes that 'the very name of cross ought utterly to be abolished'. Some writers imagined an absurd form of puritan correctness, whereby 'a country tailor [must] be said to sit [not] cross legged but Andrew-wise. A cross bow must be termed a venison or pasty bow, nor ought you say I will cross the street, but overthwart it.'[33] They advised zealous brothers to 'carry no coin about you' for money was marked by the sign of a cross; 'let not your children be instructed in the horn-book, because of the first character', the Christ cross row. Street names and personal names with 'cross' in them would all have to be changed, and much misogynist fun was had with the notion of 'cross wives' and women sitting 'cross legged'.[34] Those who denigrated the cross in this way were therefore enemies to prosperity and literacy and domestic discipline. 'Roundheads', declared one humorous writer of late 1641, 'cannot endure to see a cross, but will start and run back from it. Alas, they love good coin both in gold and silver, though the impression and figure of a cross be stamped thereon.'[35] Another cursed the covetous hypocrisy of the sectarian artisans: 'They that hate crosses, may they have worse, / And never have a cross in their purse.'[36]

London awoke on the morning of 25 January 1642 to find Cheapside Cross 'abused and defaced' with various parts missing. The monument had suffered another 'notable indignity' and some of its figures had lost their extremities. Crowds gathered and jostled in Cheapside to view the damage and 'a man could not pass that way but he must declare himself, whether for the Cross or against it'.[37] The popular press added to the commotion by quickly producing a printed commentary. Some puritans compared the indignity done to the inanimate statuary at Cheapside to the human suffering of Burton, Bastwick, and Prynne. How foolish to exhibit 'mercy and brotherly compassion towards stocks and stones', wrote one sympathizer, when godly men who were 'living images' had so recently suffered. The author of *The Crosses Case in Cheapside* contrasted the authorities' concern for the defaced London monument to their former indifference to the mutilation of the puritan martyrs.[38] Prynne himself would have savoured the irony of this latest reversal. Samuel Loveday registered the lamentation of conformists at the statue's loss of its nose and other members but, he remarked, 'such lamentation was not heard when good men lost their ears'.[39]

  If the aim of the iconoclasts was to refocus attention upon the Cross and to stimulate debate that might lead to its removal, they were entirely successful. Sir John Coke reported from London on 27 January, 'there is a great schism amongst the apprentices concerning the Cross in Cheap, whether it should be pulled down; it is often in danger and some hurt is done upon it'.[40] The attack set off a new round of pamphleteering, with conservatives berating the vandalism and ridiculing the separatists whom they blamed for the work, and radicals applauding the deed and calling for the job of demolition to be finished. Wits could not resist comparing the damage to the nose on a popish figure to the scars of an advanced syphilitic, suggesting, 'That Babel's whore looks as she'd got the pox, | Then woe to him that next takes up her smock.'[41] There was sympathy as well as scorn for the iconoclast, said to be a cooper, who received a 'deadly wound' when he 'fell upon the iron pikes standing about the Cross' in the course of removing some of its statuary.[42]

The capital was profoundly agitated at this time, with rumours of rebellion and war following the king's departure from London. Parliament's popular supporters, now known as 'prick-ears' or 'Roundheads', dominated debate in the streets. For 'the rabble rout' of 'vox populi' Cheapside Cross was an easily identified enemy.[43] Their cry was 'down with crosses, down with bishops, down with idolatry', claimed one observer, who feared that 'those that will abuse Christ in his picture would do the like, I believe, if he were here in the flesh'.[44] Another satiric pamphlet has the extremists calling for the complete destruction of 'the enigmatical emblem of impiety' represented by the Cross in Cheapside. It was now their resolve, the author suggested, to 'perfect these our zealous beginnings in the confusion thereof, not only detracting arms and legs of the superstitious bodies, but also making it level with the ground'.[45] The Cavaliers' contribution, at least in hostile satire, was a willingness to ravish the goldsmiths' wives 'at the Cross, or against the Cross, until we are ready to throw down the Cross with rumbling their wives against it'.[46]

The official response to the vandalism, and to renewed public interest in Cheapside Cross, was to mount a guard, with a captain and soldiers to watch it by night. However much London's civic leaders might share puritan sentiments, their highest commitment was to maintain public order. It was as if the Cross was terminally ill, and needed to be attended like a patient who was dying. 'The poor Cross in Cheapside is so sick, as it is nightly watched withal by the trained bands of this city,' wrote Robert Fox in February 1642.[47] Radicals dismissed these official protectors of the Cross as 'Baal's friends' who thwarted the necessary work of the Lord.[48]

Several pamphlets suggested that the attackers of Cheapside Cross would have gone further if they had more time or if they had not been disturbed by the watch. One of John Taylor's pamphlets mockingly champions a workman, a brewer's clerk, who 'courageously attempted the downfall' of the Cross, and 'if he had been but valiantly seconded he would have laid it level with the pavement'. Despite their midnight exertions, 'the Cross stands to battle and brave us'. Taylor's artisan iconoclast concludes, with wordy bluster, 'if I cannot have it overthrown, demolished, cast down, razed, confounded, overturned, defaced, delapidated, destroyed, laid waste, ruinated, subverted, or call it what you will, so it be taken away and the lead melted into bullets to kill Irish rebels, I say if I cannot have it so, I will wish it so.'[49] Taylor's own views appear in the accompanying poem:

Now my opinion of the cross is this,
It is amiss to such as make't amiss

.   .   .   .

Knaves may deface it, fools may worship it,
All which may be for want of grace or wit.
To those that wronged the Cross this is my curse,
They never may have crosses in their purse.[50]

Other writers worked to vocalize *The Dolefull Lamentation of Cheap-side Crosse* in an England 'sick of the staggers' (a farmyard falling sickness). Here the masculine 'Jasper Cross' complains of being 'assaulted and battered in the king's highway by many violent and insolent-minded people, or rather ill-affected brethren; and whether they were in their height of zeal or else overcome with passion, or new wine lately come from New England, I cannot yet be resolved'. The perpetrators are assumed to be Brownists, separatists, or radical Independents from the extremist wing of the puritan movement, contaminated by returners from the colonies. They behaved, lamented Jasper, like 'a mad and giddy headed multitude, who were gathered together to wrong my antiquity and ancient renowned name'. Jasper Cross loses more than his dignity, for the iconoclasts 'steal from me here a leg, there a head, here an arm, and there a nose'. His lamentation ends with a prophecy that was remarkably prescient: 'I will tell you, my cross brethren . . . I am but your stocking [i.e. stalking] horse, and colour for your future malice; your rage will not cease though you should pull me down and make me level with the ground . . . If you be suffered to pull down all things that are across you will dare to pull a magistrate of his horse because he rides across his horseback.'[51] Who could tell where iconoclastic folly would end?

The Dolefull Lamentation precipitated a response from Samuel Loveday, a budding baptist, who solemnly listed 'reasons why we desire the extirpation' of Cheapside Cross. It was, he said, 'a monument of idolatry . . . and may be compared to Dagon, spoken of in I Samuel 5'. It was a popish ornament, fitter for Rome than for London, 'a graven image' that risked 'the wrath of God'. Above all, for forward Protestants, it was as 'thorns in our consciences' and will 'scandalize our pure profession of religion'. The Cross should come down, Loveday concluded, but only through parliamentary authority. The work of extirpation might be that of the Lord but its execution belonged to the magistrate.[52]

Just as *The Dolefull Lamentation* saw England 'sick of the staggers', so the *Answer to the Lamentation* imagines the Cross itself as afflicted with a terminal ailment. Addressed to those who would like to keep the Cross alive, 'the doctor's judgement' is one of many lampoons investing the structure with human characteristics. It sits uneasily with Samuel Loveday's baptist solemnities, with which it is printed, reminding us not to look too hard for tonal or ideological coherence in the popular publications of the 1640s. 'The doctor's judgement' mimics contemporary medical practice while mocking conservative concern for the health of Cheapside Cross:

The aforesaid Jasper having suffered much by loss of his members from his body, your delays of relief have proved very prejudicial to his health; for being, as I suppose, put into a heat by that sudden encounter, and then being exposed to the violence of the weather, and a cold piercing his body through the open pores, and not bleeding currently, I fear it festers inwardly, whereby many radical humours are congealed therein, that in respect of his age, his disease (occasioned by their delays and obnoxions) will prove very desperately uncurable, without one medicine can be procured to apply to him, and that is a parliamentary plaster, as a preservative of his life. You do well to watch with him and pray to him, and comfort him as well as you can. Only use such medicines as may preserve his present life; for as yet the obstructions cannot be removed. If you please, you may give him a vomit, and apply a plaster to his sores.[53]

Several pamphleteers imagined that the Cross had suffered 'a mortal wound' that would lead to its burial and funeral. Bishops, Jesuits, Papists, and Cavaliers were imaginatively grouped as mourners, alongside countrymen crying 'away with the idol, down with popery, popish prelates, ceremonies, and all idolatry', in hope that its removal would bring them prosperity.[54] One publication featured 'the last will and testament of Cheapside Cross', bequeathing its popish accoutrements to Catholic co-religionists, and embracing the archbishops of Canterbury and York within this fold by appointing them as executors.[55]

A somewhat gloating publication of 1642, whose author may actually have been involved in the January assault, applauded the iconoclasts who 'wrenched off a leg and part of a thigh from that image they presumptuously call Christ, plucked away the pope's mitre, disarmed his cardinal, cracked the queen mother's crown, took away the half [of a saint] and most shamefully defaced a fifth, for its nose is gone'. *The Crosses Case in Cheapside* acknowledged that by civil standards the attack was a crime, but it appealed to higher standards such as fulfilling the will of God and anticipating the necessary work of the state. 'The person that plucked off the leaden leg and part of the thigh from the image did very well. And if the magistrate now shall break down all the images and defile their coverings, so destroying them out of Israel, he shall do better.' The Cross must come down because 'it is an offence and grief of heart to the strong Christian, a stumbling block to the weak, and a very downfall to the stubborn and wilful'. The standard puritan charge that the Cross was an idol, 'Baal's image', an offence to God, and an impediment to the reformation of religion had extra weight as England descended into the confusion of war.[56]

On 24 April 1643 Parliament appointed Sir Robert Harley, a long-time enemy of
Cheapside Cross, to chair a Commons committee to supervise the destruction
of offensive religious images in the metropolitan area. He met immediately
with the city authorities, and three days later, on 27 April 1643, the London
Court of Aldermen gave order 'for the demolishing and pulling down of the
Cross in Cheapside, in regard of the idolatrous and superstitious figures thereabout set and fixed'.[57] Most sources agree that the initiative came from the City
rather than from Westminster, although a royalist newsletter claims that the
House of Commons chose 'rather to act the business by their hands than
appear in it themselves'. There was clearly collusion between them. 'Parliament
has permitted the people to demolish [Cheapside Cross] from its foundations,'
reported the Venetian ambassador.[58] The Lord Mayor at this time was the
radical Isaac Pennington (later a regicide) who put an end to three and a half
centuries of custodianship. The volte-face in the City, turning from protecting
the Cross to destroying it, was comparable to the action of parish authorities
who changed from cherishing to eradicating such religious equipment as rood
screens and altar rails. Conservative presbyterians could take some satisfaction
that the work was done by the magistrates rather than by the mob.

Political, religious, and military factors combined in this final downfall
of the Cross in the maypole season of 1643. The Venetian ambassador thought
that the parliamentarians were made 'insolent' by such recent military success-
es as the taking of Reading (26 April) and that this emboldened them to pull
down the Cross.[59] Others in the parliamentary camp regarded the Cross as an
impediment to victory, and hoped that its downfall would bring about a flow
of blessings. Harley and Pennington seem to have been engaged in an act of
assuagement and propitiation, a kind of sacrificial cleansing with elements
of godly conjuration. If that action appears ironically superstitious, like casting
out 'the accursed thing' that compromised the covenant, it seems to have won
God's attention. The presbyterian chronicler John Vicars attributed Parliament's 'wonderful and extraordinary good success' on the battlefield to God's
pleasure at their recent iconoclastic action. 'The great success the Parliament's
forces had' at Leeds, Blackburn, Dorchester, and Reading, and the military
triumphs of Sir William Waller in Hereford and Sergeant Major Chudley in
Devon followed 'immediately after that vote against Somerset House [*residence
of the queen and her Capuchin friars*] and Cheapside Cross'. The destruction of
popish images, avowed Vicars, was 'a work most noble and much conducing to
the high honour of God, and great comfort of all good men'.[60]

The Cross began its fall on the morning of Tuesday, 2 May. The day was
'calm, clear and fair', wrote the Cavalier diarist Sir Humphrey Mildmay, when
'the Cross in Cheape [was] taken down by the Jews [*his derisive term for the*

The 2 of May, 1643. y^e Croſſe in Cheapeſide was pulled downe, a Troope of Horſe & 2 Companies of foote warted to garde it & at y^e fall of y^e tope Croſſe dromes beat trumpets, blew & multitudes of Capes warre throwne in ye Ayre. & a greate Shoute of People with ioy. ye 2 of May the Almanacke ſayeth, was ye invention of the Croſſe. & 6 day at night was the Leaden Popes burnt. in the placeringinge of Bells, & a greate Acclamation & no hurt done in all theſe actions.

10. The destruction of Cheapside Cross, 1643

puritans], the town in much disorder'.[61] The soldiers who had been guarding the cross against the attentions of iconoclasts since January 1642 now had to guard the demolition crew from harassment by defenders of the Cross who insisted 'they would rather lose their lives than it should down'.[62] The Venetian ambassador reported that the work took three days, 'always with the presence of a company of horse to prevent riots, and with a great crowd of people, the majority blessing the deed but others, although of the same religion, detesting and deploring it'. Four companies of the London Trained Bands drew up 'to guard and defend' the demolition crew and to safeguard the valuable materials they brought down.[63] Several commentators remarked on the irony that the almanac showed 2 May as *'inventio crucis'* (invention of the cross, commemorating the discovery of the true cross by St Helena) on the very day when in London the celebrated Cross was coming down.[64] It was also a day of ironic inversion, with the destruction of Dagon a festive alternative to the setting up of maypoles that were now forbidden by the puritan regime.

John Vicars's delight in the stripping and destruction of the Cross—'that mirror and amazement of abominable and shameful idolatry'—was almost uncontrollable.

The gorgeously gilt leaden coat of Cheapside Cross was plucked over its ears, and its accursed carcass also piecemeal tumbled down to the ground . . . Many thousands of people . . . came to see (and, no doubt, some popish sots to bewail) the fatal fall of that whore. Yea, and the work was both guarded and solemnized with brave bands of soldiers sounding their trumpets and shooting off their pieces, as well as shouting out with their voices, and echoing out their joyful acclamations at the happy downfall of Antichrist in England . . . Nor was this abominable idol, thus brought to her death or destruction, left without a funeral solemnity; for upon the Friday following at night a great fire was made in Cheapside, just where the Cross stood, whereinto the leaden gods, saints and popes were cast, and there melted, to make bullets yet further to bang and beat down the living idols or idolators of Rome.

The bells rang, the bonfires burned, the waits sang, trumpets sounded, drums banged, guns saluted, 'together with most jocund and joyful acclamations of mens' voices', as London celebrated the 'funeral' of Cheapside Cross. Thus ended the days of 'the most famous, or rather infamous, monument of superstition in the Christian world'.[65] To emphasize the symbolic transformation and cleansing, the Book of Sports—'that most mischievous and abominably profane and pernicious book' which had permitted such abominations as maypoles—was burned 'by the common hangman . . . in the very place where the Romish Cross in Cheapside formerly stood'.[66]

For Vicars the Cross had female, bestial, and even diabolical characteristics. Other writers continued the conceit that Cheapside Cross had been a sentient being with a social identity, brought down by 'error and schism'. 'Jasper Cross' had suffered sickness, died, and was given a memorial funeral. Like any citizen of substance, he made his will and distributed his legacies, and his executors inventoried his goods and wrote his epitaph. Awaiting his end, the Cross feels 'sick at heart' and laments pathetically, 'I shall never see the end of the merry month of May.' On the morning when his major ornaments were removed, he looked 'like a skeleton or an anatomy of his body or corpse by ten or eleven o'clock at noon'.[67] For wits less concerned than Vicars to justify the righteousness of parliament, the events of May provided opportunities for satire, for lessons in history, and observations on contemporary manners.

The mock testament of 'Jasper Cross his last will' dwells on the material worth of the structure and the new uses to which its components could be put. The gold will go to the highest bidder, the lead will provide bullets or plumbers' fittings, the iron to make swords, and so on. One curious bequest seems to promise a kind of resurrection: 'I give my body and stones to those masons and workmen that cannot tell how to frame the like again, to keep by them for a pattern; for in time there will be more crosses in London than ever there was yet.' This seems to presage the revival of Roman Catholicism, but it also prophesies the vengeance awaiting when the king regains his capital from the parliamentary rebels. In a bitter farewell, in the form of an epitaph, the Cross chastises the people as being 'like stone to all goodness', and forecasts the continuance of 'cross tricks, cross ways, and cross vanities'.[68]

'Must I then down?' asks a plaintive Cheapside Cross in a royalist verse of May 1643. The broadsheet contrasts the innocence of the Cross with the lawless rebellion of the zealous 'prick-ears' and covetous Roundheads who sought its destruction.

> They will divide my coat, my flesh, my bones,
> They'll share the gold, and give their wives the stones.
> They say they'll pluck the tower of Babel down,
> All things go right when there's no Cross ith' town.

And in a typical barb against the puritans it adds:

> They'll have no common prayer, but do abhor
> All that is common, but a common whore[69]

'What hast thou done, poor Cross, that this hard doom is laid upon thee?' enquired another ballad pamphlet of 1643. The answer, in the voice of a cavalier, was that revolutionary London was controlled by greedy fanatics, who would themselves suffer in due course.

> For now they keep the whole City in awe,
> With wrong-expounded and misconstrued law
>
> .   .   .   .
>
> May they lead lives so crossed with grief and care,
> That, at the last, may bring them to despair
>
> .   .   .   .
>
> And may they still be crossed and crossed again,
> May crosses mixed with losses be their pain
>
> .   .   .   .
>
> And to conclude, may they all lead cross lives,
> Nay, which is worse, be troubled with cross wives.[70]

As an object of veneration as well as a target of derision, the Cross braved generations of controversy to participate in the religious and ceremonial drama of the city. Now it was down and dismembered, its fate matching that of the body politic itself. Cheapside Cross was not restored at the Restoration, and appears to have faded from memory. Iconoclastic agitators of the later seventeenth century would have to find targets elsewhere.

15

THE ADAMITES EXPOSED: NAKED RADICALS IN THE ENGLISH REVOLUTION

1641 was the year when the world first turned upside down,[1] and the year when the Adamites supposedly took off their clothes. The unravelling of the kingship of Charles I, the undermining of magistracy and episcopacy, the collapse of press censorship, and the emergence of a radicalized artisan underclass, produced in 1641 a whirlwind of cultural and political confusion. Among its many by-products was the obscure and disturbing phenomenon of the Adamites. Identified as a sect of revolutionary naked fundamentalists, the Adamites were bewildering, frightening, or ridiculous, depending on one's point of view. Whether they emerged from the radical underground as daring experimental antinomians, or belonged instead to a literary tradition of burlesque and grotesque, is one of the concerns of this chapter.

The Adamites appeared amidst the explosion of sectarian enthusiasm following the assault on the Church of England and the crippling of the Caroline regime. Episcopal authority had collapsed by the summer of 1641, and parochial discipline was in shreds. Anyone could gather an audience and call it a congregation, and any congregation could deem itself a church. Conservatives complained bitterly that button-makers and other common tradesmen were proclaiming from pulpits and in private assemblies, and even women were daring to preach.[2] This was a remarkably fertile moment for religious enthusiasm and experimentation, and for the proliferation of heresies old and new, as deference and decorum disappeared.

Our knowledge of the Adamites is largely confined to printed pamphlets and tracts of the 1640s and 1650s. We know them as a textual phenomenon rather than a social movement. They featured in a spate of publications in 1641, and were mentioned from time to time in the revolutionary decades that followed. Sometimes they were cited as deluded extremists, at other times as little more than a joke. The Adamites came in at number nine in *A Discovery of 29 Sects here in London*, which the book-collector George Thomason acquired in September 1641, and no comprehensive catalogue of heresies or sects would subsequently leave them out. Some of these lists were illustrated, imprinting the image of the naked Adamite alongside that of the Seeker, the Familist, the Anti-Scriptarian, and many others.[3]

Catalogue of the several Sects and Opinions in England and other Na
With a briefe Rehearsall of their false and dangerous Tenents.

Iesuit — *Arminian* — *Arian* — *Adamite* — *Libertin*
AnteScripturian — *Soule Sleeper* — *Anabaptist* — *Familist* — *Seeker* — *Divorcer*

11. Several sects and opinions in revolutionary England

Historians have occasionally taken notice of the Adamites, alongside other fringe phenomena of the 1640s, but few have paused to ponder their significance. I have not found a single extended discussion of the Adamites in scholarly books or articles, and rarely more than a paragraph or passing reference in studies of the revolutionary era. Christopher Hill's classic *The World Turned Upside Down* gives them less than a complete sentence, while McGregor and Reay's collection on *Radical Religion in the English Revolution* makes no mention of the Adamites at all.[4] Historiographically, the Adamites are almost invisible, as if previous scholars have judged them too marginal or spurious for any mainstream account of the revolution. They were not, like Anabaptists or Quakers, the founders of modern religious denominations, nor, like the Ranters, the ancestors (or pseudo-ancestors) of left-wing antinomianism.[5] They had no spokesmen, no martyrs. As far as most accounts of the period are concerned, they might as well never have existed.

This chapter is an attempt to bring the Adamites into historical focus. But it is not simply concerned to resuscitate an obscure and neglected sect. My principal purpose is to explore the margins of early modern society and religion, and to use accounts of the Adamite phenomenon to illuminate other dark corners of the past. This will involve an excursion into the discourse on apparel, as well as brief discussions of medieval heresies and the more familiar Ranters and Quakers of revolutionary England.

Who were the Adamites, what did they believe, and how were they said to conduct themselves? What was their relationship to earlier heresies, to sectarian extremism, libertinism and Familism, and to the visionary practice, employed by some prophets, of 'going naked as a sign'? In light of the recent historiographical battle over the Ranters, as to whether that antinomian collective ever existed, should we treat the Adamites as a literary or discursive phenomenon or as a hidden revolutionary sect? Were there really practising religious nudists in pre-civil war London, or were the Adamites simply the product of prurient or fevered imaginations? Is there a story behind the story, and how do we sift out paranoid invention from hostile reporting? The key question, I will suggest, is not whether Ranters or Adamites really existed, but what the discourse in which they feature tells us about contemporary attitudes and alarms.

Since a fundamental feature of the Adamites was their rejection of clothing it may be helpful to consider how nakedness and apparel were treated in more reputable contemporary sources.

There were three interwoven discussions about clothing in early modern England. The first took account of the origins of apparel and its place in God's plan. The second focused on the function of clothing, explaining its value, purpose, and utility for ornament and protection. The third, and most virulent, addressed the abuse of apparel and the vanity, pride, and sinfulness of garments that were excessive, luxurious, or inappropriate. These discussions occupied a moral and religious sphere, largely separate from the other discourse about honest textile manufactures in which England, as a wool country, was deeply imbued.

As everyone familiar with Genesis knew, our first parents went naked and clothing was a consequence of sin.[6] Paraphrasing the Bible story, the Elizabethan Philip Stubbes related that God created man 'after his own similitude and likeness, in innocency, holiness, righteousness, and all kind of perfection'. But after our first parents sinned 'their eyes were opened, they saw their nakedness, and were not a little ashamed (and yet before sin was committed, they both being naked, were not ashamed, but sin once committed, they became unclean, filthy, loathsome, and deformed) and sewed them garments of fig leaves together, to cover their shame withal. Then the Lord pitying their misery, and loathing their deformity, gave them pelts and fells of beasts to make their garments withal, to the end that their shameful parts might less appear.' Clothing, by this account, was originally instituted to hide 'those parts which God

12. Adam and Eve in Paradise

commandeth to be covered, nature willeth to be hid, and honesty is ashamed once to behold or look upon'. It covered and contained the unruly human frame. Our apparel, Stubbes concluded, 'was given us of God to cover our shame, to keep our bodies from cold, and to be as pricks in our eyes, to put us in mind of our frailties, imperfections and sin'.[7]

This is a complicated story, from which came the core of the Adamite revolt. Prelapsarian mankind was naked and unashamed. Clothing was originally unnecessary, indeed unheard of, as God looked kindly on his creation. But everything changed with the onset of sin, which brought in human suffering, generation, and death. Bodies became sites of shame and loathing, associated with perceptions of deformity. It is as if the body itself became monstrous, not just that mankind acquired knowledge. Clothing became necessary, according to the Cambridge puritan William Perkins, 'for the covering and hiding of that deformity of our naked bodies, which immediately followed upon the transgression of our first parents; and in this respect also, were garments (after the fall) appointed by God for the use of man. . . . The end of attire is, to hide the shameful nakedness of the body from the sight of men.'[8] Visual illustrations of this transition were in common circulation in sixteenth- and seventeenth-century print, from Bibles to herbals, from devotional handbooks to Milton's *Paradise Lost*. The naked body in its Edenic setting would have been familiar to many readers, as would the image of transgression with its punishing imposition of clothes.

Moving easily from Genesis to early modern England, social and religious commentators observed that clothing served a variety of ancillary purposes. It offered protection from the hostile elements, and helped a complex society cope with social and gender distinction. 'Apparel was given for three ends,' wrote the Elizabethan minister Adam Hill: 'for honesty's sake to cover our unseemly parts; for necessity's sake, to defend us from the injury of the weather; and for dignity's sake both to distinguish men from beasts, and men of high degree from the lower sort.' God allowed clothing 'not only for necessity's sake, but also for honest comeliness', taught the Elizabethan homily on apparel. However, it went on, 'all men may not look to wear like apparel, but every one according to his degree, as God hath placed him'.[9]

Dozens of commentators repeated or elaborated these remarks. Among the 'many purposes' for which garments were invented, taught the future bishop John Williams, 'they keep private persons from the injuries of the Heavens, and the public from the injuries of the Earth'. They serve both 'as shelters of necessity' and 'as scutcheons of . . . dignity', fending off 'the injuries of the air, wetting, nipping, and scorching', as well as 'the injuries of men'. The layman William Prynne likewise pontificated that 'the end why God ordained apparel at the first was only to cover nakedness; to fence the body against cold, wind, rain, and other annoyances; to put men in mind of their penury, their mortality, their spiritual clothing from heaven, and the like; and to distinguish one sex, one nation, one dignity, office, calling, profession from another'.[10]

William Perkins's explanation of the origin and purpose of clothing is the most orthodox and comprehensive.

The ends of apparel are specially these. First, for necessity's sake; that is for the defending of the body from the extremity of parching heat and pinching cold, and consequently the preserving of life and health. This was the end for which garments were made after the fall. And the reason of it is this. Whilst man was yet in the state of innocency, before his fall, there was a perfect temperature of the air, in respect of man's body, and so there was no need of garments; and nakedness then was no shame unto man, but a glorious comeliness. Now after that Adam, and in him all mankind, had sinned, vanity came upon all creatures; and amongst the rest, upon the air a marvelous distemperature in respect of heat and cold. For the remedy whereof, it was ordained that Adam should wear apparel, which God having once made and appointed, he hath ever since blessed it as his own ordinance, as daily experience showeth.[11]

Once instituted, however, clothing began to serve other functions. It was 'necessary two ways', Perkins argued, 'first, in respect of nature, for the preservation of life and health; secondly, in respect of place, calling and condition, for the upholding and maintenance thereof'. The 'necessary raiment . . . for the scholar, the tradesman, the countryman, the gentleman . . . serveth not only to defend their bodies from cold, but . . . belongs also to the place, degree, calling, and condition of them all.' Clothing, Perkins continued, 'must be . . . answerable to our estate and dignity, for distinction of order and degree in the societies of men'.[12] Since vanity, by this account, was encoded in the origins of clothing, the practical benefits of apparel were entwined with temptation to abuse.

Commentators who discussed the origins and purposes of clothing were quick to warn of its dangers. Philip Stubbes took offence at fashions that were excessive, flamboyant, luxurious, lascivious, or foreign. Adam Hill decried 'the pride of apparel' that, with gendered precision, led men to pride and women to whoredom. Arthur Dent lambasted 'wanton, immodest and offensive apparel' that reflected 'excessive and abominable pride'. John Williams preached against 'the vanities for the rigging of the body'. And John Bunyan excoriated 'the lust-provoking fashions of the times'.[13] But none of them thought the problem could be solved by disrobing altogether.

Christians were supposed to wear clothing according to their status or degree, as God had placed them. But too often, amidst the confusing social mobility of the early seventeenth century, the outward apparel did not match the body beneath. Commoners aped the costume of their betters, and women borrowed items that belonged to male attire. Angry reformers railed against women who dressed like men and against the 'lascivious and effeminate' wretches who 'showed themselves in woman's attire'. 'Garments are set down for signs distinctive between sex and sex,' insisted Stephen Gosson, as if by abusing or removing those garments the distinction might be blurred.[14]

So too with social distinctions, the clothing made and displayed the woman or the man. The puritan Arthur Dent complained in *The Plaine Mans Path-way to Heauen*, 'nowadays few will keep within compass, few will know their places; but the most part run beyond their bounds, and leap quite out of their sockets . . . For now we cannot, by their apparel, discern the maid from the mistress, nor the waiting woman from her lady. And thus we see in this matter of apparel how all is out of joint.'[15]

Clothing helped shape and sustain the social order. There had long been anxiety about apparel, unease about the naked body, and considerable muddle about what clothes signified. This is why successive regimes imposed sumptuary laws attempting to restrict particular items of dress to specified degrees and ranks;[16] it is why social conservatives became so alarmed when people put on robes above their station or costume that created confusion about their class or sex;[17] and it is one of the reasons that revolutionary-era critics reacted with indignation when radical sectarian Adamites allegedly took off their clothes altogether.

The Adamites of 1641 were by no means the first to abandon the proprieties of apparel, for late antiquity and medieval Europe spawned recurrent movements in which naked radicals are said to have flourished. Critics and chroniclers of the 1640s were well versed in ecclesiastical history, expected significant recurrence, and were not surprised when ancient heresies re-emerged. A survey of earlier appearances will help to set the stage for the Adamites of revolutionary England.

Though Christians and Jews shared a general horror of the naked body there were special occasions in earlier times when nudity might be appropriate. Adult baptism, as a central sacrament of the primitive Church, involved 'stripping off the old man [Satan] with his deeds',[18] and could be accompanied by literal as well as symbolic undressing. It appears to have been common in the third and fourth centuries for Christian initiates to stand naked for their baptism, their nudity symbolizing entry into new life. Cyril of Jerusalem in the fourth century congratulated newly baptized Christians, 'Marvellous, you were naked in the sight of all and were not ashamed. Truly you bore the image of the first-formed Adam, who was naked in the garden and was not ashamed.' Stressing the association between clothing and sinfulness a few years later, John the Deacon told baptismal candidates that they 'put off the earthly garments of mortality' as they stepped into the water of rebirth.[19]

Fundamentalist extremists turned symbolic ritual into cultic practice. Though always derided and often persecuted, a succession of free-thinking sects promoted a version of Adamite nudity, either ostentatiously going naked as a sign or gathering in unclothed congregations. The Adamiani, for example, were a small Gnostic sect of the second and third centuries who, one scholar alleges, 'attempted to restore man's primitive innocence in paradise by practising naturism of both sexes in their worship as well as in their communal living'. A similar movement gathered in Roman Spain in the fourth and fifth centuries, associated with the Manichaean ascetic Priscillian. A canon of the Synod of Saragossa in 380 specifically forbade Priscillianist congregations from reading or interpreting the scriptures in the nude.[20]

Medieval France spawned the Turlupins, another shadowy sect supposedly given to nakedness and licentiousness. One of their followers, Jeanne Daubenta, was interrogated by the Dominicans and burned at the stake in 1372 and apparently went to her death in the nude.[21] Shadowy and intermittent phenomena of this sort recurred throughout the Middle Ages, leaving faint traces in chronicles and inquisitorial records.

Most famous of all were the European Adamites, an offshoot of the Taborite-Hussite movement in early fifteenth-century Bohemia. 'Ipsi Adamites se cognominabant ab Adam, qui in statu innocentia cum Eva nudus ambulavent,' wrote Aeneas Sylvius Piccolomini in his 1451 *Historia Bohemica*. 'Wandering through forests and hills, some of them fell into such insanity that men and women threw off their clothes and went nude, saying that clothes had been adopted because of the sin of the first parents, but that they were in a state of innocency. From the same madness they supposed that they were not sinning if one of the brethren had intercourse with one of the sisters, and if the woman conceived, she said she had conceived of the holy ghost,' said their first hostile historian, Laurence of Brezova.[22]

At the height of their strength the Bohemian Adamites numbered in the thousands, scattered through several villages and strongholds. Like their seventeenth-century English namesakes, they formed the extremist fringe of a radical movement and attracted charges of promiscuity and licentiousness that may or may not have been justified. All contemporary accounts are hostile, so it is hard to tell whether their nakedness was an article of faith, an everyday practice, a deliberate provocation, an occasional eccentricity, or an exaggeration or invention of the chroniclers. The Taborites hated them enough to hunt them down, and most were slaughtered in John Zizka's campaigns of 1421.[23]

There was, of course, no continuity between this fifteenth-century movement and the Adamites of Stuart England, but the chronicles were readily available. The 1563 edition of John Foxe's *Acts and Monuments* (but not later editions) mentions the 'abominable doings' of the Bohemian Adamites and their violent suppression, and this book would have been in many parish churches.[24] During the time of the Thirty Years War the career of Charles I's sister as Protestant Queen of Bohemia heightened English interest in all things Bohemian, and may have revived interest in the radical Hussite fringe. Naked sectarians were also known to have emerged in the course of the radical reformation in the Low Countries in the sixteenth century, and these too provided a model for the English Adamites of 1641.[25]

1641 opened with the imprisonment of Archbishop Laud and closed with the impeachment of a dozen more bishops. The established Church was under attack 'root and branch' as reformers questioned its organization and worship, and radicals rejected it altogether. It was a year of political turmoil and constitutional revolution, when parliamentarians passed the Triennial Act, brought down Lord Deputy Strafford, and abolished the courts of Star Chamber and High Commission. Part of the kingdom was in arms, part of it paralysed, as the Scots took control of the north. The country suffered from acute anxiety as rumours of plots and conspiracies compounded with the outbreak of rebellion in Ireland. The king was adrift and uncounselled, burdened by decisions he immediately regretted. The recurrence of plague in London added to the anxieties of the season, stirring fears that a day of judgement was at hand.[26]

As the Church of England disintegrated, and moderate presbyterians proved incapable of establishing an alternative, pamphleteers began to document the proliferation of radical religious sects. Just as there were eighty heresies known to Epiphanius in the fourth century and ninety in the age of St Augustine, so the troubles and distractions of Charles I's England produced sects and heresies numbering from the dozens to the hundreds. Writers exhibited list after list of outrageous beliefs and practices, making minimal discrimination between those they knew from history, those they learned about through hearsay, and those they could attest to by direct observation. They seem almost to luxuriate in the fecundity of sectarian error. The Adamites became a standard feature of these lists, which tended to copy and recirculate the same limited information.

The unmediated voices of sectarian extremists themselves are rare, and in the case of the Adamites non-existent. Perhaps because they were too busy gathering their churches and proclaiming their visions, perhaps because they shunned publicity and feared for their safety, perhaps because they and their followers had low levels of literacy, and perhaps too because they only supposititiously existed, the Adamite prophets of 1641 never set forth their positions in print. Alarmed conservatives, on the other hand, Anglican apologists as well as mainstream puritans, produced dozens of pamphlets to expose, to refute, and to ridicule extremists of all sorts. Not surprisingly the preponderance of the evidence is biased, in sources prone to panic, exaggeration, and invention.

One of the first reviews of radical separatism, John Taylor's *A Swarme of Sectaries and Schismatiques* published in June 1641,[27] ridicules tub preachers and licentious anabaptists, but makes no mention at all of the Adamites. Taylor was always keen to satirize sectarian absurdities, especially if sexual impropriety was involved, but here he said nothing about anyone going naked. The Adamites would surely have been grist to his mill if their presence were already known. It seems that they emerged later in the year, as the weather warmed up and radical sectarianism began to boil.

It may be possible to pinpoint the Adamite moment. They had emerged by early summer 1641, or at least were memorialized in print. An anonymous pamphlet of July 1641, *The Brownists Conventicle*, claims excitedly that

'Thraskites, or Sabbatarians, Banisterians, Brownists and Anabaptists', as well as Familists, had appeared in almost every English parish. 'But of all the rest which is of greatest remark, there is sprung up a new sect of Adamists, who take their denomination from our first father Adam, and these with men and women promiscuously mingled have their private meetings, where they will not hear the word preached nor have the sacrament administered to them but naked, not so much as fig-leaf breeches upon them, thinking thereby to imitate our first parents in their innocency.'[28] Adamites, the writer implied, were the most extreme extension of religious separatism, the *reductio ad absurdum* reached by abandoning all structure and discipline, order and hierarchy, learning and liturgy, and clothes.

The Adamites were, briefly, the talk of the town. A character in Richard Brome's 1641 play *A Joviall Crew* suggests going 'to London . . . to see . . . the Adamites run naked before the ladies'.[29] A 'mercury' or news-monger in a 'pleasant dialogue' of 1641 responds to a boast that the hawkers of news-sheets worked as hard as Adam by joking, 'you were true Adamites indeed, for some of you had scarce clothes enough to cover your nakedness'.[30] They entered quickly into popular printed culture, able to raise both a scare and a laugh.

There were even allusions to the Adamites in the most solemn disputes of the day about the future of the Church of England. Preaching before parliament on 20 June 1641, the presbyterian Henry Burton repudiated Archbishop Laud's claim that a Church without ceremonies was naked. ' 'Tis true, beloved, 'tis naked, and it is in spirit and truth when it is naked, and when it is in its own naked truth. Adam and Eve were never more glorious than in their naked innocency; when they put on fig-leaves to cover them, it was only a badge of shame.' Bishop Joseph Hall turned this conceit around in attacking Burton's polemical tract, *The Protestation Protested*. 'When I traced every step of your lazy and superfluous discourse . . . I found you as naked as an Adamite, not (one reason) the least piece of armour with you.'[31]

References to the Adamites multiplied as summer passed into autumn. An alarmist pamphlet of September 1641 included the Adamites in *A Discovery of 29 Sects here in London*. Whether they were truly abroad in the city and suburbs, or as esoteric and unlikely as the Britanists, the Chaldeans, and the Mahometans with whom they shared the list, is impossible to tell. Among these 'devilish and damnable' groups the Adamites stood out as 'a shameless sect; they ground their religion from our father Adam, and yet they go naked when they hear prayers or prophesying, when he hid himself from the presence of God because he was naked'.[32]

Startling claims about the Adamites appeared in another publication of September 1641 titled *A Nest of Serpents Discovered. Or, A knot of old Heretiques*

revived, Called the Adamites. Wherein their original, increase, and several ridicu-
lous tenets are plainly laid open. The title-page depicts eight naked Adamites,
five men and three women, in a room lit with a lantern. One of the Adamites,
a man, stands at a table with an open book, presumably the Bible. Another, in
a state of sexual arousal, is being corrected by a woman with a whip or stick and
the words 'down lust'. This illustration—perhaps the first depiction of an
erect penis in English popular print—was influential in shaping the image
of the Adamites, and would be reproduced several times with different wording
in later Ranter publications; but it is neither discussed nor alluded to in the
text.

Instead, the author reviews ancient and medieval nudist heresies to show
that the Devil was always 'busy to raise up dangerous and noisome heresies'
to disturb the quietness of the Church. The original Adamites, the author
believed, came from the late second century, within the Roman empire.
Meeting for religious exercises 'as naked as they were when they came from
their mothers womb . . . they lived obscurely and basely, seemed to admire
continency, though they never observed it, never admitted of marriage, and
called the place of their meeting the true Paradise'. Reviving this movement
in fifteenth-century Bohemia, their successors 'received the sacrament naked'
and fell into 'many other absurd and ridiculous positions' before being justly
destroyed. More recently, he added, another 'knot of them gathered together at
Amsterdam' at the time of the Reformation, including some who 'were so con-
ceited and so void of reason that they climbed to the tops of trees, and there
would sit naked expecting bread from heaven until they fell down half dead
with hunger, a just punishment for such presumption'. Throughout history, the
author concluded, these Adamites were 'gross dissemblers, deluding the world
with pretended holiness whereas their doctrine is the doctrine of devils'.[33]

As for the Adamites of modern-day London, details were wanting. Though
allegedly the Adamite heresy 'is of late sprung up in this nation, to the wonder-
ment of all that hear of it', the 'nest of serpents' advertised in the pamphlet was
not yet discovered. However, the author promised, 'they will ere long be
brought to light that their doings may be known and they shamed and justly
punished . . . Their meeting is sometime at Lambeth, at other times about
Saint Katherine's, sometimes in the fields or in the woods, at sometimes in
cellars; their ringleaders are laid out for, and no question but they will be
caught in the midst of their lewd and abominable exercise, which is so scandalous, blasphemous, heathenish and abominable. At their discovery more
shall be written.'[34]

Details of English Adamite activity would have to wait for Thomas Bray,
an Oxford scholar using the anagrammatic pseudonym Samoth Yarb, who

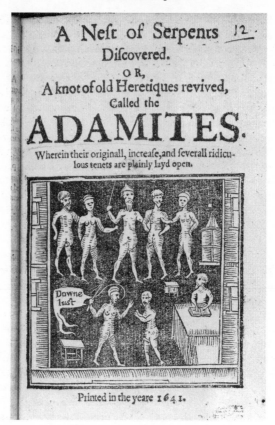

13. A nest of serpents, the Adamites of 1641

purported to have infiltrated their meetings.[35] *A New Sect of Religion Descryed, called Adamites: Deriving their Religion from our Father Adam* is hard to date precisely because it does not appear in the British Library's Thomason collection, nor was it entered in the register at Stationers' Hall, but it probably came from the second half of 1641. The subtitle summarizes the core of the Adamites' beliefs, and explains how the author came by his information: *Wherein they hold themselves to be blameless at the last day, though they sinne never so egregiously, for they challenge salvation as their due from the innocencie of the second Adam; this was first disclosed by a brother of the same sect to the author, who went*

along with this brother, and saw all these passages following. A crude illustration
shows three naked Adamites within a chamber: a long-haired woman holding a
book, her tresses obscuring her genitals, a man proclaiming from a stool in a
state of sexual arousal, and another man with a stick attempting to tame the
prophet's erection, saying 'down, proud flesh, down'. This may be derived from
the illustration to *A Nest of Serpents Discovered*, with its legend 'down lust', but
Bray claims to have been eyewitness to such a scene.[36] In both illustrations the
penis rampant implies unbridled lust which, like the abandonment of clothing,
reduces civilized Londoners to the level of savages or beasts. Uncovering the
Adamites provides an excuse for pornographic representation at a moment
when standards of all sorts were slipping. The publisher and illustrator took
full advantage of the lapse of censorship to circulate an image that had no
known antecedent in English popular print.[37]

The author establishes the context for his disclosures by referring to 'the
multitude of sects which are scattered here and there about this kingdom, and
how they lie like nests of Caterpillars, destroying our sweet smelling garden
roses'. This was a common complaint by the autumn of 1641, once again using
the imagery of infestation or swarm. He then tells how he met a melancholic
and disaffected 'brother' (never identified by name), walking in Moorfields in
London, who told him the secrets of his sect. Among the Adamites, said the
brother, 'we go all naked whensoever the word is expounded, holding it unlawful to call those vestments which we wear but fig-leaves, because our ancient
parents Adam and Eve did clothe themselves in no other when they fled from
the presence of God in the garden of Paradise'. (Another tenet of Adamite
belief, hinting at an artisan following, was that 'no man of what degree soever
he be must live idly from handiwork, because it is said in the curse, in the sweat
of thy face shalt thou eat thy bread till thou return unto the ground'.) Shocked
and intrigued by these revelations, Bray agreed to attend an Adamite assembly.
He knew he would have to take an oath 'on the bark of a tree, to be secret' (a
travesty of the oath upon the book) but casuistically 'thought with myself, that
that oath could not be very prejudicious to me', so he could reveal it to the
world.[38]

Bray's escort took him to 'a very fair house' which the author judged 'more fit
for a Lord than such fools', though he did not reveal its location. There the two
undressed without ado, 'and when we were both naked there came an ancient
man all naked also, with a long white stick in his hand, and conducted us into
a very fair chamber, where were above nine score naked persons, men and
women one with another'. The elder then inducted the newcomer, making him
swear on a piece of bark 'which our father Adam brought with him forth from
Paradise [to] keep due hours at meetings, and also keep it secret both from the

14. A new sect of religion, the Adamites of 1641

eyes and ears of the world'.[39] Apart from the peculiarities of costume, this was not unlike induction into a trade guild or initiation into any secret brotherhood, except for the presence of women.

The meeting proceeded, as radical separatist assemblies supposedly did, with 'he that was to prophecy that day' mounting a joint stool, 'where, without any ceremony at all, he began to bawl what came first to his mind. The first thing he prophesied (I remember) was the downfall of all religions except theirs, with many most blasphemous things which I am both afraid and ashamed to write.' There was nothing distinctively Adamite about this address, except that everyone present was naked. But nakedness had its problems. 'It was an order among these naked fools,' Bray explained, 'that if the planet Venus reigned in their lower parts, making them swell for pride, or rather for lust, then should the clerk with his long stick strike down the presumptuous flesh.' This misfortune affected the speaker, who became aroused at the sight of 'a zealous sister' and had to be disciplined, as shown in the illustration. 'After this hurly-burly was over,' Bray continued, 'there came many women into the chamber, all naked, also the foremost bearing a naked child,' who was christened by the prophet 'Abel, after the name of the second son of our father Adam.'[40]

It may not be unreasonable to ask whether Bray was projecting his own erotic fantasies onto his story, as well as his distaste for artisan separatism. The writing evokes the genre of the traveller's tale, and has some of the voyeuristic flavour and discursive eroticism of *A Description of the Sect Called the Familie of Love*, also published in 1641.[41] It teases the reader to assess how much is true or imagined. My guess is that Bray made the whole thing up, having heard that the Adamite heresy had been revived in revolutionary London. In that case *A New Sect of Religion* was just one more of the welter of libellous lies and 'railing fallacies' spread daily by a press that was prone to 'fictitious devisings' and 'fabulous invention'.[42]

A more detailed account of Adamite practice, superficially more plausible, appears in another pamphlet of 1641, *The Adamites Sermon: Containing their manner of Preaching, Expounding, and Prophesying: As it was delivered in Marie-bone Park, by Obadiah Couchman, a grave Weaver, dwelling in Southwark, who with his companie were taken and discovered by the Constable and other Officers of that place; by the means of a womans husband who dogged them thither. And some part likewise by meanes of a Gentlewoman, a widow, which is a Ministers daughter in the Citie of London, who was almost perswaded to become one of their Societie, if her father had not disswaded her from it. Also a Dialogue between an Adamite and a Brownist concerning their Religion, etc.* This also escaped inclusion in the Thomason collection.

The title-page features an extraordinary illustration, quite different in spirit from the indoor scenes in the two previous treatments. This has a sylvan setting that may represent Marylebone park (then a royal hunting ground, now the home of the Marylebone Cricket Club) in which a gathered community of Adamites, men and women, sit naked hand in hand while their leader proclaims from a book. Unlike most of the other works mentioning Adamites, this one is printed in black letter, which may indicate a more popular readership. The name of the publisher is given as Francis Coules, a reputable bookseller with a shop in Old Bailey.[43]

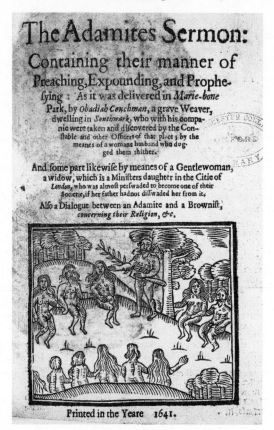

15. The Adamites' sermon in Marylebone Park, 1641

The Brownists of this account were congregational independents, often depicted as extreme sectarians, but once again the Adamites outstrip them in absurdity, ignorance, and irrationality. Persuading the Brownist to accompany him to a meeting, the Adamite proclaims, 'I am the son of Adam, who begot me in his innocency. I follow his steps before he fell; that is, I am an Adamite. And though at this present you see me clothed in garments, which in verity and truth ought not to be worn but by the wicked, yet know that when we expound we lay aside those superstitious weeds and coverings of our bodies; and as my father Adam was naked whilst he was in Paradise, so do we prophesy naked, that is to say, free from sin, as our father was whilst he was naked.'[44]

Intrigued, like Bray before him, the Brownist seeks further information. The Adamites, he learns, held three weekly meetings: on Mondays, to confer 'how to increase and augment our number, and how to secure us from them that envy our innocency'; on Wednesdays, for 'a day of humiliation, whereon we humble ourselves by fasting and praying by the Spirit'; and Fridays, 'for a day of rejoicing'. The Friday meetings began with prayer and ended in sexual abandon of the sort hinted at in the earlier pamphlets. 'On that day he on whom the Spirit falls is led in state between two sisters and mounted on a chair, circled on every side with the holy brethren and more holy sisters, where he prophecies till the spirit giveth way to the flesh, and suffers it to rebel; then he whom the Spirit so moveth by the insurrection of the flesh makes his election among the holy sisters; the rest follow his example, and so they endeavour to propagate and augment their number,' fulfilling the commandment to increase and multiply. Completely won over by what seems to be an invitation to an orgy, the Brownist accompanies the Adamite 'straight to Marylebone Park, where were gathered at least one hundred men and women . . . [who] instantly stripped themselves to the bare skin, both men and women' to listen to the Adamite's sermon.[45]

The sermon, attributed to the weaver Obadiah Couchman, is a ludicrous pastiche of sectarian ignorance, enthusiasm, and false erudition. It is a warning, or demonstration, of what can happen when the Bible is read by the unlettered. The preacher begins, perhaps redundantly, by inviting the assembly to imitate the examples of 'our first parents Adam and Eve . . . [who] were naked or without clothes; therefore let us lay aside these unsanctified and wicked weeds, these rags of ungodliness and profane relics of sin, that is to say our clothes; not only our gowns and breeches, petticoats and doublets, but also our shirts and smocks, especially because they are of the colour white and like to the Whore of Babylon's superstitious smock, with whom the wicked commit the act of adultery.'[46]

Savouring the words from Genesis, 'and they were both naked', the speaker declares, 'No question but the prophet Genesis himself was naked when he writ these words.' Clothing, the preacher continues, is simply the covering for sin. 'Those that are clothed in fine raiment, like Dives spoken of in the evangelist, have the visible marks of the beast; they are proud, haughty and ambitious, they are gluttons and surfeit with the banners of pride.' This leads to an attack on clerical garments, 'canonical cassocks . . . levitical surcingles, and . . . large surplices made of fine linen', as well as luxurious cloaks, foreign fashions and gowns of satin, 'the very name whereof is idolatry, because it is cousin german to Satan'.[47]

There follows a tirade against idolatry, especially crosses, and then a comparison of Adamite purity with the corruptions of the Church of England, parodying the puritan diatribe against artifice and ornamentation. 'This our assembly is more holy than their consecrated church; the green liberty of these trees more pleasant than their painted windows; the summer apparel of the earth more delightful and softer by far than their stones; the chirping of these pretty birds more melodious than their howling organs; and lastly, our nakedness innocence, and their vestments idolatry . . . good brethren and sisters, be not seduced by them, for they be wicked, abominable and profane.'[48] Rejecting the physical church as well as material costume, this liberated congregation privileges the greenwood over the city, nature over art. None the less, these Adamites were not completely anarchic, for like their brethren at Moorfields they retained some residue of organization, structured meetings, leadership, and even some attachment to the sacraments.

Finally, anticipating the climax of the Adamite Friday meeting, the speaker invites the followers of Adam in the state of innocence, with 'not so much as fig leaves upon us, let us therefore rejoice exceedingly and express our joy in the lively act of generation and propagation of the godly, that may be born naked as we are at this present'.[49] And there it ends, presumably on the brink of sexual congress. Despite the promises on the title-page, the pamphlet provides no further detail about the Adamite group and its apprehension. The constable, the husband, the gentlewoman, and the minister remain unnamed, and no date for the incident is given. Though the specificity of the information would seem to point toward an actual occurrence, no corroborating evidence can be found. There are no surviving records of the Marylebone constables, no incident of this sort appears in the London or Middlesex sessions records, and no other trace can be found of the weaver Obadiah Couchman.[50] We are left with an artful construction, a dialogue followed by a monologue, satirically representing what the author imagined the Adamites to have said.

Nobody else claims to have penetrated their mysteries, but several more writers of 1641 alluded to the Adamites, expecting their readers to understand the references. *The Humble Petition of the Brownists* of November 1641 (which appears to be a Catholic pamphlet in disguise) pleads for toleration of all religious sects, from Papists to the Family of Love, depicting them as harmless eccentrics living humbly and quietly in error. 'Let the Adamites preach in vaults and caves as naked as their nails and starve themselves with cold, they think themselves as innocent as Adam and Eve were in their nakedness before the fall, let them alone till some innocent Eve be so curious as to eat the forbidden fruit, and then they will all make themselves aprons of fig leaves perceiving their nakedness.'[51] More crudely mocking, *The Schismatick Stigmatised* by Richard Carter (in the bookshops by December 1641) includes the Adamites among 'the rabble of brain-sicks who are enemies to old England's peace'. None was more ludicrously deluded than 'that poor, silly, simple, senseless, sinless, shameless, naked wretch, Alice the Adamite: As bare as one's nail, she shames not her tail.'[52]

After 1641, however, the Adamite trail grows cold, with references that are muddled, repetitive, and unconvincing. A pamphlet of January 1642 listing *The Divisions of the Church of England Crept in at XV Several Doores* classified the Adamites as 'a people who would have an independent society, which neither magistrate nor church should command nor meddle with, but live as they list and labour to increase and multiply in the world, fearing neither government nor discipline, and in their societies they are so overcome with lust that they cannot pray'. The author (apparently John Taylor again) seems to have confused the Adamites with anarchic antinomians; he highlights their alleged sexual abandon but fails to mention their militant nakedness. A similar pamphlet published six months later, *Religions Lotterie, or the Churches Amazement*, ranks the Adamites at number six among sixteen 'sorts of religions', and simply paraphrases the earlier description.[53] Adamites were sometimes confused with Anabaptists, partly because Anabaptists were blamed for all sorts of sectarian excesses, and partly because their ceremonies sometimes included fullimmersion baptisms of initiates who took off all their clothes. When Daniel Featley compiled his charge against the Anabaptists, *The Dippers Dipt. Or the Anabaptists Duck'd and Plung'd*, he explicitly associated them with the Adamites, who were not ashamed to 'go naked'. The Scottish minister Robert Baillie, who had lived in London in 1641, declared the anabaptist 'nakedness in baptism' not only 'without any scriptural warrant' but also 'extremely contrary to all civility' and 'natural shame'.[54]

In 1643, in the heat of civil war, a parliamentary propagandist rather implausibly included the Adamites among the *XXXIII Religions, Sects, Societies, and Factions of the Cavaliers now in Armes against the Parliament* (1643). The Adamites, he alleged, 'have all things in common, and hold it a paradise to live so, because their discipline allows both sects [*sic; sexes?*] to court naked, in which they blush no more than Adam at his first creation. This discipline a native German first learned it in Holland, and since being in England taught it to the cavalry.' This may have been a reference to earlier Adamite heresies, but it was also a jibe at Prince Rupert, who was born in Bohemia and served in Brabant. By 1645, in a subsequent edition, the number of 'several religions held

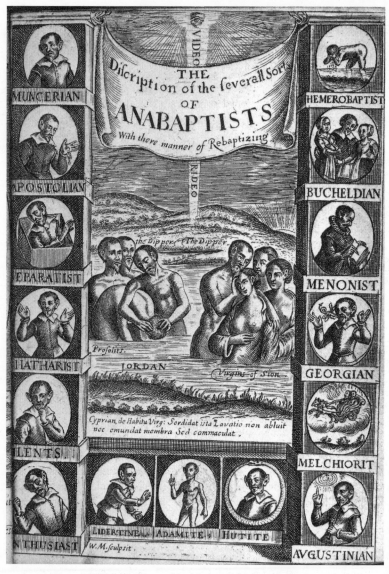

16. The several sorts of Anabaptists, with other sectarians

and maintained by the cavaliers' had grown to thirty-six, including of course the Adamites, but the information was no more specific or reliable.[55]

1645 saw the publication of Ephraim Pagitt's *Heresiography; or, a Description of the Heretickes and Sectaries of these Latter Times.* This was a monumental work that went through six editions in the next seventeen years. Like Thomas Edwards's *Gangraena* (which omits the Adamites),[56] it sought both to memorialize and to excoriate religious folly and excess. Pagitt gives several pages to the Adamites but says nothing to suggest that they were ever active in England. He seems not to know about the pamphlets of 1641, or else to mistrust them completely. Pagitt's sources are literary and historical, referring once again to early Christianity, fifteenth-century Bohemia, and the radical reformation in Amsterdam. The Adamites, he reminds readers, were 'an old heresy, of which St Augustine maketh mention, but renewed by the Anabaptists. In the assembly of the Adamites, men and women pray naked, celebrate the holy communion naked, hear sermons naked . . . They call the place of their meeting Paradise.' A certain Piccard in Bohemia 'taught his sect to go naked, and to call him Adam, and to use promiscuous marriages'. Later in Amsterdam, Pagitt continues, the followers of Theodore the tailor, seven men and five women, 'rushed into the street stark naked . . . crying horribly throughout the town, woe, woe, woe, the divine vengence', and were eventually executed for their trouble. But there is nothing about Obadiah the weaver or any of the Adamites of Stuart London. The most complete edition of *Heresiography* included a picture of a naked Adamite (upper body only) with this accompanying verse:

> What strong presumption do these monsters frame?
> Are Adam's children void of Adam's shame?
> By these no garments must be worn forsooth,
> Who say they are themselves the naked truth.[57]

Naked revolutionaries reappeared in 1650, subsumed within the new label 'Ranters'. Like 1641, the year following the execution of the king was one of deep anxiety and lost bearings. The Ranters replaced the Adamites as the most outrageous and disturbing of revolutionary sects, at least in the minds of alarmist and fanciful authors, just as the Adamites had earlier outstripped the Brownists in spiritual pride, licentiousness, and folly. Recent critical inquiry has challenged the notion that the Ranters existed as an organized group or movement, and it seems clear that some historical claims for their significance are overblown. None the less, there can be no doubt that the early 1650s saw radical libertarians experimenting with Ranter ideas, a few publications embracing Ranter philosophy, and numerous works subjecting the Ranters to ridicule or attack. If there was no Ranter movement there was at least a Ranter phenomenon that agitated religious culture in the earliest years of the Interregnum. The label was used indiscriminately to describe adepts of divine perfection, libertines who thought themselves freed from sin and its consequences, and roisterers who violated all moral norms. Viewing the Ranters in light of earlier claims about the Adamites may help to differentiate their alleged transgressions, and may help to redirect the acrimonious debate that has exercised recent scholarship on mid-seventeenth-century England.[58]

Though traceable in ancient heresies and expounded in controversial tracts, the Ranter philosophy of the pamphlets has more in common with the rake-hell reprobation and drunken good-fellowship of alehouse culture than with the rest of radical sectarianism. According to *The Ranters Religion. Or, A faithful and infallible Narrative of their damnable and diabolical opinions, with their detestable lives and actions* (1650), the Ranters 'dare impudently to affirm that that man who tipples deepest, swears the frequentest, commits adultery, incest or buggery the oftenest, blasphemes the impudentest, and perpetrates the most notorious crimes with the highest hand and rigidest devotion, is the dearest darling of heaven'. Their meetings, according to *The Routing of the Ranters,* another pamphlet of 1650, were 'spent in drunkenness, uncleanness, blasphemous words, filthy songs, and mixed dances of men and women stark naked'.[59]

Critics were quick to attach to the Ranters the worst excesses of the Adamites, as well as more outrageous antinomian crimes. One group of Ranters, according to *The Ranters Bible,* were those 'called by the name of the Familists of Love, who would have all things in common, and hold it a paradise to live so, because their discipline allows, to court naked, in which they blush no more than Adam at his first creation'. Another sort of Ranter, among seven alleged sub-groups of the sect, 'exercise themselves in nothing else but lascivious and unapparelled vices', especially promiscuous and communal sex.[60]

Iconographically, the Adamites and the Ranters were interchangeable. *The Ranters Religion* of 1650 uses the same woodblock illustration as *A Nest of Serpents Discovered* of 1641, with its chamber of naked celebrants, except that the words 'down lust' are replaced by 'behold these ranters'. But the Ranters, while shedding the last vestiges of moral restraint, seemed less fastidious about removing their clothes. Most of the time they stayed dressed. At one Ranter assembly the women allegedly 'clad themselves all in white, which they call the Emblem of Innocence', while other Ranter pamphlets describe the women 'clothed all in white lawn'.[61] Mrs Hull of Whitechapel is said to have bid a fellow Ranter to 'take up her coats and frock', and cavorted upside down 'with her coats about her ears' in a literal enactment of inversion.[62] Male Ranters too were more likely to be depicted as obscenely half-dressed than completely nude,

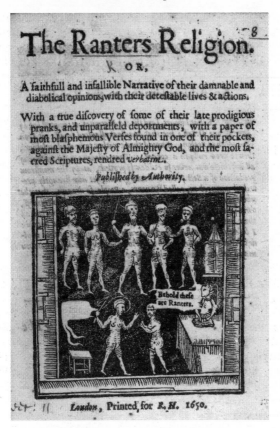

The Ranters Religion.
OR,

A faithfull and infallible Narrative of their damnable and diabolical opinions, with their deteſtable lives & actions.

With a true diſcovery of ſome of their late prodigious pranks, and unparallel'd deportments, with a paper of moſt blaſphemous Verſes found in one of their pockets, againſt the Majeſty of Almighty God, and the moſt ſacred Scriptures, rendred *verbatim*.

Publiſhed by Authority.

Behold theſe are Ranters.

London, Printed, for *R. H.* 1650.

17. Another nest of serpents, the Ranters of 1650

more inclined to 'kissing of one anothers breeches' than to disrobing altogether. At Ranter assemblies, supposedly, 'one of them lets fall his breeches, and turning his shirt aside' allows the rest to kiss his arse. Though Ranters may have behaved like this, especially in their cups, the scene may also be construed as a dramatization of the insults 'kiss my ass', 'a turd in your teeth', or the obscene anal kiss of the Devil.[63]

Whereas the Adamites had generally been presented as devout but deluded, the Ranters were depicted as depraved. Nakedness, for these fanatics, was an incidental accompaniment to debauchery, not a central expression of belief.

Nudity was never a central tenet of Ranterism, although some Ranters could barely keep their breeches on. Abiezer Coppe, the expositor and apologist for Ranterism, associated nakedness with harlotry and shame and claimed to stand, 'for clothing the naked, for the breaking of every yoke, for the letting of the oppressed go free', though he himself was said to have preached *en désha-bille*.[64] Joseph Salmon, another Ranter prophet, discussed clothing in spiritual and allegorical terms, proclaiming that God would clothe his people in alternative raiments, in 'robes of royalty' and 'garment[s] of salvation', if not in this world then the next.[65]

The Ranters of pamphlet fame only shed their clothes in the course of wild festivities, in flagrant violation of the puritan reformation of manners. One Ranter gathering near Soho in November 1650 is said to have turned Adamite when, 'after some hours spent in feasting and the like, they stripped themselves quite naked, and dancing the Adamites curranto, which was that after two or three familist gigs, hand in hand, each man should embrace his fellow female, in the flesh, for the acting of that inhuman theatre of carnal copulation'.[66] Other accounts of the Ranters 'dancing of the hay naked, at the White Lion in Petticoat Lane' and 'stark naked . . . revelling and dancing' may refer to the same cluster of incidents.[67] They may also refer to the revels in London taverns, which Laurence Clarkson described, 'where Doctor Paget's maid stripped herself naked and skipped among them'. If this was a servant to Pagitt the heresiographer, who had lost control of his household discipline, the world was truly upside down.[68]

Journalists, then as now, adopted the latest vocabulary and wrote of ordinary incidents as if they were deeply threatening. One report from this time described two prostitutes as 'she-Ranters' and described how they enticed their Johns to an alehouse where 'they all stripped themselves stark naked and fell to dancing about their room'. The next day, in violation of all good order, the women 'went stark naked about the streets', and 'being demanded if they had husbands, they replied, their husbands were within them which was God'. The report has extra resonance in a culture attuned to Adamites and Ranterism, and suggests that sexual offenders themselves, as well as popular authors, may have adopted the language of radical sectarianism and antinomian perfection.[69]

Another journalist exposé, written at York in January 1651, claims to have located 'a great company of new Ranting Adamites' at the Star drinking house in Stonegate, where they 'solaced themselves for the space of an hour, in a most inhuman, satanical and luxurious way, man and women together'. The Adamite label is attached, despite no indication that they took off their clothes. Instead, this group of carousers, partaking of illicit Christmas cheer, allegedly plotted

18. The Ranters' frolic, 1651

murder and mayhem. And although these Ranters renounced both God and the Devil, in typical wild-sectarian fashion, they none the less pledged 'all due obedience to Charles II'. Citizens of the new English republic might see this as cause for alarm, but the incongruity of their allegiance adds weight to the suggestion that the author made the story up or stretched it out of proportion. The report oscillates between savagery and buffoonery, and though it might be taken seriously as a symptom of distress in the early years of the Interregnum it throws no light at all on either Adamites or Ranters.[70]

One of the purposes of the pamphlet was to allow the author, Samuel Tilbury, to inflict on the public his atrocious verse, which had its origins in the pamphlet literature of the previous decade:

> A sect of Ranters of late revived,
> Who seem more innocent than ere Adam lived,
> Such as will naked go, and think't a sin
> To wear a garment, they're so hot within

> With lust, that they all clothing do distrain;
> Aaron's old vestments they account profane
>
> .   .   .   .   .   .
>
> The whore of Babel's smock they all detest,
> All Antichristian relics with the rest.
> All must be barely naked, 'cause they say
> Truth itself naked goes, and so should they.
> Naked as from their mothers' wombs, they wear
> Nothing that covers, only skin and hair.
> Thus marching naked sister with a brother,
> For want of clothes they cover one another.
> In some dark grange thus meet they, where 'tis fit
> That they the deed of darkness should commit
>
> .   .   .   .   .   .
>
> And when all grow proud with hot desires,
> Thus they correct and quench their fires.[71]

Though it may be questioned whether organized cultic nudity ever existed in revolutionary England, there can be no doubt that some individuals went naked in public for provocative or polemical effect. Lunatics sometimes ripped off their clothes, drunken revellers occasionally undressed, and a number of godly prophets felt called upon to remove all worldly garments and go forth naked 'as a sign'. Some of these people were labelled Adamites or Ranters, fuelling the anti-sectarian literature, but their behaviour belongs to an entirely different tradition. It may be helpful, before concluding, to review some of this freelance visionary nudism.

Old Testament prophets sometimes used nakedness to chastise their leaders, to embarrass their followers, or to symbolize their submission to God. Their naked bodies carried religious or political messages. Mainstream Bible scholars found this troubling, and sometimes cast doubt on the text. William Perkins, the leading Calvinist theologian of late Elizabethan England, dismissed the probability that Isaiah and Saul actually stripped to the nude. Though the Bible says that Isaiah loosed the sackcloth from his loins and 'walked naked and bare-foot three years for a sign and wonder' (Isaiah 20: 2, 3), Perkins objects that 'it cannot be proved that he put off the garment next to his skin'. Similarly, when Saul is said to have 'stripped off his clothes also, and prophesied before Samuel in like manner, and lay down naked all that day and all that night' (1 Samuel 19: 24), Perkins remarks that 'we are not to imagine that he prophesied naked, it being so unseemly a thing, and even against the law of nature since the fall'. Rather, he suggests, in keeping with contemporary vestiarian propriety, 'the meaning is that he stripped himself of his armour'.[72]

Other interpretations were possible, including the gloss that nakedness was a sign of exceptional religious devotion. A literal reading might justify a saint in going completely unclad. The seventeenth-century church historian Thomas Fuller recognized that Isaiah's 'going naked for three years' was 'extraordinary and mystical, having an immediate commandment of God for the same', but he took pains to disqualify this as a precedent for contemporary religious disrobing.[73] The word 'naked' in early modern usage could mean scantily or inadequately dressed as well as completely nude, and was often used in this sense to describe the Irish or the Scots or naked savages.[74] It could refer to a state of dishabille as well as full nudity, as when an Elizabethan adulteress was observed 'lying still most unhonestly all naked with her clothes still up'.[75]

Medieval saints and ascetics sometimes appeared in the nude. Believers took literally St Jerome's famous injunction, 'nudus nudum Christum sequi' (naked to follow a naked Christ), which became a popular formula in the twelfth century. The words were generally construed to favour poverty, a stripping away of worldly possessions, but some saintly enthusiasts went the whole hog (or the full monty). St Francis of Assisi is said to have stripped himself naked on at least one occasion to dramatize his message and his mission.

Quakers in north and north-west England took to going naked as a sign in the early 1650s, soon after the first flush of pamphlets about the Ranters, and may even have been inspired by accounts of Adamite godly nakedness. Thomas Fuller thought them 'no less ridiculous than erroneous' for 'the casting off of their clothes' and 'going naked'.[76] This is a part of Quaker history that later Friends sometimes attempted to suppress. Writing to the people of Ulverston, Lancashire, in 1652, George Fox commented that 'the Lord made one to go naked among you, a figure of thy nakedness, and of your nakedness, and as a sign amongst you before your destruction cometh, that you might see that you were naked and not covered with the truth'. In 1653 there were reports of a Quaker couple calling themselves Adam and Eve, who 'went for some while as some uncivilised heathen do, discovering their nakedness to the eye of every beholder'. Another in Westmorland ran 'stark naked to the cross in the view of many, and stood in that posture . . . speaking to the people', while there seems to have been an irregular procession of naked Quakers through the streets of Kendal and around the Yorkshire dales.[77]

A dozen or more Quakers felt moved to go naked in the early years of the Protectorate. Unlike the Adamites, who are alleged to have held private meetings in the nude, these were public provocations by individual believers in the midst of the worldly and unfaithful. The militant Quaker William Peres died in prison in Yorkshire in 1654 after being 'moved to strip himself naked, a figure of all the nakedness in the world'. His colleague William Simpson had more success as a naked prophet, visiting Oxford in 1654 'naked and bare' in rebuke to the Cromwellian regime. Following Simpson's example, Elizabeth Fletcher, a young Quaker woman, 'went naked through the streets' of Oxford around 1655. Simpson likened himself to the prophet Isaiah and claimed to have walked 'naked as a sign' through 'Walton, London, Colchester, Cambridge, and other towns about'. George Fox recalled that this English Isaiah 'went three years naked and in sackcloth in the days of Oliver and his parliament, as a sign to them and to the priests, showing how God would strip them of their power, and that they should be naked as he was, and should be stripped of their benefices'.[78]

The reference to 'sackcloth', which Simpson himself mentions in one of his pamphlets, redirects us to Perkins's qualification about Isaiah, and suggests that Quaker nakedness may sometimes have been incomplete. When Samuel Pepys a few years later observed a Quaker crying 'repent! repent!' through Westminster Hall he noted that the man was 'naked . . . only very civilly tied about the privities to avoid scandal'.[79] But use of the adjective 'stark' suggests that some prophets of the 1650s were less restrained.

The dying years of the Protectorate saw another outbreak of Quakers going naked for a sign. Solomon Eccles made something of a career of the practice, going naked through various parts of London, carrying fire and brimstone on his head, and crying 'remember Sodom and Gomorrah'. He was probably the man Samuel Pepys saw with only his 'privities' covered. In 1661 a northern magistrate could report that 'in all the great towns, Quakers go naked on market days . . . crying "woe to Yorkshire"'. But the practice soon faded as Quakers became more respectable, although there were isolated (and sometimes spectacular) cases of naked testifying later in the reign of Charles II, including some in the American colonies.[80]

What are we to make of all this? We could simply say that accounts of the Adamites are lurid and alarmist fabrications, and therefore not worth our attention. We could argue that behind the sensationalist pamphlets lies a grain of truth, which we seek to expose and recover. Or we could decide that the discourse itself is interesting and important for what it says about fears and attitudes in the early 1640s. The ancestry and genealogy of the Adamites would then be of less interest than their presence in a particularly troubled moment.

The propensity of some religious enthusiasts to disrobe may provide a key to the Adamite phenomenon. Rooted in Old Testament prophecy, revived in medieval heresy, and visible at the wilder extremes of the Protestant Reformation, the practice of 'going naked for a sign' recurred throughout Christian history.[81] Though it is extremely unlikely that any organized Adamite sect actually existed in 1641, with meetings and rituals of the sort so luridly described, it is easy enough to imagine that odd individuals were swept up in the experimental sectarian frenzy and felt exhilarated or courageous enough to take off their clothes. It would only take one such incident to remind writers of the earlier nudist heresies, to spawn rumours of the Adamite resurgence, and to set off the hunt for the 'nest of serpents'. Adamite revelations fed a reading public eager for sensation, willing to believe the worst about religious extremists, until the Ranters emerged to excite even more shocking alarm. Anabaptist dipping ceremonies and references to the 'naked' Church were further grist to the mill.

If the Adamites truly existed, outside of the textual world of satire and polemic, and if their meetings had been infiltrated or interrupted as some pamphleteers claimed, one might expect to find more specific references elsewhere, perhaps in diaries or judicial records. If Obadiah Couchman turns up, or if better corroborative evidence becomes available, the story may end differently. Meanwhile, our problem is one of genre as well as history, involving the sensational exposé, the religious warning, mild pornography, and the shaggy dog story.

Occupying the discursive realm of the pamphlets rather than the documented world of the streets, the Adamites of 1641 appear to have served as a stalking-horse (or whipping boys) for other sectarian groups, the Brownists and the antinomian underground. With their ludicrous theology, preposterous priesthood, outrageous sexuality, and offensive nakedness, the Adamites served to discredit the rest of the sectarian swarm. That their leaders were weavers or tailors, dependent on the manufacture of clothes, was part of the joke. But it also marks the disdain of gentle and clerical authors for artisan preachers in general, and their fear of the abandonment of hierarchy, discipline, sexual propriety, and clothes.

Once recorded, or reinvented, the Adamites were too useful to be forgotten. They lived on for decades in catalogues of sects and heresies, in ribald pamphlets, and in sermons, poetry, and jokes, as reminders of folly and excess.[82] In 1707, when a distracted 'French prophetess' stripped 'stark naked' and declaimed from the altar in the popish chapel in Lincoln's Inn Fields, the pamphleteers immediately cast her as an Adamite. Though reportedly 'frensical' and 'inspired with a pretended spirit', she did not belong to a nudist cult. The 'Adamite' label helped to categorize her action, to contain it and ridicule it, associating her bold display with the earlier Adamites of memory and text.[83]

The ludic element was always prominent in remarks about the Adamites, reminding us that bawdy entertainment was intertwined with warnings of descent into savagery and chaos. Even in 1641 the 'Adamite' pamphlets could be read for laughs as well as for signs of impending chaos. Preaching at a visitation in 1662, Henry King, bishop of Chichester, made jesting and rhetorical reference to the Adamites while advocating the proper 'dressing' or 'cladding' of sermons. To put no 'clothes' on an argument 'were to establish the heresy of the Adamites in the pulpit, and to dogmatize nakedness'. Though few in his audience could ever have seen an Adamite, all were none the less familiar with the discursive Adamite phenomenon. In a Church that was redecking itself with ceremonies, cladding itself with ornament after the naked austerities of revolution, most auditors could distinguish between rhetoric that was bare or dressed.[84]

Conclusion

A conclusion, traditionally, tells readers what they have already read or sketches out suggestions for further research. It may also be used as a form of damage control, to acknowledge gaps or shortcomings or to try to turn weaknesses into strengths. In this conclusion I respect these conventions, while attempting to draw together central themes and to highlight salient issues and connections from various parts of the book. If my arguments seem loosely structured and open-ended, some readers may detect the breath of post-modernism while others may share my sense that the past is ultimately intractable, though always worthy of pursuit. As D. H. Lawrence said of the English novel, whenever you try to nail something down in history, history gets up and walks away with the nail.

One conclusion, confirmed in every chapter, is that English society under Elizabeth I and the early Stuarts was marked by thousands of competing narratives. Every parishioner could tell a story, and every dispute had myriad dimensions. There were some tales told to quicken the authorities and to mobilize the power of the State, others designed to misinform or to deflect investigators' attention. Our tales present differing degrees of plausibility and rhetorical polish, from Agnes Bowker's explanation for her missing baby to John Stacy's explanation for his dirty boots, from Thomas Bedford's account of a monstrous birth in Devonshire to Thomas Bray's exposé of the London Adamites. Many of these stories could be further elaborated, and many more of a similar sort could be extracted from the historical record. Almost all of them illuminate social and gender relations or dealings between laity and clergy, and many shed light on contested areas of early modern culture and religion.

Drawn from both archival and textual sources, these stories display the power and perplexity of magistrates and ecclesiastical examiners and the energy of the popular press. Their themes include unwanted pregnancy and illegitimate birth; midwifery, infanticide, and abortion; murder, attempted murder, and attempted suicide; remedies for plague and cures for epilepsy; domestic and professional reputations; the flouting of ecclesiastical discipline; the persistence of traditional beliefs; the cultural significance of clothing; and opposing religious sensibilities in the reign of Charles I. They may not directly explain the progress of the Reformation or the origins of the civil war, but they help us to understand the society within which these major events happened.

Though committed to principles of uniformity and obedience, early modern England exhibited great reserves of flexibility and practical tolerance. It was a society that valued harmony, yet one that preferred to accommodate rather than eliminate difference. Parishioners did not panic when faced with aberrant behaviour or unusual phenomena, and officials usually proceeded with reason and caution. Rather than reacting with alarm when a woman allegedly gave birth to a cat they conducted a sensible series of inquiries. Agnes Bowker's stories of bestial intercourse did not set off a witchcraft scare but prompted instead a determination to get to the bottom of the mystery. Nor was there a wave of fear associated with the monstrous births, even though the authors of broadsheets and pamphlets called stridently for national repentance. Casual observers were more likely to see malformed babies as sad occurrences or passing curiosities than as messages from an angry god.

The parishioners of Elizabethan Cuckfield were more inclined to resolve their disputes by appealing to higher authorities than by direct or violent action. The battle for the Cuckfield pulpit, after the ouster of the discredited vicar, was a rare lapse of decorum among protagonists who more commonly resorted to petitions and letters. So too at Great Tew and Holton, Slaidburne and East Drayton, the acts of indiscipline and defiance that led to the intervention of the courts were relatively minor breakdowns in an otherwise orderly community. If they were acts of revolt they were limited and readily contained. Like the many altercations between clergy and laity, and the later assaults on communion rails, these lapses were usually resolved by quiet apologies and low-keyed admissions of guilt. At least until the short-lived Laudian ascendancy, the church courts were more concerned to restore harmonious relations than to punish offenders.

Women had much more agency than some contemporary moralists would allow, and more than some modern historians would credit. Though expected, in theory, to be chaste and silent, women like Rose Arnold and Lydia Downes proved voluble and resourceful when it came to telling their tales. It seems clear from these stories that women socialized freely with each other, were the guardians and attendants of childbirth, and enjoyed mixed company at the alehouse. Servants had freedom to fall in love or get into trouble; wives had business and pleasure outside the home. But female sociability was not the same as solidarity. It was the women of Harborough who supported and then questioned Agnes Bowker. It was the women of Cuckfield who helped and harassed Mercy Gould. The women of Newgate, London, were deeply divided by financial, sexual, and professional jealousies.

Midwives in particular were forceful and independent figures. Elizabeth Harrison, the midwife of Harborough and Great Bowden, stuck to her story, and may have been the originator of the tale of Agnes Bowker's cat. Clearly she had authority among the local women and did not crumble before the archdeaconry court. Denis Clarke, the midwife at Cuckfield, was outraged when her services were dispensed with and led the delegation of women that examined Mercy Gould. Her testimony went all the way to the Privy Council. Francis Fletcher of Great Tew stood her ground when faced with the intrusion of Thomas Salmon and maintained her dignity under ecclesiastical inquiry. Other midwives are glimpsed in passing, assisting in the travail of unmarried servants or at the parturition of monstrous births. Only Elizabeth Wyatt of north London appears to have been a disreputable figure, and her failings are offset by the accomplishments of the more elderly practitioners, Anna Browne and Annis Cox.

Clergymen feature throughout this book and one of them, Anthony Anderson, makes several appearances. Anderson was the diligent official who recorded the case of Agnes Bowker, and it was he who conducted his own experiments with the cat and sent his files and illustration to the Earl of Huntington. Anderson later appears as the embattled vicar of Medbourne, facing a parishioner's fury over tithes, and later still at Stepney in a shouting match with the moneyer John Pye. He was also the author of sermons against superstition and an advocate of respect for the ecclesiastical calling.

An impression might be left that there were always sour relations between clergy and laity, but this would be untrue. Edmund Curteys of Cuckfield was probably no more typical than was Thomas Banks of Slaidburne or Richard Drake of Radwinter. Notwithstanding their prevalence in this study, verbal attacks were relatively uncommon, physical assaults quite rare, and acts of violent iconoclasm extremely unusual. The majority of ministers were painstaking and competent, and most of their parishioners were suitably docile and devout. Whether they all believed the same way is another matter. The clergy included hard-line Calvinists bent on godly reformation and ceremonial Arminians in pursuit of the beauty of holiness. There were vigorous preachers and occasional sermonists, clerks with the gift of pastoral grace and others who wanted worldly wit and discretion. Many were firm in their liturgical practice, in accord with the Book of Common Prayer, but others would waver as circumstance required. Most stood on their ministerial dignity, but were torn between the demands of their superiors and the needs of their flock. Bartholomew Price of Holton may not have been unusual, under pressure from the diocesan authorities and his leading parishioners, in taking to his bed. But his lay neighbours knew exactly what they wanted, and some took matters into their own hands to achieve it: 'God's blessing on them that buried the dead.'

Lay beliefs are hard to discern, especially for men and women who were not self-consciously devout. Our stories offer hints and glimpses, which further research may clarify or confirm. The villagers of Elizabethan Leicestershire and Northamptonshire evidently believed in the possibility of cross-species gestation, though some were sceptical that in Agnes Bowker's case it had actually happened. Agnes's confession of her pact with the Devil might also strike them as strange, but it remained within the realm of possibility and experience. This was a culture accustomed to the presence of evil, committed to combating the Devil and his works.

Similar beliefs inform reactions to the spate of monstrous births. God and the Devil were locked in conflict and England was one of their battlegrounds. Monstrous births could reflect this conflict, though they were susceptible to a range of alternative readings. Evangelical reformers were inclined to extract the most sensational message from these unfortunate events, but for most people, it seems, the Devil was more a distant threat than a familiar predator, and God too appeared more like a judge in heaven than a force in the immediate local world. Francis Lane claimed that 'the devil was great with him' when he attempted to drown Rose Arnold, and Lydia Downes found the Devil incarnate in Richard Skeete. But the young men who baptized beasts and pulled down communion rails were implicated more in daredevil antics and raucous devilment than a serious engagement with Satan.

Preachers and reformers repeatedly charged that tampering with costume— adopting the apparel of the opposite sex—was an abomination unto the Lord. It was, quite literally, a travesty of gender norms. But this did not stop dozens of people, both men and women, from occasional cross-dressing. They were prepared to be admonished—that after all was their minister's job—but they did not necessarily take the reformist strictures seriously. Again, we are left with the impression of a laity that knew its duty but was not overly concerned with the predicates of evangelical Christianity.

This seems especially true in the case of those parishioners who hurled insults at their clergymen. To call one's parson an ass or a knave was bad judgement and bad manners, but it was not necessarily a sign of anticlericalism or irreligion. Heated words and physical threats were locally disruptive but they did not point to a crisis in lay–clerical relations. It is remarkable how many speech-offenders were diligent attenders at church and yet claimed to be as good a man as their minister. The redoubtable John Mynet, charged as 'an atheist, heathen or infidel' and 'a sower of dissention, discord and sedition', comes across as an unreformed conformist who knew his own way and his own mind. William Prynne, who reserved his venom for Archbishop Laud, used law and scholarship and his own well-publicized sufferings to mark a direction for the Church of England that had apparently been abandoned by its bishops.

The altar dispute in Caroline England was conducted through visitations and sermons, the discourse of priests and prelates. But it was also conducted through parish action, through the willingness or unwillingness of ordinary parishioners to co-operate and conform. Although the dispute involved sacramental faith at the heart of Christian worship, it also involved such mundane things as sight-lines and furnishings, convenience and custom. Charles I's bishops ignited a firestorm when they attempted to impose uniformity on a diverse and pluralistic religious culture. The parish elders who suffered excommunication rather than relocate their tables, and the young men who participated in the breaking of the rails, may have stood firm against Dagon but they also stood up for diversity and local independence.

Cheapside Cross was also identified with Dagon—the filthy god of the Philistines—though that seems to have been a polemical rather than a popular characterization. The crowds that gathered to watch it fall, like the crowd assembled at Chester for the burning of Prynne's picture-frames, included some who were hostile, some who were fickle, and no doubt many who were indifferent. The Cross, like the radical sects and the most bizarre of them, the Adamites, became a topic of discourse, an item for satire in print. The explosion of print at the beginning of the English revolution points to a ferment of beliefs and religious experiments, but it complicates the problem of distinguishing textual phenomena from other historical conditions. Radical sectarians who took off their clothes were no more common than women who gave birth to cats, but stories about them enriched and enlivened the world we have lost. Our store of stories reveals the multiple possibilities of experiencing and talking about that world.

Notes

INTRODUCTION

1. William Shakespeare, *Hamlet*, Act V, Scene i.
2. The phrase pays homage to Peter Laslett, *The World We Have Lost* (1965; 3rd edn., 1984). For an alternative point of entry, see Keith Thomas, *Religion and the Decline of Magic* (1971).
3. G. R. Elton, *Star Chamber Stories* (1958), 9–10. In 1996 the Royal Historical Society devoted a special session to 'The Eltonian Legacy', in which *Star Chamber Stories* was never mentioned, *Transactions of the Royal Historical Society*, 6th ser. 7 (1997), 177–336.
4. Natalie Zemon Davis, *Society and Culture in Early Modern France* (Stanford, Calif., 1975).
5. David Sabean, *Power in the Blood: Popular Culture and Village Discourse in Early Modern Germany* (Cambridge, 1984), 3, 174–98.
6. Robert Darnton, *The Great Cat Massacre and Other Episodes in French Cultural History* (New York, 1984; 1985 edn.), 3, 5, 7, 261.
7. Edward Muir and Guido Ruggiero (eds.), *Microhistory and the Lost Peoples of Europe* (Baltimore, 1991); Carlo Ginzburg, *Clues, Myths, and the Historical Method* (Baltimore, 1989); Guido Ruggiero, *Binding Passions: Tales of Magic, Marriage and Power at the End of the Renaissance* (Oxford and New York, 1993). Among the best English examples are Peter Lake, 'Puritanism, Arminianism and a Shropshire Axe-Murder', *Midland History*, 15 (1990), 37–64; Steve Hindle, 'The Shaming of Margaret Knowsley: Gossip, Gender, and the Experience of Authority in Early Modern England', *Continuity and Change*, 9 (1994), 391–419; and Wyn K. Ford, 'The Ordeal of Joan Acton', *Sussex Archaeological Collections*, 122 (1984), 127–37.

CHAPTER 1

1. This chapter is a revised version of my article, 'De la fiction dans les archives? Ou le monstre de 1569', *Annales. Économies, Sociétés, Civilisations*, 48 (1993), 1309–29.
2. David Cressy, *Birth, Marriage, and Death: Ritual, Religion, and the Life Cycle in Tudor and Stuart England* (Oxford, 1997), 35–79; Laura Gowing, 'Secret Births and Infanticide in Seventeenth-Century England', *Past and Present*, 156 (1997), 87–115; Richard Adair, *Courtship, Illegitimacy and Marriage in Early Modern England* (Manchester and New York, 1996), 48–91.
3. The Archdeacon of Leicester was the pluralist Richard Barber, also Warden of All

Souls Oxford. Terence Y. Cocks, 'The Archdeacons of Leicester, 1092–1992', *Transactions of the Leicestershire Archaeological and Historical Society*, 67 (1993), 34. For the normal workings of ecclesiastical justice at this time see Ralph Houlbrooke, *Church Courts and the People During the English Reformation 1520–1570* (Oxford, 1979) and Martin Ingram, *Church Courts, Sex and Marriage in England, 1570–1640* (Cambridge, 1987).

4. All quotations are taken from British Library, Lansdowne MS 101, fos. 21–33. The case is discussed, and the illustration reproduced, in Norman L. Jones, *The Birth of the Elizabethan Age: England in the 1560s* (Oxford, 1993), 45–7, 156–7.

5. Cf. G. R. Quaife, *Wanton Wenches and Wayward Wives: Peasants and Illicit Sex in Early Seventeenth Century England* (1979).

6. Harborough was a township and chapelry within the parish and manor of Bowden Magna, Leicestershire, across the river Welland from Little Bowden, Northamptonshire. This was an area of animal husbandry, especially cattle, horses, and sheep. A Henry Bowker, perhaps Agnes's father, had witnessed various deeds, grants and enfeoffments in and around Harborough in the 1540s, and was evidently a reputable yeoman or townsman. Other Bowkers served as workmen, ratepayers, and minor officials in Harborough into the seventeenth century. J. E. Stocks and W. B. Bragg (eds.), *Market Harborough Parish Records 1531–1837* (Oxford, 1926), 246–8 and *passim*.

7. Harborough fair commenced on 9 October, the feast of St Denis, and continued for eight days following. *Victoria County History of Leicestershire*, vol. v (1964), 141.

8. The Roos family had been accumulating land in southern Leicestershire since the beginning of the Tudor era. Robert Roos, esquire, had gone to law with Edward Griffin, esquire, over land and the advowson of Great Bowden and Harborough in 1543. A. Hamilton Thompson, *A Catalogue of Charters and Other Documents Belonging to the Hospital of William Wyggeston at Leicester* (Leicester, 1933), 183, 185–8; George F. Farnham, *Leicestershire Medieval Village Notes* (Leicester, 1933), vi. 233; *Victoria County History of Leicestershire*, v. 43. For another gentlewoman medical adviser see Linda Pollock, *With Faith and Physic: The Life of A Tudor Gentlewoman, Lady Grace Mildmay 1552–1620* (1993).

9. Cressy, *Birth, Marriage, and Death*, 55–73; David Harley, 'Historians as Demonologists: The Myth of the Midwife-Witch', *Social History of Medicine*, 3 (1990), 1–26.

10. For belief in cross-species hybridization and monstrous births see Janis L. Pallister (ed.), *Ambroise Paré On Monsters and Marvels* (Chicago, 1982), 67–73; Josef Warkany, *Congenital Malformations* (Chicago, 1971), 15. See also Chapter 2 on 'Monstrous Births and Credible Reports: Portents, Texts and Testimonies'.

11. Thomas Cooper, *Thesavrvs Lingvae Romanae & Britannicae* (1565; STC 5686), *sub* 'Mola'; Helkiah Crooke, *Microcosmographia. A Description of the Body of Man Together with the Controversies Thereto Belonging* (2nd edn., 1631; STC 6063), 297–9; Thomas Raynold (from the German and Latin of Eucharius Roesslin), *The Byrth of Mankynde* (1540, various editions including two in 1565; STC 21157/8).

12. For the association between cats and the moon, as well as between cats and

diabolism, see M. Oldfield Howey, *The Cat in the Mysteries of Religion and Magic* (New York, 1956), 28, 80, 212, 218.

13. For a midwife's oath in 1567 see John Strype, *Annals of the Reformation*, i/2 (Oxford, 1824), 242–3; Cressy, *Birth, Marriage, and Death*, 63–8. On the distinction between spells, charms, and prayers, see Keith Thomas, *Religion and the Decline of Magic* (New York, 1971), 41.

14. Marie-Helene Huet, *Monstrous Imagination* (Cambridge, Mass., 1993), 1–78.

15. Cressy, *Birth, Marriage, and Death*, 55–9; Adrian Wilson, 'The Ceremony of Childbirth and its Interpretation', in Valerie Fildes (ed.), *Women as Mothers in Pre-Industrial England* (1990), 68–107.

16. Christopher Pollard was a young man, only recently ordained, and quite possibly out of his depth. According to later *libri cleri* of the Diocese of Lincoln he was ordained on 4 March 1568 by the Bishop of Peterborough, and was parson of Houghton, Leicestershire, aged 26, in 1576, when the bishop described him as 'reasonable learned in the scriptures and Latin tongue, a teacher in his own parish'. He was still rector of Houghton in 1603. C. W. Foster, *The State of the Church in the Reigns of Elizabeth and James I as Illustrated by Documents Relating to the Diocese of Lincoln* (Lincoln, Lincoln Record Society, 23; 1926), 41, 106, 291.

17. George Walker and William Jenkinson had minor landed and commercial interests in Harborough. Jenkinson had recently built stables which encroached on the market square. In 1570, as feoffees of the town, they were described as yeomen. Christopher Pollard and Edmund Goodyear witnessed their enfeoffment, Farnham, *Leicestershire Medieval Village Notes*, vi. 234; *VCH Leics.* v. 135.

18. Turpin and Griffin were powerful landowners and magistrates along the Leicestershire–Northamptonshire border. Both were Justices of the Peace, Turpin for Leicestershire, Griffin for Northants, and they served together on Commissions of Oyer and Terminer. Griffin's father, Sir Edward Griffin of Dingley, had been Attorney General under Edward and Mary and acquired part of the manor of Harborough and Bowden Magna. In 1564 the Griffins added 'the manor, farm or grange of Braybrooke and all its appurtenances in Braybrooke and Little Bowden, co. Northants.' to their various holdings. Sir George Turpin served in early Elizabethan parliaments, held lands at Knaptoft and Carlton Curlieu, and was steward of nine Leicestershire manors of the Duke of Suffolk when Lord Henry Grey was attainted for treason. Griffin appears to have been a moderate Protestant, an accumulator of former monastic land (although his father had served under Mary). Turpin may have been more conservative in religion (although such matters are notoriously hard to determine), keeping a former Dominican as minister at Knaptoft. Farnham, *Leicestershire Medieval Village Notes*, vi. 233, 235; *Calendar of Patent Rolls, Elizabeth I*, vol. iii: *1563–1566* (1960), 24, 25, 42, 100, 286, 423; *Calendar of Patent Rolls, Elizabeth I*, vol. iv: *1566–1569* (1964), 204; *Calendar of Patent Rolls, Elizabeth I*, vol. v: *1569–1572* (1966), 17; *VCH Leics.* v. 77, 139; T. E. Hartley (ed.), *Proceedings in the Parliaments of Elizabeth I*, vol. i: *1558–1581* (Leicester, 1981), 146;

W. G. Hoskins, *Essays in Leicestershire History* (Liverpool, 1950), 86; Foster, *State of the Church*, 39.

19. Possibly the royal progress through Collyweston, Northamptonshire, in August 1566, described in John Nichols, *The Progresses and Public Processions of Queen Elizabeth* (1823), i. 204.

20. The church of St Mary in Arden, a chapelry of Bowden Magna, lay somewhat isolated to the east of Market Harborough; the porch dates from the fourteenth century and is constructed of ironstone and limestone, *VCH Leics.* v. 38, 48. Most of the church is now ruined but the porch is well preserved.

21. Its main circulation was oral. On the distribution of this material in printed form, see Tessa Watt, *Cheap Print and Popular Piety, 1550–1640* (Cambridge, 1991) and Margaret Spufford, *Small Books and Pleasant Histories: Popular Fiction and its Readership in Seventeenth Century England* (1981).

22. Less dangerous cures for the falling sickness included driving three nails into the ground where the epileptic fell, drinking wine with ashes of a frog's liver, and a host of herbal remedies, Thomas Lupton, *A Thousand Notable Things* (1579, 1631 edn.; STC 16961), 44, 75, 147; John Parkinson, *Paradisi in Sole Paradisus Terrestris: A Garden of All Sorts of Pleasant Flowers* (1629; STC 19300), 194, 335, 344, 456, 477, 502; John Gerarde (enlarged by Thomas Johnson), *The Herball or Generall Historie of Plantes* (1636; STC 11752), 106, 204, 245, 441, 465, 485, etc.

23. On witchcraft see Thomas, *Religion and the Decline of Magic*, 435–583; Clive Holmes, 'Popular Culture? Witches, Magistrates, and Divines in Early Modern England', in Steven L. Kaplan (ed.), *Understanding Popular Culture: Europe from the Middle Ages to the Nineteenth Century* (Berlin, New York, and Amsterdam, 1984), 85–111; Clive Holmes, 'Women: Witnesses and Witches', *Past and Present*, 140 (1993), 45–78; and James Sharpe, *Instruments of Darkness: Witchcraft in Early Modern England* (1996). For near-contemporary cases involving animal familiars, shape-shifting, and taking of blood, see Barbara Rosen (ed.), *Witchcraft in England, 1558–1618* (Amherst, Mass., 1991), 69, 74, 85, 234; John Philip, *The Examination and Confession of Certain Wytches at Chelmsford* (1566; STC 19845).

24. The witchcraft statute of 1563 (5 Eliz. *c.*16) made it illegal to invoke evil spirits, but witchcraft and sorcery became a capital felony only if they caused a human victim to die. Thomas, *Religion and the Decline of Magic*, 442.

25. Hastings became Lord Lieutenant of Leicestershire in 1559, succeeded to his earldom in 1560, and served on county commissions of the peace. He was recognized as a patron of puritans and as an heir presumptive to the throne. Claire Cross, *The Puritan Earl: The Life of Henry Hastings, Third Earl of Huntingdon, 1536–1595* (1966).

26. William Nicholson (ed.), *The Remains of Edmund Grindal* (Cambridge, 1863), 306. Unfortunately the Privy Council Register is missing from May 1567 to May 1570.

27. William Bullein, *A Dialogue Against the Fever Pestilence* (1564, 1573, 1578), ed. M. W. Bullen and A. H. Bullen (1888), 76. I am grateful to Norman Jones for drawing

Bullein's work to my attention. Cf. Jean Céard, *La Nature et les prodiges: L'Insolite au XVIe siècle, en France* (Geneva, 1977).

28. Christopher Hill, 'The Many-Headed Monster in Late Tudor and Early Stuart Political Thinking', in Charles H. Carter (ed.), *From the Renaissance to the Counter-Reformation* (1966), 296–324; Conyers Read, *Mr Secretary Cecil and Queen Elizabeth* (1955), 431–7; Stephen Alford, *The Early Elizabethan Polity: William Cecil and the British Succession Crisis, 1558–1569* (Cambridge, 1998), 182–208.

29. Anthony Anderson is not known as a university graduate. For his work as archdeacon's commissary in instance cases, see Leicestershire Record Office, 1. D41/11/6, fos. 83–87v. He served under Richard Barber, Archdeacon of Leicester from 1560 to 1589. In 1573 Anderson became rector of Medbourne, Leicestershire, where he later clashed with parishioners over tithes. He was appointed rector of Stepney, Middlesex, in 1587 and in 1592 became sub-dean of the Chapel Royal. In his many publications Anderson describes himself in puritan terms as a 'preacher', 'minister of the good gospel of God', and 'preacher of Christ's holy gospel'. *An Exposition of the Hymne Commonly Called Benedictus* (1573; STC 567); *A Godlie Sermon, Preached . . . at Burghley in Rutlande* (1576; STC 568); *The Shield of our* Safetie (1581; STC 572); *An Approved Medicine against the Deserved Plague* (1593; STC 566). Anderson may have been recalling his experiences at Harborough when he wrote of the 'ignorance and weakness' of 'poor country people', in *An Exposition of the Hymne*, sig. A3v. In this tract he warned upright Christians 'not to lean upon other men's reports', nor to trust 'the whispering speech of the deep dissembling heart', and went on to warn that 'in this our age the Church of England is vexed with . . . horrible imps and messengers of our enemy Satan', fos. 26v, 27, 28v. See Chapter 9, on 'Mocking the Clergy' for Anderson's later problems with his parishioners.

30. Patrick Collinson, *Archbishop Grindal 1519–1583: The Struggle for a Reformed Church* (1979); B. W. Beckingsale, *Burghley: Tudor Statesman, 1520–1598* (1967). William Cecil, made Lord Burghley in 1571, had strong attachments to the southeast midlands; Burghley House was not far from Market Harborough. He was a firm Protestant, sat in parliament for Northamptonshire, and surely knew the investigating magistrates, George Turpin and Edward Griffin. Anthony Anderson had preached at Burghley on New Year's Day 1567. Nicholas Bullingham, an impeccable anti-Romanist, was Bishop of Lincoln, 1560–71.

31. In chronological order, *A Description of a Monstrous Chyld Borne at Chichester* (1562); *The True Report of the Forme and Shape of a Monstrous Childe, Borne at Much Horkeslye . . . Essex* (1562); John Barker, *The True Description of a Monsterous Chylde, Borne in the Ile of Wight* (1564); *The True Discription of Two Monsterous Chyldren Borne at Herne in Kent* (1565); William Elderton, *The True Fourme and Shape of a Monsterous Chylde, Which was Borne in Stony Stratforde . . . Northamptonshire* (1566); John Mellys, *The True Description of Two Monsterous Children . . . Borne in the Parish of Swanburne in Buckynghamshyre* (1566); H.B., *The True Discription of a Child with Ruffes borne in . . . Micheham in the Countie of Surrey* (1566); *The Forme and Shape of a Monstrous Child, Borne at Maydstone in Kent*

(1568). See also William Fulwood, *The Shape of ii Monsters* (1562), and *The Discription of a Rare or Rather Most Monstrous Fish* (1566). These are discussed in Chapter 2, 'Monstrous Births and Credible Reports: Portents, Texts, and Testimonies'.

32. Edward Fenton, *Certaine Secrete Wonders of Nature* (translated from the French of Pierre Boaistuau, 1569).

33. Watt, *Cheap Print and Popular Piety*, 42.

34. Barnaby Googe, *The Popish Kingdom or Reigne of Antichrist* (1570), ed. R. C. Hope (1880), 26; Bullen (ed.), *Dialogue Against the Fever Pestilence* (1578 edn.), 73. William Bullein was a well-connected medical figure with friends among the Barber-Surgeons. The group's self-appointed mission appears to have been to raise the standards and status of surgeons by squashing quacks, charlatans, and 'the rabble of women' who claimed to know about medicine. I am grateful to Deborah Harkness for discussion of these issues.

35. Warkany, *Congenital Malformations*, 15; Harry Oxorn, *Human Labor and Birth* (5th edn; Norwalk, Connecticut, 1986), 113–51, 309.

36. Stephen Batman, *The Doome Warning to all Men to the Iudgement* (1581; STC 1582), 285, 315, 363; Thomas Heywood, *The Hierarchie of the Blessed Angells* (1635; STC 13327), 541. For the Norfolk woman see Marjorie Hope Nicolson (ed.), *Conway Letters . . . 1642–1684* (New Haven, 1930), 294. For the Hampshire case see Thomas Lanfiere, *The Wonder of Wonders*, in Hyder Edward Rollins (ed.), *The Pack of Autolycus* (Cambridge, Mass., 1927), 185–90.

37. Cyriacus Ahlers, *Some Observations Concerning the Woman of Godlyman* (1726); R. Manningham, *An Exact Diary of What was Observ'd during a Close Attendance upon Mary Toft* (1726); S. A. Seligman, 'Mary Toft—The Rabbit Breeder', *Medical History*, 5 (1961), 349–60; Lisa Cody, 'The Doctor's in Labour; or a New Whim Wham from Guildford', *Gender and History*, 4 (1992), 175–96; Dennis Todd, *Imagining Monsters: Miscreations of the Self in Eighteenth-Century England* (Chicago, 1995).

38. Some of these issues are raised in Hayden White, *Tropics of Discourse: Essays in Cultural Criticism* (Baltimore, 1978); Dominick LaCapra, *History and Criticism* (Ithaca, NY, 1985); Peter Novick, *That Noble Dream: The 'Objectivity Question' and the American Historical Profession* (New York, 1988); Joan W. Scott, 'The Evidence of Experience', *Critical Inquiry*, 17 (1991), 773–97; James Chandler, Arnold I. Davidson, and Harry Harootunian, 'Questions of Evidence', *Critical Inquiry*, 18 (1991), 76–8; Carlo Ginzburg, 'Checking the Evidence: The Judge and the Historian', *Critical Inquiry*, 18 (1991), 79–92.

CHAPTER 2

1. Full sources for these and other monstrous births are given below.

2. Central texts include Aristotle, *Problemata*; Cicero, *De Senectute, De Amicitia, De Divinatione*; Michel de Montaigne, *Essays or Morall, Politike and Millitarie Discourses* (1603; STC 18041); Ambroise Paré, *Des monstres et prodiges* (Paris, 1573).

3. See, for example, in order of publication, Jean Céard, *La Nature et les prodiges: L'Insolite au XVIe siècle, en France* (Geneva, 1977); Katharine Park and Lorraine J. Daston, 'Unnatural Conceptions: The Study of Monsters in France and England', *Past and Present*, 92 (1981), 20–54; William J. Beck, 'Montaigne et Paré: Leurs idées sur les monstres', *Rinascimento*, 30 (1990), 317–42; Ottavia Niccoli, *Prophecy and People in Renaissance Italy* (Princeton, 1990), esp. ch. 2, 'Monsters, Divination, and Propaganda in Broadsheets'; Lorraine Daston, 'Marvellous Facts and Miraculous Evidence in Early Modern Europe', *Critical Inquiry*, 18 (1991), 93–124; Marie-Hélène Huet, *Monstrous Imagination* (Cambridge, Mass., 1993); Dudley Wilson, *Signs and Portents: Monstrous Births from the Middle Ages to the Enlightenment* (1993); Dennis Todd, *Imagining Monsters: Miscreations of the Self in Eighteenth-Century England* (Chicago, 1995); Kathryn M. Brammall, 'Monstrous Metamorphosis: Nature, Morality, and the Rhetoric of Monstrosity in Tudor England', *Sixteenth Century Journal*, 27 (1996), 3–21; David Williams, *Deformed Discourse: The Function of the Monster in Medieval Thought and Literature* (Montreal, London, and Buffalo, 1996). See also Josef Warkany, *Congenital Malformations* (Chicago, 1971), esp. ch. 2, 'Teratology of the Past', and Harold Kalter (ed.), *Issues and Reviews in Teratology* (New York and London, 1983).

4. Brammall, 'Monstrous Metamorphosis', 5–6; Wilson, *Signs and Portents*, 1. See also William E. Burns, ' "Our Lot is Fallen into an Age of Wonders": John Spencer and the Controversy Over Prodigies in the Early Restoration', *Albion*, 27 (1995), 237–52.

5. Mid-century examples include John Locke, *A Strange and Lamentable Accident . . . at Mears-Ashby in Northamptonshire* (1642); *The most Strange and Wovnderfvll apperation of blood . . . Also the true relation of a miraculous and prodigious birth in Shoo-lane* (1645); *A Declaration, of a strange and Wonderfull Monster: Born in Lancashire . . . after the mother . . . had curst the Parliament* (1646); and *The Ranters Monster: Being a true Relation of one Mary Adams* (1652). See also *Nature's Wonder? A True Account . . . of a strange Monster* (1664) in H. E. Rollins (ed.), *The Pack of Autolycus or Strange and Terrible News* (Cambridge, Mass., 1927), 141–5, and *The Wonder of this Present Age. Or, An Account of a Monster Born in . . . Westminster* (1687) in H. E. Rollins (ed.), *The Pepys Ballads* (8 vols.; Cambridge, Mass., 1929–32), iii. 287–90; John Spencer, *Discourse on Prodigies* (1663); Jerome Friedman, *The Battle of the Frogs and Fairford's Flies: Miracles and the Pulp Press During the English Revolution* (New York, 1993).

6. See, for example, Helkiah Crooke, *Microcosmographia. A Description of the Body of Man. Together with the Controversies Thereto Belonging* (2nd edn., 1631; STC 6063), 297–9; John Sadler, *The Sick Womans Private Looking-Glasse* (1636; STC 21544), 133–42; Jacob Rueff, *The Expert Midwife, or An Excellent . . . Treatise of the generation and birth of man* (1637; STC 21442), 137, 152–7. See also Audrey Eccles, *Obstetrics and Gynaecology in Tudor and Stuart England* (Kent, Ohio, 1982), 47; Jacques Gelis, *History of Childbirth: Fertility, Pregnancy and Birth in Early Modern Europe* (Cambridge, 1991), 258–65.

7. Robert Hill, *The Pathway to Prayer and Pietie* (1610; STC 13473), 413. Daniel Featley,

Ancilla Pietatis: Or, the Hand-Maid to Private Devotion (1626; STC 10725), 498. These prayers may have been influenced by reports of a grotesquely misshapen child in *Strange Newes out of Kent* (1609).

8. William Shakespeare, *A Midsummer Night's Dream*, V. i. 409–14; *King Lear*, I. iv. 281–3.

9. Peter Lake, 'Puritanism, Arminianism and a Shropshire Axe-Murder', *Midland History*, 15 (1990), 37–64; Peter Lake, 'Deeds against Nature: Cheap Print, Protestantism and Murder in Early Modern England', in Peter Lake and Kevin Sharpe (eds.), *Culture and Politics in Early Stuart England* (London and Stanford, 1994); Frances Dolan, *Dangerous Familiars: Representations of Domestic Crime in England, 1550–1700* (Ithaca and London, 1994). Jim Sharpe, 'Witchcraft in Early Modern England: A Subject Worth Reopening?', *Social History Society Newsletter*, 16: 2 (Autumn, 1991), 3–6; James Sharpe, *Instruments of Darkness: Witchcraft in Early Modern England* (1996). Clive Holmes, 'Popular Culture? Witches, Magistrates, and Divines in Early Modern England', in Steven L. Kaplan (ed.), *Understanding Popular Culture: Europe from the Middle Ages to the Nineteenth Century* (Berlin, New York, and Amsterdam, 1984), 85–111. See also Roger Chartier, 'Culture as Appropriation: Popular Cultural Uses in Early Modern France', ibid. 229–53; Tessa Watt, *Cheap Print and Popular Piety, 1550–1640* (Cambridge, 1991); and Alexandra Halasz, *The Marketplace of Print: Pamphlets and the Public Sphere in Early Modern England* (Cambridge, 1997).

10. Adrian Wilson, 'The Ceremony of Childbirth and its Interpretation', in Valerie Fildes (ed.), *Women as Mothers in Pre-Industrial England* (London, 1990), 68–107; David Cressy, *Birth, Marriage, and Death: Ritual, Religion, and the Life Cycle in Tudor and Stuart England* (Oxford, 1997), 15–94.

11. Warkany, *Congenital Malformations*, 38.

12. John Brooke, trans. (attributed to Luther and Melanchthon), *Of two Woonderful Popish Monsters* (1579; STC 17797), sig. A ii.

13. Perhaps its most complete expression is Paré's *Des monstres et prodiges*, first published in Paris in 1573; Pallister (ed.), *Ambroise Paré On Monsters and Marvels*; Céard, *La Nature et les prodiges*. See also the section 'Of Monsters' in *The Problems of Aristotle* (1597; STC 764).

14. Pierre Boaistuau, trans. Edward Fenton, *Certaine Secrete Wonders of Nature, containing a description of sundry strange things* (1569; STC 3164.5, formerly STC 17087; first published in Paris, 1560).

15. Pallister (ed.), *Ambroise Paré*, 33–42; Warkany, *Congenital Malformations*, 12–15; Marie-Hélène Huet, *Monstrous Imagination*.

16. See above, Chapter 1. Several of these women were themselves either pregnant or recently delivered. Cf. Pallister (ed.), *Ambroise Paré*, 8–9.

17. *The true discription of two monsterous chyldren Borne at Herne in Kent* (1565).

18. *The true discripcion of a Childe with Ruffes* (1566).

19. Bedford, *A Trve and Certaine Relation of a Strange Birth, which was borne at . . . Plimmouth* (1635).

20. Francis Bacon, *Novum Organon* (1620; STC 1162), book ii, 29.

21. *The true reporte of the forme and shape of a monstrous childe, borne at Much Horkesleye* (1562); Barker, *The true description of a monsterous Chylde born in the Isle of Wight* (1564); Elderton, *The true fourme and shape of a monsterous chyld, whiche was borne in Stony Stratforde* (1566).

22. *The Description of a Monstrous Pig* (1562); Fulwood, *The Shape of ii Monsters* (1562); I.R., *A Most straunge, and true discourse, of the wonderfull iudgement of God* (1600). A similar position is taken by Stephen Batman, *The Doome warning all men to the Iudgemente: Wherein are contayned for the most parte all the straunge Prodigies hapned in the Worlde* (1581; STC 1582), epistle dedicatory.

23. *A Wonder Woorth the Reading* (1617); *Gods Handy-worke in Wonders* (1615).

24. *Certaine Secrete Wonders of Nature*, 12v.

25. *The true reporte of the forme and shape of a monstrous childe, borne at Much Horkesleye* (1562).

26. *The forme and shape of a Monstrous Child born at Maydstone* (1568).

27. I.R., *A Most straunge, and true discourse, of the wonderfull iudgement of God* (1600).

28. Ibid.

29. Mellys, *The true description of two monsterous children* (1566); Barker(?), *A discription of a monstrous Chylde, borne at Chychester* (1562); *A Most certaine report of a monster borne at Oteringham* (1595).

30. *The forme and shape of a Monstrous Child born at Maydstone* (1568).

31. *A Wonder Woorth the Reading* (1617); *The Description of a Monstrous Pig* (1562).

32. Barker, *The true description of a monsterous Chylde, borne in the Isle of Wight* (1564); Elderton, *The true fourme and shape of a monsterous chyld, whiche was borne in Stony Stratforde* (1566); *A Most certaine report of a monster borne at Oteringham* (1595); Bedford, *A Trve and Certaine Relation of a Strange Birth* (1635).

33. *The true discription of two monsterous chyldren Borne at Herne* (1565); *A right strange example of the handie worke of God* (Monmouth, 1585); *Strange Newes out of Kent* (1609); Leigh, *Strange News of a prodigious Monster* (1613).

34. *The discription of a rare or rather most monstrous fishe* (1566); Phillip, *A Meruaylous straunge deformed swyne* (1571).

35. *The true discription of two monsterous chyldren Borne at Herne* (1565); Mellys, *The true description of two monsterous children* (1566); *The true discripcion of a Childe with Ruffes* (1566).

36. Leigh, *Strange Newes of a prodigious Monster* (1613).

37. *A Wonder Woorth the Reading* (1617).

38. Leigh, *Strange Newes of a prodigious Monster* (1613); Cicero, quoted in Warkany, *Congenital Malformations*, 12. See also John Poynet, *A Short Treatise of Politike Power* (1556; STC 201178), sigs. K2v, K4v, relating political developments to recent monstrous births at Oxford, Coventry, and Fulham.

39. Barker(?), *A discription of a monstrous Chylde, borne at Chychester* (1562); Barker, *The true description of a monsterous Chylde, borne in the Isle of Wight* (1564); I.R., *A Most straunge, and true discourse, of the wonderfull iudgement of God* (1600).

40. *Gods Handy-worke in Wonders* (1615).

41. *The true discription of two monsterous chyldren Borne at Herne* (1565); Elderton, *The true fourme and shape of a monsterous chyld* (1566); Mellys, *The true description of two monsterous children* (1566); I.R., *A Most straunge, and true discourse, of the wonderfull iudgement of God* (1600).

42. Barker(?), *A discription of a monstrous Chylde, borne at Chychester* (1562); Phillip, *A Meruaylous straunge deformed swyne* (1571); *Strange Newes out of Kent* (1609).

43. Bedford, *A Trve and Certaine Relation of a Strange Birth* (1635).

44. Elderton, *The true fourme and shape of a monsterous chyld* (1566); *A right strange example of the handie worke of God* (1585); Leigh, *Strange News of a prodigious Monster* (1613); *Gods Handy-worke in Wonders* (1615).

45. J. Alan B. Somerset (ed.), *Records of Early English Drama: Shropshire* (Toronto, Buffalo, and London, 1994), 223, 226, 237; David Galloway (ed.), *Records of Early English Drama: Norwich 1540–1642* (Toronto, Buffalo, and London, 1984), 146–7, 157, 173, 227, 233.

46. *A Wonder Woorth the Reading* (1617).

47. Bedford, *A Trve and Certaine Relation of a Strange Birth* (1635). Cf. Batman, *Doome warning*, 278, for a monstrous child 'carried . . . through the cities of Italy for gain's sake'; Pallister (ed.), *Ambroise Paré*, 9–10; Keith Thomas, *Man and the Natural World* (New York, 1983), 135.

48. *The Tempest*, II. ii; Ben Jonson, *Bartholomew Fayre: A Comedie, Acted in the Yeare, 1614* (1631; STC 14753).

49. Natascha Würzbach, *The Rise of the English Street Ballad, 1550–1650* (Cambridge, 1990), 47–9, 258. See also the discussion of 'vulgar' credulity in Adam Fox, 'Rumour, News and Popular Political Opinion in Elizabethan and Early Stuart England', *Historical Journal*, 40 (1997), 599.

50. For elite notions of veracity, compare Barbara Shapiro, *'Beyond Reasonable Doubt' and 'Probable Cause': Historical Studies in the Anglo-American Law of Evidence* (Berkeley and Los Angeles, 1991); Barbara Shapiro, 'The Concept "Fact": Legal Origins and Cultural Diffusion, *Albion*, 26 (1994), 1–26; Steven Shapin, *A Social History of Truth: Civility and Science in Seventeenth-Century England* (Chicago, 1994).

51. Batman, *Doome warning*, sigs. A2–A4; MS notation on title-page, Huntington Library rare book 59456.

52. *The Winter's Tale*, IV. iv. 260. For contemporary accounts of the mooncalf see Thomas Cooper, *Thesavrvs Lingvae Romanae & Britanicae* (1565; STC 5686), *sub* 'mola', and Crooke, *Microcosmographia*, 297.

53. *The true reporte of the forme and shape of a monstrous childe, borne at Much Horkesleye* (1562).

54. Barker, *The true description of a monsterous Chylde, borne in the Isle of Wight* (1564); *The true discription of two monsterous chyldren Borne at Herne* (1565); Elderton, *The true fourme and shape of a monsterous chyld* (1566); Mellys, *The true description of two monsterous children* (1566); *The true discripcion of a Childe with Ruffes* (1566); I.R., *A Most straunge, and true discourse, of the wonderfull iudgement of God* (1600).

55. Canterbury Cathedral Archives, U3/65/1/1.

56. *The Winter's Tale*, IV. iv. 270, 283.

57. Elderton, *The true fourme and shape of a monsterous chyld* (1566); *The true discripcion of a Childe with Ruffes* (1566); *The forme and shape of a Monstrous Child born at Maydstone in Kent* (1568); *A Most certaine report of a monster borne at Oteringham* (1595). See also *The discription of a rare or rather most monstrous fishe* (1566).

58. *Strange Newes out of Kent* (1609); *A Wonder Woorth the Reading* (1617).

59. Leigh, *Strange Newes of a prodigious Monster* (1613). It is not entirely clear whether Leigh was the author of this pamphlet, employing a popular form to reach a wider audience, or whether his name was being used to lend credence to the report and respectability to the publication. Leigh's printed sermons were usually produced by Creed and Johnson, but the monster pamphlet was printed and published by Pindley and Man for more popular distribution. See Edward Arber (ed.), *A Transcript of the Registers of the Company of Stationers* (1876), iii. 526.

CHAPTER 3

1. The principle sources are Public Record Office, State Papers, SP 12/123–31.

2. Almost 3% of births in the 1570s were illegitimate. See Richard Adair, *Courtship, Illegitimacy and Marriage in Early Modern England* (Manchester and New York, 1996), 48–91; David Cressy, *Birth, Marriage, and Death: Ritual, Religion, and the Life Cycle in Tudor and Stuart England* (Oxford, 1997), 35–79.

3. SP 12/123, fo. 70.

4. SP 12/131, no. 26.1, collated with SP 12/130, fo. 128, which has the same report with minor differences in phrasing.

5. For example, 'An Elizabethan Gentlewoman: The Journal of Lady Mildmay, circa 1570–1617', ed. Rachel Weigall, *Quarterly Review*, 215 (1911), 119–38; *Diary of Lady Margaret Hoby 1599–1605*, ed. Dorothy M. Meads (1930).

6. Cressy, *Birth, Marriage, and Death*, 73–9.

7. Laura Gowing, 'Secret Births and Infanticide in Seventeenth-Century England', *Past and Present*, 156 (1997), 87–115. See also Peter C. Hoffer and N. E. H. Hull, *Murdering Mothers: Infanticide in England and New England 1558–1803* (New York, 1981).

8. The following information is based on J. H. Cooper, 'Cuckfield Families. II', *Sussex Archaeological Collections*, 42 (1899), 19–53, esp. 34–45; Wilbraham V. Cooper, *A History of the Parish of Cuckfield* (Haywards Heath, 1912), 38–43, 72–8; Percy D. Mundy (ed.), *Abstracts of Star Chamber Proceedings Relating to the County of Sussex. Henry VII to Philip and Mary*, Sussex Record Society, 16 (1913), 61–3; Ernest Straker, *Wealden Iron* (1931); J. J. Goring, 'Wealden Ironmasters in the Age of Elizabeth', in E. W. Ives, R. J. Knecht, and J. J. Scarisbrick (eds.), *Wealth and Power in Tudor England: Essays Presented to S. T. Bindoff* (1978), 204–27; C. S. Cattell, 'The 1574 Lists of Wealden Ironworks', *Sussex Archaeological Collections*, 117 (1979), 161–71; Henry Cleere and David Crossley, *The Iron Industry of the Weald* (Leicester, 1985).

9. The collision between Curteys and Bowyer is reviewed in Roger B. Manning,

Religion and Society in Elizabethan Sussex (Leicester, 1969), 113–25. Manning calls Bowyer 'an overbearing upstart', and finds it 'simply astonishing' that he later appears as a puritan, ibid. 113, 124.

10. Manning, *Religion and Society*, 103; Cooper, *History*, 37–40; J. H. Cooper, 'Pre-Reformation and Elizabethan Vicars of Cuckfield', *Sussex Archaeological Collections*, 44 (1901), 9–27.

11. See *Acts of the Privy Council, 1580–81*, 324.

12. SP 12/129, fo. 35 (no. 16.1).

13. Ninian Chaloner, the vicar's most loyal supporter, had been appointed by Curteys as a coadjutor of Cuckfield Grammar School in 1573. In 1581 he was even willing to go to prison on the minister's behalf, Cooper, 'Vicars', 14,15. He too was a prominent ironmaster, in partnership with the magistrate Sir Walter Covert, Straker, *Wealden Iron*, 416.

14. Manning classes Bishop Curteys himself as a 'puritan' and therefore assumes the bishop's enemies to have been enemies to advanced Protestantism, *Religion and Society*, 71–2. See the testimonial on behalf of Bishop Curteys, subscribed by forty-two preachers of the Diocese of Chichester, in Curteys's edition of Hugo De Sancto Victore, *An Exposition of Certayne Words of S. Paul* (1577; STC 13924), preface. It is possible that Curteys himself wrote this testimony by way of an apologia.

15. Ibid.; Manning, *Religion and Society*, 91.

16. *Dictionary of National Biography*; Manning, *Religion and Society*, 106–7.

17. SP 12/130, fo. 3 (no. 2).

18. J. S. Cockburn (ed.), *Calendar of Assize Records: Sussex Indictments. Eliz. I* (1975), 143.

19. Cf. the charges against 'scandalous and malignant' clergy in the 1640s, in, for example, Clive Holmes (ed.), *The Suffolk Committees for Scandalous Ministers 1644–1646* (Suffolk Records Society, 1970). For witchcraft and the division of the elite between the credulous and the sceptical, see Keith Thomas, *Religion and the Decline of Magic* (1971), 272, where the Curteys case is instanced; James Sharpe, *Instruments of Darkness: Witchcraft in Early Modern England* (1996).

20. SP 12/129, fo. 34 (no. 16).

21. Manning depicts Overton as 'a thorough scoundrel', an odious schemer for self-advancement, *Religion and Society*, 67–9. But Overton, like Bowyer, deserves more respect. His *Godlye and Pithie Exhortation, Made to the Iudges of Sussex* was published in 1580 (STC 18925), soon after his elevation to the see of Coventry and Lichfield.

22. SP 12/130, fo. 1.

23. Curteys appeared before High Commission but received no sentence, John Strype, *Annals of the Reformation* (3 vols.; Oxford, 1824), ii. 17. For the workings of the High Commission see Roland G. Usher, *The Rise and Fall of the High Commission* (2nd edn.; Oxford, 1968).

24. SP 12/130, fo. 42 (no. 22); Manning, *Religion and Society*, 118–20.

25. Gentlemen ushers waited in the Queen's Presence Chamber. Simon Bowyer had been at court since 1567, was promoted to daily waiter in 1571, and eventually became senior usher and Black Rod of the Garter until his death in 1597. I am

grateful to William Tighe for supplying these details. See also Cooper, 'Cuckfield Families', 41 n.

26. SP 12/131, fos. 107–108v.

27. John M. Riddle, *Contraception and Abortion from the Ancient World to the Renaissance* (Cambridge, Mass., 1992); Cressy, *Birth, Marriage, and Death*, 47–50.

28. John Gerard (enlarged by Thomas Johnson), *The Herball or Generall Historie of Plants* (1636; STC 11752), 831–3, 60, 845, 1130. T. C. (Thomas Cartwright?), *An Hospitall for the Diseased* (1579, 1598 edn.; STC 4307), sig. A3v.

29. Cressy, *Birth, Marriage, and Death*, 59–73.

30. SP 12/131, fo. 68v. The reference to 'two wives apiece now alive' more likely refers to breach of matrimonial pre-contract than to bigamy, but the relevant allegations cannot be found.

31. *APC 1580–81*, 324.

32. Cooper, *History*, 42; Cooper, 'Vicars', 24; SP 12/149, no. 78.

33. *APC 1581–82*, 334–5.

34. Cockburn (ed.), *Calendar of Assize Records: Sussex*, 165.

35. *APC 1581–82*, 113, 125, 130, 131, 140; Cooper, *History*, 41.

36. British Library, Egerton MS 1693, fo. 128: 'Certeyn reasons sett downe, by the Dean & Chapter of Chichester to the reverend father in God, the B. of Chichester against the admitting of Mr Coortesse somtyme vicar of Cuckfield to be Residensarie in that Church.' They deemed him 'not meet for this place . . . very contentious and unquiet, and . . . no preacher'. For a different interpretation see Manning, *Religion and Society*, 122–4.

CHAPTER 4

1. Lincolnshire Archives, Court Papers, box 68/2, 15. Scraptoft was an enclosed village four miles east of Leicester, at this time undergoing conversion from arable to animal husbandry. The 106 communicants reported in 1603 suggests a population of about 175. Tilton, about eight miles further east, had a similar agricultural economy and was experiencing similar changes. The Lane family had interests in the Tilton area since the reign of Henry VIII, but were not among the major landowners in the district. L. A Parker, 'The Depopulation Returns for Leicestershire in 1607', *Transactions of the Leicestershire Archaeological Society*, 23 (1947), 321–90; *Tr. Leics. Arch. Soc.* 17 (1932–3), 78–9.

2. Nicholas Fisher was vicar of Scraptoft from 1604 to 1610.

3. Laura Gowing, 'Secret Births and Infanticide in Seventeenth-Century England', *Past and Present*, 156 (1997), 87–115.

CHAPTER 5

1. J. A. Sharpe, *Crime in Seventeenth-Century England: A County Study* (Cambridge, 1983), 130, 137; David Cressy, *Birth, Marriage, and Death: Ritual, Religion, and the*

Life Cycle in Tudor and Stuart England (Oxford, 1997), 49. The case can be followed in Colchester Borough Records, Gaol Delivery Rolls 37/14, 15, 22, 23, and the Colchester Book of Examinations and Recognizances, not foliated, 12 November to 28 December 1638 (Essex Record Office, Chelmsford, microfilm T/A/465).

2. Essex Record Office, D/ACA 49, fos. 211v, 217v, 230; D/ACA 50, fo. 8v.

3. Henry Chettle, *Kind-Harts Dreame. Conyeining five Apparitions, with their Invectives against abuses raigning* (1593? STC 5123), sig. D4; Robert Humston, *A Sermon Preached at Reyfham in the Countie of Norff.* (1589; STC 13969), fo. 15. See also Keith Thomas, *Religion and the Decline of Magic* (1971), 177–88.

4. See above, Chapter 1.

5. Peter Laslett, 'The Bastardy-Prone Sub-Society', in Peter Laslett, Karla Oosterveen, and Richard M. Smith (eds.), *Bastardy and its Comparative History* (1980), 217–46; Richard Adair, *Courtship, Illegitimacy and Marriage in Early Modern England* (Manchester, 1996).

6. William Hunt, *The Puritan Moment: The Coming of Revolution in an English County* (1983); Harold Smith, *The Ecclesiastical History of Essex Under the Long Parliament and Commonwealth* (Colchester, 1932).

CHAPTER 6

1. Guildhall Library, London, MS 9057/1, fos. 2v–9v (reverse foliation). The examinations and depositions run from 3 June to 20 November 1635. All but one of the women in this case signed their depositions with a mark. The Archdeacon of London at this time was the Laudian Thomas Paske.

2. See, for example, Linda Pollock, 'Childbearing and Female Bonding in Early Modern England', *Social History*, 22 (1997), 286–306; Laura Gowing, *Domestic Dangers: Women, Words, and Sex in Early Modern London* (Oxford, 1996); Jenny Kermode and Garthine Walker (eds.), *Women, Crime and the Courts in Early Modern England* (1994); Frances E. Dolan, *Dangerous Familiars: Representations of Domestic Crime in England, 1550–1700* (Ithaca and London, 1994); Sara Mendelson and Patricia Crawford, *Women in Early Modern England* (Oxford, 1998), 202–42.

3. Doreen Evenden, 'Mothers and Their Midwives in Seventeenth-Century London', in Hilary Marland (ed.), *The Art of Midwifery: Early Modern Midwives in Europe* (1993), 9–26; Adrian Wilson, 'The Ceremony of Childbirth and its Interpretation', in Valerie Fildes (ed.), *Women as Mothers in Pre-Industrial England* (1990), 68–107; David Cressy, *Birth, Marriage, and Death: Ritual, Religion, and the Life Cycle in Tudor and Stuart England* (Oxford, 1997), 55–84. See also Laurel Thatcher Ulrich, *A Midwife's Tale: The Life of Martha Ballard, Based on Her Diary 1785–1812* (New York, 1991).

4. There was no London alderman of this era named Lamb. However, Sir Martin Lumley was alderman for Bread Street Ward from 1624 to 1634, also President of Christ's Hospital, and would have been the City magistrate most accessible to the

parties in this dispute. I am grateful to the City Archivist of the Corporation of London for supplying this information.

5. Anna Brown, midwife, aged 58, the wife of William Brown, was born in Hereford and had lived in London for fifteen years. She too signed with a mark.

6. Annis or Anne Cox, formerly wife of Henry Cox of St Andrew Wardrobe, had been licensed as a midwife in 1613, and displayed her authorization at visitations as late as 1637. I am grateful to Doreen Evenden for supplying this information.

7. Elizabeth Selby, the youngest witness and the daughter of a gentleman, was the only woman in this story to sign with a signature instead of a mark.

8. See the midwife's oath in John Strype, *Annals of the Reformation* (3 vols.; Oxford, 1824), v. 242–3; *The Book of Oaths. And the Several Forms therof, Both Ancient and Modern* (1689), 161–6.

9. Cressy, *Birth, Marriage, and Death*, 97–123.

10. Elizabeth Wyatt identified the intriguingly named Christian Hoare as a widow, but public fame suggested that her child was a bastard. There is no record of Edward Hoare's baptism or burial in the parish registers of St Andrew Holborn, Guildhall Library, London, MSS 6667/2, 6673/2.

11. See, for example, *The Batchelars Banquet*, ed. F. P. Wilson (Oxford, 1929).

12. Gowing, *Domestic Dangers*.

13. Garthine Walker, 'Expanding the Boundaries of Female Honour in Early Modern England', *Transactions of the Royal Historical Society*, 6th ser. 6 (1996), 235–45.

CHAPTER 7

1. Oxfordshire Archives, Oxford Archdeaconry Office Acts, c. 12, fo. 75. Related citations in this case, from 29 November 1633 to 15 March 1634, are on fos. 69v, 75v, 81, 151. Margaret Rymel, the fourth child of Hugh and Eleanor Rymel, was baptized on 7 November 1632. It was either her birth, or that of an unrecorded sibling a year later, that led to the events of this case.

2. For the 'Great Tew Circle' see Hugh Trevor-Roper, *Catholics, Anglicans and Puritans: Seventeenth Century Essays* (Chicago, 1988), 166–230.

3. Audrey Eccles, *Obstetrics and Gynaecology in Tudor and Stuart England* (Kent, Ohio, 1982); Adrian Wilson, 'The Ceremony of Childbirth and its Interpretation', in Valerie Fildes (ed.), *Women as Mothers in Pre-Industrial England* (1990), 68–107; David Cressy, *Birth, Marriage, and Death: Ritual, Religion, and the Life Cycle in Tudor and Stuart England* (Oxford, 1997), 55–73; Linda Pollock, 'Childbearing and Female Bonding in Early Modern England', *Social History*, 22 (1997), 286–306. Robert Herrick refers to 'the child-bed mysteries' in his poem, 'Julia's Churching, or Purification', in *Hesperides* (1648).

4. Doreen Evenden, 'Mothers and their Midwives in Seventeenth-Century London', in Hilary Marland (ed.), *The Art of Midwifery: Early Modern Midwives in Europe*

(1993), 9–26. For the midwife's oath see *The Book of Oaths* (1649 and 1689). Ben Jonson plays on women's secrets and mysteries in *Epicoene, or The Silent Woman* (1620; STC 14763), IV. ii, V. iii.

5. 'The woman shall not wear that which pertaineth unto a man, neither shall the man put on a woman's garment: for all that do are abomination unto the Lord thy God', Deuteronomy 22: 5.

6. Rudolf M. Dekker and 'Lotte C. van de Pol', *The Tradition of Female Transvestism in Early Modern Europe* (New York, 1989), 2.

7. Linda Woodbridge, *Women and the English Renaissance: Literature and the Nature of Womankind, 1540–1620* (Urbana and Chicago, 1984), 139.

8. Jean E. Howard, 'Crossdressing, the Theatre, and Gender Struggle in Early Modern England', *Shakespeare Quarterly*, 39 (1988), 418–40, quotes from 418, 419 and note 3. Howard's article has been reprinted in Lesley Ferris (ed.), *Crossing the Stage: Controversies on Cross-Dressing* (London and New York, 1993), 20–46. A modified and evolved discussion, reiterating the original question, appears in Jean Howard, *The Stage and Social Struggle in Early Modern England* (1994), esp. 94–104.

9. Howard, 'Crossdressing', 419, 436.

10. Linda Woodbridge, *Women and the English Renaissance*, 139–58; Laura Levine, *Men in Women's Clothing: Anti-theatricality and Effeminization, 1579–1642* (Cambridge and New York, 1994), 1–25; Lisa Jardine, 'Boy Actors, Female Roles, and Elizabethan Eroticism', in David Scott Kastan and Peter Stallybrass (eds.), *Staging the Renaissance: Reinterpretations of Elizabethan and Jacobean Drama* (New York and London, 1991), 57–67. See also Lisa Jardine, *Still Harping on Daughters: Women and Drama in the Age of Shakespeare* (Totowa, NJ, 1983), 9–36; Phyllis Rackin, 'Androgyny, Mimesis, and the Marriage of the Boy Heroine on the English Renaissance Stage', *PMLA* 102 (1987), 29–41; Phyllis Rackin, 'Foreign Country: The Place of Women in Shakespeare's Historical World', in Richard Burt and John Michael Archer (eds.), *Enclosure Acts: Sexuality, Property, and Culture in Early Modern England* (Ithaca, NY, and London, 1994), 70–2; Stephen Greenblatt, *Shakespearian Negotiations: The Circulation of Social Energy in Renaissance England* (Berkeley, 1988); Mary Beth Rose, *The Expense of Spirit: Love and Sexuality in English Renaissance Drama* (Ithaca, NY, 1988); Stephen Orgel, 'Nobody's perfect: or Why Did the English Stage Take Boys for Women?', *South Atlantic Quarterly*, 88 (1989), 7–29; Katherine E. Kelly, 'The Queen's Two Bodies: Shakespeare's Boy Actresses in Breeches', *Theatre Journal*, 42 (1990), 81–93; Steve Brown, 'The Boyhood of Shakespeare's Heroines: Notes on Gender Ambiguity in the Sixteenth Century', *Studies in English Literature 1500–1900*, 30 (1990), 243–63; Ursula K. Heise, 'Transvestism and the Stage Controversy in Spain and England, 1580–1680', *Theatre Journal*, 44 (1992), 357–74; Susan Zimmerman (ed.), *Erotic Politics: Desire on the Renaissance Stage* (New York and London, 1992). For somewhat more cautious accounts, see Michael Shapiro, *Gender in Play on the Shakespearian Stage: Boy Heroines and Female Pages* (Ann Arbor, Michigan, 1994) and Grace Tiffany, *Erotic Beasts and Social Monsters: Shakespeare, Jonson, and Comic Androgeny* (Newark, Delaware, 1995). Among

the few historical engagements with this subject, see Anthony Fletcher, 'Men's Dilemmas: The Future of Patriarchy in England, 1560–1660', *Transactions of the Royal Historical Society*, 6th ser. 4 (1994), 61–81; Anthony Fletcher, *Gender, Sex and Subordination in England, 1500–1800* (New Haven and London, 1995); and Susan Dwyer Amussen, '"The Part of a Christian Man": The Cultural Politics of Manhood in Early Modern England', in Susan D. Amussen and Mark Kishlansky (eds.), *Political Culture and Cultural Politics in Early Modern England* (Manchester, 1995), 213–33.

11. Judith Butler, *Gender Trouble: Feminism and the Subversion of Identity* (New York and London, 1990); Jonathan Dollimore, *Sexual Dissidence: Augustine to Wilde, Freud to Foucault* (Oxford, 1991); Marjorie Garber, *Vested Interests: Cross-Dressing and Cultural Anxiety* (New York and London, 1992); Druann Pagliassotti, 'On the Discursive Construction of Sex and Gender', *Communication Research*, 20 (1993), 472–93; David Kuchta, 'The Semiotics of Masculinity in Renaissance England', in James Grantham Turner (ed.), *Sexuality and Gender in Early Modern Europe* (Cambridge, 1993), 233–45; Mark Breitenberg, 'Anxious Masculinity: Sexual Jealousy in Early Modern England', *Feminist Studies*, 19 (1993), 377–98; Mario DiGangi, 'Reading Homoeroticism in Early Modern England: Imaginations, Interpretations, Circulations', *Textual Practice*, 7 (1993), 483–97.

12. Woodbridge, *Women and the English Renaissance*, 141, 224. Mary Beth Rose points out that Woodbridge finds 'more coherence and range' in this alleged 'transvestite movement' than the pamphlet literature can document, *Expense of Spirit*, 69 n.

13. Woodbridge, *Women and the English Renaissance*, 150, 153, 156. Woodbridge cites *The Mous Trap* (1606), *The Cuckow* (1607), *The Fair Maid of Bristow* (*c.*1604), *The Fleire* (*c.*1608), and *The Roaring Girl* (*c.*1608) among plays in which women adopt masculine attire. See also Marjorie Garber, 'The Logic of the Transvestite: *The Roaring Girl* (1608)', in Kastan and Stallybrass, *Staging the Renaissance*, 221–34; Stephen Orgel, 'The subtexts of *The Roaring Girl*', in Zimmerman (ed.), *Erotic Politics*, 12–26; Jean E. Howard, 'Sex and Social Conflict: The Erotics of *The Roaring Girl*', ibid. 170–90; and Lloyd Edward Kermode, 'Destination Doomsday: Desires for Change and Changeable Desire in *The Roaring Girl*', *English Literary Renaissance*, 27 (1997), 421–42.

14. Kelly, 'The Queen's Two Bodies', 92; Brown, 'Boyhood of Shakespeare's Heroines', 249; Susan Zimmerman, 'Disruptive Desire: Artifice and Indeterminacy in Jacobean Comedy', in her *Erotic Politics*, 42. See also Denise A. Walen, '"Lust-exciting Apparel" and the Homosexual Appeal of the Boy Actor: The Early Modern Stage Polemic', *Theatre History Studies*, 15 (1995), 87–103.

15. Winfried Schleiner, 'Male Cross-Dressing and Transvestism in Renaissance Romances', *Sixteenth Century Journal*, 19 (1988), 605–19; Laura Levine, 'Men in Women's Clothing: Anti-theatricality and Effeminization from 1579 to 1642', *Criticism*, 28 (1986), 136, 130; Jonathan Dollimore, 'Shakespeare, Cultural Materialism, Feminism and Marxist Humanism', *New Literary History*, 21 (1990), 483; Zimmerman, 'Disruptive desire', 43. Note, however, the more circumspect remarks by

Stephen Orgel on 'the eye of the beholder' and Lisa Jardine on 'textual imputation' in Zimmerman (ed.), *Erotic Politics*, 14, 28.

16. Levine, *Men in Women's Clothing*, 1–25, quotes on 5, 8, 9.

17. Wilfrid Hooper, 'The Tudor Sumptuary Laws', *English Historical Review*, 30 (1915), 433–49; Frances Elizabeth Baldwin, *Sumptuary Legislation and Personal Regulation in England* (Baltimore, 1926). We need a modern historical analysis of the economics, social semiotics, and cultural enmeshment of costume.

18. George Gascoigne, *The Steele Glas. A Satyre* (1576; STC 11645), sig. Iv. For a similar complaint against 'courtly madams which dance in men's doublets', see the ubiquitous Anthony Anderson, *The Shield of our Safetie* (1581; STC 572), sig. S4v.

19. Stephen Gosson, *Playes Confuted in Fiue Actions* (1582), in Arthur Kinney (ed.), *Markets of Bawdrie: The Dramatic Criticism of Stephen Gosson* (Salzburg, 1974), 175.

20. William Harrison, *The Description of England* (1577), ed. Georges Edelen (Ithaca, NY, 1968), 147.

21. Thomas Beard, *The Theatre of Gods Ivdgements* (1631; STC 1661), 419–20. Earlier editions appeared in 1597 and 1612.

22. John Rainolds, *The Overthrow of Stage-Playes* (Middleburgh, 1599), 97.

23. Adam Hill, *The Crie of England* (1595; STC 13465), 17.

24. Phillip Stubbes, *Anatomie of Abuses*, sigs. E7v–F5v. Cf. George Gascoigne, *The Steel Glas* (1576), sig. I1v.

25. N. E. McClure (ed.), *The Letters of John Chamberlain* (2 vols.; Philadelphia, 1939), ii. 286–7, 289, including the quote from King James.

26. *Hic Mulier: or, The Man-Woman: Being a Medicine to cure the Coltish Disease of the Staggers in the Masculine-Feminines of our Times* (1620; STC 13378); *Haec-Vir: Or, The Womanish-Man* (1620; STC 12599); *Muld Sacke: Or The Apologie of Hic Mulier* (1620; STC 21538). The three are reproduced in Barbara J. Baines (ed.), *Three Pamphlets on the Jacobean Antifeminist Controversy* (New York, 1978).

27. *Hic Mulier: or, The Man-Woman*, sigs. A3, A4, Bv–B2, C, B2v–B3. The playwright Thomas Middleton remarks on the fashion of courtesans wearing men's doublets: ' 'Tis an Amazonian time', in *A Mad World, My Masters* (1608; STC 17888), Act III, Scene iii. See also John Taylor's attack on 'shameless double-sexed hermaphrodites, Virago roaring-girls, that to their middle, to know what sex they were was half a riddle', in Bernard Capp, *The World of John Taylor the Water Poet, 1578–1653* (Oxford, 1994), 115.

28. William Prynne, *Histrio-Mastix. The Players Scovrge, or Actors Tragædie* (1633), 171–2, 179–80, also 182–3, 206–9; Thomas B. Howell (ed.), *Cobbett's Complete Collection of State Trials*, vol. iii (1809), 568.

29. Daniel Rogers, *Matrimoniall Honour: Or, the Mutual Crowne and Comfort of Godly, Loyal, and Chaste Marriage* (1642), 174.

30. Alan H. Nelson (ed.), *Records of Early English Drama: Cambridge* (Toronto, Buffalo, and London, 1989), 543, 688. Fairclough resisted being ensnared as a performer, D'Ewes as a member of the audience.

31. Robert Herrick (1591–1674), was a Devonshire minister in the 1630s. 'Delight in

Disorder' and 'Upon Julia's Clothes' come from *Hesperides*, as does 'Julia's Petticoat'.

32. Peter Laslett, 'The Wrong Way Through the Telescope: A Note on Literary Evidence in Sociology and Historical Sociology', *British Journal of Sociology*, 27 (1976), 319–42.

33. See works by Levine and Woodbridge, cited above. Cf. the treatment of men in women's clothing in William Shakespeare, *The Merry Wives of Windsor* (performed 1597) and Thomas Heywood, *The Brazen Age* (1613; STC 13310).

34. Louise Schleiner, 'Ladies and Gentlemen in Two Genres of Elizabethan Fiction', *Studies in English Literature 1500–1900*, 29 (1989), 1–20; Winfried Schleiner, 'Male Cross-Dressing and Transvestism', 605–19; Constance Jordan, *Renaissance Feminism: Literary Texts and Political Models* (Ithaca, NY, and London, 1990), 223–8.

35. John Fletcher, *Monsieur Thomas* (1639; STC 11071; performed *c*.1610–13); Francis Beaumont and John Fletcher, *The Scornful Ladie* (1616; STC 1686; repr. 1625, 1630, 1633, 1639); Thomas Dekker and John Webster, *West-ward Hoe* (1607; STC 6540); A *Pleasant Conceyted History of George a Greene, the Pinner of Wakefield* (1599; STC 12212); William Haughton, *English-men for My Money; or . . . a Woman Will Have her Will* (1616; STC 12931; repr. 1626 and 1631); Nathan Field, *Amends for Ladies* (1618; STC 10851); Thomas Middleton, *A Mad World, My Masters* (1608; STC 17888); Ben Jonson, *Epicoene, or the Silent Woman* (1620; STC 14763; first performed by the Revels children in 1609). See also Victor Oscar Freeburg, *Disguise Plots in Elizabethan Drama* (New York, 1915), 102–8, 117–19, 190–1. Among these only *Epiocene* has attracted the attention of critical scholarship.

36. Jonathan Crewe, 'In the Field of Dreams: Transvestism in *Twelfth Night* and *The Crying Game*', *Representations*, 50 (1995), 101–21.

37. Peter Stallybrass, 'Transvestism and the "Body Beneath": Speculating on the Boy Actor', in Zimmerman (ed.), *Erotic Politics*, 76.

38. Robert Charles Hope (ed.), *The Popish Kingdom or Reigne of Antichrist, written in Latin Verse by Thomas Naogeorgus and Englyshed by Barnabe Googe* (1880), 48.

39. Christopher Fetherstone, *A Dialogue Agaynst Light, Lewde, and Lascivious Dauncing* (1582; STC 10835), sig. D7. Early Stuart examples of Maytide and midsummer cross-dressing can be found in David George (ed.), *Records of Early English Drama: Lancashire* (Toronto, Buffalo, and London, 1991), lii, 26, and Audrey Douglas and Peter Greenfield (eds.), *Records of Early English Drama: Cumberland, Westmorland, Gloucestershire* (Toronto, Buffalo, and London, 1986), 201.

40. Buchanan Sharp, *In Contempt of All Authority: Rural Artisans and Riot in the West of England, 1586–1660* (Berkeley and Los Angeles, 1980), 104; Martin Ingram, 'Ridings, Rough Music and Mocking Rhymes in Early Modern England', in Barry Reay (ed.), *Popular Culture in Seventeenth-Century England* (1985), 166–97; James Stokes (ed.), *Records of Early English Drama: Somerset* (Toronto, Buffalo, and London, 1996), 62.

41. Rioters at Hereford in 1612 included the yeoman 'William Jones, alias Wicked Will, apparelled in woman's apparel', David N. Klausner (ed.), *Records of Early English Drama: Herefordshire* (Toronto, Buffalo, and London, 1990), 136. Natalie Zemon

Davis, *Society and Culture in Early Modern France* (Stanford, Calif., 1975), 147–9 cites other English examples.

42. Stephano Janiculo, an associate of Arabella Stuart, escaped a Turkish prison disguised as a woman, Mary Beth Rose, *Expense of Spirit*, 61 n.; Prince James, later James II, is said to have disguised himself as a woman while escaping from Parliamentary custody in 1648, John Loftis (ed.), *The Memoirs of Anne, Lady Halkett and Ann, Lady Fanshawe* (Oxford, 1979), 24–5. Female costume was almost *de rigueur* for escaping from the Tower of London.

43. Richard Simpson of Cambridge University adopted female disguise to make his assignations with Elizabeth Vipen, a married woman, in 1596, Cambridge University Archive, V.C.Ct III.2, fos. 261 ff. I owe this reference to Alexandra Shepard.

44. Dekker and van de Pol, *The Tradition of Female Transvestism in Early Modern Europe*, 1–14; Joad Raymond (ed.), *Making the News: An Anthology of the Newsbooks of Revolutionary England, 1641–1660* (New York, 1993), 148, 167. The diarist Walter Younge reported *c*.1627, 'there was a woman apprehended at Plymouth in the attire or habit of a man by the mayor, at the time the Earl of Denbigh and Sir Henry Martyn were to go to sea. It is said she is one Smith's wife of London, kept by Sir Henry Martyn', British Library, Additional MS 35,331, fo. 16. See also the case of Joanna Goodman in 1569, cited p. 110 and references to Mary Ambree, *c*.1584.

45. Howard, 'Crossdressing, the Theatre, and Gender Struggle', 420–2; R. Mark Benbow and Alasdair D. K. Hawkyard, 'Legal Records of Cross-Dressing', appended to Shapiro, *Gender in Play*, 225–34.

46. F. G. Emmison, *Elizabethan Life: Morals and the Church Courts* (Chelmsford, 1973), 18; William H. Hale (ed.), *A Series of Precedents and Proceedings in Criminal Causes, extending from the year 1475 to 1640; extracted from the Act-Books of the Ecclesiastical Courts of the Diocese of London* (1847), 212.

47. Hale, *Series of Precedents*, 212.

48. P. A. Mulholland, 'The date of *The Roaring Girl*', *Review of English Studies*, NS 28 (1977), 17–31; Paul A. Mulholland (ed.), *The Roaring Girl* (Manchester, 1987), 262–3. The case can be found in Greater London Record Office, DLC/310, fos. 19–20.

49. Borthwick Institute, York, Court of High Commission, Cause Papers, HCCP 1596, no. 7.

50. Historical Manuscripts Commission, *Calendar of Cecil MSS. at Hatfield House* (1899), viii. 201.

51. Arthur Husey (ed.), 'Visitations of the Archdeacon of Canterbury', *Archaeologia Cantiana*, 27 (1904), 226.

52. Stokes (ed.), *Records of Early English Drama: Somerset*, 262, 277, 281, 343, 363.

53. J. A. Sharpe, *Crime in Early Modern England 1550–1750* (1984), 178.

54. Borthwick Institute, York, Metropolitical Visitation of the Diocese of Chester, V.1633, Court Papers, fo. 113v.

55. Peter Lake, 'The Laudian Style: Order, Uniformity and the Pursuit of the Beauty of Holiness in the 1630s', in Kenneth Fincham (ed.), *The Early Stuart Church,*

1603–1642 (1993), 161–85, draws attention to the Laudian view of the church as the 'house of God'.

56. Mary Douglas, *Purity and Danger* (1969), esp. pp. 4, 113.

CHAPTER 8

1. Oxfordshire Archives, Oxford Diocesan Papers, Act Book, c. 2, fo. 144v. Subsequent citations in this case are on fos. 144v–147, 167, 172, 178–179v, 192–194v, 284v, 292.

2. Richard Burn, *Ecclesiastical Law* (7th edn., 4 vols., 1809), i. 259–65; J. V. Bullard (ed.), *Constitutions and Canons Ecclesiastical 1604* (1934), 285, 295; *Book of Common Prayer* (1662).

3. *Les Reports de Sir Gefrey Palmer* (1678), 296–7; David Cressy, 'Purification, Thanksgiving and the Churching of Women in Post-Reformation England', *Past and Present*, 141 (1993), 106–46.

4. Public Record Office, State Papers, SP 16/478/87.

5. Lichfield Record Office, B/V/1 55, p. 28.

6. Ronald A. Marchant, *The Church Under the Law; Justice, Administration and Discipline in the Diocese of York, 1560–1640* (Cambridge, 1969), 227, 205; Keith Thomas, *Religion and the Decline of Magic* (New York, 1971), 160; John Addy, *Sin and Society in the Seventeenth Century* (1989), 204. See also Martin Ingram, *Church Courts, Sex and Marriage in England, 1570–1640* (Cambridge, 1987), 3, 16, 23, 52, 57, 112, 340–65.

7. The 1572 *Admonition to the Parliament* complained of frequent excommunication by the commissary's court: 'In this court, for non payment of twopence, a man shall be excommunicated if he appear not when he is sent for, if he do not as his ordinary would . . . And as it is lightly granted and given forth, so if the money be paid, and the court discharged, it is as quickly called in again', W. H. Frere and C. E. Douglas (eds.), *Puritan Manifestoes* (1954), 33–4. A similar complaint appears in article 24 of the 'Roots and Branches' petition of 1640, in David Cressy and Lori Anne Ferrell (eds.), *Religion and Society in Early Modern England* (1996), 178.

8. Burn, *Ecclesiastical Law*, ii. 243–8. For an episcopal inquiry into the enforcement of excommunication sanctions, see *Articles to be Ministered And to be Enquired of, And answered in the first generall visitation of the reverend father in God, John, by Gods permission, Bishop of Bristol* (Oxford, 1603; STC 10143), item 27, 6. Examples of the sanction in practice include a recently delivered mother who was denied her churching in 1596 because she was excommunicated; a service at Tealby, Lincolnshire, that came to a halt in 1628 when the vicar spied an excommunicated parishioner in the congregation; and an excommunicated couple who were physically barred from entering the church in 1632.

9. Cambridge University Library, MS Mm. 4.29, fo. 57.

10. Richard Cosin, *An Apologie: Of, and For Sundrie Proceedings by Iurisdiction Ecclesiasticall* (1591; STC 5820), 64–5.

11. David Dymond and Clive Paine, *The Spoil of Melford Church: The Reformation in a Suffolk Parish* (Ipswich, 1992), vi–vii.

12. *Statutes of the Realm*, 3 Jac. I, c. 5, my emphasis.

13. 'Archbishop Bancroft's Letter Regarding Catholic Recusants, 1605', in David Cressy and Lori Anne Ferrell (eds.), *Religion and Society in Early Modern England* (1996), 134.

14. Margaret Blundell (ed.), *Cavalier Letters of William Blundell to his Friends 1620–1698* (1933), 245. Cf. the claim by the fictitious Martin Marprelate that he would rather be buried 'in some barn, outhouse or field' than in any church or churchyard that had been polluted by the bishops, *Martins Months Minde* (1589; STC 17452), sig. F4v. Writing in 1600 Francis Tate remarked, 'such as die excommunicate are, for the most part, buried without the *procession* as they call it, and that is either without the bounds of the church yard, which was the circuit of the lesser procession, or in the limits or meres of the parish, where commonly is an *interstitium*, much like that of the Romans', in Thomas Hearne (ed.), *A Collection of Curious Discourses Written by Eminent Antiquaries* (2 vols.; 1771), i. 220; Margaret Blundell (ed.), *Cavalier Letters of William Blundell to his Friends 1620–1698* (1933), 245.

15. Henry Barrow, *The Writings of Henry Barrow 1587–1590*, ed. Leland H. Carlson (1962), 459–60; John Veron, *The Huntyng of Purgatorye to Death* (1561; STC 24683), fo. 37; Oliver Heywood, *The Rev. Oliver Heywood, B.A. 1630–1702; His Autobiography, Diaries, Anecdote and Event Books*, ed. J. Horsfall Turner (4 vols.; Brighouse, 1882–5), ii. 250.

16. Theo Brown, *The Fate of the Dead: A Study in Folk-Eschatology in the West Country After the Reformation* (Totowa, NJ, 1979); Michael MacDonald and Terence R. Murphy, *Sleepless Souls: Suicide in Early Modern England* (Oxford, 1990); David Cressy, *Birth, Marriage, and Death: Ritual, Religion, and the Life Cycle in Tudor and Stuart England* (Oxford, 1997), 114–17.

17. Bishop Matthew Wren in 1635 described the churchyards as 'a dormitory or place for Christians to sleep in . . . to be raised again at the last day', Public Record Office, C115/N9/8876; Cressy, *Birth, Marriage, and Death*, 465.

18. Katherine Chidley, *The Iustification of the Independent Churches of Christ* (1641), 58.

19. Wheatley was a chapelry within the parish of Cuddesdon, and lacked a consecrated church of its own. Strictly speaking, Mrs Horseman should have been buried at Cuddesdon, but inhabitants of Wheatley used Holton on an informal basis. Mary D. Lobel (ed.), *Victoria County History of Oxford*, vol. v (1957), 98, 114–15, 174–6.

20. Price was BA in 1579 and MA in 1583 at St Mary's Hall Oxford. He was presented to the rectory of Holton in 1584 but the lord of the manor retained the tithes. Losing a long ecclesiastical suit for restitution of tithes, Price settled in 1610 for a salary of £60 a year. Joseph Foster (ed.), *Alumni Oxonienses: The Members of the University of Oxford, 1500–1714* (4 vols.; Oxford, 1891), iii, *sub* 'Price'; *VCH Oxford*, v. 175.

21. David Cressy, *Bonfires and Bells: National Memory and the Protestant Calendar in Elizabethan and Stuart England* (1989), 16; Cressy, *Birth, Marriage, and Death*, 421–5.

22. Hugh Barker, Chancellor of the Diocese of Oxford, had been Doctor of Law since 1605. He died in 1632 and was buried in New College chapel. He excommunicated dozens of offenders in 1629 and 1630, but Elizabeth Horseman is not among them. Earlier diocesan act books are missing.

23. Burn, *Ecclesiastical Law*, i. 271.

24. Her will describes Mrs Horseman as a widow of Wheatley, and mentions a son, George Horseman and a daughter, Mary, wife of John Hampton of Innbourne, Gloucestershire, clerk. Administration was granted to Mary Horseman alias Hampton on 2 April 1631, with instructions to exhibit a probate inventory by 20 July. None of these documents makes reference to her excommunication or the extraordinary treatment of her body; Oxford Diocesan Papers, wills 31/3/1. Unfortunately the Holton burial register does not survive before 1633.

25. *VCH Oxford*, v. 98, 298, 308.

26. Peter Lake, 'The Laudian Style: Order, Uniformity and the Pursuit of the Beauty of Holiness in the 1630s', in Kenneth Fincham (ed.), *The Early Stuart Church, 1603–1642* (1993), 161–85; Julian Davies, *The Caroline Captivity of the Church: Charles I and the Remoulding of Anglicanism* (Oxford, 1992), esp. chs. 2 and 6. Millenarians might also be reminded of the opening of the fifth seal in Revelation 6: 9, revealing 'under the altar the souls of them that were slain for the word of God'.

27. See, for example, Edmund Grindal's letter to Secretary Cecil in 1569, excusing the night-time burial of Edmund Bonner, the Marian bishop of London. Who died excommunicate and unabsolved, 'Wherefore by the law Christian sepulture might have been denied him; but we thought not good to deal so rigorously, and therefor permitted him to be buried in St. George's church yard' in Southwark, William Nicholson (ed.), *The Remains of Edmund Grindal* (Cambridge, 1863), 307–8. For seventeenth-century examples see Clare Gittings, *Death, Burial and the Individual in Early Modern England* (1984), 76–8.

28. This is one of the conclusions of my *Birth, Marriage, and Death*. Thomas Fuller compares James I's flexibility in this regard with hardening religious divisions in the late 1630s, observing, 'If moderate men had had the managing of these matters, the accommodation had been easy with a little condescension on both sides. But as a small accidental heat or cold (such as a healthful body would not be sensible of) is enough to put him into a fit, who was formerly in *latitudine febris*, so mens minds distempered in this age with what I may call a mutinous tendency, were exasperated with such small occasions which otherwise might have been passed over and not notice taken.' *Church History of Britain* (1656), book 11, 151.

29. Guildhall Library, MS 9064/18, fos. 22, 97v.

30. Oxfordshire Archives, Oxford Diocesan Papers, c. 2, fo. 191v.

31. The phrase is from Canon 68 in Bullard (ed.), *Constitutions and Canons Ecclesiastical*, 285.

32. See, for example, *The Late Commotion of Certaine Papists in Herefordshire. Occasioned by the death of one Alice Wellington, a Recusant, who was buried after the*

Popish maner, in the Towne of Allens-Moore, neere Hereford, upon Tuesday in Whitsun weeke last past (1605; STC 25232.5).

33. Oxford Archdeaconry Papers, c. 5, fo. 148.

34. Oxford Diocesan Papers, c. 2, fos. 7v–8.

35. Borthwick Institute, York, Y/V/CB/1, fo. 34v.

36. Lichfield Record Office, B/V/1 61, p. 23.

37. Durham Archives, DCD/SJB 7, fo. 6v. Cf. the case of John Vernon, vicar of Cookham, Berkshire, who allowed two excommunicated recusants to be buried in his churchyard at night in the 1620s. Vernon said that the first burial took him by surprise, and that he tried to forestall the second by impounding the key to the church, Bodleian Library, Rawlinson MS D 363, fos. 270–322.

38. Berkshire Record Office, D/A2.C74, fos. 406–407v.

39. Sidney A. Peyton (ed.), *The Churchwardens' Presentments in the Oxfordshire Peculiars of Dorchester, Thame and Banbury* (Oxfordshire Record Society, Oxford, 1928), 116, 141, 204; T. F. Thisleton-Dyer, *Church-Lore Gleanings* (1892), 139.

40. Buckinghamshire Record Office, D/A/V/ 2. For more examples of clandestine burials of recusants see Hugh Aveling, *Northern Recusants: The Catholic Recusants of the North Riding of Yorkshire 1558–1790* (1966), 148.

41. *The Acts of the High Commission within the Diocese of Durham* (Surtees Society, 34; 1858), 142; Lichfield Record Office, B/V/1 61, p. 9.

42. Greater London Record Office, DL/C/319, fo. 141.

43. Borthwick Institute, York, C/V/CB/2, fos. 77v. She was excommunicated in 1632. For a similar case at Staynton Thornaby, Yorkshire, ibid., fos. 98v–99. See also Marchant, *The Church Under the Law; Justice, Administration and Discipline in the Diocese of York, 1560–1640*, 139 n., 220 n. In 1679, four days after her interment in the Quaker burying ground at Fakenham, Norfolk, the body of Mary Lardner was exhumed 'in an inhuman manner, breaking the coffin, so as they were forced to tie it together, lest the corpse should fall out', and was set up in the market place 'to the great amazement of many people, who were troubled at the sight thereof', Joseph Harrison, *The Lamentable Cry of Oppression* (1679), 28.

44. A. G. Matthews, *Walker Revised. Being a Revision of John Walker's Sufferings of the Clergy during the Grand Rebellion 1642–60* (Oxford, 1948), 151; Percival A. Moore (ed.), 'The Metropolitical Visitation of Archdeacon [*sic*] Laud', in *Associated Architectural Societies Reports and Papers*, 29 (1907), 516.

45. Patricia Crawford, *Women and Religion in England 1500–1720* (1993); Cressy, *Birth, Marriage, and Death*, 19–20.

46. Bodleian Library, Tanner MS 42, fo. 221.

47. Tanner MS 38, fo. 111. For another comment on 'popish buryings' see *Calendar of State Papers, Domestic, 1679–80*, 24.

48. Hereford Record Office, Registrar's Files, 1674/8.

49. Oxfordshire Archives, Oxford Archdeaconry Papers, c. 23, fo. 163; All Saints, Oxford, parish register transcript at Oxfordshire Archives.

50. Tanner MS 35, fos. 190–190v.

CHAPTER 9

1. Borthwick Institute, York, High Commission Cause Papers, 1597/12; Lincolnshire Archives, Court Papers, box 61/1, 19, 49; Buckinghamshire Record Office, D/A/V4, fo. 53v; Norfolk Record Office, DN/VIS/7/1; Borthwick Institute, Visitation Court Book 1636, fo. 65; J. S. Cockburn (ed.), *Western Circuit Assize Orders 1629–1648* (Camden Society, 4th ser. 17; 1976), 198–9; Public Record Office, SP 16/3362/96; SP16/470/55.

2. Important discussions of lay–clerical relations in early modern England include Christopher Hill, *The Economic Problems of the Church from Archbishop Whitgift to the Long Parliament* (Oxford, 1956); Rosemary O'Day, *The English Clergy: The Emergence and Consolidation of a Profession 1558–1642* (Leicester, 1979), esp. chs. 13 and 14; Eamon Duffy, 'The Godly and the Multitude in Stuart England', *The Seventeenth Century*, 1 (1986), 31–55; Christopher Haigh, 'Anticlericalism and the English Reformation', in Christopher Haigh (ed.), *The English Reformation Revised* (Cambridge, 1987), 56–74; Patrick Collinson, ' "Shepherds, Sheepdogs, and Hirelings": The Pastoral Ministry in Post-Reformation England', in W. J. Sheils and Diana Wood (eds.), *The Ministry: Clerical and Lay* (Studies in Church History, 26; Oxford, 1989), 185–220. I am grateful to Eric Josef Carlson for letting me see his unpublished paper, 'Anticlericalism, Social Discipline, and the Parish in Tudor and Stuart England', delivered at the North American Conference on British Studies in October 1995. For continental comparisons see Ian Green, ' "Reformed Pastors" and *Bons Curés*: The Changing Role of the Parish Clergy in Early Modern Europe', in Sheils and Wood (eds.), *The Ministry: Clerical and Lay*, 249–86; Andrew Pettegree, 'The Clergy and the Reformation: From "Devilish Priesthood" to New Professional Elite', in Andrew Pettegree (ed.), *The Reformation of the Parishes: The Ministry and the Reformation in Town and Country* (Manchester and New York, 1993), 1–21. It is worth pointing out that the word 'anticlericalism' entered the English language in the nineteenth century, and was unknown in early modern discourse.

3. Similar 'scandalous, malicious and contemptuous words' hurled against lay officials can sometimes be found in Quarter Sessions records, as when a Hertfordshire man called a constable 'rascal knave . . . jackanapes . . . scurvy knave, also a busy fellow', W. J. Hardy (ed.), *Hertfordshire County Records. Notes and Extracts from the Sessions Rolls 1581 to 1698*, vol. i (Hertford, 1905), 42; when a Yorkshireman declared, 'I care not a fart for Sir Francis Wortley's warrants', and another berated 'a bankrupt, roguish and knavish constable', John Lister (ed.), *West Riding Sessions Records, ii: Orders, 1611–1642. Indictments, 1637–1642* (Yorkshire Archaeological Society, 53; 1915), 60, 160, 332; and when a Cheshire labourer told his churchwarden, 'thou art a base fellow, a home breed rogue, a white livered rascal', J. H. E. Bennett and J. C. Dewhurst (eds.), *Quarter Sessions Records with other Records of the Justices of the Peace for the County Palatine of Chester 1559–1760* (Record Society of Lancashire and Cheshire, 94; 1940), 110.

4. By the end of James I's reign it was normal for a prospective cleric to have a univer-

sity degree, O'Day, *English Clergy*, 142. The very success of clerical higher education, at a time when few others attended Oxford or Cambridge, may have contributed to a cultural estrangement between incumbents and parishioners.

5. George Herbert, 'A Priest to the Temple or, The Country Parson' [*c*.1632], in F. E. Hutchinson (ed.), *The Works of George Herbert* (Oxford, 1941), 237, 265.

6. Ibid. 233; Martin Ingram, *Church Courts, Sex and Marriage in England, 1570–1640* (Cambridge, 1987), 111.

7. Greenham allegedly left Dry Drayton, Cambridgeshire, in 1591, after a ministry of twenty years, because of 'the untractableness and unteachableness of that people among whom he had taken such exceeding great pains', Eric Josef Carlson, *Marriage and the English Reformation* (Oxford, 1994), 159, quoting Samuel Clarke, *The Lives of Thirty-Two English Divines*. Baxter's efforts in Worcestershire are described in Richard Baxter, *Confirmation and Restauration* (1658), 157–65, and Matthew Sylvester (ed.), *Reliquiae Baxterianae: Or, Mr Richard Baxter's Narrative of the most Memorable Passages of his Life and Times* (1696). For more friction between clergy and laity see Christopher Haigh, 'The Church of England, the Catholics and the People', in Christopher Haigh (ed.), *The Reign of Elizabeth I* (1984), 207–8, 215–16; and Susan Dwyer Amussen, ' "The Part of a Christian Man": The Cultural Politics of Manhood in Early Modern England', in Susan D. Amussen and Mark Kishlansky (eds.), *Political Culture and Cultural Politics in Early Modern England* (Manchester, 1995), 224.

8. William Attersoll, *A Commentarie Vpon the Epistle of Saint Pavl to Philemon* (1612; STC 890), 150; Historical Manuscripts Commission, *Report on the Manuscripts of the Family of Gawdy* (1885), 23. Thaxter explicitly compared his frustrations in the country to his former success at Cambridge.

9. William Harrison, *The Difference of Hearers* (1614; STC 12870), 31, 39. Attempting to promote Protestantism in a part of the country 'addicted to popery and impiety', Harrison likened his message to the seed that fell on stony ground. The fault, he insisted, lay with the hearers, not with the preacher or his message, ibid., sigs. A5, A6, 6–15, 213.

10. Ralph Cudworth, senior, in 1617, quoted in Tom Webster, *Godly Clergy in Early Stuart England: The Caroline Puritan Movement, c.1620–1643* (Cambridge, 1997), 54.

11. *A Remonstrance on the behalfe of Cumberland and Westmerland* (1641), 3.

12. Edward Dering, 'A Briefe and Necessary Catechism' [1572], in *Maister Derings Workes* (Middleburg, 1590?), 'to the Christian reader', not paginated. See also Anthony Anderson, *The Shield of our Safetie* (1581; STC 572), sig. U2.

13. Samuel Crooke, *The Ministeriall Husbandry and Building* (1615; STC 6069), epistle dedicatory; Charles Richardson, *A Workeman That Needeth Not to be Ashamed: Or the Faithfull Steward of Gods House* (1616; STC 21019), 39; Attersoll, *Commentarie*, 34; George Downame, *Two Sermons, The One Commending the Ministerie in Generall: The Other Defending the Office of Bishops* (1608; STC 7125), 30, 40, 65–6. Insisting on 'the burden and honour' as well as 'the duty and dignity' of the ministry, Downame set forth his view of the clerical calling: 'to instruct the ignorant, to reduce the erroneous, to heal the diseased, to seek the lost, to admonish the

disorderly, to comfort the distressed, to support the weak, to be patient to all', as well as to preach and to read. Not surprisingly he added, 'to abuse the ministry by word or deed, is a sin highly displeasing unto God, and grievously provoking his anger', ibid. 16, 68. See also Richard Bernard, *The Faithfull Shepherd* (1621; STC 1941), 1, on 'the high calling of the ministry', and Stephen Egerton, *The Boring of the Ear* (1623; STC 7527.5), 20 for the claim that 'the contempt of any true minister is the contempt of God himself'.

14. William Hardwick, *Conformity with Piety, Requisite in God's Service* (1638; STC 12766), 8. For a recent study of clerical claims, see Andrew Foster, 'The Clerical Estate Revitalised', in Kenneth Fincham (ed.), *The Early Stuart Church, 1603–1642* (1993), 139–60.

15. William Perkins, *A Direction for Gouernment of the Tongue* (1593, 1611 edn.; STC 19691), sigs. A2, 2, also 57, 63, 74, 102.

16. Anthony Anderson, *An Exposition of the Hymn Commonly Called Benedictus* (1574; STC 567), sig. 30v; idem, *The Shield of our Safetie*, sig. T4v.

17. See esp. George Gifford, *A Briefe Discourse of Certaine Points of the Religion, Whiche is Among the Common Sorte of Christians: Which May be Termed the Country Divinitie* (1582; STC 11846). On the intermingling of godliness and alehouse culture see Tessa Watt, *Cheap Print and Popular Piety, 1550–1640* (Cambridge, 1991).

18. Charles Gibbon, *The Praise of a Good Name. The Reproach of an Ill Name* (1594; STC 11819), 45; Attersoll, *Commentarie*, 34, 93, 475.

19. Joseph Bentham, *The Societie of the Saints: or, A Treatise of Good-fellowes, and their Good-fellowship* (1630, 1638 edn.; STC 1889), 125; Herbert, 'Priest to the Temple', 268–9; Duffy, 'The Godly and the Multitude', 33.

20. Robert Bolton, *Some Generall Directions for a Comfortable Walking with God* (1625; 5th edn., 1638; STC 3254), sig. A4, 112–13. For more on Christian reproof, and the dangers of jeering retaliation, see Thomas Trescot, *The Zealous Magistrate* (1642), 13–14.

21. Bolton, *Some Generall Directions*, 115–16; Hardwick, *Conformity with Piety*, 8.

22. Attersoll, *Commentarie*, 119–20.

23. Anderson, *Shield of our Safetie*, sig. A3v.

24. Perkins, *Direction for the Gouernment of the Tongue*, 106–14; John Dod and Robert Cleaver, *A Godly Forme of Houshold Gouernment* (1598, 1630 edn.; STC 5388), sig. R3; Bentham, *Societie of the Saints*, 126.

25. Anderson, *Exposition*, fos. 2v–3; Thomas Beard, *The Theatre of Gods Ivdgements* (1597, 1631 edn.; STC 1661), 207, 562. See also Attersoll, *Commentarie*, 204; Downame, *Two Sermons*, 70; Henry Burton, *A Divine Tragedy Lately Acted, or A Collection of sundry memorable examples of Gods judgements upon Sabbath-breakers* (1636; STC 4140.7), *passim*.

26. Canons 18 and 111 of 1604, in J. V. Bullard (ed.), *Constitutions and Canons Ecclesiastical* (1934), 255–6, 309.

27. Kenneth Fincham (ed.), *Visitation Articles and Injunctions of the Early Stuart*

Church, vol. i (Church of England Record Society, Woodbridge, Suffolk, 1994), 2, 78, 106, 166.

28. O'Day, *English Clergy*, chs. 10–15; Hill, *Economic Problems of the Church*, part 3.

29. J. A. Sharpe, *Defamation and Sexual Slander in Early Modern England: The Church Courts at York* (York, 1980); Laura Gowing, *Domestic Dangers: Women, Words, and Sex in Early Modern London* (Oxford, 1996).

30. For comparative studies of anger, abuse, and reconciliation, see J. A. Sharpe, '"Such Disagreement betwyxt Neighbours": Litigation and Human Relations in Early Modern England', in John Bossy (ed.), *Disputes and Settlements: Law and Human Relations in the West* (Cambridge, 1983), 167–87; David Parkin, 'Exchanging Words', in Bruce Kapferer (ed.), *Transaction and Meaning: Directions in the Anthropology of Exchange and Symbolic Behavior* (Philadelphia, 1976), 163–90; Cheryl English Martin, 'Popular Speech and Social Order in Northern Mexico, 1650–1830', *Comparative Studies in Society and History*, 32 (1990), 305–24; David Garrioch, 'Verbal Insults in Eighteenth-Century Paris', in Peter Burke and Roy Porter (eds.), *The Social History of Language* (Cambridge, 1987), 104–19.

31. Canterbury Cathedral Archives, X.1.1, fos. 27v–30. The Epistle for Michaelmas is the terrifying account, from Revelation 12, of the battle between the angels and the dragon, pitting salvation by 'the blood of the lamb' against the power of the devil who 'is come down unto you' in wrath, William Keating Clay (ed.), *Liturgical Services. Liturgies and Occasional Forms of Prayer set forth in the Reign of Queen Elizabeth* (Cambridge, 1847), 176.

32. Canterbury Cathedral Archives, X.1.1, fo. 156v. See also the case of Edward Carpenter, an alderman of Canterbury, who called churchwarden Hopper a 'knave' in 1561 for demanding 6s. 8d. for burying his wife in the church, and Thomas Wells of Hawkhurst, who was presented in 1564 'for assaulting and railing on the minister'. Ibid. X.1.1, fo. 3v; X.1.6, fos. 48, 53.

33. Westminster Abbey Muniments, book 15, fo. 88.

34. A. L. Rowse, *Tudor Cornwall* (New York, 1969), 320–41; Christopher Haigh, *English Reformations: Religion, Politics and Society under the Tudors* (Oxford, 1993), 174–5, 268, 339. See also 'The View of the State of the Church in Cornwall', in Albert Peel (ed.), *The Seconde Part of a Register: Being a Calendar of Manuscripts under that Title intended for Publication by the Puritans about 1593* (2 vols.; Cambridge, 1915), ii. 98–110.

35. Lincolnshire Archives, Court Papers, box 69/1, 15; Leicestershire Record Office, 1D 41/4/213–223. Anderson had previously distinguished himself as the Commissary of the Archdeacon of Leicester who had handled the case of Agnes Bowker's cat and referred it to the Earl of Huntingdon, British Library, Lansdowne MS 101, and Chapter 1, above.

36. Guildhall Library, MS 9064/13, fos. 42v–43.

37. Morris Palmer Tilley, *A Dictionary of the Proverbs in England in the Sixteenth and Seventeenth Centuries* (Ann Arbor, Michigan, 1950), 377, 688.

38. Guildhall Library, MS 9064/13, fo. 114. Anderson was not alone in thinking his

parishioners' 'rebellions, presumptions, scorning' the cause of the latest plague, Anthony Anderson, *An Approved Medicine against the deserved Plague* (1593; STC 566), sig. A3v.

39. William H. Hale (ed.), *A Series of Precedents and Proceedings in Criminal Causes* (1847), 208; Proverbs 10: 8 and 10.

40. Lori Anne Ferrell, 'Kneeling and the Body Politic', in Donna Hamilton and Richard Strier (eds.), *Religion, Literature, and Politics in Post-Reformation England* (Cambridge, 1995), 70–92.

41. Borthwick Institute, York, High Commission Cause Papers, 1597/12.

42. Ibid. The same court in 1590 dealt with John Huddlestone, gentleman, of Kirton, Nottinghamshire, who addressed his parson as 'whoreson, drunken slave' and complained that 'his preaching is naught', in Claire Cross, 'Sin and Society: The Northern High Commission and the Northern Gentry in the Reign of Elizabeth I', in Claire Cross, David Loades, and J. J. Scarisbrick (eds.), *Law and Government Under the Tudors: Essays Presented to Sir Geoffrey Elton* (Cambridge, 1988), 207. Cf. the Nottinghamshire labourer in 1634 who told his local magistrate, 'he was sometimes a justice of peace, and sometimes a just-ass', H. Hampton Copnall (ed.), *Nottinghamshire County Records: Notes and Extracts from the Nottinghamshire County Records of the 17ᵗʰ Century* (Nottingham, 1915), 25.

43. Lincolnshire Archives, Court Papers, box 61/1, 19, 49.

44. For example, Staffordshire Record Office, B/V/1 61, 25; Guildhall Library, MS 9064/21, fo. 67v; Greater London Record Office, DL/C/319, fo. 69; Norfolk Record Office, DN/VIS 6 and 7; Borthwick Institute, York, Visitation Court Book 1636, fos. 31, 58, 90, 139v, 258.

45. Buckinghamshire Record Office, D/A/V3, fo. 114.

46. Staffordshire Record Office, B/V/1 66. See also the case of Edmund Booth of Holton, Suffolk, cited in 1633 'for misbehaving himself in service time in church by laughing, and in March last there was a fart let in the church in sermon time and he was vehemently suspected for the same', Norfolk Record Office, DN/VIS/6/4.

47. Keith Thomas. 'The Place of Laughter in Tudor and Stuart England', *TLS* (21 January 1977), 77–81.

48. A. Percival Moore (ed.), 'The Metropolitical Visitation of Archdeacon [*sic*] Laud', in *Associated Architectural Societies' Reports and Papers*, 29 (1907), 508.

49. Norfolk Record Office, ANF/1/4.

50. Buckinghamshire Record Office, D/A/V4, fo. 53v.

51. John White, *The Way to the True Church* (1608, 1616 edn.; STC 25397), 'to the reader'.

52. The Earl of Warwick and the Bishop of Lincoln almost came to blows in the House of Lords in 1641 when the earl thought that the bishop had called him 'sirrah' instead of 'sir'.

53. Borthwick Institute, Visitation Court Book 1636, fo. 65.

54. Public Record Office, SP16/375/82.

55. SP16/362/96. For the curse of Meroz see Judges 5: 23.

56. SP16/470/55. See also the case of Walter Bayley, tailor, who called the rector of

Bridport, Dorset, 'a base knave, a dangerous knave, a base rogue, a dangerous rogue', and was bound over in March 1640 to appear at the next assize, Cockburn (ed.), *Western Circuit Assize Orders*, 198–9.

57. In *King Lear*, Act II, Scene ii the disguised Duke of Kent calls Oswald 'knave . . . rascal . . . rogue . . . and varlet', in a powerful cascade of abuse. Timon in *Timon of Athens* cries, 'Rogue, rogue, rogue', and Patroclus in *Troilus and Cressida*, 'varlet . . . rogue'. Similar words were frequently directed at churchwardens in the course of collecting the parish assessments.

58. Laura Gowing, 'Gender and the Language of Insult in Early Modern London', *History Workshop Journal*, 35 (1993), 1–21; Gowing, *Domestic Dangers, passim*. See also J. A. Sharpe, *Defamation and Sexual Slander in Early Modern England: The Church Courts at York* (Borthwick Papers, no. 58; York, 1980).

59. Guildhall Library, MS 9064/15, fo. 19; MS 9064/16, fo. 206v. Cf. the case in Cambridgeshire in 1602 in which parishioners conducted a charivari, one of them dressed in a black gown, to mock their vicar for allowing himself to be beaten by his wife, Ely Diocesan Records, B/2/18, fos. 174v–175, cited in Carlson, 'Anticlericalism, Social Discipline, and the Parish', 3.

60. Mocking insults did not have to be verbal, and did not always reach the courts. The minister of Ovington, Norfolk, endured a parishioner who disturbed and vexed him during sermon time, 'by frowning, putting out his mouth, setting his teeth, knitting his brows, whispering to himself, clapping his hand upon his knee with malcontented gestures . . . stamping with his feet to the offence of others', John Trendle to Sir Bassingbourne Gawdy, August 1598, HMC *Gawdy*, 62.

61. Herbert, 'Priest to the Temple', 268–9. For more advice on reproof and reprehension, see Perkins, *Direction for the Gouernment of the Tongue*, 63.

62. J. F. Williams (ed.), *Diocese of Norwich: Bishop Redman's Visitation 1597* (Norfolk Record Society, Norwich, 1946), 78.

63. Lincolnshire Archives, Ch. P/6, 26.

64. Ibid.

65. A. G. Matthews, *Walker Revised. Being a Revision of John Walker's Sufferings of the Clergy during the Grand Rebellion 1642–66* (Oxford, 1948), 322, 334, 344; O'Day, *English Clergy*, 203; House of Lords Main Papers, Petition of 6 February 1641.

66. John Rushworth, *Historical Collections: The Third Part* (1692), 59. See also Tai Liu, *Puritan London: A Study of Religion and Society in the City Parishes* (London and Newark, NJ, 1986), 143–4 n.

67. Bernard, *Faithfull Shepherd*, 32–3. See also John Dod, *A Remedy Against Privat Contentions* (1609; STC 6940), sigs. Bv, E4; Samuel Hieron, 'Penance for Sinne', in *The Workes of Mr Sam. Hieron* (2 vols.; 1620, 1635 edn.; STC 13384), ii. 75, 137.

68. Public Record Office, SP16/261, fos. 83–86; Kenneth Fincham, *Prelate as Pastor: The Episcopate of James I* (Oxford, 1990), 224–5, 259.

69. SP16/261, fos. 121–3, 195v. His excommunication was lifted within six months, ibid., fo. 207.

70. SP16/261, fos. 165v–69.

71. *Calendar of State Papers, Domestic, 1634*, 318; *CSPD 1634–35*, 110, 329; *CSPD 1635*, 227; *CSPD 1635–36*, 105–7, 115. For more on Stephen Dennison and his adversaries, see the forthcoming work of Peter Lake.

72. Trescot, *Zealous Magistrate*, 13–14.

73. Geoffrey Chaucer, 'General Prologue', *The Canterbury Tales*.

CHAPTER 10

1. Borthwick Institute, York, Court of High Commission, Cause Papers, 1590/5. There is a brief note of this case in G. E. Aylmer, 'Unbelief in Seventeenth Century England', in Donald Pennington and Keith Thomas (eds.), *Puritans and Revolutionaries: Essays in Seventeenth-Century History Presented to Christopher Hill* (Oxford, 1978), 31–2. It also warrants a note by Veronica M. O'Mara, 'A Middle English Sermon Preached by a Sixteenth Century Atheist: A Preliminary Account', *Notes and Queries*, 232 (1987), 183–5.

2. The complaint was signed by the minister John Hutton, and laymen Anthony Rayner, Nicholas Rayner, John Prinell, and Richard Pickhaven, and marked by George Harrison and Edward Holmes, the churchwardens. East Drayton, with its dependent chapels of Askham and Stokeham, was a peculiar of the Dean and Chapter of York. John Hutton, BA (aged 32 at the time of his trouble with Mynet) became vicar on 22 January 1586 and was succeeded by George Ormerode on 11 December 1590. K. S. S. Train (ed.), 'Lists of the Clergy of North Nottinghamshire', *Thoroton Society Record Series*, 20 (Nottingham, 1961), 47–8. He was, then, a relative newcomer to the parish and left (or died) soon after his collision with Mynet. He may have been the John Hutton who matriculated at Trinity College Cambridge in 1577, was ordained in 1584, and became rector of Gateshead, Durham, in 1592. It is possible, though not proven, that he was a kinsman of Matthew Hutton, Dean of York from 1567 to 1589 and later bishop of Durham and archbishop of York. The archbishop of York from 1589 to 1594 was John Piers, formerly bishop of Salisbury, who replaced Edwin Sandys. For the legal and administrative framework within which Mynet's case was handled, see Claire Cross, 'Sin and Society: The Northern High Commission and the Northern Gentry in the Reign of Elizabeth I', in Claire Cross, David Loades, and J. J. Scarisbrick (eds.), *Law and Government Under the Tudors: Essays Presented to Sir Geoffrey Elton* (Cambridge, 1988), 195–209.

3. Though his status is not explicitly stated, one of the papers in the case refers to him as 'Mr. Mynett'. There had been Mynets among the parish notables since early Tudor times, and two kinsmen or descendants, William and Robert Mynet (or Mynnett) were among the twelve 'owners of East Drayton' in 1612, John Throsby, *Thoroton's History of Nottinghamshire: Republished with Large Additions* (3 vols.; 1797), ii. 240. There were Mynets (or Minnitts) among the modest Hearth Tax payers of East Drayton in the reign of Charles II, W. F. Webster (ed.), 'Nottinghamshire Hearth Tax 1664: 1674', *Thoroton Society Record Series*, 37 (Nottingham,

1988), 35, 121. Neither Mynet nor Hutton appears in the Elizabethan State Papers or Acts of the Privy Council, and neither left a will surviving in York or Nottinghamshire records.

4. York, HC AB 11, 21 Feb. 1589/90. The case can be followed on fos. 223v, 230v, 234v, 251v, and 284, from February to August 1590.

5. Anthony Anderson, *The Shield of our Safetie* (1581; STC 572), sig. T4, and more attacks on 'the atheists of our days', sigs. Bv, B2, B4; John Dove, *A Confutation of Atheisme* (1605; STC 7078), 2–4; Henry Smith, *God's Arrow Against Atheists* (1593; 1604 edn.; STC 22737), 5, 100. See also Adam Hill, *The Crie of England* (1595; STC 13465), 32, 36; Thomas Beard, *The Theatre of Gods Ivdgements* (1597; 1631 edn.; STC 1661), 141–51; Arthur Dent, *The Plaine Mans Path-way to Heaven* (1601; 1631 edn.; STC 6634), 129; Martin Fotherby, *Atheomastix: Clearing Four Truthes, Against Atheists and Infidels* (1622; STC 11205).

6. Michael Hunter, 'The Problem of "Atheism" in Early Modern England', *Transactions of the Royal Historical Society*, 5th ser. 35 (1985), 135–57; Aylmer, 'Unbelief in Seventeenth-Century England', 22–46; Michael Hunter and David Wooton (eds.), *Atheism from the Reformation to the Enlightenment* (Oxford, 1992); Nicholas Davidson, 'Christopher Marlowe and Atheism', in Darryll Grantley and Peter Roberts (eds.), *Christopher Marlowe and English Renaissance Culture* (Aldershot, Hants, and Brookfield, Vermont, 1996), 129–47; Patrick Collinson, 'Hooker and the Elizabethan Establishment', in Arthur Stephen McGrade (ed.), *Richard Hooker and the Christian Community* (Tempe, Arizona, 1997), 163–5.

7. A. C. Wood (ed.), 'The Nottinghamshire Presentment Bills of 1587', *Thoroton Society Record Series*, 11 (1943), 20, 36.

8. Brett Usher, 'Expedient and Experiment: The Elizabethan Lay Reader', a paper presented at the Ecclesiastical History Society conference at St Andrews, 1997. I owe this reference to Peter Marshall.

9. David Cressy, *Bonfires and Bells: National Memory and the Protestant Calendar in Elizabethan and Stuart England* (1989), 25–8, 80–4; Ronald Hutton, *The Rise and Fall of Merry England: The Ritual Year 1400–1700* (Oxford, 1994), 37–9, 111–52; Ronald Hutton, *The Stations of the Sun: A History of the Ritual Year in Britain* (Oxford, 1996), 311–21. See also Martin Marprelate's mockery of the bishop John Bullingham's sermon upon St John's Day, 'John, John, the grace of God, the grace of God, gracious John, not graceless John, but gracious John; John, holy John, holy John, not John full of holes, but holy John', in *Oh Read Over D. John Bridges, for it is a Worthy Worke: Or an Epitome* (1588), 47. I am grateful to Patrick Collinson for redirecting me to this source.

10. Deponents included John Hutton, clerk, aged 32; Nicholas Rayner, yeoman, 27; Richard Pickhaven, yeoman, 30; Richard Bingham, yeoman, 26; and Thomas Nicholson, husbandman, 40.

11. Carlo Ginzburg, *The Cheese and the Worms: The Cosmos of a Sixteenth-Century Miller* (Baltimore, 1980).

12. Jacobus de Voragine [*The Golden Legend*] (1527; STC 24880), fos. 139–141, 228–230, has the stories of John the Baptist. Pliny [Caius Plinius Secundus], *The Secrets and*

Wonders of the World (1585; STC 20032x), sig. D2, discusses elephants and dragons. 'St. Byllet', the authority on dragons and bones, turns out to have been John Beleth, author of the twelfth-century *Summa de Ecclesiasticis Officiis*, whose canonization is unrecorded.

13. Theodor Erbe (ed.), *Mirk's Festial: A Collection of Homilies by Johannes Mirkus* (Early English Text Society, 1905), 182–6; John Mirk, *The Festyvall* (1532; STC 17975); David B. Foss, 'John Mirk's *Instructions for Parish Priests*', in W. J. Sheils and Diana Wood (eds.), *The Ministry: Clerical and Lay* (Studies in Church History, 26; 1989), 131–40.

14. Bodleian Library, MS Lat. Liturg. B.5, described in Adrian Henstock, 'Medieval Service Books', *Transactions of the Thoroton Society*, 99 (1995), 13.

15. Contrast Patrick Collinson, *The Religion of Protestants: The Church in English Society 1559–1625* (Oxford, 1982) and Christopher Haigh, *English Reformations: Religion, Politics, and Society under the Tudors* (Oxford, 1993), esp. 235–95.

16. Alexandra Walsham, *Church Papists: Catholicism, Conformity and Confessional Polemic in Early Modern England* (Woodbridge, 1993); Haigh, *English Reformations*, 291–3; Judith Maltby, ' "By This Book": Parishioners, the Prayer Book and the Established Church', in Kenneth Fincham (ed.), *The Early Stuart Church, 1603–1642* (1993), 115–37.

CHAPTER 11

1. Thomas Edwards, *The Third Part of Gangraena* (1646), 17; Christopher Hill, *The World Turned Upside Down: Radical Ideas During the English Revolution* (New York, 1972).

2. Edwards, *Third Part of Gangraena*, 17. Work-in-progress by Ann Hughes on civil war Presbyterians confirms the reliability of many of Edwards's reports.

3. Edwards, *Third Part of Gangraena*, 18.

4. Thomas Edwards, *Gangraena: or a Catalogue and Discovery of many of the Errours, Heresies, Blasphemies and Pernicious Practices of the Sectaries of this time* (1646), 28, 67.

5. See, for example, *The Wicked Resolution of the Cavaliers* (1642); Joad Raymond (ed.), *Making the News: An Anthology of the Newsbooks of Revolutionary England 1641–1660* (New York, 1993).

6. *Mercurius Aulicus*, week ending 26 October 1644. The author is presumed to be John Berkenhead; Charles Carlton, *Going to the Wars: The Experience of the British Civil Wars 1638–1651* (1992), 77.

7. Charles Edward Long (ed.), *Diary of the Marches of the Royal Army During the Great Civil War* (Camden Society, 74; 1859), 67.

8. A. G. Matthews, *Walker Revised. Being a Revision of John Walker's Sufferings of the Clergy during the Grand Rebellion 1642–60* (Oxford, 1948), 274.

9. An exception is *One Argument More Against the Cavaliers: Taken from their Violation of Churches* (1643).

10. David Cressy, *Birth, Marriage, and Death: Ritual, Religion, and the Life Cycle in Tudor and Stuart England* (Oxford, 1997), 173–80, on 'baptism in times of distraction'.

11. Folger Shakespeare Library, Washington, DC, Folger MS V.a.436, fo. 151.

12. William Dugdale, *A Short View of the Late Troubles in England* (Oxford, 1681), 560. This story is repeated in Edward Pettit, *Visions of the Reformation* (1683), 117.

13. J. C. Jeaffreson (ed.), *Middlesex County Records* (1888), iii. 179.

14. William Dunn Macray (ed.), *A Register of the Members of St Mary Magdalen College, Oxford* (1894), vol. i, pp. v, 48–51, 58; Susan Brigden, *London and the Reformation* (Oxford, 1991), 180.

15. John Gough Nichols (ed.), *The Diary of Henry Machyn, Citizen and Merchant-Taylor of London, from A.D. 1550 to A.D. 1563* (Camden Society, 1848), 58–60; Susan Brigden, *London and the Reformation*, 550. There is no English counterpart of the old German practice of drowning a condemned man in a sack with two animals, but it was not unknown for cats to be stuffed in sacks with gunpowder to add their noise to the burning of an effigy or the flaming of a bonfire. In 1638 the New Year's Day service at Ely was disturbed 'by the roasting of a cat tied to a spit by one William Smith, and there was a fire made about it, whereby much people were gathered together and a great profanation made both of the day and the place'. The cat was tortured just outside the cathedral choir, and was an obvious affront to the disciplinarian bishop Matthew Wren, who was particularly keen on music and harmony in church.

16. Historical Manuscripts Commission, *Calendar of the Manuscripts . . . Preserved at Hatfield House, part X* (1904), 450. The word 'partlet' referred to a chicken, which may have accompanied the cat to baptism; it also meant a kind of neckerchief, in which case it was a costume accessory for the cat. The name Gurlypot refers to rumbling or roaring or 'gurling' noises, and may have been the kind of name given to a witch's familiar or a cat.

17. Dorothy M. Meads (ed.), *Diary of Lady Margaret Hoby 1599–1605* (1930), 192.

18. Walter C. Renshaw, 'Notes from the Act Books of the Archdeaconry Court of Lewes', *Sussex Archaeological Collections*, 49 (1906), 53, 54.

19. H. R. Wilton Hall (ed.), *Records of the Old Archdeaconry of St Alban's. A Calendar of papers A.D. 1575 to A.D. 1637* (St Albans, 1908), 141–2.

20. Ibid.

21. George Ornsby (ed.), *The Correspondence of John Cosin* (2 vols.; Durham, 1869), i. 2.

22. James Stokes (ed.), *Records of Early English Drama: Somerset* (Toronto and London, 1996), 107–9, 901.

23. Ibid. 901.

24. *Calendar of State Papers, Domestic, 1611–18*, 538, 536, 540.

25. Buckinghamshire Record Office, D/A/V4, fo. 111v.

26. William Lilly, *Mr William Lilly's History of His Life and Times, from the Year 1602, to 1681* (1715), 41.

27. *CSPD 1631–33*, 145–6, 256; Public Record Office, SP16/210/47; SP16/211/70. The

dispute dated back at least two years, *Acts of the Privy Council July 1628 to April 1629*, 361; *APC May 1629 to May 1630*, 1, 50, 207–98; *APC June 1630 to June 1631*, 193, 218, 225.

28. Ibid. See also John Southerden Burn, *The High Commission. Notices of the Court, and its Proceedings* (1865), 60; S. R. Gardiner (ed.), *Reports of Cases in the Courts of Star Chamber and High Commission* (1886), 275–6.

29. British Library, Sloan MS 1457, fo. 19v; Keith Thomas, *Religion and the Decline of Magic* (New York, 1971), 75.

30. William H. Hale (ed.), *A Series of Precedents and Proceedings in Criminal Causes, extending from the year 1475 to 1640; extracted from the Act-Books of the Ecclesiastical Courts of the Diocese of London* (1847), 223; Greater London Record Office, DL/C/307, fo. 27; Guildhall Library, MS 9064/18, fo. 61v. For similar escapades see GLRO, DL/C/316, fo. 57v; Lichfield Record Office, B/V/1, 66.

31. Oxfordshire Archives, Archdeaconry Papers, c. 13, fo. 34. See also the mock marriages at the Restoration court, high jinx among the high-born, in R. C. Latham and W. Matthews (eds.), *The Diary of Samuel Pepys* (10 vols.; Berkeley and Los Angeles, 1970–6), i. 27; iv. 37; E. S. de Beer (ed.), *The Diary of John Evelyn* (6 vols.; Oxford, 1955), ii. 589.

32. Oxfordshire Archives, Diocesan Papers, c. 4, fo. 55v.

33. Cheshire Record Office, EDC 5 (1962), no. 5, cited in John Addy, *Sin and Society in the Seventeenth Century* (1989), 68.

34. Richard Hooker, 'Of the Laws of Ecclesiastical Politie', in *The Works of that Learned and Judicious Divine, Mr Richard Hooker* (1723), 217.

35. Thomas Comber, *A Brief Discourse Upon the Offices of Baptism and Confirmation* (1674), appended to his *A Companion to the Altar* (1675), 358, 411.

36. Cressy, *Birth, Marriage, and Death*, 97–194.

37. Natalie Zemon Davis, *Society and Culture in Early Modern France* (Stanford, Calif., 1975), 97–123; Barbara A. Babcock (ed.), *The Reversible World: Symbolic Inversion in Art and Society* (Ithaca, NY, 1978), 14, 29; Stuart Clark, 'Inversion, Misrule and the Meaning of Witchcraft', *Past and Present*, 87 (1980), 99–106. For attempts to discern a distinctive youth culture in England see Paul Griffiths, *Youth and Authority: Formative Experience in England, 1560–1640* (Oxford, 1996).

38. Keith Thomas, *Religion and the Decline of Magic*, 37.

39. Edwards, *Gangraena*, 67.

CHAPTER 12

1. Relevant recent scholarship on the religious disputes of early Stuart England includes Nicholas Tyacke, *Anti-Calvinists: The Rise of English Arminianism, c.1590–1640* (Oxford, 1987); Julian Davies, *The Caroline Captivity of the Church: Charles I and the Remoulding of Anglicanism* (Oxford, 1992); Peter White, *Predestination, Policy and Polemic: Conflict and Consensus in the English Church from the*

Reformation to the Civil War (Cambridge, 1992); Kenneth Fincham (ed.), *The Early Stuart Church, 1603–1642* (1993). A major study of the Caroline altar policy is forthcoming from Fincham and Tyacke.

2. House of Lords, Main Papers (hereafter HL), Petition of 30 June 1641. The rector was William Cooper. Only one of the subscribers made a mark. For the Protestation see *Fifth Report of the Royal Commission on Historical Manuscripts* (1876), part 1, appendix 3.

3. HL Petition of 1 July 1641. Twelve of the 41 subscribers made marks instead of signatures. On Blackwell and his son, see Keith Lindley, *Popular Politics and Religion in Civil War London* (1997), 39–40, 224; Tai Liu, *Puritan London: A Study of Religion and Society in the City Parishes* (London and Newark, NJ, 1986), 134–5; Robert Brenner, *Merchants and Revolution: Commercial Change, Political Conflict, and London's Overseas Traders, 1550–1653* (Princeton, 1993), 527, 548–9.

4. Tyacke, *Anti-Calvinists*, 199; John Cosin, 'Notes and Collections on the Book of Common Prayer' [1619 and 1638], in *The Works of the Right Reverend Father in God, John Cosin* (5 vols.; Oxford, 1843–55), v. 85–8, 308–45. Nehemiah Wallington, *Historical Notices of Events Occurring Chiefly in the Reign of Charles I* (2 vols.; 1869), i. 23, quotes with alarm from a letter from Cambridge dated 1635 which claims that Dr Collins, Provost of King's College, 'maintains transubstantiation and many points of popery'. See also Tom Webster, *Godly Clergy in Early Stuart England: The Caroline Puritan Movement, c.1620–1643* (Cambridge, 1997), 117, for puritan enthusiasm for the sacrament as 'the bond of mutual amity betwixt the faithful'; E. Brooks Holifield, *The Covenant Sealed: The Development of Puritan Sacramental Theology in Old and New England, 1570–1720* (New Haven and London, 1974); and Kenneth Stevenson, *Covenant of Grace Renewed: A Vision of the Eucharist in the Seventeenth Century* (1994).

5. *Articles Whereupon it was Agreed by the Archbishoppes and Bishoppes* (1571; STC 10039), article 28.

6. William Keatinge (ed.), *Liturgical Services: Liturgies and Occasional Forms of Prayer Set Forth in the Reign of Queen Elizabeth* (Cambridge, 1847), 180, 193, 195. See also the 1559 Injunctions, in Edward Cardwell (ed.), *Documentary Annals of the Reformed Church of England* (2 vols.; Oxford, 1844), i. 234.

7. British Library, Lansdowne MS 8, fo. 16, 'Varieties in service and administrations used', quoted in Henry Gee, *The Elizabethan Prayer Book and Ornaments* (1902), 164–5; Patrick Collinson, *Religion of Protestants: The Church in English Society 1559–1625* (Oxford, 1982), 32.

8. J. V. Bullard (ed.), *Constitutions and Canons Ecclesiastical 1604* (1934), canons 18, 20–2, 26–8, 82.

9. Kenneth Fincham (ed.), *Visitation Articles and Injunctions of the Early Stuart Church*, vol. i (Church of England Record Society, Woodbridge, Suffolk, 1994), 10, 31, 70, 100.

10. J. Charles Cox and Alfred Harvey, *English Church Furniture* (1908), 18; George Yule,

'James VI and I: Furnishing the Churches in his Two Kingdoms', in Anthony Fletcher and Peter Roberts (eds.), *Religion, Culture and Society in Early Modern Britain: Essays in Honour of Patrick Collinson* (Cambridge, 1994), 193.

11. Kenneth Fincham, *Prelate as Pastor: The Episcopate of James I* (Oxford, 1990). For the re-sacralizing of eucharistic gestures in this period see Lori Anne Ferrell, 'Kneeling and the Body Politic', in Donna Hamilton and Richard Strier (eds.), *Religion, Literature, and Politics in Post-Reformation England, 1540–1688* (Cambridge, 1995), 70–92; David Cressy, 'Conflict, Consensus and the Willingness to Wink: The Erosion of Community in Charles I's England', *Huntington Library Quarterly* (forthcoming).

12. Thomas Fuller, *The Church-History of Britaine* (1655), book 11, 151.

13. Tyacke, *Anti-Calvinists*, 116–17, 199–205; Davies, *Caroline Captivity*, 205–50; Webster, *Godly Clergy*, 237; Kevin Sharpe, *The Personal Rule of Charles I* (1992), 333–45; Peter Lake, 'The Laudian Style: Order, Uniformity and the Pursuit of Holiness in the 1630s', in Fincham (ed.), *Early Stuart Church*, 161–85.

14. Thomas Wilson of Debden, Essex, was later charged as 'so notorious an innovator as that he set up the rails at his own charge, and that a year or two before any injunction', Jim Sharpe, 'Scandalous and Malignant Priests in Essex: The Impact of Grass-roots Puritanism', in Colin Jones, Malyn Newitt, and Stephen Roberts (eds.), *Politics and People in Revolutionary England: Essays in Honour of Ivan Roots* (Oxford, 1986), 261.

15. Williams to the Mayor of Leicester, 18 September 1633, Historical Manuscripts Commission, *Hastings*, vol. ii (1930), 74. See also the case of the vicar of Grantham whose attempt to instal an altar in 1627 met with opposition from the townsmen and the bishop, John Williams, *The Holy Table, Name and Thing* (1637; STC 25724), 6–10.

16. This version of the battle of the altars can be followed in Williams, *Holy Table, Name and Thing*; Peter Heylin, *A Coale from the Altar* (1636; STC 13270); Peter Heylin, *Antidotum Lincolniense* (1637; STC 13267); John Pocklington, *Altare Christianum* (1637; STC 20075); and William Prynne, *A Quench-Coale* (Amsterdam, 1637; STC 20474). For a lay observation in 1637 that 'so bitter are our churchmen now in their invectives one against the other, that it grieveth all good people to see it, and maketh us to fear the event', see Historical Manuscripts Commission, *Report on the Manuscripts of the Right Honourable Viscount De L'Isle*, vol. vi (1966), 95. See also C. E. Welch, 'The Downfall of Bishop Williams', *Transactions of the Leicestershire Archaeological and Historical Society*, 40 (1964–5), 42–58.

17. Norfolk Record Office, Norwich, VIS 6/4, not foliated.

18. Tyacke, *Anti-Calvinists*, 199–205; Davies, *Caroline Captivity*, 215–21; John Fielding, 'Arminianism in the Localities: Peterborough Diocese, 1603–1642', in Fincham (ed.), *Early Stuart Church*, 104–5; A. Percival Moore (ed.), 'The Metropolitical Visitation of Archdeacon [*sic*] Laud', in *Associated Architectural Societies' Reports and Papers*, 29 (1907), 488, 507. Wren's raising of chancel steps, installation of rails, and setting tables altarwise formed three of the articles of impeachment against

him in 1641, *Articles of Impeachment of the Commons . . . Against Matthew Wren* (1641), 4. Laud was blamed for similar innovations but his own visitation articles followed the more traditional form, locating the table in 'convenient sort, within the chancel or church', in *Articles to be Inquired of in the Metropolitical Visitation . . . in and for the Dioces of London* (1636; STC 102265.5), sig. A3.

19. Bodleian Library, Rawlinson MS D. 158, fo. 46v. See also Tyacke, *Anti-Calvinists*, 202–6; Kenneth Fincham, 'Episcopal Government, 1603–1640', in Fincham (ed.), *Early Stuart Church*, 80, for Brent's instructions at Dover in 1637.

20. Fincham (ed.), *Visitation Articles and Injunctions*, 91; Ronald Marchant, *The Puritans and the Church Courts in the Diocese of York* (1960), 56.

21. Borthwick Institute, York, Visitation Court Book 1636, fos. 83v, 449v, 492; the parishes of Anstey, Gresley, and Trowell in Nottinghamshire also lacked rails about their communion tables, ibid., fos. 506, 510, 522v.

22. For example, at St Edmund's, Salisbury, under the eye of the cathedral, the church-wardens spent four pounds late in 1633 'for making the rail in the chancel' and other work about the communion table, Henry J. F. Swayne (ed.), *Churchwardens Accounts of S. Edmund & S. Thomas, Sarum, 1443–1702* (Salisbury, 1896), 200. At Lambeth, Surrey, in Archbishop Laud's back yard, the churchwardens paid £1. 7s. 2d. in 1635 'to the joiner for removing the communion table'. Only fifteen years earlier they had paid £8. 15s. for major masonry and carpentry setting the table in the chancel; and in 1642 they would be at charge again 'for taking down the rails that were about the communion table', Charles Drew (ed.), *Lambeth Churchwardens Accounts 1504–1645* (Surrey Record Society, 1943), 109, 18, 171. Following Matthew Wren's visitation in 1636, the churchwardens of Cratfield, Suffolk, laid out two pounds 'the 6th day of September to Abraham Ellis for setting up the rails in the church', and an extra 3s. 4d. 'for fetching the rails from Laxfield', William Holland (ed.), *Cratfield. A Transcript of the Accounts of the Parish, from A.D. 1490 to A.D. 1642* (1895), 172. In Cheshire the churchwardens of Wilmslow railed their table in 1635; at Tilston they paid 'for railing in the holy table' in 1635; but at Middlewich no rail was erected until 1639, Judith Maltby, *Prayer Book and People in Elizabethan and Early Stuart England* (Cambridge, 1998), 200, 211, 222.

23. Laud in 1637, in *The Works of . . . William Laud, D.D.*, ed. W. Scott and J. Bliss (7 vols.; Oxford, 1847–60), vi. 57, qu. in Tyacke, *Anti-Calvinists*, 202; John Rushworth, *Historical Collections: The Second Volume of the Second Part* (1680), 126–7; Pock-lington, *Altare Christianum*, 132.

24. 'The priest being within the rail shall administer the same to the people without the rail.' *Calendar of State Papers, Domestic, 1640–41*, 346. See also G. W. O. Addleshaw and Frederick Etchells, *The Architectural Setting of Anglican Worship* (1948), 122–45.

25. *CSPD 1637*, 225.

26. *Articles of Enquiry and Direction for the Diocese of Norwich . . . 1638* (1638; STC 10299), sig. C4v; 'Constitutions and Canons Ecclesiastical . . . 1640', in *Works of . . . William Laud*, v. 625. See also Williams, *Holy Table, Name and Thing*; Heylin, *A Coale from the Altar*; Heylin, *Antidotum Lincolniense*; Pocklington, *Altare*

Christianum; and Joseph Mede, *The Name of Altar, or* ΘΥΣ ΙΑΣΤΗΡΙΟΝ, *anciently given to the Holy Table* (1637; STC 17768.5).

27. Moore (ed.), 'Metropolitical Visitation of Archdeacon [*sic*] Laud', 524; J. A. Robinson (ed.), 'Documents of the Laudian Period', in *Collecteana II*, Somerset Record Society, vol. 43 (1928), 183, 190. Kevin Sharpe, *Personal Rule*, 335, insists that Charles rather than Laud was the author of these instructions. For the related argument that to use God's table to collect money was to invite wrangling and swearing, see Walter Balcanquall, *The Honour of Christian Churches* (1634; STC 1238), 116–17.

28. Addleshaw and Etchells, *Architectural Setting of Anglican Worship*, 124; *CSPD 1640–41*, 204; Bodleian Library, Rawlinson MS D. 158, fo. 50v; 'Constitutions and Canons Ecclesiastical . . . 1640', in *Works of . . . William Laud*, v. 625.

29. Public Record Office, SP/16/388/41; Borthwick Institute, York, V.1640, fo. 130; Bodleian Library, Rawlinson MS D. 1480, fo. 118; Leicestershire Record Office, RO, 1 D 41/21.

30. *Articles exhibited against Benjamin Spencer* (1642), 4.

31. Ephraim Udall, *Communion Comlinesse* (1641), 12–13.

32. Thomas Cheshire, *A True Copy of that Sermon which was preached at S. Pauls the tenth day of October last* (1641), 12.

33. *Articles to be Inquired of within the Diocese of Ely* (1638; STC 10197).

34. Ibid., sigs. A2v, A3. See also Wren's 'Particular Orders, Directions, and Remembrances Given in the Dioces of Norwich . . . 1636', in Cardwell (ed.), *Documentary Annals*, ii. 253–8; Parliamentary charges against Wren in 1641, in Wallington, *Historical Notices*, i. 154–66.

35. *Articles of Enquiry and Direction for the Diocese of Norwich . . . 1638* (1638; STC 10299), sigs. A2v, A4v, B, C4, C4v. See also Brian Duppa's 1638 articles for Chichester, in Addleshaw and Etchells *Architectural Setting of Anglican Worship*, 128.

36. Among the ministers ejected in Suffolk, Jeremiah Raven, the rector of Great Blakenham, allegedly had so much 'zeal for the bringing in of innovations' that 'contrary to his parishioners' knowledge and consent [he] set men to work to make and set up rails [and] raise[d] the ground in the chancel three steps high'. Theodore Beale of Ash Bocking was cited as 'a solemn cringer and bower toward the east end of the chancel and towards the communion table' who 'denied the sacrament unto such as would not come to the rail'. Robert Sugden of Benhall likewise 'caused the communion table to be turned altarwise and to be set at the upper end of the chancel under the east window and commonly bowed to the said table'. So fierce was he for exact conformity, his enemies alleged, that even old, lame, and blind parishioners were denied the sacrament if they did not 'kneel before the rail'. Clive Holmes (ed.), *The Suffolk Committees for Scandalous Ministers 1644–1646* (Suffolk Records Society, Ipswich, 1970), 18–19, 40, 41–2, 68, 91.

37. *The Petition and Article Exhibited in Parliament against Doctor Heywood* (1641), 1, 5–7, 9.

38. Tyacke, *Anti-Calvinists*, 239; *The Works of . . . William Laud*, v. 624–6.

39. Ibid. 626; Davies, *Caroline Captivity*, 251–87, esp. 261, where it is again pointed out

that Laud himself did not go so far as Wren and some others in enforcing communion at the rails.

40. William Juxon, *Articles to be Enquired of Within the Diocese of London* (1640; STC 10267), sig. A3v.

41. See, for example, Wallington, *Historical Notices*, i. 23–8.

42. Charles Chauncey, *The Retraction of Mr Charles Chancy formerly Minister of Ware in Harfordshire. Wherein is proved the unlawfulness and danger of Rayling in Altars or Communion Tables* (1641), 6.

43. William Prynne, *A Breviate of the Prelates Intolerable Usurpations* (Amsterdam, 1637; STC 20454), 108–9. [William Prynne?] *Newes from Ipswich* (1641 edn.), sig. A3.

44. *CSPD 1634–35*, 22; *CSPD 1636–37*, 37; *CSPD 1640*, 272, 528; *CSPD 1640–41*, 126.

45. Public Record Office, SP16/372/109, fo. 1. Comments of this sort spread surreptitiously in the late 1630s, to emerge as a cascade of accusation in 1640 and 1641.

46. John Ley, *A Letter (Against the erection of an Altar) Written Iune 29, 1635* (1641), 2–5; John Ley, *A Discourse Concerning Puritans* (1641), 14. For Bishop Bridgeman's adoption of the Laudian programme, see Maltby, *Prayer Book and People*, 139–41.

47. HL undated petition of 1640.

48. Robinson (ed.), 'Documents of the Laudian Period', 183–202; Thomas Garden Barnes, *Somerset 1625–1640: A County's Government During the 'Personal Rule'* (Cambridge, Mass., 1961), 16–17; J. S. Cockburn (ed.), *Western Circuit Assize Orders 1629–1648* (Camden Society, 4th ser. 17; 1976), 143, 169, 198. The churchwardens were gaoled on a writ *de excommunicate capiendo*, and were eventually absolved after performing penance. One of them allegedly suffered 'a consumption through grief' and died soon after. The Beckington case was one of the first to concern the House of Commons at the end of 1640, and was cited in *Articles of Accusation and Impeachment Of the House of Commons, and all the Commons of England Against William Pierce Doctor of Divinitie and Bishop of Bath and Wells* (1642), 6; John Rushworth, *Historical Collections, The Second Part* (1680), 300.

49. Ibid. 5.

50. *CSPD 1641–43*, 525.

51. Historical Manuscripts Commission, *The Manuscripts of the House of Lords*, xi: *Addenda 1517–1714* (1962), 253.

52. HL Petition of 8 January 1641.

53. HL Order of 22 December 1640.

54. HL Petition of 6 February 1641. The diarist Robert Woodford, steward of Northampton, recorded further details of this struggle over the table. By Woodford's account, diocesan officials ordered the table set altarwise in August 1637, and it was moved 'to the very top' of the church in November. The churchwardens' refusal to instal rails brought them before Dr Clark in December 1637 when, instead of conforming, they defiantly moved the table down from the 'top' and 'set it longwise in the body of the chancel'. Within a month they were excommunicated, and the table was presumably set altarwise again. The disputed rail was installed in March 1638. A year later, in time for the Easter communion in April 1639, the table

was 'brought down' to its former place, and Woodford prayed, 'Lord, keep us still from sinful innovations', 'The Diary of Robert Woodford', in Historical Manuscripts Commission, *Ninth Report* (1884), appendix, 496–8. See also John Fielding, 'Opposition to the Personal Rule of Charles I: The Diary of Robert Woodford, 1637–1641', *Historical Journal*, 31 (1988), 769–88, esp. 783–5; and Webster, *Godly Clergy*, 216–23.

55. *CSPD 1640–41*, 351.

56. Historical Manuscripts Commission, *Reports of Manuscripts in Various Collections* (1907), iv. 306. Here too churchwardens were excommunicated for their non-cooperation.

57. R. F. B. Hodgkinson (ed.), 'Extracts from the Act Books of the Archdeacons of Nottingham', *Transactions of the Thoroton Society*, 31 (1928), 136–7.

58. Guildhall Library, MS 9064/21, fo. 23v.

59. Huntington Library, San Marino, MS STTM, box 20/25. The parish is probably Burton Dasset, Warwickshire. Parishioners complained of the 'new fashions' their minister had introduced, 'things out of use and not known in our church till he came', and his suppression of other practices which were 'according to the ancient fashion in our church'.

60. Bodleian Library, Rawlinson MS D. 158, fos. 50v, 46–46v. These observations conflate Drake's response to the Committee on Religion in 1641 and his answer to further complaints in 1643.

61. Ibid., fos. 43–55.

62. *CSPD 1640*, 486.

63. *CSPD 1640*, 517, 522; Public Record Office, SP/16 463/27; Webster, *Godly Clergy*, 213; Mark Charles Fissel, *The Bishops' Wars; Charles I's Campaigns against Scotland. 1638–1640* (Cambridge, 1994), 264–9. Richard Drake, the Laudian minister of Radwinter, claimed that the soldiers 'were invited to the fact. They were but instrumental', working on behalf of disaffected parishioners, Bodleian Library, Rawlinson MS D. 158, fo. 50. Wallington, *Historical Notices*, i. 122–3, adds to the report the information that the soldiers tied the Radwinter images to a tree and whipped them, and tossed a dead duck into Drake's church with an ominous play on his name. The symbolism may also have been aimed at Arthur Duck, the chancellor of the diocese of London who had encouraged Drake in his innovations.

64. *CSPD 1640*, 580.

65. John Vicars, *A Sight of ye Trans-actions of these latter yeares* (1646), 6, 7 and illustration. Cf. William Hawkins to the Earl of Leicester in August 1640, 'our soldiers in divers places commit great disorders, even in our churches, pulling down the rail about the communion table in a strange manner', HMC *De L'Isle*, iv. 318.

66. *CSPD 1640*, 7, 12, 22; Public Record Office, SP16/466/23, fos. 67–73. For the bitter background to the battle of the altar rails at Rickmansworth, see Wallington, *Historical Notices*, i. 70–1. Legally it only took three people to make a riot.

67. W. J. Hardy (ed.), *Hertford County Records. Notes and Extracts from the Sessions Rolls 1581 to 1698* (Hertford, 1905), 64–5. Richard Mose, Matthew Osborne, and George

Thoroughgood apparently undertook the iconoclasm at the behest of local men George Nobnall, Thomas Pomfret, and John Skingle.

68. *CSPD 1640–41*, 69–70, 140; Public Record Office, SP16/467/79 (2, 4, 7, and 17 September 1640).

69. SP16/470/55; Mary Anne Everett Green (ed.), *The Diary of John Rous* (Camden Society, 1856), 99; Wallington, *Historical Notices*, i. 123–6.

70. Essex Record Office, Chelmsford, Q/Sba 2/41. Exodus 20 includes the Ten Commandments. Exodus 20: 25–6 appears to forbid hewn altars and altar steps.

71. *CSPD 1641–43*, 473, 507, 517.

72. Marchant, *Puritans and the Church Courts*, 61, 67–8, 194–7; *The Petition and Articles Exhibited by the Parishioners of Pont Iland and others in the County of Northumberland, against Dr Gray* (1641), sig. A3, complaining that 'Gray caused the table to be removed and placed altarwise close to the wall of the east end of the choir, according to the lord of Canterbury's fashion'.

73. Holmes (ed.), *Suffolk Committees*, 9–10.

74. *The Petition and Articles or Severall Charge exhibited in Parliament against Edward Finch* (1641); Edward Finch, *An Answer to the Articles Preferred Against Edward Finch* (1641); *Articles Exhibited in Parliament against Master Iohn Sqvire, Vicar of Saint Leonard Shoreditch, August 7th. 1641* (1641); HL Petition of 13 May 1641 against Richard Etkins, of Kensington, Middlesex; British Library, Add. MS 22,084, fos. 8–8v, against Thomas Lawrence of Bemerton, Wiltshire; HL Petition of 13 January 1641 against John Pocklington; *The Petition and Articles, or Severall Charge exhibited in Parliament against John Pocklington* (164). See also John Rushworth, *Historical Collections: The Third Part* (1692), 58–9 for the charge against Edward Layfield of All Hallows, Barking; H. Parker, *The Altar Dispute, or A Discovrse Concerning the Severall Innovations of the Altar* (1641), 7, 28, 33, 66.

75. HL Petitions of 20 and 22 July 1641; John Nalson, *An Impartial Collection of the Great Affairs of State* (2 vols.; 1683–4), ii. 328; Maltby, *Prayer Book and People*, 122.

76. Lindley, *Popular Politics and Religion*, 41

77. William Grant, *The Vindication of the Vicar of Isleworth* (1641), 18.

78. Historical Manuscripts Commission, *The Manuscripts of His Grace the Duke of Portland Preserved at Welbeck Abbey* (1894), iii. 76, 80.

79. Bruno Ryves on Chelmsford in 1641, in *Mercurius Rusticus: Or, the Countries Complaint* (1646), 22.

80. *The Brownists Conventicle* (1641), 5.

81. HMC *Various*, ii. 259–60. Bishop John Williams of Lincoln, acting dean of Westminster, was said to be 'very ready to yield' to these reconversions. See also Nalson, *Impartial Collection of the Great Affairs of State*, i. 507, 537.

82. Orders of 16 January and 1 March reprinted in John Williams, *Articles to be enquired of Within the Diocese of Lincoln* (1641), sig. C2.

83. *A Declaration of the Commons in Parliament made Septemb. 9. 1641* (1641), sig. A2v; *The Orders from the Hovse of Commons for the Abolishing of Superstition, and*

Innovation, in the Regulating of Church Affaires (1641), 1–3; Public Record Office, SP16/484/16; *CSPD 1641–43*, 120; John Morrill, *The Nature of the English Revolution* (1993), 87–8, 170; Conrad Russell, *The Fall of the British Monarchies 1637–1642* (Oxford, 1995), 368, 404.

84. Chauncey, *Retraction of Mr Charles Chancy*; H. Parker, *The Altar Dispute, or A Discovrse Concerning the Severall Innovations of the Altar* (1641), 33, 67; H. Jacob, *Kneeling in the Act of Eating and Drinking at The Lords Table is a Sinne* (1641); J.W., *Certain Affirmations In Defence of the Pulling Down of Communion Rails, by divers rash and misguided people judiciously and religiously answered* (1641), 3–6.

85. John Williams, *Articles to be enquired of Within the Diocese of Lincoln* (1641), sigs. A2, A3v, B2v, B3v. For a caustic review of Williams's part in the altar controversy, see Richard Dey, *Two Looks over Lincolne, or A View of his Holy Table, Name and Thing, Discovering his Erronious and Popish Tenets and Positions* (1641).

86. *The Heads of Several Petitions and Complaints* (1641), 2, 4.

87. *Articles exhibited against Benjamin Spencer* (1642), 2.

88. John Bond, *A Doore of Hope* (1641), 48, 53.

89. Holmes (ed.), *Suffolk Committees*, 64, 73, 81, 87.

90. HL Petition of 9 February 1641.

91. *The Curates Conference* (1641), 6–7; *CSPD 1641–43*, 89.

92. Henry Ellis (ed.), 'Letters from a Subaltern officer of the Earl of Essex's Army, Written in the Summer and Autumn of 1642', *Archaeologia*, 35 (1853), 321–3. The writer is Nehemiah Wharton.

93. Huntington Library, Ellesmere MS 7765.

94. Margaret Aston, *England's Iconoclasts*, i: *Laws Against Images* (Oxford, 1988), 62, 73; Thomas Paske, *The Copy of a Letter sent to an Honourable Lord* (1642), 4; Bruno Ryves, *Mercurius Rusticus* (1646; 1685 edn.), 136, 139, 140, 154. See also, with caution, William Dugdale, *A Short View of the Late Troubles in England* (Oxford, 1681), 557–60.

95. C. H. Firth and R. S. Rait (eds.), *Acts and Ordinances of the Interregnum, 1642–1660* (3 vols.; 1911), i. 265.

96. C. H. Evelyn White (ed.), *The Journal of William Dowsing* (Ipswich, 1885), 15–33; J. G. Cheshire (ed.), 'William Dowsing's Destructions in Cambridgeshire', *Cambridgeshire and Huntingdonshire Archaeological Society Transactions*, 3 (1909–14), 77–91. See also John Morrill, 'William Dowsing, the Bureaucratic Puritan', in John Morrill, Paul Slack, and Daniel Woolf (eds.), *Public Duty and Private Conscience in Seventeenth-Century England* (Oxford, 1993), 173–203.

CHAPTER 13

1. William Prynne, *A New Discovery of the Prelates Tyranny in their Late Prosecutions of Mr William Pryn* (1641), 1.

2. S. R. Gardiner (ed.), *Documents Relating to the Proceedings Against William Prynne,*

   in 1634 and 1637 (Camden Society, NS 18; 1877); Ethyn Williams Kirby, *William Prynne: A Study in Puritanism* (Cambridge, Mass., 1931); William M. Lamont, *Marginal Prynne 1600–1669* (1963).

3. Cf. Kevin Sharpe, *The Personal Rule of Charles I* (New Haven and London, 1992), esp. 285, 360, 610, 676, 680–2, 758–65.

4. Michel Foucault, *Discipline and Punishment* (New York, 1977); Peter Lake and Michael Questier, 'Agency, Appropriation and Rhetoric Under the Gallows: Puritans, Romanists and the State in Early Modern England', *Past and Present*, 153 (1996), 64–107.

5. William Prynne, *Histrio-Mastix. The Players Scovrge, or, Actors Tragaedie* (1633; STC 20464).

6. William Prynne to Archbishop Laud, 11 June 1634, in Gardiner (ed.), *Documents*, 42.

7. (John Marston?), *Histrio-Mastix. Or. The Player Whipt* (1610; STC 13529). This play, performed by the boys of St Paul's in 1599, presented play-going as a proper pastime for citizens and lawyers, and associated the actors with harmony and peace. The presumed author, John Marston, gave up the theatre for the Church, becoming minister of Christchurch, Hampshire, from 1616 to 1631. He was still alive when Prynne's *Histrio-Mastix* was published, dying in London in 1634. A Latin comedy with a similar title, *Fucus Sive Histrio-Mastix*, was perfomed at Cambridge in 1623, Alfred Harbage, *Annals of English Drama, 975–1700* (revised edn., Philadelphia, 1964), 64–5, 94–5.

8. Prynne, *Histrio-Mastix*, 9, 830.

9. 'The best actors in the world, either for tragedy, comedy, history, pastoral, pastoral-comical, historical-pastoral, tragical-historical, tragical-comical-historical-pastoral', William Shakespeare, *Hamlet*, Act II, Scene ii.

10. *Histrio-Mastix* was published 'about Christ-tide 1632' according to Prynne, *New Discovery*, 8.

11. William Prynne, *The Church of Englands Old Antithesis to New Arminianisme* (1629; STC 20457).

12. Prynne, *Histrio-Mastix*, 821.

13. Borthwick Institute, York, Cause Papers, H.2046.

14. Public Record Office, SP 16/231/71, 16/242/50, 16/245/6; Bulstrode Whitelock, *Memorials of English Affairs* (1732), 18.

15. John Rushworth, *Historical Collections. The Second Part* (1680), 220–41.

16. Thomas B. Howell (ed.), *Cobbett's Complete Collection of State Trials*, vol. iii (1809), 563, 566; Gardiner (ed.), *Documents*, 1–13.

17. Howell (ed.), *State Trials*, iii. 564–5; Gardiner (ed.), *Documents*, 14–15.

18. Howell (ed.), *State Trials*, iii. 574, 577–8; Gardiner (ed.), *Documents*, 20–1.

19. Howell (ed.), *State Trials*, iii. 582–3. The reference is to the biblical Achan, who troubled Israel by secreting 'the accursed thing', Joshua 7: 1–26. See also Blair Worden, 'Oliver Cromwell and the Sin of Achan', in Derek Beales and Geoffrey Best (eds.), *History, Society, and the Churches: Essays in Honour of Owen Chadwick* (Cambridge, 1985), 125–45.

20. Howell (ed.), *State Trials*, iii. 576.

21. Ibid.; Prynne, *New Discovery*, 10–11.

22. Howell (ed.), *State Trials*, iii. 585, 58; Gardiner (ed.), *Documents*, 25.

23. Charles Ripley Gillett, *Burned Books: Neglected Chapters in British History and Literature* (New York, 1932), 190, 223, 245.

24. Gardiner (ed.), *Documents*, 29.

25. William Knowler (ed.), *The Earl of Strafforde's Letters and Dispatches* (2 vols.; 1739), i. 261; Kirby, *William Prynne*, 29–31.

26. Sharpe, *Personal Rule*, 676.

27. *Calendar of State Papers, Domestic, 1633–34*, 524.

28. Gardiner (ed.), *Documents*, 33.

29. Prynne, *New Discovery*, 7; Henry Burton, *A Divine Tragedie Lately Acted* (1636; STC 4140.7). Noy died in 1634.

30. Burton, *Divine Tragedie*, 44.

31. Wallington quoted in Kirby, *William Prynne*, 30; *William Whiteway of Dorchester His Diary 1618 to 1635* (Dorset Record Society, 12; 1991), 144.

32. Huntington Library, San Marino, MS HM 55603, not foliated.

33. Gardiner (ed.), *Documents*, 32–56.

34. Ibid.; Knowler (ed.), *Earl of Strafforde's Letters*, ii. 266.

35. William Prynne, *A Breviate of the Prelates Intolerable Usurpations, both upon the Kings Prerogative Royall, and the Subjects Liberties* (Amsterdam, 1637; STC 20454); *Briefe Instructions for Church-wardens* (1637? STC 20454.5); *The Vnbishoping of Timothy and Titvs* (1636; STC 20476); *Newes from Ipswich* (Edinburgh ? 1636; STC 20469).

36. *Newes from Ipswich*, sigs. A2–B2. A slightly less explosive version, with some of the more insulting adjectives removed, was republished in London in 1641 (British Library, E.177 (12)).

37. Burton, *Divine Tragedie*. See also Henry Burton, *For God and the King. The Summe of Two Sermons* (1636; STC 4141).

38. HMC, *Report on the Manuscripts of the Right Honourable Viscount De L'Isle* (*Sidney Papers*), vol. vi (1966), 96.

39. *CSPD 1636–37*, 565; *CSPD 1637*, 49; HMC *De L'Isle*, vi. 105, 108; Rushworth, *Historical Collections. The Second Part*, 380–5.

40. Gardiner (ed.), *Documents*, 75–6; HMC *De L'Isle*, vi. 112; Henry Burton, *A Narrative of the Life of Henry Burton* (1643), 12.

41. *CSPD 1637*, 249; Gardiner (ed.), *Documents*, 62–9.

42. Thomas Fuller, *The Church History of Britain* (1655), book 11, 153–4; Prynne, *New Discovery*, 65. For a modern analysis of the state's use of pain to silence and negate opponents, see Elaine Scarry, *The Body in Pain: The Making and Unmaking of the World* (New York, 1985). Prynne, decisively, refused to be silenced or negated.

43. Public Record Office, SP16/363/42; Gardiner (ed.), *Documents*, 90; Prynne, *New Discovery*, 65–6; Lamont, *Marginal Prynne*, 39.

44. *CSPD 1637*, 209.

45. HMC *De L'Isle*, vi. 112, 115.

46. Quoted in Sharpe, *Personal Rule*, 697.

47. *CSPD 1638–39*, 587.

48. Gardiner (ed.), *Documents*, 86–7; Public Record Office, SP16/362/42. See also George Garrard's newletters, in Knowler (ed.), *Earl of Strafforde's Letters*, ii. 85, and Prynne's own account in *New Discovery*, 33–4, 44, 64–5.

49. Fuller, *Church History of Britain*, book 11, 153.

50. *CSPD 1637*, 332, 344. Prynne himself retold the story of the people who 'dipped their handkerchers in [the blood] as a thing most precious', in *New Discovery*, 59.

51. SP16/372/109; Burton, *Narrative of the Life*, 14; Kirby, *William Prynne*, 47.

52. Gardiner (ed.), *Documents*, 91.

53. *CSPD 1637–38*, 139.

54. SP16/361/117.

55. SP16/375/82.

56. SP16/472/48; SP16/406/88.

57. Wallington quoted in Kirby, *William Prynne*, 44; Prynne, *New Discovery*, 33.

58. Burton, *Narrative of the Life*, 14.

59. HMC *De L'Isle*, vi. 120.

60. *CSPD 1637*, 332.

61. Gardiner (ed.), *Documents*, 66; *CSPD 1637*, 414, 456.

62. *CSPD 1637*, 433, 434.

63. *CSPD 1637*, 403, 492; Prynne, *New Discovery*, 92–3; Knowler (ed.), *Earl of Strafforde's Letters*, ii. 115; Edward Burghall, 'Providence Improved', in T. Worthington Barlow (ed.), *Cheshire: Its Historical and Literary Associations* (Manchester and London, 1859), 156.

64. The Revd Canon Blomfield, 'On Puritanism in Chester in 1637: An Account of the Reception of William Prynne', *Journal of the Architectural, Archaeological and Historic Society, for the County, City, and Neighbourhood of Chester*, 3 (1885), 284. The story is also told in R. C. Richardson, *Puritanism in North-West England: A Regional Study of the Diocese of Chester to 1642* (Manchester, 1972), 182–3.

65. *CSPD 1638–39*, 1142.

66. Prynne, *New Discovery*, 103

67. Ibid. 218–20, 221.

68. Ibid. 104–5.

69. Kenneth Fincham, *Prelate as Pastor: The Episcopate of James I* (Oxford, 1990), 31, 289–91.

70. Prynne, *New Discovery*, 107. On the same day as the bonfire the authorities secured public penance from the principal citizens of Chester who had treated Prynne with compassion, Chester City Record Office, Corporation Assembly Book, A/B/2 (1624–8), fo. 42v. Some of them were heavily fined and detained for a month in York castle, John Southerton Burn, *The High Commission. Notices of the Court and its Proceedings* (1865), 64–5.

71. Lawrence M. Clopper (ed.), *Records of Early English Drama: Chester* (Toronto, 1979).

72. Prynne, *New Discovery*, 105.

73. Ibid. 214.

74. Ibid. 112.

75. William Prynne, *Health's Sicknesse: Or a Compendious Discourse Proving the Drinking of Healthes to be Sinfull* (1628; STC 20462).

76. SP16/473/113; SP16/473/48. A royalist broadsheet of 1643 also rhymed derisively about 'Saint Prynne', *A Vindication of Cheapside Cross* (Oxford, 1643).

77. Prynne, *New Discovery*, 114–15; Burton, *Narrative of the Life*, 41.

78. Historical Manuscripts Commission, *The Manuscripts of the Earl Cowper Preserved at Melbourne Hall, Derbyshire* [Coke MSS] (1888), ii. 267.

79. Historical Manuscripts Commission, *Report on the Manuscripts of the Duke of Buccleuch* [Montague papers, second series] (vol. iii, 1926), 395.

80. New College Oxford, MS 9502, 'Robert Woodforde's Diary', 28 November 1640.

81. HMC *De L'Isle*, vi. 346; HMC, *The Manuscripts of Lord Kenyon* (1894), 60; HMC *Manuscripts of S. H. Le Fleming, Esq. Of Rydal Hall* (1890), 18.

82. David Laing (ed.), *The Letters and Journals of Robert Baillie* (3 vols., Edinburgh, 1841), i. 277; 'Robert Woodforde's Diary', 28 November 1640.

83. Laing (ed.), *Letters and Journals of Robert Baillie*, i. 277.

84. Allen B. Hinds (ed.), *Calendar of State Papers and Manuscripts, Relating to English Affairs, Existing in the Archives and Collections of Venice*, vol. xxv: *1640–1642* (1924), 103.

85. Robert Chestlin, *Persecutio Undecima: The Churches Eleventh Persecution* (1648), 21.

86. Hobbes quoted in Kirby, *William Prynne*, 53.

87. W. Dunn Macray (ed.) *The History of the Rebellion and Civil Wars . . . by Edward, Earl of Clarendon* (6 vols.; Oxford, 1888), i. 269.

88. Prynne, *New Discovery*, 116.

89. *CSPD 1641*, 531; Prynne, *New Discovery*, *passim*.

90. *CSPD 1641*, 587; Prynne, *New Discovery*, 144; Kirby, *William Prynne*, 56.

91. Prynne, *New Discovery*, 201, 226.

CHAPTER 14

1. Richard Carter, *The Schismatick Stigmatized* (1641), 1, 13.

2. *The Dolefull Lamentation of Cheap-side Crosse: or old England sick of the Staggers* (1641), 8.

3. John Gough Nichols (ed.), *The Diary of Henry Machyn, Citizen and Merchant-Taylor of London, from A.D. 1550 to A.D. 1563* (Camden Society, 1848), 58–60.

4. Edward Dering, 'A Briefe and Necessary Catechism' (1572), in *Maister Derings Workes* (Middleburg, 1590?), 'to the Christian reader', not paginated.

5. John Stow, *Annales, or a Generall Chronicle of England* (1631; STC 23340), 694. In

another account, 'the Virgin . . . was robbed of her son, and her arms broken, by which she stayed him on her knees; the whole body was haled by ropes and left ready to fall', William Andrews, *Old Church Lore* (Hull, 1891), 143.

6. Ryhen Pameach [Henry Peacham], *A Dialogue Between the Crosse in Cheap, and Charing Crosse* (1641), sig. A2v.

7. *Analytical Index of the Series of Records Known as the Remembrancia, Preserved Among the Archives of the City of London, AD 1579–1664* (1878), 65–6; Corporation of London Records Office, Repertories 5, fo. 291; 6, fos. 59v, 69v; 13, fos. 167, 189v; 14, fo. 102; 20, fo. 216v; Margaret Aston, *The King's Bedpost: Reformation and Iconography in a Tudor Group Portrait* (Cambridge, 1993), 110.

8. Corporation of London Records Office, Journal 25, fo. 230v; Repertories 25, fos. 24, 263v.

9. *Cheap-side Crosse Censured and Condemned by a Letter Sent from the Vicechancellour* (1641), 3–10.

10. *Cheap-side Crosse Censured and Condemned*, 7, 8. The pious king Hezekiah had smashed the images and idols of Judah, 2 Kings 18: 4. Edward VI, who had presided over the iconoclasm of 1547–8, was often recalled as 'the young Hezekiah'.

11. Kenneth Fincham and Peter Lake, 'The Ecclesiastical Policy of James I', *Journal of British Studies*, 24 (1985), 188, 195.

12. Jacqueline Eales, *Puritans and Roundheads: The Harleys of Brampton Bryan and the Outbreak of the English Civil War* (Cambridge, 1990), 47.

13. Corporation of London Record Office, Repertories 30, fo. 244v; 35, fo. 243; 39, fo. 219v; 40, fos. 337–337v, 342v; 41, fo. 336v.

14. *Cheapsides Triumphs, and Chyrones Crosses Lamentation*, in Hyder Edward Rollins (ed.), *The Pepys Ballads* (8 vols.; Cambridge, Mass., 1929–32), ii. 49–53.

15. Peacham, *Dialogue Between the Crosse in Cheap, and Charing Crosse*, sig. A2v.

16. Ibid., sig. A2.

17. Allen B. Hinds (ed.), *Calendar of State Papers and Manuscripts, Relating to English Affairs, Existing in the Archives and Collections of Venice*, vol. xxvi: 1642–43 (1924), 272; *The Downe-fall of Dagon, or the taking downe of Cheap-side Crosse* (1643), not paginated. The author used the name 'Dagon' ironically, making clear in his text that he disagreed with the puritan view that the Cross was akin to an idol.

18. Peter Lake and Michael Questier, 'Agency, Appropriation and Rhetoric Under the Gallows: Puritans, Romanists and the State in Early Modern England', *Past and Present*, 153 (1996), 77, citing William Allen, *Brief Historie of the Glorious Martyrdom* (1908), 12.

19. *Analytical Index of the . . . Remembrancia*, 66.

20. *Cheap-side Crosse Censured and Condemned*, 7, 6, 5.

21. *Cheap-side Crosse Censured and Condemned*, 12, 14.

22. *A Discovery of 29 Sects here in London* (1641), 3.

23. *The Popes Proclamation: Together with . . . Six Articles Exhibited Against Cheapside Crosse* (1641), sig. A4. The same point was made in Henry Burton, *Englands*

Bondage and Hope of Deliverance. A Sermon Preached before the Honourable House of Parliament . . . Iune 20. 1641 (1641), 30.

24. *The Crosses Case in Cheapside* (1642), 22.

25. *Downe-fall of Dagon*, n.p.; Historical Manuscripts Commission, *Report on the Manuscripts of Lord Montagu of Beaulieu* (1900), 147.

26 *Cheap-side Crosse Censured and Condemned*, 1, 11; *The Crosses Case in Cheapside*, 6, 8; Abraham Cowley, *A Satyre Against Seperatists* (1642), 6. Much-cited verses included 2 Kings 18: 4, Judges 8: 27, Judges 2: 11–14, Judges 16: 23, and Joshua 7: 13.

27. *Cheap-side Crosse Censured and Condemned*, 13–14.

28. Burton, *Englands Bondage*, 30.

29. *The Brownists Conventicle: Or an Assembly of Brownists, Separatists, and Non-Conformists* (1641), 7. See also John Taylor, *The Anatomy of the Separatists, alias, Brownists, the factious Brethren, in these Times* (1642), 4.

30. *The Adamites Sermon* (1641), 7.

31. T. J., *A Medicine for the Times. Or, An Antidote Against Faction* (1641), sig. A3.

32. Peacham, *Dialogue Between the Crosse in Cheap, and Charing Crosse*, sig. A3. This complaint was repeated in *The Downe-fall of Dagon* (1643), with the addition that the Brownists directed stones at the Cross as well as spit.

33. Peacham, *Dialogue Between the Crosse in Cheap, and Charing Crosse*, sig. A4v.

34. *A Medicine for the Times*, sigs. A2v–A3.

35. *A Remonstrance of Londons Occurrences* (1641), sig. A2.

36. *The Resolution of those Contemners that will have no Crosses* (1641), sig. A4. A similar couplet appears in Thorny Ailo [John Taylor], *A full and compleat Answer against the Writer of a late Volume . . . Together with some excellent verses on the defacing of Cheap-side Crosse* (1642), 6.

37. *The Crosses Case in Cheapside* (1642), sig. A3, 1.

38. Ibid. 9, 11, 27, 46.

39. Samuel Loveday, *An Answer to the Lamentation of Cheap-side Crosse* (1642), 5. 4.

40. Historical Manuscripts Commission, *12th Report*, appendix, pt. 2, *The Manuscripts of the Earl Cowper, K.G., Preserved at Melbourne Hall, Derbyshire*, vol. ii (1888), 304.

41. Richard Overton, *Articles of High Treason Exhibited Against Cheapside Crosse* (1642), 4. See also John Taylor, *A Tale of a Tub* (1641), 2, 4, which purports to give comfort to the Brownist iconoclasts who attempted 'the holy destruction of that nest of idols' and who 'bare away the lead'.

42. *The Distractions of Our Times* (1642), 5.

43. Overton, *Articles of High Treason Exhibited Against Cheapside Crosse*, 1, 2. See also Robert Chestlin, *Persecutio Undecima. The Churches Eleventh Persecution* (1648), 66 for a history of 'the nightly tumults about pulling down Cheapside Cross' and the providential punishment of some of the iconoclasts.

44. *The Resolution of those Contemners that will have no Crosses*, sigs. A2v, A3. Cf. Carter, *Schismatick Stigmatized*, 1.

45. *The Resolution of the Round-Heads, To pull downe Cheap-side Crosse* (1641), 3. This work is sometimes attributed to John Taylor.

46. *The Wicked Resolution of the Cavaliers* (1642), 2–3.

47. *Calendar of State Papers, Domestic, 1642*, 274; *The Crosses Case in Cheapside*, 4, 15.

48. Ibid. 4.

49. Taylor, *Full and compleat Answer*, 6.

50. Ibid. 7–8.

51. *The Dolefull Lamentation of Cheap-side Crosse*, 7–8. The name Jasper suggests a slightly ridiculous personality as well as the bright display of the gemstone.

52. Loveday, *Answer to the Lamentation*, sigs. A2–A2v.

53. Ibid. 5.

54. *The Remarkable Fvneral of Cheapside-Crosse* (1642), sigs. A2, A3v.

55. Overton, *Articles of high Treason*, 5.

56. *The Crosses Case in Cheapside*, 1, 8, 17.

57. Corporation of London Record Office, Journal 40, fo. 58v.

58. *Mercurius Aulicus*, 30 April–6 May 1643; John Vicars, *Jehovah-Jireh. God in the Mount. Or, Englands Parliamentarie-Chronicle* (1644), 32; *CSP Venetian 1642–43*, 272. George Thomason picked up a copy of *Cheap-side Crosse Censured and Condemned* (1641) in April 1643, just a few days before the authorities oversaw its final destruction.

59. *CSP Venetian 1642–43*, 272.

60. Vicars, *Jehovah-Jireh*, 321.

61. 'Diary of Sir Humphrey Mildmay, 1633–52', British Library, Harleian MS 454, fo. 50. Mildmay was 'a whimsical and feckless country gentleman' from Danbury, Essex, according to William Hunt, *The Puritan Moment* (Cambridge, Mass., 1983), 269.

62. *Downe-fall of Dagon.*

63. *CSP Venetian 1642–43*, 272; *Downe-fall of Dagon.*

64. *Downe-fall of Dagon*; Vicars, *Jehovah-Jireh*, 327.

65. Ibid. 327–8.

66. Ibid. 328. See also John Vicars, *A Sight of ye Trans-actions of these latter yeares* (1646), 20–1 and illustration.

67. *Downe-fall of Dagon.*

68. 'Jasper Cross his last will' in *Downe-fall of Dagon.*

69. *A Vindication of Cheapside Crosse against the Roundheads* (Oxford, 1643).

70. 'The Downfall of Cheapside-Cross, May 2, 3, 4, 1643', in *Rump: or an exact Collection of the Choycest Poems and Songs relating to the Late Times* (1662; 1874 edn.), 138–9.

Chapter 15

1. Christopher Hill, *The World Turned Upside Down: Radical Ideas During the English Revolution* (1972).

2. See, for example, *A Curb for Sectaries and Bold Propheciers* (1641); *A Discoverie of Six women preachers* (1641).

3. *A Discovery of 29 Sects here in London* (1641), 4; *A Catalogue of the severall Sects and*

Opinions in England and other Nations. With a briefe Rehearsall of their false and dangerous Tenents (1647).

4. Hill, *World Turned Upside Down*, 253; J. F. McGregor and B. Reay, *Radical Religion in the English Revolution* (Oxford, 1984). The Adamites are mentioned briefly in Jerome Friedman, *Blasphemy, Immorality, and Anarchy: The Ranters and the English Revolution* (Athens, Ohio, 1987), 283–4, and *The Battle of the Frogs and Fairford's Flies: Miracles and the Pulp Press During the English Revolution* (New York, 1993), 94–6. Continental Adamites of the fifteenth and sixteenth centuries make brief appearances in George Huntson Williams, *The Radical Reformation* (3rd edn.; Kirksville, Missouri, 1992), 318, 584, 761, 1069. The Adamites are mentioned, but not discussed, in James Grantham Turner, *One Flesh: Paradisal Marriage and Sexual Relations in the Age of Milton* (Oxford, 1987), 37, 82, 84, 85, and in Dagmar Freist, *Governed by Opinion: Politics, Religion and the Dynamics of Communication in Stuart London 1637–1645* (1997), 86, 128, 141, 172; they are absent from Keith Lindley, *Popular Politics and Religion in Civil War London* (1997).

5. Hill, *World Turned Upside Down*, 158–85; J. C. Davis, *Fear, Myth, and History: The Ranters and their Historians* (Cambridge, 1986).

6. Genesis 2: 25, 3: 16–21; John Williams, *A Sermon of Apparell* (1620; STC 25728), 25. For another commentary on 'naked truth', prelapsarian 'naked innocency', and the naked marriage of Ish and Isha (Adam and Eve) before their fall into sin, see William Austin, *Haec Homo* (1639; STC 976), 171–3.

7. Philip Stubbes, *The Anatomie of Abuses* (1583; STC 23376) sigs. C3v–C4v. See also Anthony Anderson, *The Shield of our Safetie* (1581; STC 572), sigs. T–Tv, on the fall of man, the origin of clothing, and the errors of 'the Adamites which run naked, to counterfeit Adam and Evah'.

8. William Perkins, *The Whole Treatise of the Cases of Conscience* (1608; STC 19670), 105–7.

9. Adam Hill, *The Crie of England* (1595; STC 13465), 38; *Certain Sermons or Homilies appointed to be read in Churches* (2 vols.; 1623), ii. 102–3. Stephen Gosson likewise taught that clothing was instituted 'for comeliness, as to keep off the injury of the air', and for social, cultural, occupational, and gender identification: Stephen Gosson, *Playes Confuted in Five Actions* (1582), in Arthur Kinney (ed.), *Markets of Bawdrie: The Dramatic Criticism of Stephen Gosson* (Salzburg, 1974), 189.

10. Williams, *Sermon of Apparell*, 25–6; William Prynne, *Histrio-Mastix* (1633; STC 20464), 207.

11. Perkins, *Whole Treatise of the Cases of Conscience*, 104–5.

12. Ibid. 97, 99–100.

13. Stubbes, *Anatomie of Abuses*, sigs. C3v–C4v; Hill, *Crie of England*, 40–2; Arthur Dent, *The Plaine Mans Path-way to Heauen* (1601; 1612 edn.) 45, 47; Williams, *Sermon of Apparell*, 23; John Bunyan, *The Barren Fig-Tree, or, The Doom and Downfall of the Fruitless Professor*, in George Offor (ed.), *The Whole Works of*

John Bunyan, vol. iii (1862), 565; see also Bunyan's verse on the immoral use of apparel:

> God gave us clothes to hide our nakedness,
> And we by them do it expose to view.
> Our pride and unclean minds to an excess,
> By our apparel, we to others show.

A Book for Boys and Girls; or, Temporal Things Spiritualized, ibid. 752.

14. Thomas Beard, *The Theatre of God's Judgements* (1597; 1631 edn.); Gosson, *Plays Confuted*, ed. Kinney, 175.

15. Dent, *Plaine Mans Path-way*, 52–3.

16. Wilfrid Hooper, 'The Tudor Sumptuary Laws', *English Historical Review*, 30 (1915), 433–49; Francis Elizabeth Baldwin, *Sumptuary Legislation and Personal Regulation in England* (Baltimore, 1926).

17. David Cressy, 'Gender Trouble and Cross Dressing in Early Modern England', *Journal of British Studies*, 35 (1996), 438–65.

18. Colossians 3: 9; Ephesians 4: 22–4.

19. Jonathan Z. Smith, 'The Garments of Shame', *History of Religions*, 5 (1965–6), 217–38; Margaret R. Miles, *Carnal Knowing: Female Nakedness and Religious Meaning in the Christian West* (New York, 1991), 25–6, 33–6.

20. Enrico S. Molnar, 'The Adamites of Bohemia: A Movement of Naturist Dissent within the Matrix of Christian History and Theology', bound with his *Hussite Essays* (Claremont, 1971), 4, 6.

21. Ibid. 8–9.

22. Laurence of Brezova, *Chronicle of the Hussite Wars* [1431], in Howard Kaminsky, *A History of the Hussite Revolution* (Berkeley and Los Angeles, 1967), 430.

23. Kaminsky, *History of the Hussite Revolution*, 418, 429; Molnar, 'Adamites of Bohemia', 2, 12, 15.

24. John Foxe, *Acts and Monuments of the Latter and Perilous Dayes* (1563; STC 11222), 252–3. I am grateful to Thomas Freeman for directing me to this source. Foxe is the most likely English source for Anthony Anderson's reference to 'the Adamites which run naked', *Shield of our Safetie*, sig. Tv.

25. Williams, *Radical Reformation*, 584, 761.

26. For the political narrative see Conrad Russell, *The Fall of the British Monarchies 1637–1642* (Oxford, 1991), and Anthony Fletcher, *The Outbreak of the English Civil War* (1981). I plan to explore more of the social and cultural history of the period November 1640–February 1642 in a work provisionally titled *England on Edge: The Revolution of 1641*.

27. John Taylor, *A Swarme of Sectaries and Schismatiques* (1641). The date is from the Thomason collection, British Library, E.158.1. Taylor was away from London most of the summer on one of his celebrated rowing tours, and may have missed this emergent phenomenon. See also *Religions Enemies. With a Brief and Ingenious*

Relation, as by Anabaptists, Brownists, Papists, Familists, Atheists, and Foolists, sawcily presuming to tosse Religion in a Blanquet (1641; E.170.7).

28. *The Brownists Conventicle: Or an assemble of Brownists, Separatists, and Non-Conformists* (1641; E.164.13), 2.

29. Richard Brome, *A Joviall Crew: or, The Merry Beggars. Presented in a Comedie, at the Cock-Pit in Drury-Lane, in the yeer 1641* (1652), Act II, Scene. i, sig. D3. The play was written to be staged about 25 April 1641, and may have been performed on 2 September, the last acting day before the theatres were closed; Ann Haaker (ed.), *Richard Brome. A Jovial Crew* (Lincoln, Nebraska, 1968), xi–xii. Like many plays of the period, the text could have been altered at any time between first scripting and ultimate printing.

30. *The Downefall of Temporizing Poets, unlicenst Printers, upstart Booksellers, trotting Mercuries, and bawling Hawkers* (1641), 2. Using a similar conceit a few years later, William Golding suggested that the English colonists of Bermuda 'had long since turned Adamites out of necessity', had they not found means of illegal commercial subsistence, William Golding, *Servants on Horse-back, or, A Free-People Bestrided in their Persons and Liberties* (1648), 7. I owe this reference to Carla Pestana.

31. Henry Burton, *Englands Bondage and Hope of Deliverance* (1641), 28; Joseph Hall, *A Survay of That Foolish, Seditious, Scandalous, Prophane Libell, The Protestation Protested* (1641), 2–3. For more on the innocent nakedness of Adam and Eve and the wholesomeness of a Church stripped naked of ceremonies, see Henry Burton, *A Replie to a Relation of the Conference Betweene William Laude and Mr. Fisher the Jesuit* (1640), 99–104. For the conformist complaint that religion 'is left stark naked', see also *A Plea for Moderation* (1642), 8.

32. *A Discovery of 29 Sects*, 4.

33. *A Nest of Serpents Discovered. Or, A knot of old Heretiques revived, Called the Adamites. Wherein their original, increase, and several ridiculous tenets are plainly laid open* (1641; E.168.12), 2–5.

34. Ibid. 6.

35. Thomas Bray, of Abingdon, Berkshire, had matriculated at Pembroke College in 1637. Using the same pseudonym, Samoth Yarb, 'an Oxfordshire gentleman', he published *The Anatomy of Et Caetera. Or the Unfolding of that Dangerous Oath* (1641).

36. Thomas Bray ('Samoth Yarb'), *A New Sect of Religion Descryed, called Adamites: Deriving their Religion from our Father Adam* (1641). It is also possible that *A New Sect of Religion Descryed* came before *A Nest of Serpents*, and that Bray's description and illustration provided the inspiration for the latter.

37. Cf. Lynn Hunt (ed.), *The Invention of Pornography: Obscenity and the Origins of Modernity, 1500–1800* (New York, 1993), esp. editor's introduction, 9–45.

38. Bray, *New Sect of Religion Descryed*, 3–6.

39. Ibid. 6.

40. Ibid. 6–7.

41. *A Description of the Sect Called the Familie of Love: With their common place of resi-*

dence. Being discovered by one Mrs. Susanna Snow of Pirford near Chersey in the County of Surrey, who was vainly led away for a time through their base allurements, and at length fell mad, till by a great miracle shewn from God, she was delivered (1641). See also Thomas Middleton, *The Family of Love* (1608), Act III, Scene ii, in which the merchant Dryfat seeks admission to the orgiastic Family and learns their password. An important corrective is Christopher W. Marsh, *The Family of Love in English Society, 1550–1630* (Cambridge, 1994).

42. Martin Parker, *The Poets Blind Mans Bough* (1641), title-page, sigs. A2, A3, A4v, B; *A Presse Full of Pamphlets* (1642), sigs. Av, A3v. See also John Taylor, *The Liar. Or, A Contradiction of those who in the titles of their Books affirmed them to be true, when they were false* (1641), especially sig. A2, regarding a lady who crossed the Thames 'stark naked, without swimming' (presumably by boat).

43. *The Adamites Sermon* (1641). Coules was renowned as a ballad publisher, 'his ballads were invariably illustrated with curious woodcuts', Henry R. Plomer, *A Dictionary of the Booksellers and Printers Who Were at Work in England, Scotland and Ireland from 1641 to 1667* (1907), 49–50.

44. *The Adamites Sermon*, 3.

45. Ibid. 3–4.

46. Ibid. 4.

47. Ibid. 4–5.

48. Ibid. 6–8.

49. Ibid. 8. The Wing catalogue lists a 1651 reprint of *The Adamites Sermon* at the UCLA Clark Library (Wing A475C) but this seems to be a ghost. Compare the mock sermon in John Taylor, *A Tale in a Tub or, A Tub Lecture As it was delivered by My-heele Mendsoale, an inspired Brownist . . . In a meeting house neere Bedlam* (1641).

50. There were people named Couchman in early Stuart London, but no Obadiah Couchman can be found.

51. *The Humble Petition of the Brownists* (1641), 4. For its authorship see W. K. Jordan, *The Development of Religious Toleration in England . . . 1640–1660* (Cambridge, Mass., 1940), 439–40; G. E. Aylmer, 'Did the Ranters Exist?', *Past and Present*, 117 (1987), 218.

52. Richard Carter, *The Schismatick Stigmatised* (1641), 15.

53. (John Taylor), *The Divisions of the Church of England Crept in at XV Several Doores* (1642), sig. A2v; *Religions Lotterie, or the Churches Amazement* (1642), sig. A2v. 'An Adamite' appears among eight imagined attendants at *The Remarkable Funeral of Cheapside-Cross* (1642), sig, A4.

54. Daniel Featley, *The Dippers Dipt. Or the Anabaptists Duck'd and Plung'd* (1645; 1660 edn.), 27, 34–5; Robert Baillie, *Anabaptism, The True Fountaine of Independency, Antinomy, Brownism, Familisme* (1647), 173. For more on ritual nakedness among the anabaptists, see Thomas Edwards, *The Third Part of Gangraena* (1646), 189.

55. *XXXIII Religions, Sects, Societies, and Factions of the Cavaliers now in Armes against the Parliament* (1643), sig. Av; idem (1645), sigs. A2v–A3.

56. Thomas Edwards, *Gangraena* (1646); *The Second Part of Gangraena* (1646). Edwards made no mention of the Adamites, perhaps because he was not convinced of their reality; but he did repeat the charge that some of the anabaptists delighted in handling and dipping naked young women, *The Third Part of Gangraena* (1646), 189.

57. Ephraim Pagitt, *Heresiography; or, a Description of the Heretickes and Sectaries of these Latter Times* (1645), 85–7, qu. on 86. See also *A Relation of Severall Heresies* (1646); *A Brief Collection Out of Master Pagitts Book* (1646); Ephraim Pagitt, *Heresiography* (1662), 117.

58. Davis, *Fear, Myth, and History*; Aylmer, 'Did the Ranters Exist?', 208–19; Christopher Hill, 'Abolishing the Ranters', in his *A Nation of Change and Novelty: Radical Politics, Religion and Literature in Seventeenth-Century England* (1990), 186–8; J. C. Davis, 'Fear, Myth and Furore: Reappraising the "Ranters" ', *Past and Present*, 129 (1990), 79–103; and debate among J. F. McGregor, Bernard Capp, Nigel Smith, B. J. Gibbons, and J. C. Davis in *Past and Present*, 140 (1993), 155–210. See also Nigel Smith (ed.), *A Collection of Ranter Writings from the Seventeenth Century* (1987).

59. Davis, *Fear, Myth, and History*, 158, 163.

60. Ibid. 169, 171.

61. Ibid. 164, 176; *The Arraignment and Tryall with a Declaration of the Ranters* (1650), 6.

62. *The Ranters Recantation* (1650), in Davis, *Fear, Myth, and History*, 181.

63. *Strange Newes from Newgate* (1651), in Davis, *Fear, Myth, and History*, 184, 186; *The Routing of the Ranters*, ibid. 165; *The Ranters Ranting* (1650), title-page. See also Smith (ed.), *Collection of Ranter Writings*, 19.

64. *A Fiery Flying Roll*, in Smith (ed.), *Collection of Ranter Writings*, 113; *Copp's Return to the wayes of Truth* (1651), ibid. 145. For Coppe's nakedness see *Dictionary of National Biography*.

65. *A Rout, A Rout*, in Smith (ed.), *Collection of Ranter Writings*, 192–3, 201. It was about this time, perhaps inspired by contemporary discussions of nudity and Adamism, that the scholar John Hall published his witty proposition 'that women ought to go naked', John Hall, *Paradoxes* (1650), 54–77. Just as nakedness for Adam and Eve was 'the great mark of their liberty and uprightness', he argued, so 'truth . . . is naked' and 'nakedness restores women to themselves', ibid. 57, 63, 67.

66. *The Ranters Bible* (1650), in Davis, *Fear, Myth, and History*, 169.

67. *The Ranters Declaration* (1650), title-page; for another version of this print, with altered words, see *The Declaration of John Robins* (1651), in Davis, *Fear, Myth, and History*, 203; for a similar image, featuring two erect penises, see *Strange Newes from Newgate* (1651), ibid. 187. J. F. McGregor cites corroborative evidence of Bacchanalian Ranter disturbances in his contribution to the debate on 'Fear, Myth and Furore', 160.

68. *The Lost Sheep Found* (1660), in Smith (ed.), *Collection of Ranter Writings*, 183. Not all public nakedness was attributed to Adamite or Ranter antinomianism. When a woman disrobed in the middle of a sermon at Whitehall in 1652 the minister thought her more mad than wicked, David Brown, *The Naked Woman, or a Rare*

Epistle Sent to Mr Peter Sterry (1652), 16, 8–10. When Mary Combe was caught wandering naked in her Somerset village in the mid-1650s she was regarded as sexually promiscuous and mentally unbalanced, rather than religiously inspired, G. R. Quaife, *Wanton Wenches and Wayward Wives: Peasants and Illicit Sex in Seventeenth Century England* (1979), 156–7. See also John Philips, *A Satyr Against Hypocrites* (1655), 20, which has a Maytide dancer advising her partner:

> Martha put off thy clothes, for time is come
> That men may bauble show and women bum,
> For that the seed of them that do profess
> Shall only need be clothed with righteousness.

69. *Mercurius Fumigosus*, 12 (16–23 August 1654), in Joad Raymond (ed.), *Making the News: An Anthology of the Newsbooks of Revolutionary England, 1641–1660* (New York, 1993), 159–60.

70. Samuel Tilbury, *Bloudy Newse from the North, and the Ranting Adamites Declaration* (1650), 1–5.

71. Ibid. 6.

72. William Perkins, *The Whole Treatise of the Cases of Conscience* (1608; STC 19670), 105, 106.

73. Thomas Fuller, *The Church History of Britain* (1656), preface to book 8.

74. For examples of this usage, see *Calendar of State Papers, Domestic, 1640*, 39, 52; *CSPD 1641*, 435; *CSPD 1641–43*, 164.

75. Laura Gowing, *Domestic Dangers: Women, Words, and Sex in Early Modern London* (Oxford, 1996), 189.

76. Fuller, *Church History*, preface to book 8.

77. Francis Higginson, *A Brief Relation of the Irreligion of the Northern Quakers* (1653), 29–30; Kenneth L. Carroll, 'Early Quakers and "Going Naked as a Sign"', *Quaker History*, 67 (1978), 75–8.

78. Ibid. 78–80.

79. Ibid. 81.

80. Ibid. 81–3. The Yorkshire minister Abraham de la Pryme recalled an incident from the time of the Restoration, when a Quaker 'who was revelation mad' went 'to the church to reprehend the congregation . . . stark naked', Charles Jackson (ed.), *The Diary of Abraham de la Pryme* (Surtees Society, 54; Durham, 1870), 149–50.

81. The 1990s saw a revival of Christian naturism in North America, with widely publicized gatherings in North Carolina and elsewhere, *Wall Street Journal* (11 August 1997, section A, 1). Note also the activities of such groups as Naturist Life International, Christian Naturists, and Fig Leaf Forum who promote Adamite nudist ideas over the internet.

82. For example, 'I saw a vision yesternight | Enough to sate a Seeker's sight . . . It was a she so glittering bright | You'd think her soul an Adamite', John Cleveland, 'To the State of Love, or, The Senses Festival', in Brian Morris and Eleanor Withrington (eds.), *The Poems of John Cleveland* (Oxford, 1967), 47; Henry More, *Divine*

Dialogues (1668), Edward Pettit, *The Visions of the Reformation* (1683), 93; R.D., *The Strange and Prodigious Religions, Customs, and Manners, of Sundry Nations* (1683), 40; *The Adamite, or the Loves of Father Rock* (1683); George Saville (Marquis of Halifax), *The Anatomy of an Equivalent* (1688), 9.

83. *The French Prophetess Turn'd Adamite* (1707).

84. Mary Hobbs (ed.), *The Sermons of Henry King* (1992), 258. For another reference to the clothing and dressing of sermons, see Thomas Trescot, *The Zealous Magistrate* (1642), 'to the reader'.

Index